Scott Foresman-Addison Wesley
enVisionMATH™
Florida

Authors

Randall I. Charles
Professor Emeritus
Department of Mathematics
San Jose State University
San Jose, California

Janet H. Caldwell
Professor of Mathematics
Rowan University
Glassboro, New Jersey

Mary Cavanagh
Executive Director of Center for
Practice, Research and Innovation
in Mathematics Education (PRIME)
Arizona State University
Mesa, Arizona

Dinah Chancellor
Mathematics Consultant,
Carroll ISD, Southlake, Texas
Mathematics Consultant,
Kerrville ISD, Kerrville, Texas

Juanita V. Copley
Professor Emeritus, College of Education
University of Houston
Houston, Texas

Warren D. Crown
Professor Emeritus of Mathematics Education
Graduate School of Education
Rutgers University
New Brunswick, New Jersey

Francis (Skip) Fennell
Professor of Education
McDaniel College
Westminster, Maryland

Alma B. Ramirez
Sr. Research Associate
Math Pathways and Pitfalls WestEd
Oakland, California

Kay B. Sammons
Coordinator of Elementary Mathematics
Howard County Public Schools
Ellicott City, Maryland

Jane F. Schielack
Professor of Mathematics
Associate Dean for Assessment and
Pre K–12 Education, College of Science
Texas A&M University
College Station, Texas

William Tate
Edward Mallinckrodt Distinguished
University Professor in Arts & Sciences
Washington University
St. Louis, Missouri

John A. Van de Walle
Professor Emeritus, Mathematics Education
Virginia Commonwealth University
Richmond, Virginia

Consulting Mathematicians

Edward J. Barbeau
Professor of Mathematics
University of Toronto
Toronto, Canada

Sybilla Beckmann
Professor of Mathematics
Department of Mathematics
University of Georgia
Athens, Georgia

David Bressoud
DeWitt Wallace Professor of Mathematics
Macalester College
Saint Paul, Minnesota

Gary Lippman
Professor of Mathematics and Computer Science
California State University East Bay
Hayward, California

Glenview, Illinois • Boston, Massachusetts • Chandler, Arizona • Upper Saddle River, New Jersey

Consulting Authors

Charles R. Allan
Mathematics Education Consultant
(Retired)
Michigan Department of Education
Lansing, Michigan

Stuart J. Murphy
Visual Learning Specialist
Boston, Massachusetts

Grant Wiggins
Researcher and Educational Consultant
Hopewell, New Jersey

Center Activities Author

Ruth I. Champagne
Mathematics Education Specialist
FRIENDLY MATH, LLC
Chicago, Illinois

ELL Consultant/Reviewers

Jim Cummins
Professor
The University of Toronto
Toronto, Canada

Alma B. Ramirez
Sr. Research Associate
Math Pathways and Pitfalls WestEd
Oakland, California

Florida Reviewers

Ralph Blose
Curriculum Support Specialist
Miami-Dade County

Lynda Cihanowic
Teacher
Okaloosa County

Janice Demers
Teacher
Pinellas County

Carmen Elliott
Teacher
Brevard County

David Hyers
Teacher
Nassau County

Noreen Kraebel
Math Resource Specialist
Pasco County

Susan Petrek
Math Resource Specialist
Osceola County

Virginia Sanchez
Teacher
Miami-Dade County

Anita Saunders
Math and Science Coach
Collier County

Gay Street
Math Coach
Marion County

ISBN-13: 978-0-328-44657-5
ISBN-10: 0-328-44657-2

Topic Titles

Florida

BIG IDEAS · SUPPORTING IDEAS

Grade 5
Big Ideas and Supporting Ideas

Big Idea 1 Develop an understanding of and fluency with division of whole numbers.
Benchmarks: MA.5.A.1.1, MA.5.A.1.2, MA.5.A.1.3, MA.5.A.1.4

Big Idea 2 Develop an understanding of and fluency with addition and subtraction of fractions and decimals.
Benchmarks: MA.5.A.2.1, MA.5.A.2.2, MA.5.A.2.3, MA.5.A.2.4

Big Idea 3 Describe three-dimensional shapes and analyze their properties, including volume and surface area.
Benchmarks: MA.5.G.3.1, MA.5.G.3.2

Supporting Ideas Algebra
Benchmarks: MA.5.A.4.1, MA.5.A.4.2

Supporting Ideas Geometry and Measurement
Benchmarks: MA.5.G.5.1, MA.5.G.5.2, MA.5.G.5.3, MA.5.G.5.4

Supporting Ideas Number and Operations
Benchmarks: MA.5.A.6.1, MA.5.A.6.2, MA.5.A.6.3, MA.5.A.6.4, MA.5.A.6.5

Supporting Ideas Data Analysis
Benchmarks: MA.5.S.7.1, MA.5.S.7.2

K–5 Math Strand Colors

- Number and Operations
- Algebra
- Geometry and Measurement
- Data Analysis
- Problem Solving

Topic 1

Number Sense: Division

BIG IDEA 1 · SUPPORTING IDEAS

Big Idea 1 MA.5.A.1.1, MA.5.A.1.2, MA.5.A.1.3

Supporting Ideas Number and Operations MA.5.A.6.5

enVisionMATH™ Florida
Scott Foresman-Addison Wesley

Florida Contents

Topic 8

Adding and Subtracting Fractions with Unlike Denominators

Big Idea 2 MA.5.A.2.1, MA.5.A.2.2,
MA.5.A.2.3

**Supporting Ideas Number and
Operations** MA.5.A.6.1

Topic 9

Adding and Subtracting Mixed Numbers

Big Idea 2 MA.5.A.2.1, MA.5.A.2.2,
MA.5.A.2.3

Problem-Solving Handbook

Use this Problem-Solving Handbook throughout the year to help you solve problems.

Everybody can be a good problem solver!

Don't give up!

There's almost always more than one way to solve a problem!

Don't trust key words.

Pictures help me understand!

Explaining helps me understand!

Problem-Solving Process

Read and Understand

❓ What am I trying to find?
- Tell what the question is asking.

❓ What do I know?
- Tell the problem in my own words.
- Identify key facts and details.

Plan and Solve

❓ What strategy or strategies should I try?

❓ Can I show the problem?
- Try drawing a picture.
- Try making a list, table, or graph.
- Try acting it out or using objects.

❓ How will I solve the problem?

❓ What is the answer?
- Tell the answer in a complete sentence.

Strategies
- Show What You Know
  - Draw a Picture
  - Make an Organized List
  - Make a Table
  - Make a Graph
  - Act It Out/ Use Objects
- Look for a Pattern
- Try, Check, Revise
- Write an Equation
- Use Reasoning
- Work Backward
- Solve a Simpler Problem

Look Back and Check

❓ Did I check my work?
- Compare my work to the information in the problem.
- Be sure all calculations are correct.

❓ Is my answer reasonable?
- Estimate to see if my answer makes sense.
- Make sure the question was answered.

Using Bar Diagrams

Use a bar diagram to show how what you know and what you want to find are related. Then choose an operation to solve the problem.

Problem 1

Carrie helps at the family flower store in the summer. She keeps a record of how many customers come into the store. How many customers came into the store on Monday and Wednesday?

Customers

Days	Customers
Monday	124
Tuesday	163
Wednesday	151
Thursday	206
Friday	259

Bar Diagram

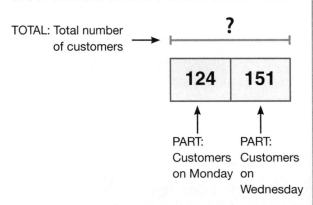

TOTAL: Total number of customers → ?

| 124 | 151 |

PART: Customers on Monday   PART: Customers on Wednesday

$$124 + 151 = \blacksquare$$

 Think I can add to find the total.

Problem 2

Kim is saving to buy a sweatshirt from the college her brother attends. She has $18. How much more money does she need to buy the sweatshirt?

$32

Bar Diagram

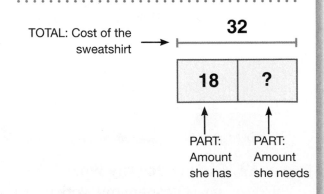

TOTAL: Cost of the sweatshirt → 32

| 18 | ? |

PART: Amount she has   PART: Amount she needs

$$32 - 18 = \blacksquare$$

 Think I can subtract to find the missing part.

Pictures help me understand!

Don't trust key words!

Season tickets to the community theater cost only $105 each no matter what age you are. What is the cost of tickets for four people?

Bar Diagram

TOTAL: Total cost of the tickets →

?

| 105 | 105 | 105 | 105 |

PART:
Cost of
each ticket

$$4 \times 105 = \blacksquare$$

 Think I can multiply because the parts are equal.

Thirty students traveled in 3 vans to the zoo. The same numbers of students were in each van. How many students were in each van?

Bar Diagram

TOTAL: Total number of students →

30

| ? | ? | ? |

PART:
Number in
each van

$$30 \div 3 = \blacksquare$$

 Think I can divide to find how many are in each part.

Problem-Solving Strategies

Strategy	Example	When I Use It
Draw a Picture	The race was 5 kilometers. Markers were at the starting line and the finish line. Markers showed each kilometer of the race. Find the number of markers used.	Try drawing a picture when it helps you visualize the problem or when the relationships such as joining or separating are involved.
Make a Table	Phil and Marcy spent all day Saturday at the fair. Phil rode 3 rides each half hour and Marcy rode 2 rides each half hour. How many rides had Marcy ridden when Phil rode 24 rides?	Try making a table when: • there are 2 or more quantities, • amounts change using a pattern.
Look for a Pattern	The house numbers on Forest Road change in a planned way. Describe the pattern. Tell what the next two house numbers should be.	Look for a pattern when something repeats in a predictable way.

Draw a Picture example diagram:

Start Line — Finish Line

Start Line 1 km 2 km 3 km 4 km Finish Line

Make a Table example:

Rides for Phil	3	6	9	12	15	18	21	24
Rides for Marcy	2	4	6	8	10	12	14	16

Look for a Pattern example: house numbers 3, 6, 10, 15, ?, ?

Everybody can
be a good
problem solver!

Strategy	Example	When I Use It
Make an Organized List	How many ways can you make change for a quarter using dimes and nickels?	Make an organized list when asked to find combinations of two or more items.
	1 quarter = 1 dime + 1 dime + 1 nickel 1 dime + 1 nickel + 1 nickel + 1 nickel 1 nickel + 1 nickel + 1 nickel + 1 nickel + 1 nickel	
Try, Check, Revise	Suzanne spent $27, not including tax, on dog supplies. She bought two of one item and one of another item. What did she buy? $8 + $8 + $15 = $31 $7 + $7 + $12 = $26 $6 + $6 + $15 = $27	Use Try, Check, Revise when quantities are being combined to find a total, but you don't know which quantities. **Dog Supplies Sale!** Leash .... $8 Collar .... $6 Bowls .... $7 Medium Beds .... $15 Toys $12
Write an Equation	Maria's new CD player can hold 6 discs at a time. If she has 204 CDs, how many times can the player be filled without repeating a CD? Find $204 \div 6 = n$.	Write an equation when the story describes a situation that uses an operation or operations.

Problem-Solving Handbook

xv

Even More Strategies

Strategy	Example	When I Use It
Act It Out	How many ways can 3 students shake each other's hand?	Think about acting out a problem when the numbers are small and there is action in the problem you can do.
Use Reasoning	Beth collected some shells, rocks, and beach glass. **Beth's Collection** 2 rocks 3 times as many shells as rocks 12 objects in all How many of each object are in the collection?	Use reasoning when you can use known information to reason out unknown information.
Work Backward	Tracy has band practice at 10:15 A.M. It takes her 20 minutes to get from home to practice and 5 minutes to warm up. What time should she leave home to get to practice on time?	Try working backward when: • you know the end result of a series of steps, • you want to know what happened at the beginning.

Time Tracy leaves home **?** ← 20 minutes ← Time warm up starts ← 5 minutes ← Time practice starts **10:15**

I can think about when to use each strategy.

Strategy	Example	When I Use It

Solve a Simpler Problem 	Each side of each triangle in the figure at the left is one centimeter. If there are 12 triangles in a row, what is the perimeter of the figure?
	
	 I can look at 1 triangle, then 2 triangles, then 3 triangles.
	
	  perimeter = 3 cm
	
	  perimeter = 4 cm
	
	  perimeter = 5 cm
		Try solving a simpler problem when you can create a simpler case that is easier to solve.

Make a Graph	Mary was in a jump rope contest. How did her number of jumps change over the five days of the contest? 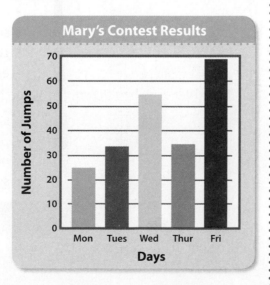	Make a graph when: • data for an event are given, • the question can be answered by reading the graph.

Writing to Explain

Here is a good math explanation.

Writing to Explain What happens to the area of the rectangle if the lengths of its sides are doubled?

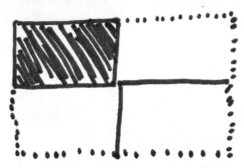

■ = $\frac{1}{4}$ of the whole rectangle

The area of the new rectangle is 4 times the area of the original rectangle.

Tips for Writing Good Math Explanations....

A good explanation should be:
- correct
- simple
- complete
- easy to understand

Math explanations can use:
- words
- pictures
- numbers
- symbols

This is another good math explanation.

Writing to Explain Use blocks to show 13 × 24.
Draw a picture of what you did with the blocks.

First we made a row of 24 using 2 tens and 4 ones. Then we made more rows until we had 13 rows. Then we said 13 rows of 2 tens is 13 × 2 tens = 26 tens or 260. Then we said 13 rows of 4 ones is 13 × 4 = 52. Then we added the parts. 260 + 52 = 312 So, 13 × 24 = 312.

Problem-Solving Recording Sheet

Name __Jane__

Problem-Solving Recording Sheet

Problem:
On June 14, 1777, the Continental Congress approved the design of a national flag. The 1777 flag had 13 stars, one for each colony. Today's flag has 50 stars, one for each state. How many stars were added to the flag since 1777?

Find?

Number of stars added to the flag

Know?

Original flag
13 stars

Today's flag
50 stars

Strategies?

Show the Problem
☑ Draw a Picture
☐ Make an Organized List
☐ Make a Table
☐ Make a Graph
☐ Act It Out/Use Objects

☐ Look for a Pattern
☐ Try, Check, Revise
☑ Write an Equation
☐ Use Reasoning
☐ Work Backwards
☐ Solve a Simpler Problem

Show the Problem?

| 50 |
| 13 | ? |

Solution?

I am comparing the two quantities.
I could add up from 13 to 50. I can also subtract 13 from 50. I'll subtract.

$$\begin{array}{r} 50 \\ -\ 13 \\ \hline 37 \end{array}$$

Answer?

There were 37 stars added to the flag from 1777 to today.

Check? Reasonable?

37 + 13 = 50 so I subtracted correctly.

50 − 13 is about 50 − 10 = 40
40 is close to 37. 37 is reasonable.

Name **Benton**

Teaching Tool
1

Problem-Solving Recording Sheet

Problem:

Suppose your teacher told you to open your math book to the facing pages whose page numbers add to 85. To which two pages would you open your book?

Find?

Two facing page numbers

Know?

Two pages.
Facing each other.
Sum is 85.

Strategies?

Show the Problem
- ☑ Draw a Picture
- ☐ Make an Organized List
- ☐ Make a Table
- ☐ Make a Graph
- ☐ Act It Out/Use Objects

- ☐ Look for a Pattern
- ☑ Try, Check, Revise
- ☑ Write an Equation
- ☐ Use Reasoning
- ☐ Work Backwards
- ☐ Solve a Simpler Problem

Show the Problem?

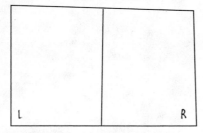

L + R = 85
L is 1 less than R

Solution?

I'll try some numbers in the middle.
40 + 41 = 81, too low
How about 46 and 47?
46 + 47 = 93, too high
Ok, now try 42 and 43.
42 + 43 = 85.

Answer?

The page numbers are 42 and 43.

Check? Reasonable?

I added correctly.
42 + 43 is about 40 + 40 = 80
80 is close to 85.
42 and 43 is reasonable.

Topic 1

Number Sense: Division

1 How many strings are on the guitars used by Tejano musicians? You will find out in Lesson 1-6.

2 Radar measures over 19 hands. How many feet tall is Radar? You will find out in Lesson 1-4.

Review What You Know!

Vocabulary

Choose the best term from the box.

> • rounding • multiple
> • difference • product

1. The number 800 is a __?__ of 100.

2. One way to estimate is to use __?__.

3. In the equation 12 × 4 = 48, the number 48 is the __?__.

Place Value

Write each number in expanded form.

4. 473 **5.** 826 **6.** 340

7. 208 **8.** 56 **9.** 591

Fact Families

Write the fact family for each set of numbers.

10. 3, 7, 21 **11.** 9, 4, 36 **12.** 4, 4, 16

13. 8, 5, 40 **14.** 9, 9, 81 **15.** 6, 8, 48

Rounding

Round each number to the place value of the underlined digit.

16. 4̲56 **17.** 3̲8 **18.** 1̲,600

19. 3,6̲48 **20.** 2̲5 **21.** 99̲9

22. 2̲39 **23.** 6,72̲9 **24.** 7̲9

25. Writing to Explain Explain how to round 768 to the hundreds place.

3

The roadrunner prefers to run rather than to fly. What is the roadrunner's top speed? You will find out in Lesson 1-5.

4

Passengers on cruise ships often set sail from the Port of Miami. This is one of the world's busiest cruise ports. How can division be used to find the number of tables in the dining room of a small cruise ship? You will find out in Lesson 1-2.

Topic Essential Questions

- What is the relationship between multiplication and division?
- How can quotients be estimated?
- What are remainders in division and how are they interpreted?

MA.5.A.1.1 Describe the process of finding quotients involving multi-digit dividends using models, place value, properties and the relationship of division to multiplication.

Relating Multiplication and Division

How can you use the relationship between multiplication and division to divide?

A group of 300 students boarded a 6-car monorail in equal groups. How many students were in each car?

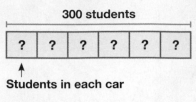

300 students

| ? | ? | ? | ? | ? | ? |

↑
Students in each car

6-car monorail

Guided Practice*

Do you know HOW?

Copy and complete.

1. $3 \times \boxed{} = 15$

$15 \div 3 = \boxed{}$

$3 \times \boxed{} = 150$

$150 \div 3 = \boxed{}$

2. $6 \times \boxed{} = 24$

$24 \div 6 = \boxed{}$

$6 \times \boxed{} = 240$

$240 \div 6 = \boxed{}$

Do you UNDERSTAND?

3. If you know that $8 \times 60 = 480$, what related division equation can you write?

4. In the example above, if 240 students boarded the monorail, how many students would be in each car?

Independent Practice

Leveled Practice Copy and complete.

5. $5 \times \boxed{} = 40$

$40 \div 5 = \boxed{}$

$5 \times \boxed{} = 400$

$400 \div 5 = \boxed{}$

6. $4 \times \boxed{} = 28$

$28 \div 4 = \boxed{}$

$4 \times \boxed{} = 280$

$280 \div 4 = \boxed{}$

7. $7 \times \boxed{} = 63$

$63 \div 7 = \boxed{}$

$7 \times \boxed{} = 630$

$630 \div 7 = \boxed{}$

8. $8 \times \boxed{} = 16$

$16 \div 8 = \boxed{}$

$8 \times \boxed{} = 160$

$160 \div 8 = \boxed{}$

In **9** through **16**, use the relationship between multiplication and division to find each quotient.

9. $270 \div 9 = \boxed{}$

10. $360 \div 6 = \boxed{}$

11. $210 \div 3 = \boxed{}$

12. $320 \div 4 = \boxed{}$

13. $560 \div 8 = \boxed{}$

14. $150 \div 5 = \boxed{}$

15. $360 \div 4 = \boxed{}$

16. $540 \div 9 = \boxed{}$

For another example, see Set A on page 22.

What You Think

You can use multiplication and division facts.

$6 \times 5 = 30$

So, $30 \div 6 = 5$

To find $300 \div 6$, think: $6 \times \boxed{} = 300$.

What You Think

You know how to multiply by multiples of 10.

$6 \times 50 = 300$

What You Write

You can use what you know about multiplication facts and multiplying by multiples of 10 to find $300 \div 6$.

$6 \times 50 = 300$

So, $300 \div 6 = 50$

There were 50 students in each car.

Problem Solving

17. The table shows Percy's hourly pay for summer jobs. If he weeds gardens for 2 hours, cleans garages for 4 hours, and walks dogs for 3 hours, how much money does he earn?

Data

Percy's Summer Jobs

Job	Hourly Pay
Weed Gardens	$3
Clean Garages	$5
Walk Dogs	$4

18. **Writing to Explain** How can you use what you know about multiplication facts and multiplying by multiples of 10 to find $560 \div 7$?

Critical THINKING

19. The Ortega family paid $150 for 5 new bicycle helmets. Each helmet was the same price. What was the price of each helmet?

20. Craig has 56 postcards from Japan, 41 postcards from Canada, and 23 postcards from France. He pasted 6 postcards on each page of his scrapbook. How many pages did he fill?

21. Su Ling used 240 beads to make 8 necklaces. She put the same number of beads on each necklace. How many beads did Su Ling put on each necklace?

22. There are 360 students in a spelling bee. The students are put in 6 equal groups. How many students are in each group?

A 6

B 36

C 60

D 160

23. **Estimation** Ben attends school for 180 days each year. The school day is about 7 hours long. About how many hours is Ben at school each year?

MA.5.A.1.2 Estimate quotients or calculate them mentally depending on the context and numbers involved.
Also MA.5.A.1.1

Dividing Multiples of 10 and 100

How can you divide mentally?

Five friends want to share these comic books equally. Can you use mental math to find how many comic books each friend will get?

Choose an Operation Divide to find how many are in each group.

Find $1,000 \div 5$.

1,000 comic books

Guided Practice*

Do you know HOW?

In **1** through **6**, use mental math to find each quotient.

1. $540 \div 9$ **2.** $490 \div 7$

3. $28,000 \div 4$ **4.** $48,000 \div 6$

5. $360 \div 6$ **6.** $81,000 \div 9$

Do you UNDERSTAND?

7. Writing to Explain How can you use the division fact $54 \div 9$ to find $5,400 \div 9$?

8. In the example at the top, how many comic books would each friend get if there were 300 comic books?

9. How could you use multiplication to check your answer of 200 comic books per person?

Independent Practice

In **10** through **29**, use mental math to find each quotient.

10. $22 \div 2$ **11.** $220 \div 2$ **12.** $2,200 \div 2$ **13.** $22,000 \div 2$

14. $63 \div 9$ **15.** $630 \div 9$ **16.** $6,300 \div 9$ **17.** $63,000 \div 9$

18. $72 \div 8$ **19.** $720 \div 8$ **20.** $7,200 \div 8$ **21.** $72,000 \div 8$

22. $36 \div 3$ **23.** $360 \div 3$ **24.** $3,600 \div 3$ **25.** $36,000 \div 3$

26. $42 \div 6$ **27.** $420 \div 6$ **28.** $4,200 \div 6$ **29.** $42,000 \div 6$

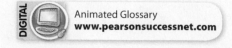

DIGITAL   Animated Glossary
www.pearsonsuccessnet.com

*For another example, see Set B on page 22.

Notice the pattern.

$10 \div 5 = 2$

$100 \div 5 = 10 \text{ tens} \div 5 = 2 \text{ tens} = 20$

$1,000 \div 5 = 10 \text{ hundreds} \div 5 = 2 \text{ hundreds} = 200$

$10,000 \div 5 = 10 \text{ thousands} \div 5 = 2 \text{ thousands} = 2,000$

Use the division fact $10 \div 5 = 2$.

Count the additional zeros in the dividend (the number you are dividing). The number you are dividing by, in this case 5, is the divisor.

There are two more zeros in 1,000 than in 10. Annex the additional zeros to the quotient (the number that is the result of dividing).

So, $1,000 \div 5 = 200$.

Each friend will get 200 comic books.

Problem Solving

30. A small cruise ship leaving from the Port of Miami can transport 240 passengers. If 8 people can be seated at each table in the dining room and each table is filled, how many tables are there?

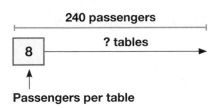

31. THINK SOLVE EXPLAIN Explain how can you find the quotient of $56,000 \div 7$ mentally. Find the quotient.

32. Estimation Estimate the sum of 184 and 179 by rounding each number to the nearest hundred. Will the estimate be an underestimate or an overestimate? Why?

33. Algebra If $180 \div n = 30$, then what is the value of n?

34. Writing to Explain Why does $3,600 \div 6$ have the same quotient as $1,800 \div 3$?

35. If a cyclist rides 200 miles in 5 days and rides the same distance each day, how many miles does the cyclist ride each day?

36. DVDs at the mall are on sale 3 for $25. If 400 DVDs are put on 5 shelves with an equal number on each shelf, how many DVDs are on each shelf?

    A 8   **C** 800

    B 80   **D** 8,000

37. 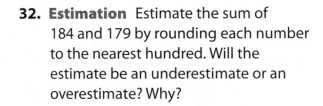 **Science** Saturn's average distance from the Sun is 886,000,000 miles. Jupiter's average distance from the Sun is 484,000,000 miles. How many miles farther is Saturn from the Sun than Jupiter?

38. Number Sense For each pair, Critical THINKING determine if the quotient is the same or different. Explain.

    a $72,000 \div 9$ and $40,000 \div 5$

    b $3,600 \div 12$ and $1,800 \div 6$

MA.5.A.1.1 Describe the process of finding quotients involving multi-digit dividends using models, place value, properties and the relationship of division to multiplication. Also MA.5.A.1.2

Breaking Apart to Divide

How can you break apart numbers to divide?

At a festival, balloons lifted off in equal groups from 5 locations. How many balloons were in each group?

Choose an operation.
Divide to find the number of balloons in each group.

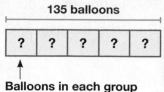

135 balloons

?	?	?	?	?

↑
Balloons in each group

135 balloons

Guided Practice*

Do you know HOW?

Copy and complete.

1. $48 \div 4 = (40 + 8) \div 4$
$= \left(\dfrac{40}{4} + \dfrac{8}{4}\right)$
$= (10 + \boxed{})$
$= \boxed{}$

2. $824 \div 8 = (800 + 24) \div 8$
$= \left(\dfrac{800}{8} + \dfrac{24}{8}\right)$
$= (\boxed{} + \boxed{})$
$= \boxed{}$

Do you UNDERSTAND?

3. If the example above were $816 \div 8$, would you break apart the dividend by using place value or by using compatible numbers? Explain your reasoning.

4. To find $324 \div 3$, how would you break apart 324 using place value? How would you break apart 324 using compatible numbers?

Independent Practice

Leveled Practice Copy and complete. Use place value or compatible numbers to break apart the dividend.

5. $88 \div 4 = (\boxed{} + 8) \div 4$
$= \left(\dfrac{80}{\boxed{}} + \dfrac{8}{\boxed{}}\right)$
$= (20 + \boxed{})$
$= \boxed{}$

6. $515 \div 5 = (500 + \boxed{}) \div 5$
$= \left(\dfrac{\boxed{}}{5} + \dfrac{15}{\boxed{}}\right)$
$= (\boxed{} + 3)$
$= \boxed{}$

7. $75 \div 5$

8. $66 \div 6$

9. $96 \div 3$

10. $633 \div 3$

11. $482 \div 2$

12. $545 \div 5$

13. $824 \div 4$

14. $963 \div 3$

Animated Glossary
www.pearsonsuccessnet.com

*For another example, see Set C on page 22.

Some dividends can be broken apart using place value to make dividing easier. The sum of the quotients of the parts gives the quotient.

$$135 \div 5 = (100 + 30 + 5) \div 5$$
$$= \frac{100}{5} + \frac{30}{5} + \frac{5}{5}$$
$$= 20 + 6 + 1$$
$$= 27$$

Tip $100 \div 5 = \frac{100}{5}$

Some dividends can be broken apart into compatible numbers. These are numbers that are easy to compute with mentally. The sum of the quotients of the compatible numbers gives the quotient.

$$135 \div 5 = (100 + 35) \div 5$$
$$= \frac{100}{5} + \frac{35}{5}$$
$$= 20 + 7$$
$$= 27$$

There were 27 balloons in each group.

Problem Solving

15. There are 155 cornstalks in 5 rows. Each row has the same number of cornstalks. How many cornstalks are in each row?

16. Draw a Diagram Odessa is cutting a square cake into 8 equal pieces. What is the least number of cuts she can make?

Use the table for **17** and **18**.

17. The table shows the number of cans Tony collected for 3 days of the canned food drive. Tony packed the cans in 3 boxes. He put an equal number of cans in each box. How many cans are in each box?

Data

Canned Food Drive	
Day	**Cans Collected**
Mon.	140
Tues.	96
Wed.	100

18. Use the table above. Suppose the number of cans Tony collects on Thursday is double the number he collected on Monday and Wednesday combined. How many cans will Tony collect on Thursday?

19. Estimation A restaurant serves about 425 customers each day. About how many customers does the restaurant serve in 7 days?

20. A pencil manufacturer shipped 448 pencils in boxes to an office supply store. There are 4 pencils in each box. How many boxes of pencils did the manufacturer ship?

  A 211

  B 122

  C 121

  D 112

21. Writing to Explain What steps would you follow to divide 525 by 5 using place value to break apart the dividend? Show your work.

Critical THINKING

22. Dave filled one bag with 22 pounds of corn and another bag with 19 pounds of corn. How much more corn is needed to have a total of 50 pounds of corn?

Lesson

1-4

MA.5.A.1.2 Estimate
quotients or calculate them
mentally depending on
the context and numbers
involved.

Estimating Quotients

How can you estimate quotients?

Jorge is putting shells into 6 boxes. He wants to put about the same number in each box. About how many shells could Jorge put in each box?

Choose an Operation Divide to separate an amount into equal groups.

258 total shells

Guided Practice*

Do you know HOW?

In **1** through **8**, estimate each quotient.

1. 520 ÷ 4

2. 444 ÷ 8

3. 640 ÷ 6

4. 310 ÷ 5

5. 683 ÷ 2

6. 297 ÷ 3

7. 700 ÷ 9

8. 507 ÷ 7

Do you UNDERSTAND?

9. Reasonableness In the rounding example above, how do you know the actual quotient should be less than 50?

10. In the example above, about how many shells could Jorge put into each box if he had 8 boxes? Is your estimate an underestimate or an overestimate?

Independent Practice

In **11** through **22**, use rounding to estimate each quotient.

11. 312 ÷ 5

12. 792 ÷ 4

13. 834 ÷ 2

14. 518 ÷ 4

15. 586 ÷ 5

16. 419 ÷ 7

17. 635 ÷ 8

18. 287 ÷ 2

19. 975 ÷ 5

20. 359 ÷ 6

21. 695 ÷ 7

22. 187 ÷ 4

In **23** through **34**, use compatible numbers to estimate each quotient.

23. 263 ÷ 3

24. 317 ÷ 7

25. 477 ÷ 6

26. 378 ÷ 9

27. 641 ÷ 6

28. 433 ÷ 4

29. 256 ÷ 3

30. 182 ÷ 7

31. 545 ÷ 8

32. 239 ÷ 5

33. 772 ÷ 7

34. 324 ÷ 8

One Way

Use rounding to estimate 258 ÷ 6.

Remember that you can round to the nearest tens or hundreds.

Round 258 to 300.

300 ÷ 6 = 50

50 shells is an overestimate, since 258 was rounded to 300.

Another Way

Use compatible numbers.

Replace 258 with 240.

240 and 6 are compatible, since 24 ÷ 6 = 4. You can use mental math to find 240 ÷ 6 = 40.

40 shells is an underestimate, since 258 was rounded to 240.

Jorge should put between 40 and 50 shells in each box.

Problem Solving

35. Mr. Turner's class planted 4 rows of 17 pansies in the school garden. Mrs. Moreno's class planted 5 rows of 14 petunias. How many flowers did the two classes plant in all?

36. THINK SOLVE EXPLAIN If you want to use compatible numbers to estimate 262 ÷ 7, is it better to use 210 ÷ 7 or 280 ÷ 7? Explain.

37. Seven friends collected coats for a clothing drive. The students gathered 61 coats. Each person collected about the same number. About how many coats did each student collect?

38. The town of Kingswood just completed building a new auditorium. There are 7 sections in the auditorium. The auditorium seats 560 people. How many seats are in each section?

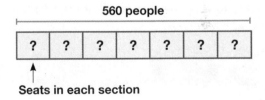

560 people

| ? | ? | ? | ? | ? | ? | ? |

Seats in each section

39. Toby earned $596 in 3 months by mowing lawns. If he was paid the same amount each month, about how much did he earn per month?

40. Think About the Process **Critical THINKING** A digital camera costs $499. A laser printer for the camera costs $277. If you have $100 to spend, which expression can you use to find how much more money you need to save to buy the digital camera?

    A 499 − 100   **C** 499 + 100

    B 277 + 100 + 499   **D** 277 − 100

41. Horses are measured in hands. Three hands equal 1 foot. Radar, the world's tallest horse, is about 19 hands high. About how many feet tall is Radar?

    F 5 feet   **H** 7 feet

    G 6 feet   **I** 8 feet

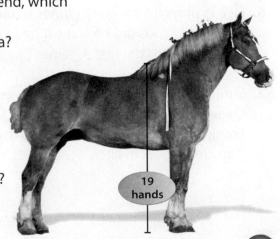

19 hands

MA.5.A.6.5 Solve non-routine problems using various strategies including "solving a simpler problem" and "guess, check, and revise."

Problem Solving

Missing or Extra Information

A 1920 antique bicycle that had once belonged to 2 owners recently sold for $850. A 2008 lightweight mountain bike recently sold for 3 times as much. What was the cost of the 2008 bike?

Guided Practice*

Do you know HOW?

For **1** and **2**, decide if each problem has extra or missing information. Solve if possible.

1. An adult male gorilla eats about 40 pounds of food each day. An adult female gorilla eats about half as much. How many pounds of food does an adult male gorilla eat in one week?

2. Lacey is buying dried fruit to feed her pet bird. How much will it cost to feed the bird for one month?

Do you UNDERSTAND?

3. Draw a diagram to show what you know and want to find in Problem 1.

4. **Writing to Explain** Why is it important to find the extra or missing information before solving a problem?

5. **Write a Problem** Write a real-world problem that does not include all of the information to solve it. Under the problem, write the missing information.

Independent Practice

For **6** and **7**, decide if each problem has extra or missing information. Solve if possible.

6. Eli has played 5 baseball games so far this season. How many runs did he score if he scored 2 runs each game for the first 4 games?

7. Sonja posted 45 band concert flyers in 2 days. Over the next 2 days, Elsie posted 60 flyers, and Frank posted 30 flyers. How many flyers did the 3 students post in all?

Stuck? Try this....

- What do I know?
- What am I asked to find?
- What diagram can I use to help understand the problem?
- Can I use addition, subtraction, multiplication, or division?
- Is all of my work correct?
- Did I answer the right question?
- Is my answer reasonable?

For another example, see Set E on page 23.

Read and Understand

Draw a diagram to show what you know and want to find.

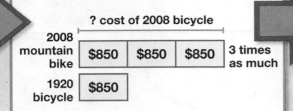

? cost of 2008 bicycle

| 2008 mountain bike | $850 | $850 | $850 | 3 times as much |
| 1920 bicycle | $850 |

Plan

Is there extra information not needed to solve the problem?

Yes. The years, 1920 and 2008, are not needed. Also, it does not matter that the antique bike once had 2 owners.

Solve

Is there missing information needed to solve the problem?

No. All the information I need is given in the problem.

Since 3 × $850 = $2,550, the cost of the 2008 bike was $2,550.

---

8. Mrs. Torance has invited 16 people to a party. What information is missing if she wants to serve enough submarine sandwiches at her party?

Each sub feeds 3 children or 2 adults

9. Kara and her 4 friends went camping. Each day they hiked 2 miles before lunch and 3 miles after lunch. How many total miles did all the girls hike on their camping trip? Provide possible information needed to solve the problem, then solve it.

10. Fox Meadow Farm boards show horses. Fifteen of their horses are in the arena. The other 21 horses are in the barn. How many horses board at the farm? Draw a picture and write an equation to solve.

11. **Reasoning** One decade equals 10 years and one century equals 100 years. Are there more years in 11 decades or 1 century?

Critical THINKING

12. **Science** Roadrunners live year-round throughout the southwestern part of the United States. At top speed, how far can a roadrunner run in 30 seconds?

top speed—22 feet per second

13. There are 6 students setting up chairs for the school play. They arrange 480 chairs in 8 equal rows. How many chairs are in each row?

A 6

B 60

C 80

D 488

14. Karen has a coin collection. She keeps an equal number of coins in each of 9 folders. How many coins are in each folder? Provide possible information needed to solve the problem, then solve it.

15. **Writing to Explain** There are 24 hours in one day. How can you use addition to find the number of hours in one week? How can you use multiplication?

MA.5.A.1.3 Interpret solutions to division situations including those with remainders depending on the context of the problem.

Understanding Remainders

counters

How many are left over?

23 soccer balls

Luisa is packing soccer balls into crates. Each crate will hold 5 soccer balls. How many crates will she fill? Are any soccer balls left?

Choose an Operation You want to separate 23 into equal groups of 5, so you can divide.

Each crate will hold 5 soccer balls.

Another Example **What do you do with the remainder?**

Ned has 27 soccer cards to put in an album. He can put 6 cards on each page. He knows that 27 ÷ 6 = 4 with a remainder of 3.

There are 3 ways to interpret a remainder.

Example A	**Example B**	**Example C**
How many pages can Ned fill?	How many pages will Ned work on?	How many cards will Ned put on the 5th page?
Find how many groups of 6 there will be.	Find how many groups are filled or started.	Find how many are left after 4 pages are filled.
The remainder can be ignored.	Add 1 to the quotient.	The remainder is the answer.
Ned can fill 4 pages.	Ned will work on 5 pages.	Ned will put 3 cards on the 5th page.

Explain It

1. Why are the answers to the examples different?

2. Janie has 34 photos to put in an album. She can put 4 photos on each page. How many photos will be on the 9th page?

Step 1	**Step 2**	**Step 3**

Step 1

Show the total number of items.

Use counters to show 23.

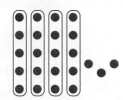

Step 2

Divide them into equal groups.

Make equal groups with 5 counters in each group.

Step 3

Write the number of equal groups and the number left over.

23 ÷ 5 = 4 with 3 left over

Luisa will fill 4 crates. There will be 3 soccer balls left over.

The part that is left over when we divide is called the remainder.

Guided Practice*

Do you know HOW?

Use counters or draw a picture to find the number of groups and the number left over.

1. 17 oranges, 3 oranges in each box

   17 ÷ 3 = ▢ with ▢ left over

2. 9 ÷ 2 = ▢ with ▢ left over

Do you UNDERSTAND?

3. **Writing to Explain** Can the remainder be greater than the divisor?

4. Dave is packing 23 sweaters into boxes. Each box will hold 3 sweaters. How many boxes will he fill? How many boxes will he need in all?

Independent Practice

For **5** through **10**, find the number of groups and the number left over. Use counters or draw a picture to help.

5. 18 jars, 4 jars in each box
   18 ÷ 4 = ▢ with ▢ left over

6. 22 shirts, 6 shirts in each box
   22 ÷ 6 = ▢ with ▢ left over

7. 27 ÷ 7 = ▢ with ▢ left over

8. 13 ÷ 2 = ▢ with ▢ left over

9. 31 ÷ 8 = ▢ with ▢ left over

10. 32 ÷ 9 = ▢ with ▢ left over

For **11** through **13**, interpret each remainder.

11. 7 football cards, 3 cards on each page How many pages can Alex complete?

12. 11 baseball cards, 4 cards on each page How many cards are on the 3rd page?

13. 34 stickers, 5 stickers on each page How many pages will have some stickers?

DIGITAL Animated Glossary, eTools
www.pearsonsuccessnet.com

*For another example, see Set F on page 23.

Lesson 1-6   **15**

Use the table for **14** through **16**.

14. Samuel has 45 prize tickets. How many marbles can he get?

15. Inez got 3 rings and 2 stickers. How many tickets did she use?

16. Milt had 28 prize tickets. He traded tickets for 3 yo-yos. How many prize tickets does he have left?

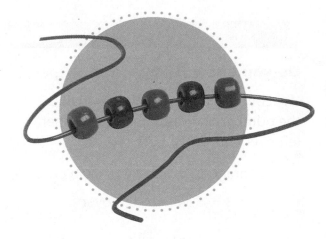

Ticket Exchange	
Prize	Number of Tickets
Yo-yo	8
Ring	9
Marble	7
Sticker	4

17. Strategy Focus Solve. Use the Draw a Picture strategy.

Keiko makes necklaces like the one in the picture on the right. She has 19 blue beads and 13 red beads.

a How many more blue beads than red beads does Keiko have?

b How many necklaces can she make?

18. Number Sense There are 38 students going to a museum. Each van can hold 8 students. How many vans will be needed?

Critical THINKING

19. Jack is making muffins. He will use 5 raisins to decorate each muffin. If he has 21 raisins, how many muffins can he decorate?

20. Jada bought a bag of 8 apples. She and her 3 sisters will share the apples equally. How many apples will each person get? Will there be any apples left over? If so, how many?

21. 🎵 **Music** How many strings in all are used to make 4 guitars like the ones in the picture below?

22. There are 39 children at a park. They want to make teams with 9 children on each team. How many teams can they make?

A 4   **C** 9

B 5   **D** 28

Tejano music uses 12-string guitars.

Find the product. Estimate to check if the answer is reasonable.

1.   692
     ×   4

2.   365
     ×   2

3.   45
     × 36

4.   444
     ×   22

5.   73
     × 52

6.   605
     ×   7

7.   117
     ×   15

8.   75
     × 62

Find the quotient.

9. 720 ÷ 9

10. 3,200 ÷ 8

11. 30,000 ÷ 5

12. 48,000 ÷ 6

13. 54,000 ÷ 9

14. 21,000 ÷ 7

15. 40,000 ÷ 5

16. 2,700 ÷ 3

Error Search Find each answer that is not correct.
Write it correctly and explain the error.

17. 42,000 ÷ 7 = 6,000

18.   308
      ×   62
      18,686

19. 180 ÷ 6 = 20

20.   123
      ×   33
        369

Number Sense

Estimating and Reasoning Write whether each statement is
true or false. Explain your reasoning.

21. The quotient of 388 ÷ 8 is closer to 50 than 40.

22. The sum of 495 + 368 is 5 more than 868.

23. The product of 5 and 3,003 is 15 more than 15,000.

24. The product of 28 and 485 is greater than 15,000.

25. The quotient of 432 ÷ 6 is closer to 80 than 70.

26. The product of 7 and 409 is greater than the product of 4 and 709.

27. The quotient of 42,000 ÷ 6 is greater than 700 and less than 70,000.

MA.5.A.1.3 Interpret solutions to division situations including those with remainders depending on the context of the problem.

Problem Solving

Reasonableness

There are 60 students attending a field trip. One chaperone is needed for every 8 students. How many chaperones are needed?

Answer: $60 ÷ 8 = 7$ with 4 left over
So, 7 chaperones are needed.

After you solve a problem, check to see if your answer is reasonable.

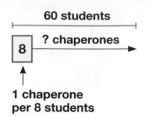

60 students

8 ? chaperones

1 chaperone
per 8 students

Guided Practice*

Do you know HOW?

Look back and check. Tell if the answer is reasonable. Explain why or why not.

1. Myrna has 26 daisies. She can plant 3 daisies in each pot. How many pots can she completely fill?

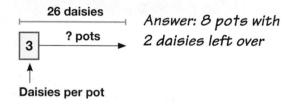

26 daisies

3 ? pots

Daisies per pot

Answer: 8 pots with 2 daisies left over

Do you UNDERSTAND?

2. In the problem above, why did the remainder need to be interpreted before the final answer was given?

3. **Write a Problem** Write a real-world problem that you can solve by dividing. Give an answer to be checked for reasonableness.

Independent Practice

In **4** through **6**, look back and check. Tell if the answer is reasonable. Explain why or why not.

4. In the school cafeteria, each table holds 10 students. There are 48 students who will eat lunch. How many tables are needed to seat all of the students?

Answer: Four tables with 8 students left over

Stuck? Try this....

- What do I know?
- What am I asked to find?
- What diagram can I use to help understand the problem?
- Can I use addition, subtraction, multiplication, or division?
- Is all of my work correct?
- Did I answer the right question?
- Is my answer reasonable?

For **5** the table at the right shows how many students can use each case of a supply.

Art Supplies	
Item	**Number of Students**
Case of pastels	3
Case of paints	4
Case of charcoals	6

Data

5. Mrs. Goia has 29 students in her art classes. She is ordering art supplies.

   a How many cases of pastels does she need to order?

   Answer: 10 cases

   b How many cases of charcoals does she need to order?

   Answer: 4 cases

6. Lionel is buying ice chests to hold 60 bottles of lemonade for a picnic. Each ice chest holds 8 bottles. How many ice chests should he buy?

   Answer: 8 chests

7. Estimation Bridget sold 62 tickets to a school concert at $3.95 each. About how much money did she collect for all 62 tickets?

8. Number Sense How many 6-bottle packages of bottled water must Rashmi's mom buy if she plans to serve 1 bottle to each of the 28 people who will attend the school fair?

Critical THINKING

9. Marcia has 27 red beads and 42 blue beads. How many beads does she have in all? Write an equation and solve.

b	
27	42

10. Pia needs 100 red beads to make a necklace. She already has 38 red beads. How many more red beads does she need? Write an equation and solve.

100	
38	r

11. A wood carver has made 70 carved animals. The animals will be shipped in boxes that hold 8 animals each. How many boxes will be completely filled? How many animals will be left over?

1 Which related multiplication equation could help you find $180 \div 6$? (1-1)

    A. $2 \times 3 = 6$

    B. $3 \times 2 = 6$

    C. $6 \times 30 = 180$

    D. $36 \times 5 = 180$

2 If $2,400 is divided evenly among 3 charities, how much does each charity get? (1-2)

    F. $8,000

    G. $800

    H. $80

    I. $60

3 How could you break apart 525 and find $525 \div 5$ by using compatible numbers? (1-3)

    A. $(524 + 1) \div 5$

    B. $(500 + 2 + 3) \div 5$

    C. $(425 + 50) \div 5$

    D. $(500 + 25) \div 5$

4 About 775 people attended 4 performances of a rock concert. About how many people attended each concert? (1-4)

    F.   About 20

    G.   About 40

    H.   About 200

    I.   About 400

5 Harry is packing 712 whistles in 8 boxes. He uses compatible numbers to estimate the number of whistles he puts in each box. Which of the following expressions uses compatible numbers to estimate $712 \div 8$? (1-4)

    A. $700 \div 8$

    B. $720 \div 8$

    C. $730 \div 8$

    D. $750 \div 8$

6 The Parker family used 9,000 gallons of water in 3 months. If they used the same amount of water each month, how many gallons of water did they use each month? (1-2)

    F.   3 gallons

    G.   30 gallons

    H.   300 gallons

    I.   3,000 gallons

7 There are 46 people at a banquet, and 6 people can be seated at each table. Which answer is reasonable if you are asked to find how many tables are needed to seat everyone? (1-7)

    A.   7 tables since $46 \div 6 = 7$ with a remainder of 4

    B.   8 tables since $46 \div 6 = 7$ with a remainder of 4, and 1 more table is needed for the remaining 4 people

    C.   4 tables because the remainder is 4 when you divide 46 by 6

    D.   6 tables since you must subtract 1 from the quotient when you divide 46 by 6

8 Mr. Sanchez worked at a hospital for 320 hours in 8 weeks. He worked the same number of hours each week. Which multiplication equation could you use to find 320 ÷ 8? (1-1)

F. $4 \times 8 = 32$

G. $8 \times 4 = 32$

H. $8 \times 40 = 320$

I. $32 \times 10 = 320$

9 A shipping company delivered 284 packages in 4 days. The same number of packages were delivered each day. How could you break apart 284 to find 284 ÷ 4 by using place value? (1-3)

A. $(283 + 1) \div 4$

B. $(260 + 24) \div 4$

C. $(250 + 34) \div 4$

D. $(200 + 80 + 4) \div 4$

10 Ling has soccer practice 2 hours a day, 3 days a week. She practices the piano for 1 hour each day, 5 days a week. How many hours does Ling practice soccer in 8 weeks? (1-5)

F. 48 hours

G. 10 hours

H. 8 hours

I. 6 hours

11 Rafael is decorating picture frames with seashells. He has 30 seashells. If he uses 7 seashells to decorate each picture frame, how many picture frames can Rafael decorate completely? (1-6)

A. 3

B. 4

C. 5

D. 7

12 Beth took 44 photographs when she was on vacation. She can paste 6 photographs on each page of her photo album. How many photos will be left after she has filled 7 pages? (1-6)

13 THINK SOLVE EXPLAIN Students are hiking on the Creekside Trail. They hike 6 miles on Thursday and 8 miles on Friday. How many miles do they need to hike on Saturday to reach the end of the trail? Provide possible information needed to solve the problem. Then solve it. (1-5)

Reteaching

Set A, pages 4–5

Find 420 ÷ 7.

Use related multiplication and division facts and multiplying by multiples of 10 to find the quotient.

$7 \times 6 = 42$ $7 \times 60 = 420$
$42 \div 7 = 6$ $420 \div 7 = 60$

Remember that you can use the relationship between multiplication and division to help you divide.

Copy and complete.

1. $8 \times \blacksquare = 320$ **2.** $5 \times \blacksquare = 150$
    $320 \div 8 = \blacksquare$ $150 \div 5 = \blacksquare$

Set B, pages 6–7

Find 48,000 ÷ 6.

Identify a basic fact. $48 \div 6 = 8$

Look for a pattern. $480 \div 6 = 80$
$4,800 \div 6 = 800$
$48,000 \div 6 = 8,000$

Remember to use basic facts and patterns to divide mentally.

Find each quotient.

1. $810 \div 9$ **2.** $4,500 \div 9$

3. $2,400 \div 6$ **4.** $42,000 \div 7$

Set C, pages 8–9

Find 336 ÷ 3.

Use place value or compatible numbers to break apart the dividend.

$$336 \div 3 = (300 + 30 + 6) \div 3$$
$$= \frac{300}{3} + \frac{30}{3} + \frac{6}{3}$$
$$= 100 + 10 + 2$$
$$= 112$$

Remember that dividends can be broken apart to make dividing easier.

Find each quotient.

1. $82 \div 2$ **2.** $66 \div 3$

3. $535 \div 5$ **4.** $808 \div 4$

5. $969 \div 3$ **6.** $642 \div 2$

Set D, pages 10–11

Estimate 330 ÷ 8.

Think of a number close to 33 that is a multiple of 8 so a basic fact can be used. Then divide.

$32 \div 8 = 4$
$320 \div 8 = 40$

So, 330 ÷ 8 is about 40.

Remember to use rounding or compatible numbers when estimating quotients.

Estimate.

1. $410 \div 6$ **2.** $653 \div 8$

3. $246 \div 5$ **4.** $641 \div 7$

Set E, pages 12–13

Decide if the problem has missing or extra information. Solve if possible.

Kay has 3 folders. Each folder has 6 pockets. How many sheets of paper are in each folder?

What you know: 3 folders, 6 pockets in each folder

What you want to find: The number of sheets of paper in each folder.

Can you solve? No, the problem does not mention the number of sheets of paper

Remember that some problems have too much information, but they can still be solved.

1. Mario had $40.20. He went to the store and bought apples, cereal, and bread. How much change did he get back?

2. Ana bought 6 books. Each book cost $13 and each bookmark cost $2. How much did Ana spend on books?

Set F, pages 14–16

Tom is putting 14 apples into bags. Each bag holds 4 apples. How many bags can Tom fill? Will any apples be left over?

Use counters to model $14 \div 4$.

$14 \div 4 = 3$ with 2 left over

Tom can fill 3 bags. There will be 2 apples left over.

Remember to make sure you put the correct number of items in each group.

1. 21 books, 5 books in each box
   $21 \div 5 = $ ▢ with ▢ left over

2. 40 stickers, 6 stickers on each page
   $40 \div 6 = $ ▢ with ▢ left over

3. 23 days, 7 days in each week
   $23 \div 7 = $ ▢ with ▢ left over

Set G, pages 18–19

A company ships 4 basketballs in a box. How many boxes are needed to ship 30 balls?

Divide.

$30 \div 4 = 7$ with 2 left over

Seven boxes will be completely filled, but another box is needed to hold the remainder of 2 balls. It is reasonable to say that 8 boxes are needed to ship 30 balls.

Remember to check the reasonableness of a solution by interpreting the remainder.

1. Sarah will store her collection of 75 CDs in a cabinet that can hold 9 CDs on each shelf. How many shelves will Sarah fill completely with her collection?

2. There are 46 people going to a baseball game in cars that can each seat 6 people. How many cars are needed for everyone to go to the game?

Developing Fluency: Dividing by One-Digit Divisors

1 During the Gold Rush, cattle herding was an important part of the economy. How many cattle could each cowboy have been responsible for? You will find out in Lesson 2-4.

2 Scientists have been tagging turtles at Turtle Island for years in order to study turtle behavior. How many turtles have the scientists tagged? You will find out in Lesson 2-4.

3 A hiking trail through Ocala National Forest in Florida winds through hills and swamps. How long is this trail? You will find out in Lesson 2-6.

Vocabulary

Choose the best term from the box.

> • compatible numbers • divisor
> • dividend   • quotient

1. In the equation 45 ÷ 9 = 5, the number 5 is the __?__ .

2. In the equation 63 ÷ 7 = 9, the number 63 is the __?__.

3. One way to estimate is to use __?__.

④ Selenium is an element found in certain materials, such as these selenite crystals. It is often used to conduct electricity. Some of the tallest selenite crystals are found in Chihuahua, Mexico. You will find out how many times as tall as they are than a 4-foot-tall student in Lesson 2-2.

Multiplication

Copy and complete.

4. 128 × 3   5. 944 × 5

6. 471 × 8   7. 640 × 6

Dividing Mentally

Copy and complete.

8. 3,600 ÷ 9 9. 5,600 ÷ 7 10. 1,200 ÷ 4

11. 350 ÷ 5 12. 60,000 ÷ 3 13. 6,300 ÷ 7

Estimating Quotients

Use rounding or compatible numbers to estimate each quotient.

14. 341 ÷ 7 15. 27,116 ÷ 3 16. 4,321 ÷ 6

Writing to Explain Write an answer to the question.

17. Explain how knowing division facts can help you estimate 5,321 ÷ 9.

Topic Essential Question

• What is the standard algorithm for division and why does it work?

MA.5.A.1.1 Describe the process of finding quotients involving multi-digit dividends using models, place value, properties and the relationship of division to multiplication.

Using Models to Divide

Hands-On
Place-value blocks

How can place value help you divide?

Mrs. Lynch displayed 57 student drawings on 3 walls in her art classroom. If she divided the drawings equally, how many drawings are on each wall?

Estimate: $60 \div 3 = 20$

57 student drawings

drawings on each wall

Another Example How do you model remainders?

Four students equally share 55 paper plates for an art project. How many plates does each student get? How many plates are left?

Step 1 Divide the tens.

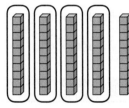

Division is used to find the number in equal groups.

$$\begin{array}{r} 1 \\ 4\overline{)55} \\ -\underline{4} \\ 1 \end{array}$$

There is 1 ten in each group and 1 ten left.

Step 2 Regroup the 1 ten as 10 ones and divide.

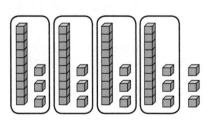

$$\begin{array}{r} 13 \text{ R3} \\ 4\overline{)55} \\ -\underline{4} \\ 15 \\ -\underline{12} \\ 3 \end{array}$$

Trade the extra ten for ten ones. The 1 ten and 5 ones make 15. There are 3 ones in each group and 3 left. The remainder is shown in the quotient as R3.

The four students will each get 13 paper plates. There will be 3 plates left over.

Explain It

1. In the first step above, what does the 1 in the quotient represent?

2. **Reasonableness** How can you check that the answer is correct?

Use place-value blocks to show 57.

Divide the tens into three equal groups.

$$\begin{array}{r} 1 \\ 3\overline{)57} \\ -3 \end{array}$$ 3 tens used

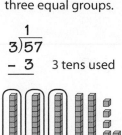

Trade the extra tens for ones.

$$\begin{array}{r} 1 \\ 3\overline{)57} \\ -3 \\ \hline 27 \end{array}$$ 3 tens used / 27 ones left

Divide the ones.

$$\begin{array}{r} 19 \\ 3\overline{)57} \\ -3 \\ \hline 27 \\ -27 \\ \hline 0 \end{array}$$ 27 ones used

There are 19 drawings on each wall.

Guided Practice*

Do you know HOW?

In **1** through **4**, use place-value blocks or draw pictures. Tell how many are in each group and how many are left.

1. 76 magazines
   5 boxes

2. 56 marbles
   3 bags

3. 82 muffins
   7 boxes

4. 72 photos
   3 albums

Do you UNDERSTAND?

5. Describe another way to show 57 using place-value blocks.

6. Mrs. Lynch displayed 48 paintings in 3 sets. If each set had the same number of paintings, how many were in each set?

Independent Practice

Leveled Practice In **7** through **10**, use the model to complete each division sentence.

7. 71 ÷ ▢ = ▢ R2

8. ▢ ÷ 4 = ▢

9. ▢ ÷ ▢ = ▢

10. ▢ ÷ ▢ = ▢ R ▢

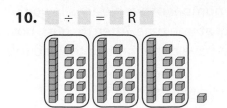

eTools
www.pearsonsuccessnet.com

DIGITAL

Independent Practice

In **11** through **30**, use place-value blocks or draw pictures to solve.

11. $3\overline{)46}$ **12.** $8\overline{)96}$ **13.** $4\overline{)55}$ **14.** $2\overline{)51}$ **15.** $5\overline{)89}$

16. $6\overline{)76}$ **17.** $7\overline{)36}$ **18.** $3\overline{)72}$ **19.** $2\overline{)63}$ **20.** $4\overline{)92}$

21. $3\overline{)44}$ **22.** $4\overline{)67}$ **23.** $6\overline{)85}$ **24.** $3\overline{)56}$ **25.** $5\overline{)97}$

26. $2\overline{)39}$ **27.** $4\overline{)31}$ **28.** $5\overline{)87}$ **29.** $7\overline{)82}$ **30.** $5\overline{)22}$

Problem Solving

31. Maya used place-value blocks to divide 87. She made groups of 17 with 2 left. Use place-value blocks or draw pictures to determine how many groups Maya made.

32. Writing to Explain Harold has 64 toy cars in 4 equal boxes. To find the number in each box, he divided 64 by 4. How many tens did he regroup as ones?

33. **Think About the Process** **Critical THINKING** Jake walks dogs and delivers papers to earn money. This month, he earned $52 delivering papers and $43 walking dogs. Each month, he puts half of his money into the bank. Which shows how much Jake saved this month?

    A $(52 + 43) + 2$ **C** $(52 + 43) \div 2$

    B $(52 + 43) \times 2$ **D** $(52 + 43) - 2$

34. Number Sense Tina has 50 berries. She wants to have the same number of berries each day for lunch. How many can she have each day if she eats them all in 5 days?

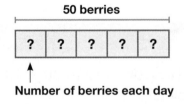

50 berries

?	?	?	?	?

Number of berries each day

35. The 4 fifth-grade classes from Jameson Elementary School took a trip to the United States Capitol. Each class had 24 students. At the Capitol, the students were divided into 6 equal groups. How many students were in each group?

36. A maximum number of people are allowed on a tour of the Capitol at one time. After 16 tours, how many people could have gone through the Capitol?

Tour maximum
40 people

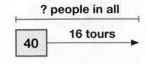

? people in all

40	16 tours

Algebra Connections

Completing Tables

Remember that multiplication and division have an inverse relationship.

Since $9 \times 7 = 63$, you also know:

$$63 \div 9 = 7$$
$$63 \div 7 = 9$$

You can use inverse relationships to help complete tables.

Example:

There are 4 quarts in a gallon. Complete the table.

gallons	1	3	8	▦
quarts	4	12	▦	40

You can multiply the number of gallons by 4 to find the number of quarts.

$8 \times 4 = 32$. So, 8 gallons = 32 quarts.

You can divide the number of quarts by 4 to find the number of gallons.

$40 \div 4 = 10$. So, 40 quarts = 10 gallons.

Copy and complete each table below.

1. Each box holds 5 pencils.

Pencils	15	30	35	40	45
Boxes	3	▦	▦	▦	9

2. Each shelf has 10 books.

Shelves	2	3	4	▦	▦
Books	20	▦	▦	50	90

3. A frame holds 4 photos.

Frames	2	3	▦	5	▦
Photos	▦	▦	16	▦	36

4. Each package has 8 markers.

Packages	2	4	5	▦	▦
Markers	▦	▦	▦	72	80

5. Mallory swims 2 miles per day.

Days	1	3	▦	10	▦
Miles	▦	▦	16	▦	60

6. Each week has 7 days.

Weeks	2	4	▦	▦	12
Days	▦	▦	35	63	▦

MA.5.A.1.4 Divide multi-digit whole numbers fluently, including solving real-world problems, demonstrating understanding of the standard algorithm and checking the reasonableness of results. Also MA.5.A.1.1

Dividing 2-Digit by 1-Digit Numbers

76 cans of soup in all

What is a common way to record division?

At the school food drive, Al needs to put the same number of soup cans into four boxes. How many soup cans will go in each box?

Choose an Operation Divide to find the number in each group.

Another Example **How do you divide with a remainder?**

Al collects 58 cans of vegetables. He puts the same number of cans in four boxes. How many cans of vegetables will go in each box? How many cans will be left over?

A 14 cans, 2 cans left over   **C** 16 cans, 2 cans left over

B 15 cans, 2 cans left over   **D** 18 cans, 2 cans left over

Step 1

Divide the tens.

Regroup the remaining ten as 10 ones.

$$\begin{array}{r} 1 \\ 4)\overline{58} \\ -4 \\ \hline 1 \end{array}$$

Divide. $5 \div 4 \approx 1$
Multiply. $1 \times 4 = 4$
Subtract. $5 - 4 = 1$
Compare. $1 < 4$

Step 2

Bring down the ones.

Divide the ones.

Multiply and subtract.

$$\begin{array}{r} 14 \text{ R2} \\ 4)\overline{58} \\ -4\downarrow \\ \hline 18 \\ -16 \\ \hline 2 \end{array}$$

Divide. $18 \div 4 \approx 4$
Multiply. $4 \times 4 = 16$
Subtract. $18 - 16 = 2$
Compare. $2 < 4$

Step 3

Check by multiplying and adding: $14 \times 4 = 56$ and $56 + 2 = 58$.

There will be 14 cans of vegetables in each box and 2 cans left.

The correct choice is **A**.

Explain It

1. How are the steps *divide, multiply, subtract,* and *compare* used in division?

2. When you check division using multiplication, what do you do with the remainder?

Divide the tens.

```
    1
4)76
  - 4
    3
```

 Think There is **1** ten in each group and **3** tens left over.

Divide the ones.

```
    19
4)76
  - 4
   36
 - 36
    0
```

Think Trade the 3 tens for 30 ones.

30 ones and 6 ones make **36** ones.

There will be 19 soup cans in each box.

Check by multiplying.

```
     3
    19
  ×  4
    76
```

The answer checks.

Guided Practice*

Do you know HOW?

In **1** and **2**, copy and complete each calculation.

1.
```
      4
  2)94
   -
      4
   - 1
      0
```

2.
```
      6R
  5)82
   - 5
   -
```

Do you UNDERSTAND?

3. Explain how you would estimate to find the answer in Exercise 2.

4. Al collects 85 cans of fruit. He puts the same number of fruit cans in 4 boxes. Will he have any cans left over? If so, how many cans?

Independent Practice

Leveled Practice In **5** through **8**, copy and complete each calculation. Check your answers.

5.
```
  7)84
   - 7
      4
   - 1
      0
```

6.
```
       6
  3)78
   -
      8
   - 1
      0
```

7.
```
      R
  4)93
   - 8
   - 1
      1
```

8.
```
     1 R
  6)80
   -
   -
```

For **9** through **18**, find each quotient. Check your answers.

9. 3)63

10. 7)88

11. 6)96

12. 4)52

13. 5)73

14. 5)93

15. 3)87

16. 4)72

17. 6)77

18. 2)37

In **19** through **28**, find each quotient. Check your answers.

19. 3)46   **20.** 7)65   **21.** 8)27   **22.** 9)86   **23.** 4)66

24. 8)59   **25.** 4)92   **26.** 3)74   **27.** 5)68   **28.** 2)89

Problem Solving

For **29** and **30**, use the graph at the right.

29. **Science** Some of the tallest selenite crystals in a cave in Chihuahua, Mexico, are 50 feet tall. About how many times as tall are the tallest crystals than a 4-foot-tall student?

30. The title of a graph gives the main idea. What would be an appropriate title for the graph?

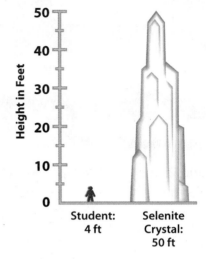

31. **Geometry** Zelda has a piece of fabric that is 74 inches long. She wants to divide it into 2 equal pieces. What is the length of each piece?

Use the recipe at the right for **32** and **33**.

32. How many ounces of Tasty Trail Mix are made using the ingredients in the recipe?

33. Maggie is making trail mix. She makes 4 batches of the recipe shown. Then she divides it into 3 equal sized bags. How many ounces are in each bag?

Tasty Trail Mix	
Granola	8 oz
Nuts	5 oz
Raisins	2 oz
Cranberries	3 oz

Data

34. **Writing to Explain** Why does $51 \div 4$ have two digits in the quotient, while $51 \div 6$ has only one digit in the quotient?

35. **Write a Problem** Write a problem that could be solved by dividing 78 by 5.

36. **Estimation** Paulo has 78 cattle on his ranch. He needs to divide them equally among 3 pastures. Which shows the best way to estimate the number of cattle in each pasture?

    A $60 \div 3$
    C $75 \div 3$
    B $66 \div 3$
    D $90 \div 3$

37. **Social Studies** Every year, the city of San Marcos holds a Cinco de Mayo festival. If 60 students perform in 5 equal groups, how many students are in each group?

    F 10
    H 25
    G 12
    I 55

Mixed Problem Solving

A state song is an official symbol of the state it represents. Each of the 50 states, with the exception of New Jersey, has at least one state song. Some of the states chose songs that are famous on their own, while other states chose a song that is known only as a state song. Here are a few examples of some of the state songs:

United States State Songs

State	Song Title	Year Written	Year Adopted
Florida	"The Swanee River"	1851	1935
Kentucky	"My Old Kentucky Home"	1853	1928
Oklahoma	"Oklahoma"	1943	1953
Maryland	"Maryland, My Maryland"	1861	1939

For **1** through **5**, use the table above.

1. How many years passed between the time Kentucky's state song was written before it was adopted?

2. How many years earlier was *"Maryland, My Maryland"* written than *"Oklahoma"*?

3. One decade equals 10 years. About how many decades passed between the writing of *"The Swanee River"* and its adoption? About how many years is this?

4. One century equals 100 years. Name a song that was written and another song that was adopted between which a century occurred. How many decades occurred between these two events?

5. **Writing to Explain** A lustrum is a period of 5 years. Richard said that about 15 lustrums occurred between Florida's state song being written and then adopted by the state. Is he correct? Explain.

6. **Strategy Focus** Decide if the problem has missing or extra information. Solve if possible.

   One decade occurred between the year *"Oklahoma"* was written and the year it was adopted. How many years occurred between the year *"The Swanee River"* was adopted and the year *"Oklahoma"* was adopted?

MA.5.A.1.1 Describe the process of finding quotients involving multi-digit dividends using models, place value, properties and the relationship of division to multiplication.

Connecting Models and Symbols

How can you use money to model division?

Abbott Middle School raised $148 selling spaghetti at the school's fund-raiser dinner. How can the principal divide the money equally among 4 school projects?

Choose an Operation Divide since you are sharing.

Another Example How can you record division?

Suppose 4 people need to share $148.

What You Think

The $100 bill needs to be shared. Exchange the $100 bill for ten $10 bills. There are now fourteen $10 bills.

Each person gets three $10 bills (4 × 3 = 12).

Two $10 bills are left to share. Exchange the $10 bills for twenty $1 bills.

That gives 28 $1 bills to be divided into four groups.

Each person gets seven $1 bills (4 × 7 = 28).

After each person gets seven $1 bills, there is no money left to share.

What You Write

```
    3
4)148
 - 12
    2
```

```
   37
4)148
 - 12
   28
 - 28
    0
```

Each person gets $37.

Explain It

1. Explain how you can exchange bills to divide four $10 bills equally among 5 people.

2. Suppose Abbott Middle School raised $76 more. In all, how much would each of the 4 projects receive?

Exchange the $100 bill for ten $10 bills. There are now fourteen $10 bills. Share the $10 bills. Each project gets three $10 bills. Two $10 bills are left.

Exchange the two remaining $10 bills for twenty $1 bills. This gives twenty-eight $1 bills.

Each project gets a total of $37.

Guided Practice*

Do you know HOW?

In **1** through **4**, use models to help you divide.

1. $3\overline{)69}$

2. $7\overline{)490}$

3. $9\overline{)225}$

4. $3\overline{)186}$

Do you UNDERSTAND?

5. **Writing to Explain** In the example above, why do you have to exchange the two remaining $10 bills?

6. If 4 people divide $244 equally, how much will each person get?

Independent Practice

Leveled Practice In **7**, use play money or draw diagrams of the bills shown at the right to symbolize division. Copy and complete the calculation as you answer the questions below.

five $100 bills

7. Six people need to share $576 equally.

a All $100 bills are replaced with $10 bills. How many $10 bills are there altogether?

b How many $10 bills will each person get?

seven $10 bills

c How many $10 bills are left?

d Replace the remaining $10 bills with $1 bills. How many $1 bills are left in all to divide among 6 people?

e What is the total amount each person gets?

$$
\begin{array}{r}
6\overline{)576} \\
-\ \blacksquare\blacksquare \\
\hline
6 \\
-\ \blacksquare\blacksquare
\end{array}
$$

six $1 bills

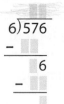

eTools
www.pearsonsuccessnet.com

*For another example, see Set C on page 54.

In **8** through **17**, copy and complete. You may use play money to help you divide.

8. 5)355   **9.** 7)693   **10.** 4)364   **11.** 6)492

12. 484 divided by 4   **13.** 672 divided by 6

14. 312 divided by 2   **15.** 765 divided by 5

16. 385 divided by 7   **17.** 759 divided by 3

Problem Solving

18. Milo is adding Spanish olives to salads for a party. A can of these olives is on sale for $1.45. Each can contains 38 olives. If Milo puts 3 olives on each salad, how many complete salads can he make?

19. Paulo helped his grandmother with her garden for five days after school. He worked for two hours each day. Paulo's grandmother gave him $75. How much money did Paulo earn each day?

20. Number Sense Nick and 3 friends unloaded 224 folding chairs for the community theater. Each person unloaded the same number of chairs. How many chairs did Nick unload?

21. Explain how division facts and patterns can help you find $20,000 \div 5$.

THINK
SOLVE
EXPLAIN

22. The Stanton Ferry transports a maximum of 756 people to Green Island in 4 trips. How many people can the ferry transport in 1 trip?

   A 151   **C** 189

   B 164   **D** 199

23. The Napoleon Bonaparte Broward Bridge is 10,646 feet long. The Sunshine Sky Bridge is 29,040 feet long. Which bridge is shorter and by how much?

24. Writing to Explain Why is 3.892 greater than 3.289?

25. Think About the Process The art museum sold 1,770 tickets to the modern art exhibit on Sunday. Each ticket cost $12. The ticket holders were divided into five groups to organize the viewing for that day. Which expression tells how to find the number of people in each group?

Critical THINKING

   F $1,770 \div \$12 + 5$

   G $1,770 \div 5 + \$12$

   H $1,770 \div \$12$

   I $1,770 \div 5$

26. Kirstin is starting a swimming club. She is the only member the first month. If club membership triples each month, how many members will the club have at the end of 4 months?

27. Find the next three numbers in the pattern shown below.

   10   15   12   17   14   ▪   ▪   ▪

Algebra Connections

Completing Number Sentences

Remember that a number sentence has two numbers or expressions that are connected by the symbols >, <, or =.

Mental math can often be used to see if the left or right side is greater.

Copy and complete the comparisons using estimation. Check your answers.

Remember:
> means "is greater than."
< means "is less than."
= means "is equal to."

Example: $81 \div 3 \bigcirc 8 \times 4$

Think I know that 8×4 is a basic fact.

The quotient of $81 \div 3 = 27$.
Complete the comparison with "<."

$$81 \div 3 < 8 \times 4$$

This means 81 separated into 3 groups is less than 8 groups of 4.

Copy and complete. Write <, >, or = in the circle.

1. $48 \div 6 \bigcirc 54 \div 6$

2. $40 \div 5 \bigcirc 45 \div 5$

3. $56 \div 7 \bigcirc 56 \div 8$

4. $84 \div 7 \bigcirc 24 \div 2$

5. $3 + 2 \bigcirc 49 \div 7$

6. $72 \div 8 \bigcirc 8 \times 1$

7. $18 \div 2 \bigcirc 18 - 10$

8. $3 \times 8 \bigcirc 72 \div 4$

9. $68 - 53 \bigcirc 48 \div 3$

10. $20 \div 4 \bigcirc 2 \times 2$

11. $30 \div 5 \bigcirc 28 \div 4$

12. $87 - 80 \bigcirc 48 \div 8$

For **13** and **14**, write a number sentence to help solve each problem.

13. Marina bought a lavender backpack for herself and a green backpack for her brother. Charley bought an orange backpack. Who spent more money?

$9

$20

14. Mr. Wozniak purchased a green backpack. Ms. Chivas purchased 4 lavender backpacks. Who paid more?

15. **Write a Problem** Write a word problem using the price of the backpacks.

$40

$50

MA.5.A.1.4 Divide multi-digit whole numbers fluently, including solving real-world problems, demonstrating understanding of the standard algorithm and checking the reasonableness of results.

Dividing 3-Digit by 1-Digit Numbers

Why use division?

Six students sold 432 candles. Each student sold the same number of candles. How many candles did each student sell?

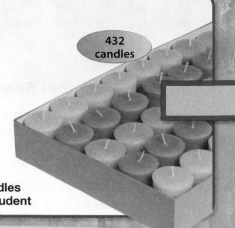

432 candles

432 candles

| ? | ? | ? | ? | ? | ? | ← Number of candles sold by each student

---

Another Example How do you find a quotient with a remainder?

2-digit quotient with remainder

Find 380 ÷ 6.

Estimate to place the first digit in the quotient.
360 ÷ 6 = 60, so the first digit goes in the tens place.

$$
\begin{array}{r}
6 \\
6\overline{)380} \\
-36 \\
\hline
2
\end{array}
$$

$$
\begin{array}{r}
63\ \text{R2} \\
6\overline{)380} \\
-36\downarrow \\
\hline
20 \\
-18 \\
\hline
2
\end{array}
$$

To check a division problem with a remainder, multiply the divisor and the quotient. Then add the remainder.

$$
\begin{array}{r}
63 \\
\times\ 6 \\
\hline
378 \\
+\ 2 \\
\hline
380
\end{array}
$$

3-digit quotient with remainder

Find 547 ÷ 4.

$$
\begin{array}{r}
1 \\
4\overline{)547} \\
-4 \\
\hline
1
\end{array}
$$

$$
\begin{array}{r}
13 \\
4\overline{)547} \\
-4\downarrow \\
\hline
14 \\
-12 \\
\hline
2
\end{array}
$$

$$
\begin{array}{r}
136\ \text{R3} \\
4\overline{)547} \\
-4 \\
\hline
14 \\
-12\downarrow \\
\hline
27 \\
-24 \\
\hline
3
\end{array}
$$

Check:

$$
\begin{array}{r}
136 \\
\times\ 4 \\
\hline
544 \\
+\ 3 \\
\hline
547
\end{array}
$$

Explain It

1. Name the quotient, divisor, remainder, and dividend in these two examples.

2. Why did the second example have a 3-digit quotient?

Find 432 ÷ 6.

Estimate. Decide where to place the first digit in the quotient.

Use compatible numbers.
$420 ÷ 6 = 70$
The first digit is in the tens place.

Divide the tens.
Multiply and subtract.

$$
\begin{array}{r}
7 \\
6{\overline{)432}} \\
-\,42 \\
\hline
1
\end{array}
$$

Divide. $43 ÷ 6 ≈ 7$
Multiply. $7 × 6 = 42$
Subtract. $43 − 42 = 1$
Compare. $1 < 6$

Bring down the ones.
Divide the ones. Multiply and subtract.

$$
\begin{array}{r}
72 \\
6{\overline{)432}} \\
-\,42\downarrow \\
\hline
12 \\
-\,12 \\
\hline
0
\end{array}
$$

Divide. $12 ÷ 6 = 2$
Multiply. $2 × 6 = 12$
Subtract. $12 − 12 = 0$
Compare. $0 < 6$

Each student sold 72 candles.

Guided Practice*

Do you know HOW?

In **1** through **6**, find each quotient.

1. $9{\overline{)270}}$ **2.** $6{\overline{)684}}$

3. $3{\overline{)65}}$ **4.** $5{\overline{)339}}$

5. $5{\overline{)564}}$ **6.** $4{\overline{)724}}$

Do you UNDERSTAND?

7. Writing to Explain How can estimating with compatible numbers help you find the quotient?

8. In the first example, find the quotient if the total number of candles is 561.

Independent Practice

In **9** through **16**, use compatible numbers to estimate each quotient. Then decide where to place the first digit of the quotient.

9. $5{\overline{)762}}$ **10.** $3{\overline{)289}}$ **11.** $8{\overline{)607}}$ **12.** $3{\overline{)567}}$

13. $6{\overline{)960}}$ **14.** $7{\overline{)973}}$ **15.** $5{\overline{)373}}$ **16.** $9{\overline{)462}}$

In **17** through **28**, copy and complete the calculation. Check your answers.

17. $8{\overline{)616}}$ **18.** $6{\overline{)486}}$ **19.** $4{\overline{)448}}$ **20.** $9{\overline{)828}}$

21. $2{\overline{)131}}$ **22.** $9{\overline{)836}}$ **23.** $5{\overline{)413}}$ **24.** $5{\overline{)469}}$

25. $7{\overline{)644}}$ **26.** $2{\overline{)995}}$ **27.** $4{\overline{)139}}$ **28.** $5{\overline{)625}}$

29. THINK SOLVE EXPLAIN How can you tell, before you divide 387 by 4, that the first digit of the quotient is in the tens place?

30. Writing to Explain **Critical THINKING** Why is the following incorrect? 296 ÷ 6 = 48 R8. Write your answer before you complete the calculation.

31. **Think** About the Process A team of 10 people in the Netherlands rolled a 140-lb barrel a distance of 164 miles in 24 hours. Each person rolled the same distance. Which of the following shows how to determine how many miles each person rolled the barrel?

A 164 ÷ 24   **C** 140 ÷ 24

B 164 ÷ 10   **D** 140 ÷ 10

32. Ray walked for 9 hours to raise money for his favorite charity. He raised $225. How much money did he raise for each hour he walked?

33. Over 9 years scientists tagged 450 turtles at Turtle Island. How many turtles did they tag each year if each year they tagged the same number of turtles?

	450 turtles							
?	?	?	?	?	?	?	?	?

34. The High Sierra Trail at Mt. Whitney is 49 miles long each way. Park rangers report that to walk the trail one way takes hikers 6 days. About how many miles must the hikers walk each day to finish all 49 miles in 6 days?

F 6 miles   **H** 10 miles

G 8 miles   **I** 12 miles

35. Algebra What is the value of c in the equation $c \times 3 = 324$?

A 18   **C** 180

B 108   **D** 1,080

36. Algebra Find the value of n.

$3 \times 7 = n \times 3$

37. Geometry What is the perimeter of the rectangle in inches? (Hint: 1 ft = 12 in.)

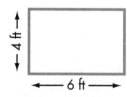

38. Suppose 8 cowboys herded 416 cattle. If each cowboy herded the same number of cattle, how many animals was each cowboy responsible for?

39. Willis Tower in Chicago is 1,450 feet tall. A hotel in Miami is 789 feet tall. How many feet taller is Willis Tower than the hotel in Miami? Finish drawing the picture. Write an equation and then solve. Let h = the difference in height.

	h

Finding Remainders

Tell how to find $573 \div 7$, including the remainder, on a calculator.

Step 1   Divide 573 by 7.

Press: 573 [÷] 7 [ENTER =]

Display: 81.857143

Step 2   Interpret the result and find the remainder.

The result means $573 \div 7$ is 81 with a remainder.
To find the remainder, multiply 7 by 81 and
subtract the result from 573.

Press: 7 [×] 81 [ENTER =]

Display: 567

Press: 573 [−] 567 [ENTER =]

Display: 6

$573 \div 7 = 81$ R6

Press (Clear) before starting a new problem.

Practice

Find each quotient and remainder.

1. $312 \div 5$ **2.** $295 \div 4$ **3.** $529 \div 9$

4. $158 \div 8$ **5.** $254 \div 3$ **6.** $191 \div 2$

7. $697 \div 6$ **8.** $413 \div 3$ **9.** $329 \div 5$

10. $9\overline{)651}$ **11.** $7\overline{)412}$ **12.** $4\overline{)381}$

13. $9\overline{)766}$ **14.** $6\overline{)218}$ **15.** $9\overline{)852}$

16. $5\overline{)689}$ **17.** $8\overline{)284}$ **18.** $4\overline{)359}$

MA.5.A.1.4 Divide multi-digit whole numbers fluently, including solving real-world problems, demonstrating understanding of the standard algorithm and checking the reasonableness of results.

Zeros in the Quotient

When do you write a zero in the quotient?

On vacation the McQueen family drove a total of 830 miles in four days. What is the average number of miles they drove each day?

Choose an Operation Divide to find how many miles per day.

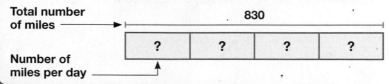

Total number of miles → 830

Number of miles per day → ? | ? | ? | ?

Another Example When do you write a zero in the ones place in the quotient?

Find 520 ÷ 4.

Step 1 Estimate. Decide where to place the first digit in the quotient. Use compatible numbers. 400 ÷ 4 = 100

$$\begin{array}{r} 1 \\ 4\overline{)520} \\ -4 \\ \hline 1 \end{array}$$
5 ÷ 4 ≈ 1
1 × 4 = 4
5 − 4 = 1
1 < 4

The first digit in the quotient is in the hundreds place.

Divide the hundreds. Multiply, subtract, and compare.

Step 2 Bring down the tens.
Divide the tens.
Multiply, subtract, and compare.

$$\begin{array}{r} 13 \\ 4\overline{)520} \\ -4\downarrow \\ \hline 12 \\ -12 \\ \hline 0 \end{array}$$
12 ÷ 4 = 3
3 × 4 = 12
12 − 12 = 0
0 < 4

Step 3 Bring down the ones.
There are 0 ones.
Write 0 in the ones place in the quotient.

$$\begin{array}{r} 130 \\ 4\overline{)520} \\ -4 \\ \hline 12 \\ -12\downarrow \\ \hline 00 \end{array}$$
There are 0 ones. Write 0 in the ones place in the quotient.

Explain It

1. In the example at the top, why is the zero in the tens place of the quotient, but in the ones place in Another Example?

2. Explain how to check your answers in both examples.

Step 1

Find $830 \div 4$.

Estimate first. Use compatible numbers. $800 \div 4 = 200$
So, the first digit in the quotient is in the hundreds place. Divide the hundreds.

$$
\begin{array}{r}
2 \\
4\overline{)830} \\
-8 \\
\hline
0
\end{array}
$$

Divide. $8 \div 4 = 2$
Multiply. $2 \times 4 = 8$
Subtract. $8 - 8 = 0$
Compare. $0 < 4$

Step 2

$$
\begin{array}{r}
20 \\
4\overline{)830} \\
-8\downarrow \\
\hline
03
\end{array}
$$

You cannot divide the tens. Write 0 in the tens place.

Step 3

$$
\begin{array}{r}
207 \ \text{R2} \\
4\overline{)830} \\
-8\downarrow \\
\hline
030 \\
-28 \\
\hline
2
\end{array}
$$

$30 \div 4 \approx 7$
$7 \times 4 = 28$
$30 - 28 = 2$
$2 < 4$

The McQueens drove about 207 miles each day.

Guided Practice*

Do you know HOW?

In **1** through **4**, find each quotient. Check your answers.

1. $9\overline{)972}$ **2.** $7\overline{)714}$

3. $5\overline{)453}$ **4.** $2\overline{)941}$

Do you UNDERSTAND?

5. **Writing to Explain** In the example at the top, what would happen if you do not bring down the zero in the ones place?

6. Suppose the McQueens only drove 424 miles in 4 days. If they drove an equal number of miles each day, how many miles did they drive in 1 day?

Independent Practice

In **7** through **24**, find each quotient. Check your answers.

7. $2\overline{)880}$ **8.** $5\overline{)540}$ **9.** $6\overline{)840}$

10. $3\overline{)323}$ **11.** $7\overline{)563}$ **12.** $3\overline{)624}$

13. $2\overline{)801}$ **14.** $5\overline{)180}$ **15.** $8\overline{)816}$

16. $3\overline{)912}$ **17.** $5\overline{)547}$ **18.** $7\overline{)284}$

19. $9\overline{)455}$ **20.** $2\overline{)420}$ **21.** $6\overline{)648}$

22. $4\overline{)816}$ **23.** $3\overline{)512}$ **24.** $7\overline{)776}$

*For another example, see Set E on page 55.

25. Elena spent $25 on a ring. She paid using $10, $5, and $1 bills. If Elena gave the clerk 8 bills, how many of each bill did she give the clerk?

26. Raul bought a collection of 856 baseball cards for $40. If only 8 cards can fit on one page of an album, how many pages will Raul have to buy?

27. The grandstand at the stadium has 648 seats. There are 6 equal sections. How many seats are in each section?

28. Ali ran 120 kilometers over a 4-week period. On average, how many kilometers did he run each week?

29. Number Sense Harry filled one box with 9 pints of blueberries. He picked 97 pints of blueberries. If Harry filled 10 boxes, how many pints were left for the last box?

30. A school raised $306 washing cars. The money will be used to buy new recycling containers for the school. If each container costs $8, how many containers can the school buy?

31. Writing to Explain Clare's teacher has a box of 180 stickers for a group of students to share equally. Does each student get more stickers if there are 6 students or if there are 9 students?

32. Each car of the roller coaster can hold 6 people. If 63 people are waiting in line to ride the roller coaster, how many cars will be needed?

33. Dora has 24 pairs of earrings. She keeps them in 6 boxes. Each box has the same number of earrings. Each pair of earrings costs between $10 and $20. How many pairs of earrings are in each box?

   A 4

   B 8

   C 10

   D 12

34. **Think About the Process** A home and garden show ran for two days. Tickets cost $2 each. On the first day, ticket sales totaled $322. On the second day, ticket sales were $294. Which of the following shows how to determine the number of tickets sold?

   F $(322 + 294) \div 2$

   G $322 \times 294 \div 2$

   H $(322 + 294) \times 2$

   I $322 \div 2 + 294$

35. The world's longest cartoon strip has 242 panels. It was drawn by 35 artists in about 8 hours. About how many panels were drawn in one hour?

   A 15   **B** 20   **C** 30   **D** 45

Choose a Computation Method

In many airports, people ride minibuses between terminals. The minibuses leave only when they are full. If a minibus carried 297 passengers in a day, and it holds 9 passengers at a time, how many times did it fill up?

Step 1   Draw a picture and choose an operation.

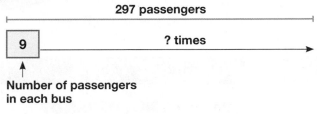

Divide 297 ÷ 9.

Step 2   Choose the best computation method. Decide whether to use mental math, paper and pencil, or a calculator.

Use a calculator.

Step 3   Solve.

Press: 297 ÷ 9 ENTER =   Display: 33

The minibus filled up 33 times.

Practice

For each problem, draw a picture and choose an operation. Then choose the best computation method and solve.

1. If each of the 297 passengers paid $2, how could the driver find the amount of money he collected? How much did he collect?

2. Four drivers had 293, 147, 307, and 284 passengers. How many passengers did the four drivers have in all?

3. One of the drivers had 150 passengers on Monday and 250 passengers on Tuesday. How many passengers does he need on Wednesday to have 500 passengers for the week?

4. A special pass for frequent travelers cost $50 a year. If 200 travelers bought the special pass, how much was the bus company paid?

MA.5.A.1.2 Estimate quotients or calculate them mentally depending on the context and numbers involved.
Also MA.5.A.1.4

More Dividing by 1-Digit Divisors

How can you use estimation to decide if your quotient is reasonable?

Eight students planted 392 sunflower seeds around the school. Each student planted the same number of seeds. How many seeds did each student plant?

```
|-------------- 392 seeds --------------|
| ? | ? | ? | ? | ? | ? | ? | ? |
 ↑
 └── Number of seeds planted by each student
```

392 seeds

Sunflower Seeds Kit

Guided Practice*

Do you know HOW?

1. Complete the estimation for 512 ÷ 9.

   ▢ ÷ ▢ = ▢

2. Find the actual quotient for 512 ÷ 9.

3. Compare your estimate for 512 ÷ 9 with the actual quotient to see if it is reasonable.

Do you UNDERSTAND?

4. Which would give the better estimate for 438 ÷ 7? Explain.

   a 440 ÷ 10   **b** 420 ÷ 7

5. **Writing to Explain** Vickie estimated a quotient of 85 and calculated an actual quotient of 48. Is her actual quotient reasonable? Explain.

Independent Practice

In **6** through **13**, estimate first. Then find each quotient. Use your estimate to check if your answer is reasonable.

6. 412 ÷ 3   **7.** 802 ÷ 7   **8.** 691 ÷ 8   **9.** 247 ÷ 5

10. 6)1,384   **11.** 9)2,871   **12.** 7)4,733   **13.** 6)3,980

In **14** through **21**, estimate first. Tell if the answers are reasonable. If the answer is not reasonable, find the correct answer.

14. 723 ÷ 5 = 44 R3   **15.** 367 ÷ 6 = 61 R1   **16.** 317 ÷ 8 = 39 R5   **17.** 548 ÷ 9 = 160 R8

18.   36 R2   **19.**   977   **20.**   911 R6   **21.**   93 R8
        4)1,142   3)2,931   7)3,582   9)1,745

*For another example, see Set E on page 55.

Step 1

Estimate: 392 is close to 400, and 400 and 8 are compatible numbers.

$400 \div 8 = 50$

Step 2

Divide.

$$\begin{array}{r} 49 \\ 8\overline{)392} \\ -32 \\ \hline 72 \\ -72 \\ \hline 0 \end{array}$$

Step 3

Compare the actual quotient to your estimate.

49 is close to 50.

So, the answer is reasonable.

Each student planted 49 sunflower seeds.

Problem Solving

22. A hiking trail through Ocala National Forest in Florida is 75 miles long. A fifth-grade hiking club completes the trail in 5 days, hiking an equal distance each day. How many miles did they hike each day?

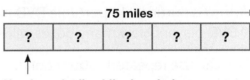

	75 miles			
?	?	?	?	?

↑

Number of miles hiked each day

23. 🎵 **Music** A square dance set requires 4 couples (8 dancers), with each couple standing on one side of a square. There are 150 people at a square dance. What is the greatest number of sets possible at the dance?

A 18　　　**C** 37

B 19　　　**D** 38

24. Alycia has 164 treats for the 7 goats at the petting zoo. Each goat gets an equal share of the treats. How many treats will each goat get? How many treats will Alycia have left over?

25. Mr. Girard sells fishing supplies to shops in Florida. He traveled 527 miles from Jacksonville to Miami. He made 6 stops, including his final stop, at equal intervals along the way. About how many miles did he travel between stops?

26. THINK SOLVE EXPLAIN Michelle traveled 498 miles from Lakeside to West Little River. She made 7 stops along the way. Michelle estimated that she drove about 50 miles between stops. Is her estimate reasonable? Explain.

27. Number Sense The Florida Aquarium in Tampa offers an eight-person membership for $160. A single-person membership costs $50. If 8 people equally share the cost of the eight-person membership, how much will each person save over the cost of a single-person membership?

Critical THINKING

MA.5.A.1.1 Describe the process of finding quotients involving multi-digit dividends using models, place value, properties and the relationship of division to multiplication.

Draw a Picture and Write an Equation

There are 112 campers going boating. The size of the boat and number of people it can hold is shown at the right. How many boats will be needed to hold all the campers?

Another Example

Arturo is putting 114 portable DVD players into boxes. Each box holds 9 DVD players. How many boxes will Arturo need?

You can use repeated subtraction to find the answer. Take one group of 9 and subtract it from 114. Keep subtracting 9 until you can no longer subtract.

$114 - 9 = 105$
$105 - 9 = 96$
$96 - 9 = 87$
$87 - 9 = 78$
$78 - 9 = 69$
$69 - 9 = 60$
$60 - 9 = 51$
$51 - 9 = 42$
$42 - 9 = 33$
$33 - 9 = 24$
$24 - 9 = 15$
$15 - 9 = 6$ You cannot subtract 9 from 6, so 6 players are left over.

114 DVD players

b boxes →

| 9 |

↑
Players per box

Tip *You can also draw a picture and write an equation to solve.*

Let b = the number of boxes needed.

$114 \div 9 = b$
$b = 12 \text{ R}6$

Since you can subtract 9 *twelve times* and have 6 *left over*,
$114 \div 9 = 12 \text{ R}6$.

Since there are 6 players left without a box, Arturo needs 13 boxes to pack all 114 DVD players.

Explain It

Why does Arturo need 13 boxes and not 12?

What do I know? There are 112 campers. Six people can fit in a boat.

What am I asked to find? The number of boats needed to hold all the campers.

Draw a picture.

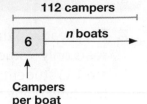

112 campers

6   *n* boats

Campers per boat

Write an equation.

Let *n* = the number of boats needed.

$$112 \div 6 = n$$

$$n = 18 \text{ R4}$$

For all campers to go boating, 19 boats will be needed.

```
      18 R4
6)112
    - 6
     52
   - 48
      4
```

Guided Practice*

Do you know HOW?

Solve. Copy and complete the picture. Then, write an equation.

1. If each van holds 9 people, how many vans will be needed to take 137 people to a concert?

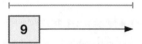

9

Do you UNDERSTAND?

2. How do you know your answer for Exercise 1 is reasonable?

3. **Write a Problem** Write a real-world problem that you can solve by drawing a picture and writing an equation.

Independent Practice

In **4** through **8**, draw a picture, write an equation, and then solve.

4. Steven has 140 photos. A page from a photo album contains 8 photos. How many pages does Steven have?

5. If you buy a digital music player for $246, including tax, and are allowed to pay for it in 6 equal payments, how much will each payment be?

6. There are 7 players on each academic team. If there are 175 total players in the tournament, how many teams are there?

Stuck? Try this....

- What do I know?
- What am I asked to find?
- What diagram can I use to help understand the problem?
- Can I use addition, subtraction, multiplication, or division?
- Is all of my work correct?
- Did I answer the right question?
- Is my answer reasonable?

7. The theater in the wilderness exhibit seats only 9 students at a time. If there are 106 students attending the field trip, how many times will the movie be shown so that all students can view it?

8. Joanna's family is driving to their summer cottage that is 441 miles away. It takes them 7 hours to drive there. If they travel an equal number of miles each hour, how far do they travel in 1 hour?

9. Brenda says a good estimate for 50 × 31 is 800. Is she correct? Explain.

10. Reasoning Wanda needs to buy at least 50 stickers. Will this 1 sheet of stickers be enough? How do you know?

11. Jin's friends collected 149 bottles of water for riders going on a bike trip. If each rider needs 4 bottles, how many riders can they supply with water?

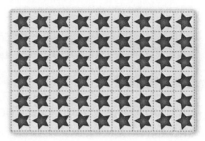

12. Writing to Explain Tell how you can check to see if 54 R2 is the quotient for 164 ÷ 3.

13. If you divide 152 flowers into 7 equal arrangements, how many flowers should there be in each arrangement?

14. 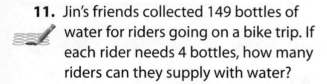 **Science** Brown bats sleep 20 hours each day. How many hours per week are they awake? How many hours per year are they awake? (Note: 1 week = 7 days; 1 year = 365 days.)

15. **Social Studies** In 1916, the first international women's ice hockey tournament was held in Cleveland, Ohio. In 1998, women's ice hockey was represented for the first time in the Winter Olympics. Give the number of years between these two events.

Think About the Process

16. A ticket to Los Angeles costs $390, and a ticket to New York costs $425. Which equation can you solve to show how much less the ticket to Los Angeles cost?

 A $390 + $425 = c

 B $425 − $390 = c

 C $425 × $390 = c

 D (2 × $390) + (2 × $425) = c

17. Each shelf holds 24 books. There are 8 shelves. Which equation would you solve to find how many books there are in all?

 F 24 + 8 = b

 G 24 − 8 = b

 H 24 × 8 = b

 I 24 ÷ 8 = b

Algebra Connections

Properties and Equations

Remember that number properties help you solve equations. Examples of each property are shown.

Commutative Properties

Addition $3 + 7 = 7 + 3$

Multiplication $7 \times 9 = 9 \times 7$

Associative Properties

Addition $3 + (7 + 5) = (3 + 7) + 5$

Multiplication $2 \times (4 \times 3) = (2 \times 4) \times 3$

Identity Properties

Addition $10 + 0 = 10$

Multiplication $13 \times 1 = 13$

Zero Property of Multiplication

$9 \times 0 = 0$

Distributive Property

$3 \times (10 + 4) = (3 \times 10) + (3 \times 4)$

Example:

Solve the following equation.

$8 \times (10 + 2) = (8 \times 10) + (y \times 2)$

Think The Distributive Property means that $8 \times (10 + 2) = (8 \times 10) + (8 \times 2)$

So, $y = 8$

Use the number properties to help you solve each equation.

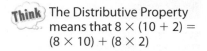 **Tip** Remember that $3 \times m$ can be written as $3m$.

1. $z + 37 = 37 + 4$

2. $38y = 38$

3. $8 + (3 + 9) = (8 + 3) + x$

4. $8y = 0$

5. $21 + z = 21$

6. $17 \times 25 = 25 \times t$

7. $10 \times (3 \times 9) = (10 \times 3) \times z$

8. $16 + (y + 4) = (16 + 3) + 4$

9. $8 \times (10 + 3) = (8 \times 10) + (8 \times y)$

10. $346y = 346$

11. One display in a store has 12 rows of 4 photos. Another display has the same number of photos arranged in 4 rows. How many photos are in each row of the second display?

12. Write a Problem Write a real-world problem that can be solved by writing and solving the equation $3 + 10 = x + 3$.

1 If the money shown is to be divided among 4 people, what should be the first step? (2-3)

A. Exchange the $100 bill for eight $10 bills and twenty $1 bills.

B. Exchange the four $10 bills for forty $1 bills.

C. Exchange the $100 dollar bill for a hundred $1 bills.

D. Exchange the $100 dollar bill for ten $10 bills.

2 Louise used this model to divide. Which division sentence does the model show? (2-1)

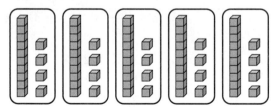

F. $70 \div 5 = 14$

G. $60 \div 5 = 14$

H. $54 \div 5 = 14$

I. $48 \div 5 = 14$

3 Four friends shared 283 marbles equally. What is $283 \div 4$? (2-5)

A. 73

B. 71

C. 70 R3

D. 70 R1

4 The baker made 52 rolls. He put an equal number of rolls in each of the 4 baskets in the display case. How many rolls did he put in each basket? (2-2)

F. 9

G. 12

H. 13

I. 14

5 Raquel's team raised 4 times the amount that Jeremy's team raised. How much did Jeremy's team raise? (2-5)

Team Leader	Amount Raised
Raquel	$836
Jeremy	
Charles	$448

A. $209

B. $204

C. $112

D. $29

6 During an overnight camping trip, 128 campers slept in bunkhouses. Twelve campers slept in each bunkhouse. Which equation can be used to find *n*, the number of bunkhouses used by the campers? (2-7)

128 campers

12 — *n* bunkhouses →

Campers per bunkhouse

F. $128 - 12 = n$

G. $128 + 12 = n$

H. $128 \times 12 = n$

I. $128 \div 12 = n$

7 The student council has 186 members divided as evenly as possible into 8 committees. How many members are on each committee? (2-4)

    A. There are 194 members in the student council.

    B. There are 23 members on each committee with 2 members left.

    C. There are 22 members on each committee.

    D. There are 22 members on each committee with 2 members left.

8 Steven solved the division problem $41 \div 4$ correctly. Which model did he use? (2-1)

    F.
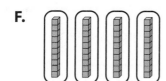

    G.
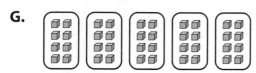

    H.
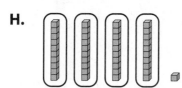

    I.
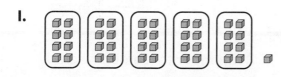

9 What is the quotient of $97 \div 5$? (2-2)

    A. 18 R2

    B. 19

    C. 19 R1

    D. 19 R2

10 A florist is making flower arrangements. She has 108 roses to place in 9 arrangements. Which of the following equations can be used to find r, the number of roses in each arrangement? (2-7)

108 roses

r	r	r	r	r	r	r	r	r

↑
Roses in each arrangement

    F. $108 + 9 = r$

    G. $108 - 9 = r$

    H. $108 \times 9 = r$

    I. $108 \div 9 = r$

11 A biologist banded 296 birds over 8 days. If she banded the same number of birds each day, how many birds did she band each day? (2-4)

12 A school has $1,016 for scholarships. The money was awarded equally to 8 students. Find the amount of money each student received. Show all of your work. (2-6)

THINK
SOLVE
EXPLAIN

Set A, pages 26–28

Find 56 ÷ 4.

Make 56 using place-value blocks.

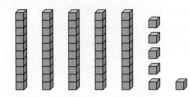

Divide the blocks into 4 equal groups. Trade 1 ten for 10 ones.

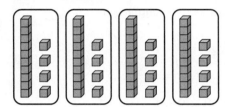

Write the division problem.

$$
\begin{array}{r}
14 \\
4\overline{)56} \\
-4 \\
\hline
16 \\
-16 \\
\hline
0
\end{array}
$$

Remember to trade 1 ten for 10 ones if you need to.

Use place-value blocks or pictures to divide.

1. 42 ÷ 7

2. 67 ÷ 5

3. 80 ÷ 9

4. 49 ÷ 6

5. 37 ÷ 2

6. 99 ÷ 8

Set B, pages 30–32

Find 85 ÷ 3.

Divide the tens.
Multiply and subtract.

$$
\begin{array}{r}
2 \\
3\overline{)85} \\
-6 \\
\hline
2
\end{array}
$$

Regroup. Divide the ones. Multiply and subtract.

$$
\begin{array}{r}
28 \text{ R1} \\
3\overline{)85} \\
-6 \\
\hline
25 \\
-24 \\
\hline
1
\end{array}
$$

Write the remainder in the quotient.

Remember to regroup when necessary.

Find each quotient. Check your answers.

1. 91 ÷ 7   **2.** 85 ÷ 6

3. 68 ÷ 9   **4.** 61 ÷ 8

5. 79 ÷ 4   **6.** 80 ÷ 5

Set C, pages 34–36

Tell how much money each person will get if 4 people share $212 equally.

Exchange the two $100 bills for twenty $10 bills. Each person gets five $10 bills. Exchange the one $10 bill and two $1 bills for twelve $1 bills. Divide the twelve $1 bills by 4. $12 ÷ 4 = $3.

Each person will get $53.

Remember to regroup when necessary.

Use play money to divide. Tell how much each person will get.

1. 6 people share $240 equally

2. 5 people share $510 equally

3. 3 people share $252 equally

4. 6 people share $336 equally

Set D, pages 38–40

Find 549 ÷ 6. Estimate first. 540 ÷ 6 = 90.

```
      91 R3
  6)549
   - 54
     09
    -  6
      3
```

Check:
```
      91
   ×   6
     546
   +   3
     549
```

The quotient 91 R3 is close to the estimate, 90.

Remember that you can use your estimate to check that your answer is reasonable.

Divide.

1. 74 ÷ 5   2. 89 ÷ 9

3. 232 ÷ 4   4. 488 ÷ 8

5. 682 ÷ 7   6. 492 ÷ 6

Set E, pages 42–44, 46–47

Find 839 ÷ 4. Estimate first. 800 ÷ 4 = 200.

```
     209 R3
  4)839
   - 8
     03
    - 0
     39
    - 36
      3
```

Check:
```
     209
   ×   4
     836
   +   3
     839
```

The quotient 209 R3 is close to the estimate, 200.

Remember that you sometimes need to write a zero in the quotient.

Divide. Estimate to check that your answer is reasonable.

1. 720 ÷ 6   2. 661 ÷ 3

3. 4)424   4. 3)914

5. 125 ÷ 3   6. 411 ÷ 8

7. 4)542   8. 6)923

Set F, pages 48–50

Eight friends want to share 131 postcards. How many postcards will each person get if each person gets the same number of cards? Draw a picture and write an equation to solve.

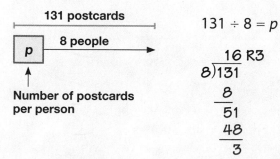

$131 \div 8 = p$

```
      16 R3
  8)131
     8
     51
     48
      3
```

p = 16 R3. Since there is a remainder of 3 postcards, there are not enough for each person to get 17 cards. Each friend will receive 16 postcards.

Remember that you can draw a picture and write an equation to solve each division problem.

1. A total of 60 students are being separated into 5 equal teams. How many students are on each team?

2. Nancy has 35 bottles of water that she wants to put into portable coolers. Each cooler can hold 6 bottles. How many coolers will Nancy need?

Developing Fluency: Dividing by Two-Digit Divisors

1 How fast can the Thorny Devil Lizard eat ants, which is one of its favorite foods? You will find out in Lesson 3-5.

2 How tall is Devil's Tower National Monument in Wyoming? You will find out in Lesson 3-2.

Review What You Know!

Vocabulary

Choose the best term from the box.

- place
- period
- digit
- remainder

1. Each group of three number places is called a __?__.

2. The position of a digit in a number is called its __?__.

3. $15 \div 6 = 2$ with a __?__ of 3.

Multiplication

Find each product.

4. 12×38 5. 47×61 6. 39×78

7. 15×208 8. 67×394 9. 52×485

Division

Use estimation to check if each given quotient is reasonable. If the quotient is not reasonable, find the correct quotient.

10. $59 \div 4 = 14$ R3   11. $287 \div 6 = 47$ R5

12. $509 \div 7 = 82$ R5   13. $3,152 \div 9 = 350$ R2

Writing to Explain Write an answer to the question.

14. Juanita is running the craft table at her camp. There will be 20 campers participating. Each camper gets 1 T-shirt. Juanita can order T-shirts in packages of 3. How many packages should she order? Explain.

3

Some comets can be seen from Earth fairly often. About how many of these comets are seen each year? You will find out in Lesson 3-2.

Topic Essential Questions

- What is a standard procedure for dividing by two-digit divisors?
- How can greater quotients be estimated?

Lesson

3-1

MA.5.A.1.2 Estimate
quotients or calculate them
mentally depending on
the context and numbers
involved.
Also MA.5.A.1.1

Using Patterns to Divide

How can patterns help you divide large multiples of 10?

A jet carries 18,000 passengers in 90 trips. The plane is full for each trip. How many passengers does the plane hold?

Choose an Operation Divide to find how many people were on each trip.

18,000 passengers
in 90 trips

Guided Practice*

Do you know HOW?

In **1** through **4**, find each quotient. Use mental math.

1. 210 ÷ 30 = 21 tens ÷ 3 tens = ▊

2. 480 ÷ 60 = 48 tens ÷ 6 tens = ▊

3. 8,100 ÷ 90 = ▊

4. 2,800 ÷ 70 = ▊

Do you UNDERSTAND?

5. In Exercise 1, why is 210 ÷ 30 the same as 21 tens ÷ 3 tens?

6. In the example at the top, if the jet carried 10,000 people in 40 trips, how many people did it carry for each trip?

7. What basic fact did you use to find the quotient in Exercise 3?

Independent Practice

In **8** through **23**, use mental math to find the missing numbers.

8. 560 ÷ 70 = 56 tens ÷ 7 tens = ▊   **9.** 360 ÷ 60 = 36 tens ÷ 6 tens = ▊

10. 6,000 ÷ 50 = 600 tens ÷ 5 tens = ▊   **11.** 24,000 ÷ 60 = 2,400 tens ÷ 6 tens = ▊

12. 2,000 ÷ 20 = ▊   **13.** 6,300 ÷ 90 = ▊   **14.** 240 ÷ 10 = ▊

15. 21,000 ÷ ▊ = 700   **16.** 8,100 ÷ 90 = ▊   **17.** 72,000 ÷ ▊ = 200

18. 30,000 ÷ ▊ = 600   **19.** 7,200 ÷ ▊ = 80   **20.** 56,000 ÷ ▊ = 800

21. 10,000 ÷ 100 = ▊   **22.** 25,000 ÷ 50 = ▊   **23.** 45,000 ÷ 90 = ▊

For another example, see Set A on page 78.

Think of a basic fact to help you find 18,000 ÷ 90.

$$18 ÷ 9 = 2$$

Think about multiples of 10:

$180 ÷ 90 = 18$ tens ÷ 9 tens = 2
$1,800 ÷ 90 = 180$ tens ÷ 9 tens = 20
$18,000 ÷ 90 = 1,800$ tens ÷ 9 tens = 200

The pattern shows us that
$18,000 ÷ 90 = 200$.

So, the jet can hold 200 people during each trip.

You can multiply to check your answer.

$$200 × 90 = 18,000$$

Problem Solving

For **24** and **25**, use the information at the right.

24. If all the flights were full and all planes carried the same number of passengers, how many people were on each flight?

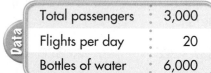

Total passengers	3,000
Flights per day	20
Bottles of water	6,000

25. If each flight was stocked with the same number of bottles of water, how many bottles were on each flight?

26. There are 12 school campuses in the community. Each campus has a 14-member volleyball team. How many students play volleyball?

27. Cell phones are packaged 20 to a box. Reliable Cell Company needs 150 cell phones. How many boxes will the company need to order?

28. **Think About the Process** Dividing 480 by 60 is the same as

A dividing 48 ones by 6 tens.

B dividing 48 tens by 6 ones.

C dividing 48 tens by 6 tens.

D dividing 48 hundreds by 6 tens.

29. Suppose there are 1,500 pencils in 20 bins. You want to put the same number of pencils in each bin. Which expression shows how to find the number of pencils in each bin?

F $1,500 + 20$ **H** $1,500 × 20$

G $1,500 - 20$ **I** $1,500 ÷ 20$

30. One dozen eggs is 12 eggs. A farmer harvested 1,260 eggs from the henhouse. Which expression shows how to find how many dozen eggs the farmer harvested?

A $1,260 + 12$ **C** $1,260 ÷ 12$

B $1,260 - 12$ **D** $1,260 × 12$

31. It takes 18,000 kilograms of sand to fill 600 school sandboxes. How many kilograms of sand will a construction company need to put in each of the 600 sandboxes to fill it for the new school year?

Lesson

3-2

MA.5.A.1.2 Estimate quotients or calculate them mentally depending on the context and numbers involved.

Estimating Quotients with 2-Digit Divisors

How can you use compatible numbers to estimate quotients?

$159 for 75 bracelets

Betty made $159 by selling 75 bracelets. Each bracelet costs the same. About how much did each bracelet cost?

Choose an Operation We know the total amount made and the number of bracelets. Divide to find the price.

Guided Practice*

Do you know HOW?

In **1** through **6**, estimate using compatible numbers.

1. 287 ÷ 42   **2.** 320 ÷ 11

3. 208 ÷ 72   **4.** 554 ÷ 62

5. 1,220 ÷ 59   **6.** 3,390 ÷ 42

Do you UNDERSTAND?

7. Writing to Explain If you use rounding to estimate in the example above, can you divide easily? Explain.

8. Reasonableness Betty has 425 more bracelets to sell. She wants to store these in plastic bags that hold 20 bracelets each. She estimates she will need about 25 bags. Is she right? Why or why not?

Independent Practice

In **9** through **29**, estimate using compatible numbers.

9. 412 ÷ 84   **10.** 288 ÷ 37   **11.** 2,964 ÷ 73

12. 228 ÷ 19   **13.** 1,784 ÷ 64   **14.** 7,620 ÷ 53

15. 2,280 ÷ 12   **16.** 485 ÷ 92   **17.** 540 ÷ 61

18. $32\overline{)1,710}$ **19.** $67\overline{)2,740}$ **20.** $81\overline{)4,322}$

21. $58\overline{)5,700}$ **22.** $44\overline{)7,810}$ **23.** $88\overline{)6,395}$

24. $74\overline{)4,877}$ **25.** $48\overline{)2,495}$ **26.** $93\overline{)6,284}$

27. $32\overline{)6,527}$ **28.** $91\overline{)3,758}$ **29.** $64\overline{)5,849}$

 For another example, see Set B on page 78.

The question asks, "About how much?" So, an estimate is enough.

Use compatible numbers to estimate 159 ÷ 75.

Find compatible numbers for 159 and 75.

Think 16 can be divided evenly by 8.

160 and 80 are close to 159 and 75.

So, 160 and 80 are compatible numbers.

Divide.

160 ÷ 80 = 2.

So, each bracelet cost *about* $2.

Compatible numbers are often used to estimate quotients.

Problem Solving

30. **Social Studies** Devil's Tower National Monument was established as our country's first national monument in 1906. Each year, many rock climbers climb to the top. If it takes two climbers 6 hours to climb from the base to the top, estimate how many feet they climbed each hour.

Top

867 feet

Base

31. **Science** A comet orbits the Sun 39 times in 129 years. About how long does it take the comet to complete one orbit?

32. Leon wants to buy 8 CDs on sale for $88. Will three $20 bills and five $5 bills be enough money for Leon to buy the CDs?

33. Estimate the product for the following expression.

805 × 62

A 4,800

B 48,000

C 54,000

D 64,000

34. Which property does the following equation illustrate?

2 + (11 + 19) = (2 + 11) + 19

F Commutative Property of Addition

G Associative Property of Addition

H Identity Property of Addition

I Commutative Property of Multiplication

35. Donald bought a clock radio. The radio weighs 18 ounces. Donald paid $12 less than the normal sales price. If the normal sales price was $38, how much did Donald spend on the radio?

36. **Writing to Explain** Autumn needs **Critical THINKING** to estimate the quotient 817 ÷ 91. Explain how she can use compatible numbers to make a reasonable estimate.

MA.5.A.1.4 Divide multi-digit whole numbers fluently, including solving real-world problems, demonstrating understanding of the standard algorithm and checking the reasonableness of results.
Also MA.5.A.1.2

Dividing by Multiples of 10

What are the steps in dividing by a multiple of ten?

Ms. Jones is distributing a jar of color tiles equally to 20 students in art class. If the jar contains 249 tiles, what is the greatest number of tiles she can give each student?

Choose an Operation Divide to find the number of tiles for each student.

249 tiles

Guided Practice*

Do you know HOW?

In **1** through **6**, divide.

1. $30\overline{)345}$ **2.** $20\overline{)282}$

3. $50\overline{)467}$ **4.** $60\overline{)841}$

5. $40\overline{)413}$ **6.** $80\overline{)766}$

Do you UNDERSTAND?

7. In the example above, if there were only 173 tiles to distribute, how many tiles could Ms. Jones give each student?

8. Reasoning In the example above, why is 12 an appropriate estimate for 249 ÷ 20?

Independent Practice

Leveled Practice Copy and complete.

9.
```
       5 R1
 20)318
    2
    1
    1
    1
```

10.
```
      1  R 2
 60)712
    6
    1
    6
    2
```

11.
```
      1  R
 30)328
    0
    2
```

12. $40\overline{)348}$ **13.** $70\overline{)618}$ **14.** $80\overline{)939}$

15. 697 ÷ 90   **16.** 114 ÷ 30   **17.** 766 ÷ 50

18. 724 ÷ 60   **19.** 841 ÷ 20   **20.** 222 ÷ 30

21. 936 ÷ 40   **22.** 295 ÷ 20   **23.** 479 ÷ 60

*For another example, see Set C on page 78.

Step 1

Find 249 ÷ 20.

Estimate: 240 ÷ 20 = 12
Divide the tens.

$$\begin{array}{r} 1 \\ 20)\overline{249} \\ -20 \\ \hline 4 \end{array}$$

Divide.   24 ÷ 20 = 1
Multiply.   1 × 20 = 20
Subtract.   24 − 20 = 4
Compare.   4 < 20

Step 2

Bring down the ones. Divide the ones.

$$\begin{array}{r} 12\ R9 \\ 20)\overline{249} \\ -20\downarrow \\ \hline 49 \\ -40 \\ \hline 9 \end{array}$$

Divide.   49 ÷ 20 = 2
Multiply.   2 × 20 = 40
Subtract.   49 − 40 = 9
Compare.   9 < 20

Ms. Jones can give each student 12 tiles, with 9 tiles left over.

The answer is reasonable since it matches the estimate of 12.

Problem Solving

Use the table to answer **24** through **26**.

24. Rita's family is driving from Tallahassee to Kissimmee first to visit Rita's aunt. From Kissimmee, they will travel to Sarasota, then return directly from Sarasota to Tallahassee. How many miles will the family drive?

Data	
Kissimmee to Key Largo	269 miles
Pensacola to Sarasota	470 miles
Tallahassee to Kissimmee	255 miles
Sarasota to Tallahassee	284 miles
Kissimmee to Sarasota	119 miles

25. A truck driver ran into construction delays on her trip from Kissimmee to Key Largo. She averaged 40 miles each hour. About how many hours did the trip take?

26. Charlie changes the CD he is listening to every 30 miles on his trip from Pensacola to Sarasota. How many times does Charlie change CDs?

27. Alachua County School District has 28,378 students, while Osceola County School District has 52,743 students. How many more students are in the Osceola district than in the Alachua district?

28. The Port Lavaca fishing pier is 3,200 feet long. If there was one person fishing every 10-foot length of the pier, then how many people would be fishing from the pier?

29. Each person on a boat ride pays $26 for a ticket. There are 63 passengers. How much money is collected from all the passengers?

  A $89
  B $504
  C $1,538
  D $1,638

30. **Think About the Process** What is the first step in finding 383 ÷ 30?

  F Regroup 8 tens as 80 ones
  G See how many are in the remainder
  H Regroup 3 hundreds as 30 tens
  I Multiply 3 by 38

MA.5.A.1.4 Divide multi-digit whole numbers fluently, including solving real-world problems, demonstrating understanding of the standard algorithm and checking the reasonableness of results.

1-Digit Quotients

What are the steps for dividing by 2-digit numbers?

Nadia is setting up 64 science kits equally. The science lab has a bin with 428 rocks and minerals. What is the greatest number of rocks and minerals she can put in each kit?

Choose an Operation Divide to find the number of rocks and minerals in each kit.

428 rocks and minerals

Another Example **How do you revise an estimate when dividing?**

Find 330 ÷ 42.

Step 1

Estimate first.

330 ÷ 42 is about 320 ÷ 40, or 8.

Tip *Think of 32 tens ÷ 4 tens = 8.*

Step 2

Divide the ones. Multiply and subtract.

8 × 42 = 336

Since 336 > 330, my estimate is too high.

$$\begin{array}{r} 8 \\ 42\overline{)330} \\ -336 \\ \hline \text{Oops!} \end{array}$$

Step 3

Revise your estimate. Since 8 was too high, try 7 and divide.

7 × 42 = 294

330 − 294 = 36

36 < 42, so I do not have to divide again.

$$\begin{array}{r} 7 \\ 42\overline{)330} \\ -294 \\ \hline 36 \end{array}$$

Answer: 7 R36

Step 4

Check your work.

Multiply the divisor by the quotient. Add the remainder.

$$\begin{array}{r} 42 \\ \times \quad 7 \\ \hline 294 \\ + \quad 36 \\ \hline 330 \end{array}$$

Explain It

1. In Step 1, how did the estimate tell you to start dividing ones?

2. In Step 2, how did you know that your first estimate of 8 was too high?

Step 1

Estimate to help decide where to place the first digit in the quotient.

$428 \div 64$ is about $420 \div 70$, or 6.

Start dividing ones.

Step 2

Divide the ones. Multiply and subtract.

$$\begin{array}{r} 6 \text{ R}44 \\ 64\overline{)428} \\ -\underline{384} \\ 44 \end{array}$$

$428 \div 64 = 6 \text{ R}44$

Step 3

Check your work:

$$\begin{array}{r} 64 \\ \times\ \ 6 \\ \hline 384 \\ +\ \ 44 \\ \hline 428 \end{array}$$

Nadia can put 6 rocks and minerals in each kit, with 44 left over.

Guided Practice*

Do you know HOW?

Copy and complete.

1. $12\overline{)115}$ R

2. $31\overline{)243}$ R

Do you UNDERSTAND?

3. Can the remainder in either example be greater than the divisor? Why or why not?

4. In the example above, if there were 612 rocks and minerals, how many would Nadia put in each kit?

Independent Practice

Leveled Practice Copy and complete.

5.   R2
$$\begin{array}{r} 38\overline{)325} \\ -3 \\ \hline 2 \end{array}$$

6.   7 R 9
$$\begin{array}{r} 52\overline{)403} \\ -\ \ 4 \\ \hline 9 \end{array}$$

7.   R 7
$$\begin{array}{r} 74\overline{)693} \\ -\ 66 \\ \hline 7 \end{array}$$

8.   R
$$\begin{array}{r} 33\overline{)301} \\ - \\ \hline \end{array}$$

In **9** through **28** divide. Check your answers.

9. $57\overline{)550}$

10. $29\overline{)254}$

11. $46\overline{)260}$

12. $56\overline{)528}$

13. $51\overline{)293}$

14. $19\overline{)119}$

15. $91\overline{)628}$

16. $40\overline{)180}$

17. $396 \div 42$

18. $275 \div 38$

19. $179 \div 22$

20. $345 \div 85$

21. $214 \div 28$

22. $748 \div 81$

23. $671 \div 79$

24. $476 \div 68$

25. $429 \div 72$

26. $127 \div 34$

27. $551 \div 84$

28. $197 \div 21$

29. Use the table at the right to answer the following questions.

   a What is the total capacity for all four exhibits at the History Museum?

   b How many class groups of 28 could view the showing at the Interactive Exhibit at the same time?

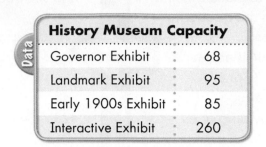

History Museum Capacity	
Governor Exhibit	68
Landmark Exhibit	95
Early 1900s Exhibit	85
Interactive Exhibit	260

30. Chen's band put on a concert at school. There were 702 people in the audience. Each ticket cost $8. The audience was seated in 13 sections. If each section had the same number of people, how many people were in each section?

31. The video room of the Little White House Museum can seat 32 people. If each group fills all 32 seats, how many groups will there be if a total of 273 people want to view the video?

32. Mr. Nolan changes the oil in his car every 3,000 miles. He uses 4 quarts of oil each time. How many quarts of oil will he have used after 12,000 miles?

33. If you estimate 124 × 22 by rounding to the nearest ten, will you get an overestimate or an underestimate? Explain.

34. Twenty members of the photography club took 559 pictures. If they use memory cards that hold 85 pictures per card, how many cards will they use?

35. The annual music festival featured different posters for sale. The sale of jazz band posters brought in $1,312. If each poster cost $16, how many were sold?

36. **Writing to Explain** Explain how you know the answer to the problem shown below has an error.

$$\begin{array}{r} 8\text{ R}24 \\ 16)\overline{152} \\ -\ 128 \\ \hline 24 \end{array}$$

37. Rachel wanted to get 8 hours of sleep before a test. She went to bed at 9:00 P.M. and woke up at 6:00 A.M. How many more hours of sleep did Rachel get than the 8 hours she wanted?

   A 3 more hours   **C** 1 more hour

   B 9 more hours   **D** No more hours

38. Explain why 0.2 and 0.02 are NOT equivalent.

THINK
SOLVE
EXPLAIN

39. In a large restaurant, there are 9 times as many chairs as tables. The restaurant is famous for its very spicy chili. If the restaurant has 342 chairs, how many tables are in the restaurant?

Mixed Problem Solving

In the Harappan Civilization, in what is now northern India, grain was used to pay workers in the city of Mohenjo-Daro.

1. If 120 bags of grain were used to pay 30 workers evenly, how many bags did each worker get paid? Solve the equation $120 \div 30 = x$.

2. In Exercise 1, how could you check to see if the workers got paid the correct amount of bags of grain?

3. Grain was divided equally among 12 workers. If each worker got 6 bags of grain, how many bags of grain were there to begin with? Solve the equation $12 \times 6 = x$.

4. Suppose there were 30 carts with bags of grain to be handed out, and there were 8 bags in each cart. How many bags in all were there?

5. In Exercise 3, how could you check to see if they got the right amount of bags of grain?

....

The Harappan artisans made beautiful crafts. The traders met outside the city to trade goods, such as beads and vases.

6. One of the Harappan women had 700 beads to trade. If she traded 35 beads to each person, how many people traded for her beads? Solve the equation $700 \div 35 = x$.

7. Use estimation to tell about how many pottery vases were sold to 19 people if each person bought 4 vases.

....

The Harappans built their houses with bricks. Each brick was the same size because the brickmakers used exact measurements.

8. If 215 bricks were used for 1 wall of a square house, how many bricks were needed for all 4 walls? Solve the equation $215 \times 4 = x$.

x			
215	215	215	215

MA.5.A.1.4 Divide multi-digit whole numbers fluently, including solving real-world problems, demonstrating understanding of the standard algorithm and checking the reasonableness of results.

2-Digit Quotients

How can you divide greater numbers?

At the cooking school, each of the 15 students is given the same number of tortillas to test new recipes. How many tortillas will each student get?

Choose an Operation Divide to find the number of tortillas.

467 tortillas

Guided Practice*

Do you know HOW?

Copy and complete.

1. 47)985
   ▦▦ R ▦▦
   − ▦▦
   ▦▦

2. 33)678
   ▦▦ R ▦▦
   − ▦▦
   ▦▦

For **3** and **4**, divide.

3. 16)298

4. 23)292

Do you UNDERSTAND?

5. **Writing to Explain** In the problem above, why do you drop the remainder?

6. How can 15 students share 627 tortillas equally?

7. How do you decide where to place the first digit in the quotient for Exercises 1–4?

Independent Practice

Leveled Practice Copy and complete. Check your work.

8. 36)584
   ▦▦ R
   − ▦▦
   ▦▦▦
   − ▦1
   8

9. 45)981
   ▦▦ R ▦▦
   − ▦0
   1
   − ▦▦
   ▦▦

10. 56)674
   ▦▦ R ▦▦
   − ▦▦
   ▦▦▦
   − ▦▦▦
   ▦▦

In **11** through **22**, divide. Check your work.

11. 76)864

12. 23)279

13. 63)710

14. 18)638

15. 48)582

16. 26)784

17. 13)989

18. 72)2,532

19. 4,328 ÷ 93

20. 678 ÷ 27

21. 980 ÷ 45

22. 717 ÷ 31

*For another example, see Set D on page 79.

Estimate to help decide where to place the first digit in the quotient.

Use compatible numbers.

$450 \div 15 = 30$

Start dividing tens.

Divide the tens. Multiply and subtract. Continue the process.

```
      31 R2
15)467
   - 45
     17
   - 15
      2
```

Check your work:

```
      31
    × 15
     155
  + 310
     465
```

$465 + 2 = 467$

So each student will get 31 tortillas.

Problem Solving

23. If you are asked to find $621 \div 59$, how do you know the quotient will be greater than 10 before you actually divide?

24. Tickets to the air show cost $5 for a child and $15 for an adult. This year, 319 children and 853 adults watched the show. How much money was raised at the air show?

25. An outdoor concert company is putting on 12 concerts this summer. Each concert is sold out. The company sold a total of 972 seats. How many people will attend each performance?

A 8   **C** 80

B 79   **D** 81

26. Julio spends about $\frac{1}{2}$ hour reading every night. He owns 8 science fiction books, 12 mystery books, and 7 history books. He wants to add enough books to his collection to have 40 books. How many more books does he need?

27. There are 120 minutes in 2 hours. How many minutes are there in 15 hours?

28. What compatible numbers can you use to estimate $803 \div 86$?

29. One of the Thorny Devil lizard's favorite foods is ants. It can eat up to 45 ants in 1 minute. How long would it take it to eat 540 ants?

F 9 minutes

G 10 minutes

H 12 minutes

I 15 minutes

45 ants each minute

30. Number Sense Decide if each statement is true or false. Explain.

a $710 \div 20$ is greater than 30.

b $821 \div 40$ is less than 20.

c $300 \div 15$ is exactly 20.

31. Braedy had $5 when she left the county fair. At the fair, she spent $11 on her ticket, $6 on lunch, and $17 on games and rides. How much money did Braedy bring to the fair?

MA.5.A.1.4 Divide multi-digit whole numbers fluently, including solving real-world problems, demonstrating understanding of the standard algorithm and checking the reasonableness of results.

More Dividing by 2-Digit Divisors

832 grapefruit seedlings

How can you use estimation to decide if your quotient is reasonable?

Orchard workers have grapefruit seedlings to plant in 23 equal rows. How many seedlings will be in each row?

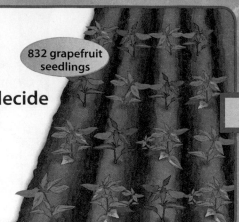

Guided Practice*

Do you know HOW?

1. Estimate 452 ÷ 21.

2. Copy and complete

$$21\overline{)452}$$

Do you UNDERSTAND?

3. For Exercise 2, how can you use estimation to decide where to place the first digit of the quotient?

4. Writing to Explain How can you use estimation to check if a quotient is reasonable?

Independent Practice

Leveled Practice Copy and complete.

5. $18\overline{)471}$

6. $49\overline{)658}$

7. $80\overline{)929}$

8. $36\overline{)176}$

In **9** through **20**, estimate and then find the quotient. Use your estimate to check your answer for reasonableness.

9. 804 ÷ 25

10. 730 ÷ 33

11. 896 ÷ 77

12. 510 ÷ 29

13. $52\overline{)387}$

14. $21\overline{)783}$

15. $35\overline{)298}$

16. $83\overline{)716}$

17. 3,158 ÷ 64

18. 5,722 ÷ 92

19. 8,114 ÷ 46

20. 6,253 ÷ 71

*For another example, see Set E on page 79.

Estimate the quotient. Use compatible numbers.

832 is about 800
23 is about 20

$800 \div 20 = 40$

The first digit is in the tens place. Start by dividing tens.

$$\begin{array}{r} 4 \\ 23\overline{)832} \\ -92 \end{array}$$

The estimate is too high. Try 3.

$$\begin{array}{r} 3 \\ 23\overline{)832} \\ -69 \\ \hline 14 \end{array}$$

Bring down the ones. Continue dividing.

$$\begin{array}{r} 36 \text{ R4} \\ 23\overline{)832} \\ -69 \\ \hline 142 \\ -138 \\ \hline 4 \end{array}$$

Check your answer against the estimate. 36 is close to 40. So the answer is reasonable.

There will be 36 grapefruit seedlings in each row.

Problem Solving

For **21** through **23**, use the table at the right.

21. Bob's Citrus and Nursery sells citrus gift cartons. They have 5,643 oranges to pack into gift cartons. How many cartons can they fill?

Bob's Citrus Gift Cartons	
Citrus Fruit	Number per Carton
Grapefruit	18
Oranges	24
Tangelos	12

22. Of the 4,325 grapefruits harvested so far, Bob's has used 1,250 for citrus sampler packs. How many gift cartons can they fill with the remaining grapefruits? How many grapefruits will be left over?

23. Bob's sells tangelo gift cartons each December. Last year, they shipped 3,300 tangelos in all. If each carton sells for $28, how much money did Bob's earn from the tangelo gift cartons sold?

24. A "score" is 20 years. The first colony in Florida was established in 1521. How many scores ago is that?

Critical THINKING

25. Lydia spends the same number of minutes on each exercise. Today she spent 90 minutes working out with 15 different exercises. How long did she spend on each exercise?

A 7 minutes   **C** 5 minutes

B 6 minutes   **D** 4 minutes

26. Jason packed his raspberry harvest in 245 containers to sell. If each container held 45 raspberries, how many raspberries did Jason harvest?

27. Estimation A farmer has 4,700 carrots to put in bunches of 15. He plans to sell the carrots for $5 per bunch at his farm stand. About how many bunches will the farmer make?

28. At an automobile plant, each car is inspected by 34 different people before it is shipped out to a dealer. Today 9,690 inspections were performed. How many cars were shipped out? Explain.

THINK
SOLVE
EXPLAIN

Lesson

3-7

MA.5.A.1.4 Divide multi-digit whole numbers fluently, including solving real-world problems, demonstrating understanding of the standard algorithm and checking the reasonableness of results. Also MA.5.A.1.2

Estimating and Dividing with Greater Numbers

How do you divide greater numbers?

Maria purchased 43 computers for her business. Because she bought so many, the final cost was $11,094. What was the cost of one computer?

Choose an Operation Divide to find $11,094 broken into 43 same-size groups.

Guided Practice*

Do you know HOW?

For **1** and **2**, estimate each quotient.

1. 22,649 ÷ 29   **2.** 34,143 ÷ 62

For **3** and **4**, divide. Check by multiplying.

3. 12)14,555   **4.** 23)31,897

Do you UNDERSTAND?

5. Writing to Explain How can you use multiplication to check if the quotient in the problem above is correct?

6. For Exercises 3 and 4, how do you know the first digit of each quotient is in the thousands place?

Independent Practice

For **7** through **10**, estimate each quotient.

7. 5,185 ÷ 17   **8.** 18,852 ÷ 38   **9.** 13,014 ÷ 56   **10.** 52,846 ÷ 93

Leveled Practice Copy and complete.

11.
```
        3
   97)3,298
     ■■1
      38
    − ■8
       0
```

12.
```
         2  R62
   72)23,390
      2■■
      17■
      1 4
       3■
       28■
        6■
```

13.
```
     ■,4■  R■
   31)44,573
      ■■
      35
      ■■■
      11■
      ■■
      24■
      2■
       6
```

14.
```
     ■,■■■  R■
   45)99,740
      ■■
      ■■
      ■■
      ■■■
      ■■■
```

15. 51)57,928   **16.** 68)72,743   **17.** 83)87,282   **18.** 76)18,240

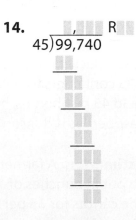

For another example, see Set E on page 79.

Step 1	Step 2	Step 3	Step 4
Estimate. Decide where to place the first digit. $12{,}000 \div 40 = 300$ The first digit in the quotient is in the hundreds place. Start dividing hundreds.	$\begin{array}{r} 3 \\ 43\overline{)11{,}094} \\ -\ 129 \\ \hline Oops! \end{array}$ $3 \times 43 = 129$ The estimate is too high. Try 2. $\begin{array}{r} 2 \\ 43\overline{)11{,}094} \\ -\ 86 \\ \hline 24 \end{array}$	Bring down the tens. Continue dividing. $\begin{array}{r} 25 \\ 43\overline{)11{,}094} \\ -\ 86\downarrow \\ \hline 249 \\ -\ 215 \\ \hline 34 \end{array}$	Bring down the ones. $\begin{array}{r} 258 \\ 43\overline{)11{,}094} \\ -\ 86 \\ \hline 249 \\ -\ 215\downarrow \\ \hline 344 \\ -\ 344 \\ \hline 0 \end{array}$ Each computer costs $258.

Problem Solving

19. The city of St. Petersburg held a chess tournament. The table below shows the fees charged for the tournament.

Data

Chess Tournament	
Student entry fee	$15
Adult entry fee	$18
Reserve a chess board	$12

a The total student entry fees paid were $3,105. How many students participated?

b There are about ten times as many students as adults registered for the tournament. About how many adults are registered?

20. 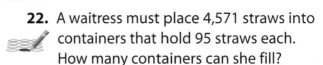 **Social Studies** The Arches National Park in Utah covers over 73,000 acres and has 2,000 stone arches. A 40-mile round-trip paved road in the park takes visitors past most of the arches. If a visitor drove the entire paved road, about how many arches would he or she see per mile?

A 20   **C** 50

B 26   **D** 75

21. Number Sense Give three factors whose product is about 10,000.

Critical THINKING

22. A waitress must place 4,571 straws into containers that hold 95 straws each. How many containers can she fill?

23. There are 1,185 words that may be used for a spelling bee. This number is 15 times as many as the number of words that will actually be used. How many words will be used in the spelling bee?

F 69   **H** 709

G 79   **I** 790

24. Tabitha's class is making flash cards to study the 1,185 words for the spelling bee. There are 5 teams in her class. How many flash cards will each team need to make?

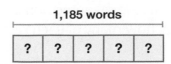

1,185 words

?	?	?	?	?

MA.5.A.6.5 Solve non-routine problems using various strategies including "solving a simpler problem" and "guess, check, and revise." Also MA.5.A.1.1

Multiple-Step Problems

For three months, a fifth-grade class held a fun fair to raise money for charities. The funds raised are shown in the table. If the class divides the money equally among 30 different organizations, how much will each organization receive?

Funds Raised	
September	$435
October	$460
November	$605

Guided Practice*

Do you know HOW?

1. A keyboardist has a digital camera that holds 156 photos. Of these photos, 114 were taken on a vacation, and the rest at a concert. The keyboardist wants to print and mount the photos of the concert on 7 pages of an album with the same number of photos on each page. How many photos will be on each page?

Do you UNDERSTAND?

2. What is the hidden question and answer in Problem 1?

3. **Writing to Explain** Were you able to use mental math in Problem 1?

4. **Write a Problem** Write a real-world multiple-step problem that can be solved by using division.

Independent Practice

In **5** through **9**, write and answer the hidden question or questions. Then solve.

5. Ralph's Nursery sold 62 cherry trees, 36 orange trees, and 42 fig trees during 14 days. If the nursery sold the same number of trees each day, how many trees were sold each day?

6. A high-rise apartment building in Miami has 15 floors with 26 apartments on each floor. There are 3 kinds of apartments in the building: one-, two-, and three-bedroom. If there is the same number of each kind of apartment, how many of each kind are in the building?

Stuck? Try this....

- What do I know?
- What am I asked to find?
- What diagram can I use to help understand the problem?
- Can I use addition, subtraction, multiplication, or division?
- Is all of my work correct?
- Did I answer the right question?
- Is my answer reasonable?

What do I know?

A class raised $435, $460, and $605. Thirty charities will receive the same amount of money from the total amount raised.

What am I asked to find?

The amount of money each charity will receive.

Find the hidden question or questions.

How much money was raised altogether?

? total amount raised

$435	$460	$605

$435 + $460 + $605 = $1,500

Solve. Use mental math.

$1,500 ÷ 30 = ▢

Think 150 tens ÷ 3 tens = 50

Each charity will receive $50.

---

7. The table at the right shows the typical number of calories for certain kinds and amounts of food. Which combination of food items contains more calories: 1 apple and 1 cooked fish stick or 1 slice of Italian bread and 1 ounce of cheddar cheese? How many more calories?

Calories in Food

Food Description	Calories
1 apple	125
1 slice Italian bread	85
1 cooked fish stick	70
1 oz cheddar cheese	115

8. Nina has enrolled in a Salsa dance class. The class meets the same number of hours each day, Monday through Friday, for 6 weeks. If the total number of hours is 90, how many hours does Nina spend in class each weekday?

9. Franco changes the oil in his car every 3,000 miles. If Franco uses 4 quarts of oil for each oil change, how many quarts of oil has he already used if his car has been driven 24,000 miles?

10. During school spirit week, Lynn sold 85 green and gold spirit ribbons in 5 days. How many ribbons did Lynn sell each day if she sold the same number of ribbons each day? Draw a picture, write an equation, then solve.

11. In 2009, Preston wrote a 5-page paper on the life of Martin Luther King Jr. One of the events Preston wrote about was Reverend King's famous *I Have a Dream* speech. The speech was given in 1963. How many years after this speech was Preston's paper written?

12. Melanie took a bag containing 700 quarters to the bank and exchanged them for dollar bills. How much money did she receive?

   A $400   C $175

   B $350   D $70

13. Tony bought *n* football cards. He gave half of them to Karen. Then he gave 2 cards to Jeff and had 6 cards left. How many cards did Tony buy?

Critical THINKING

1 Palm Beach County is the largest county in Florida, with 2,578 square miles. A township is 36 square miles. How many full-size townships would fit in Palm Beach County? (3-6)

A. 70 R22

B. 71

C. 72

D. 72 R22

2 Which of the following is the best way to estimate 487 ÷ 67 with compatible numbers? (3-2)

F. 480 divided by 70

G. 485 divided by 60

H. 490 divided by 60

I. 490 divided by 70

3 There are 40 windows on each floor of a 20-story building. If a window washer can wash 50 windows in one day, which of the following can be used to find how long it will take to wash all the windows in the building? (3-8)

A. 20 × 40 ÷ 50 = 16 days

B. 20 + 40 ÷ 50 = 21 days

C. 20 × 50 ÷ 40 = 25 days

D. 40 × 50 ÷ 20 = 100 days

4 The carnival committee has purchased 985 small prizes. If the prizes are to be divided among the 20 game booths, how many prizes will each booth have and how many prizes will be left over? (3-3)

F. 44 per booth with 5 left over

G. 49 per booth with none left over

H. 49 per booth with 5 left over

I. 490 per booth with 5 left over

5 Which of the following is another way to think of 27,000 ÷ 30? (3-1)

A. 27 tens ÷ 30 tens

B. 27 tens ÷ 3 tens

C. 270 tens ÷ 3 tens

D. 2,700 tens ÷ 3 tens

6 There are 12,156 special agents who work for the FBI. If the special agents are to be divided into groups of 32, about how many agents would be in each group? (3-7)

F. About 4,000

G. About 3,000

H. About 400

I. About 300

7 Shady Rivers summer camp has 188 campers this week. If there are 22 campers assigned to each cabin, what is the least number of cabins needed? (3-4)

A. 7

B. 8

C. 9

D. 10

8 Mrs. Delgato needs to buy 160 begonias for her flowerbed. According to the prices shown, how much would she save if she bought them by the flat instead of buying them separately? (3-8)

F. $8

G. $10

H. $40

I. $80

Begonia Prices	
One Plant	$2
One Flat (20 plants per flat)	$30

9 Alberto is saving for an item that costs $384. If he saves $30 each week, how long will it take him to save enough to buy the item? (3-3)

A. 11 weeks

B. 12 weeks

C. 13 weeks

D. 20 weeks

10 The lengths of two canals are given in the table. About how many times longer is the Erie Canal than the Chesapeake and Delaware Canal? (3-2)

Data

Ship Canal	Length (in miles)
Chesapeake and Delaware Canal	14
Erie Canal	363

F. 10

G. 30

H. 60

I. 360

11 A company ordered 384 note pads. If there are 48 note pads in each box, how many boxes were ordered? (3-4)

A. 7

B. 8

C. 9

D. 12

12 The cost to rent a lodge for a reunion is $975. If 65 people attend, and pay the same price each, how much will each person pay? (3-5)

F. $150

G. $35

H. $25

I. $15

13 In 2007, the average annual number of miles driven per vehicle in the U.S. was 12,396. What was the average number of miles driven per week? (HINT: There are 52 weeks in a year.) (3-7)

A. 238

B. 238 R20

C. 1,033

D. 1,239 R6

14 Morning Star Farm purchased 2,400 apple trees. If 80 trees can be planted on each acre of land, how many acres will be needed to plant all the trees? (3-1)

15 Myrna knows it is exactly 425 steps from one end of the football field to the other. During the band routine, Myrna has to stop every 32 steps and march in place. How many times does Myrna stop? Explain your answer. (3-5)

THINK
SOLVE
EXPLAIN

Set A, pages 58–59

Find 32,000 ÷ 80 using mental math.

Use basic facts and patterns to help.

32 ÷ 8 = 4

320 ÷ 80 = 4

3,200 ÷ 80 = 40

32,000 ÷ 80 = 400

Think 32,000 ÷ 80 is the same as 3,200 tens ÷ 8 tens.

Remember that if the basic fact has a zero in the dividend, that zero should NOT be used to find the number of zeros in the quotient.

1. 360 ÷ 40 =
2. 270 ÷ 90 =
3. 180 ÷ 20 =
4. 750 ÷ 50 =
5. 2,100 ÷ 30 =
6. 4,800 ÷ 80 =
7. 5,400 ÷ 60 =
8. 6,300 ÷ 90 =
9. 30,000 ÷ 50 =
10. 21,000 ÷ 30 =
11. 72,000 ÷ 80 =
12. 81,000 ÷ 90 =

Set B, pages 60–61

Estimate 364 ÷ 57.

Use compatible numbers and patterns to divide.

364 ÷ 57
↓   ↓
360 ÷ 60 = 6

So, 364 ÷ 57 is about 6.

Remember that compatible numbers are numbers that are easy to compute in your head.

1. 168 ÷ 45
2. 525 ÷ 96
3. 379 ÷ 63
4. 234 ÷ 72
5. 8,916 ÷ 27
6. 6,213 ÷ 65
7. $613 ÷ 93
8. $748 ÷ 92

Set C, pages 62–63

Find 461 ÷ 50.

Estimate to decide where to put the first digit in the quotient.

Use compatible numbers. 450 ÷ 50 = 9

Start dividing the ones. Multiply and subtract. Compare the remainder to the divisor.

```
    9 R11
50)461
-  450
    11
```
The answer is reasonable since it is close to the estimate.

Remember that if the product of your first quotient and the divisor is larger than the dividend, your estimate is too high. Try dividing again with the next lower number.

1. 20)428
2. 30)547
3. 40)387
4. 50)653
5. 60)589
6. 70)912
7. 80)698
8. 90)849

Set D, pages 64–66, 68–69

Find 789 ÷ 19.

Estimate first.

800 ÷ 20 = 40.

Divide the tens. Multiply, subtract, and compare.

Bring down the ones. Divide the ones. Multiply, subtract, and compare. Check the quotient against your estimate.

$$\begin{array}{r} 41\ R10 \\ 19\overline{)789} \\ -\ 76 \\ \hline 29 \\ -\ 19 \\ \hline 10 \end{array}$$

Remember that you can check your answer by multiplying the quotient by the divisor, and then adding the remainder to that product. The sum should be your dividend.

1. $74\overline{)389}$ 2. $28\overline{)119}$
3. $36\overline{)234}$ 4. $38\overline{)792}$
5. $42\overline{)523}$ 6. $58\overline{)721}$
7. $23\overline{)1,955}$ 8. $17\overline{)237}$

Set E, pages 70–71, 72–73

Find 4,321 ÷ 21.

Estimate first to help decide where to put the first digit in the quotient. Use compatible numbers: 4,000 ÷ 20 = 200

Carry out the division.

$$\begin{array}{r} 205\ R16 \\ 21\overline{)4,321} \\ 42 \\ \hline 121 \\ 105 \\ \hline 16 \end{array}$$

Remember that you can use your estimate to check your answer for reasonableness.

Estimate and then find each quotient. Check each answer for reasonableness.

1. 612 ÷ 21 2. 932 ÷ 32
3. 5,100 ÷ 24 4. 1,777 ÷ 88
5. $47\overline{)51,908}$ 6. $15\overline{)4,485}$
7. $11\overline{)1,224}$ 8. $96\overline{)63,333}$

Set F, pages 74–75

The football coach spent a total of $875 for jerseys and socks for the team. The price of the socks was $105. If the coach bought 35 new jerseys, what was the price of one jersey?

Identify the hidden question or questions.

How much did all the jerseys cost?

$875 − $105 = $770

Solve the problem.

$770 ÷ 35 = $22   Each jersey cost $22.

Remember that you need to identify the hidden question or questions and answer them before solving the problem.

Write and answer the hidden question or questions. Then solve.

1. At the city triathlon, athletes bike 25 miles, run 6 miles, and swim. If the total distance of this triathlon is 33 miles, how far do the athletes swim?

Expressions and Equations

1 One of the tallest trees in the world is a sequoia known as General Grant. How many times as tall as a typical oak tree is General Grant? You will find out in Lesson 4-6.

2 There is a viewing area in the giraffe exhibit at the Jacksonville Zoo and Gardens in Jacksonville, Florida. It allows visitors to get closer to the giraffes. How many times as tall as a fifth-grade student is a giraffe? You will find out in Lesson 4-6.

3

This superflag hung over Hoover Dam during the 1996 Olympic Torch relay. How many grommets did it take to hang the flag over the dam? You will find out in Lesson 4-2.

4

The area of Lake Victoria, in Africa, is 26,828 square miles. How does the area of Lake Victoria compare to the area of Lake Michigan, in the United States? You will find out in Lesson 4-5.

Topic Essential Questions

- How are the values of algebraic expressions and numerical expressions found?
- How are equations involving one operation solved?

Review What You Know!

Vocabulary

Choose the best term from the box.

- estimate   · operations
- factors   · addend

1. Addition, subtraction, multiplication, and division are all __?__.

2. Numbers that are multiplied to get a product are called __?__.

3. Rounding can be used to find a(n) __?__.

Multiplication

Use mental math to find each product.

4. 7×100 **5.** $40 \times 1{,}000$ **6.** 60×200

7. 30×800 **8.** 700×600 **9.** $4 \times 40{,}000$

Patterns

Write a rule for each pattern.

10.

Number of Books	15	30	45
Number of Shelves	1	2	3

11.

Original Price	$100	$150	$200
Sale Price	$75	$125	$175

12. Writing to Explain The number of miles Lin walked each month for 4 months forms a pattern.

Number of miles: 8 12 16 20

Explain how to find this pattern. Describe the pattern.

MA.5.A.6.2 Use the order of operations to simplify expressions which include exponents and parentheses.

Exponents

How can you use exponents to write large numbers?

A box of cubes has 5 layers. Each layer has 5 rows, with 5 cubes in each row.

There are $5 \times 5 \times 5$ cubes in the box.

You can use exponential notation to represent repeated multiplication of the *same* number such as $5 \times 5 \times 5$.

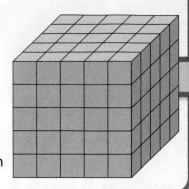

Other Examples

Exponential notation

Write $4 \times 4 \times 4$ in exponential notation.

$4 \times 4 \times 4 = 4^3$

As multiplication

Write 10^4 as multiplication.

$10^4 = 10 \times 10 \times 10 \times 10$

Standard form

Write 2^5 in standard form.

$2^5 = 2 \times 2 \times 2 \times 2 \times 2$
$\quad = 32$

An exponent is also called a power. You can read 4^6 as "4 to the sixth power." The second and third powers have special names. Read 3^2 as "3 to the second power," or 3 squared. Read 6^3 as "6 to the third power," or 6 cubed.

Guided Practice*

Do you know HOW?

1. Write 3^5 as multiplication.

2. Write 2^4 in standard form.

3. Write $7 \times 7 \times 7 \times 7 \times 7$ using exponential notation.

4. Write 5^4 as multiplication and in standard form.

5. Write 6 squared in standard form.

Do you UNDERSTAND?

6. In 3^5, what is the base? The exponent?

7. In the example at the top, how is 125 written as multiplication?

8. What is the standard form of 3 squared? For 6 cubed?

9. Why is the standard form of 3 squared and 3^2 the same?

DIGITAL

Animated Glossary
www.pearsonsuccessnet.com

*For another example, see Set A on page 102.

The base is the number to be multiplied.

The exponent is the number that tells how many times the base is used as a factor.

$$\underset{\text{base}}{5} \times 5 \times 5 = 5^3$$

factors   exponent

Numbers involving exponents may be written in different ways.

In exponential notation	5^3
As multiplication	$5 \times 5 \times 5$
In standard form	125

Independent Practice

In **10** through **16**, write in exponential notation.

10. $10 \times 10 \times 10 \times 10 \times 10$ **11.** $9 \times 9 \times 9$ **12.** 81×81 **13.** $5 \times 5 \times 5 \times 5$

14. $7 \times 7 \times 7$ **15.** $13 \times 13 \times 13 \times 13 \times 13 \times 13$ **16.** $6 \times 6 \times 6 \times 6$

In **17** through **24**, write as multiplication.

17. 17^5 **18.** 35 squared   **19.** 4^3 **20.** 7^6

21. 55^4 **22.** 11^6 **23.** 8 cubed   **24.** 1^9

In **25** through **32** write in standard form.

25. 5^4 **26.** 10^3 **27.** $4 \times 4 \times 4$ **28.** 12 squared

29. 1^{10} **30.** 2^6 **31.** 3 cubed   **32.** 9^4

Problem Solving

33. Why is the standard form of 8^2 NOT equal to 16?

THINK
SOLVE
EXPLAIN

34. Number Sense Find the number that equals 81 when it is squared.
Critical
THINKING

35. Darnell earned $10 each week for 10 weeks walking a neighbor's dog.

   a How much did he earn?

   b Write the amount Darnell earned using exponential notation.

36. Which of the following, when written in standard form, is equal to the standard form of 2^6?

   A 6^2 **C** 8^2

   B 3^4 **D** 4^4

MA.5.A.6.2 Use the order of operations to simplify expressions which include exponents and parentheses.

Order of Operations

How do you know which operation to perform first?

Evaluate $14 + 8 \times 6$.

Adding first gives:

$14 + 8 \times 6$

22×6

132

Multiplying first gives:

$14 + 8 \times 6$

$14 + 48$

62

Other Examples

Evaluate $20 + (30 - 10) \div 5$.

Using order of operations:

$20 + (30 - 10) \div 5$ ← **Compute inside the parentheses first.**

$20 + 20 \div 5$ ← **Next, divide.**

$20 + 4$ ← **Finally, add.**

24

Using a scientific calculator:

Press:

20 [+] 30 [−] 10 [÷] 5 [ENTER =]

Display will read: 24

Evaluate $4^2 - (4 + 6) \div 2$.

Using order of operations:

$4^2 - (4 + 6) \div 2$ ← **Compute inside the parentheses first.**

$4^2 - 10 \div 2$ ← **Evaluate exponents.**

$16 - 10 \div 2$ ← **Then divide.**

$16 - 5$ ← **Finally, subtract.**

11

Using a scientific calculator:

Press:

4 2 [−] 4 [+] 6 [÷] 2 [ENTER =]

Display will read: 11

Explain It

1. Each of the two expressions below has the same numbers and operations. Why do they each have different values?

   $10 - (4 + 5) \qquad (10 - 4) + 5$

2. In the second example using the scientific calculator, what is the purpose of the [^] key?

Mathematicians use a set of rules known as order of operations, the order in which to perform operations in calculations.

1. Compute inside parentheses.
2. Evaluate terms with exponents.
3. Multiply and divide from left to right.
4. Add and subtract from left to right.

Using the correct order of operations, $14 + 8 \times 6 = 62$.
A scientific calculator uses order of operations.

Press: 14 [+] 8 [×] 6 [ENTER/=]

Display will read: 62

Guided Practice*

Do you know HOW?

Evaluate each expression.

1. $36 \div 6 + 6$ **2.** $36 \div (6 + 6)$

3. $24 \div (4 + 8) + 2$ **4.** $48 \div (4 + 8) + 2^2$

5. $24 \div 4 + 8 + 2$ **6.** $48 \div 4 + 8 + 2^2$

Do you UNDERSTAND?

7. Where could you insert parentheses to make this number sentence true?
$80 \div 8 \times 5 + 4 = 90$

8. Donavan entered $12 + 4 \times 3 - 6$ into Lidia's scientific calculator. The display showed 18. In what order did the calculator complete the operations?

Independent Practice

In **9** through **22**, evaluate each expression.

9. $3^3 - 8 \times 3$ **10.** $(5^2 + 7) \div 4$ **11.** $6 \times 4 - 4 + 2$ **12.** $18 - 3 \times 5 + 2$

13. $49 - 4 \times (49 \div 7)$ **14.** $(64 \div 8) \times 3 + 6$ **15.** $72 \div (4 + 4) \times 5$ **16.** $(3 \times 3) \times (2 \times 2) \div 36$

17. $5 + 4^2 \times 3$ **18.** $9 \times 0 + 4$ **19.** $5^2 - 6 \times 0$

20. $8 \times (9 - 2) - 3$ **21.** $(5 + 4) \times 3 \times 3$ **22.** $(6 + 3) \times (21 \div 3)$

In **23** through **28**, use parentheses to make each equation true.

23. $5^2 - 6 \times 0 = 0$ **24.** $8 \times 9 - 2 - 3 = 53$ **25.** $1 + 2 \times 3 + 4 = 21$

26. $2^2 + 4 \times 6 = 48$ **27.** $5 \times 6 \times 8 - 7 = 30$ **28.** $6^2 + 7 + 9 \times 10 = 133$

DIGITAL
Animated Glossary
www.pearsonsuccessnet.com

*For another example, see Set B on page 102.

29. Number Sense Use the symbols 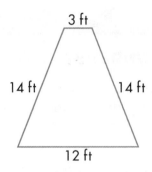 +, −, ×, and ÷ to make the equation true.

(3 ☐ 5) ☐ 4 ☐ (14 ☐ 2) = 12

30. Meredith bought 3 T-shirts for $12 each. Her grandmother paid for half the total cost. To find how much Meredith paid, evaluate the expression: (3 × 12) ÷ 2.

31. Luke needs a new fence around his garden, but the gate across the narrow end of the garden will not be replaced. To find how many feet of fencing Luke needs, evaluate the expression: 12 + (2 × 14).

3 ft

14 ft   14 ft

12 ft

32. Writing to Explain If p is greater than zero, tell which of these expressions has the higher value: (2 × p) + 5 or 2 × (p + 5). Explain how you know.

33. Jaron walked 15 blocks north and then 3 blocks west to school. Marisol walked 3 blocks east and then 15 blocks south to school. Write an equation to show that each traveled the same distance.

34. On Saturday, every seat in Mazen Theater was full. The balcony has 10 rows with 22 seats in each. The main floor has 25 rows with 30 seats each. To find the number of people at the theater, evaluate the following expression: (10 × 22) + (25 × 30).

A 16   **C** 970

B 87   **D** 14,100

35. On her math test, Bianca scored 5 points on each of 5 questions, 2 points on each of 2 questions, and 3 points on each of 4 questions. To find the number of points she scored, evaluate the expression: $5^2 + 2^2 + (3 \times 4)$.

F 26   **H** 41

G 40   **I** 84

36. **Social Studies** The world's largest flag, which was hung over Hoover Dam in 1996, measured 505 feet × 225 feet. The flag hung by a cable through grommets on one of the shorter sides. There is a grommet every 30 inches. If there is a grommet at each end, evaluate the expression 1 + (225 × 12) ÷ 30 to find out how many grommets were used to hang the flag.

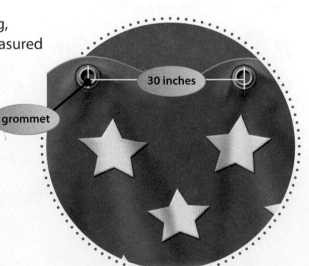

grommet

30 inches

Exponents and Order of Operations

Evaluate 5^6 on a calculator two ways.

Step 1 Use the exponent key .

Press: 5 [∧] 6 [ENTER =]

Display: `15625`

Step 2 Use repeated multiplication.

5 [×] 5 [×] 5 [×] 5 [×] 5 [×] 5 [ENTER =]

Display: `15625`

Evaluate $9^3 + (27 \div 3 + 47)$ on a calculator two ways.

Step 1 Use the calculator's order of operations.

9 [∧] 3 [+] [( ] 27 [÷] 3 [+] 47 [ )] [ENTER =]

Display: `785`

Step 2 Follow order of operations to verify that the calculator used the correct order of operations.

27 [÷] 3 [ENTER =]   [+] 47 [ENTER =]

Display: `9`   `56`

9 [∧] 3 [ENTER =]   [+] 56 [ENTER =]

Display: `729`   `785`

Practice

Evaluate each expression two ways.

1. 8^5

2. 7^4

3. $8 \times 19 - 36 + 12^5$

4. $(72 \div 9) + 6 \times 3^5$

5. 3^7

6. $1{,}204 \div 14 - 2^5 + 178$

Lesson

4-3

MA.5.A.6.2 Use the order of operations to simplify expressions which include exponents and parentheses.

Expressions

How can you evaluate an algebraic expression?

Jerome keeps track of the amount of money he earns each month. The number of lawns he mows changes each month. In July, Jerome mowed 3 lawns and earned a $20 allowance. How much did he earn in July?

> **Money Earned in July**
>
> I was paid $6 for each lawn I mowed.
>
> I got an allowance of $20.

Guided Practice*

Do you know HOW?

Use the given value for each variable and the order of operations to evaluate each expression.

1. $3 + 4n$; $n = 4$ **2.** $5 - b$; $b = 2$

3. $16 \times (3 - l)$; $l = 3$ **4.** $5p - 5$; $p = 9$

Do you UNDERSTAND?

5. What steps do you follow to evaluate the expression $2s - 3$ if $s = 2$?

6. In the example above, if Jerome had mowed 5 lawns and if he got an allowance of $15, how much would he have earned?

Independent Practice

In **7** through **18**, use the given value for each variable and the order of operations to evaluate each expression.

7. $10 - s$; $s = 4$

8. $(5 \times p) - 6$; $p = 4$

9. $2 + 6n$; $n = 5$

10. $18 \div (b + 5)$; $b = 1$

11. $9 \times (11 - s)$; $s = 2$

12. $7a + 3$; $a = 5$

13. $3h + 20$; $h = 10$

14. $3 \times n - 6$; $n = 5$

15. $18 \div (6 + s)$; $s = 3$

16. $t + 6$; $t = 9$

17. $63 - n$; $n = 21$

18. $6p - 1$; $p = 10$

For **19** through **21**, evaluate the expressions for $t = 6$.

19. $18 - 3t$

20. $t - 3$

21. $3^2 \times t$

Animated Glossary
www.pearsonsuccessnet.com

DIGITAL

For another example, see Set C on page 102.

A variable is a letter or symbol that represents a number that can vary or change.

Let a = The number of lawns Jerome mows each month

An algebraic expression is a mathematical phrase involving variables, numbers, and operations. An algebraic expression can be used to represent the problem.

$6 \times a + 20$

↑ Number of lawns

You can write $6 \times a$ as $6a$.

So, $6 \times a + 20$ is the same as $6a + 20$.

Substitute the value for a and use the order of operations to evaluate the expression.

$6a + 20$

$6 \times 3 + 20$ ←— Multiply and divide first.

$18 + 20$ ←— Then add.

38

Jerome earned $38 in July.

Problem Solving

22. 🌐 **Social Studies** Inside the Lincoln Memorial in Washington, D.C., is a statue of Abraham Lincoln sitting in a chair. If the statue were standing, it would be 28 feet tall. Write an equation that could be used to find the difference between the height of the statue if it were standing and the actual statue height. What is the difference?

19 feet

23. At an apple orchard, workers place 9 apples into each bag to be sold at the local market. If 523 apples were picked, how many bags will be completely filled?

24. Jeff added $\frac{4}{5}$ cup of water to $\frac{2}{3}$ cup of lemonade concentrate. Is there more water or concentrate in the mixture?

25. Which is of the following is the value of the expression $5 + 3 \times t$, if $t = 8$?

A 56 **C** 16

B 29 **D** 8

26. 🔍 **Science** A bacteria cell splits in half when it reaches a certain size. After the first split, there are 2 cells. After the second split, there are 4 cells. How many cells will there be after the fifth split?

27. Writing to Explain In the expression $g \div (12 - 7)$ why should you subtract before you divide?

28. How are the expressions $7 - g$ and $g - 7$ different?

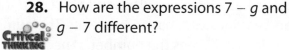

29. Julio sold homemade dog biscuits at the school fair. He sold 5 large dog biscuits and 4 bags of small dog biscuits. The total number of dog biscuits Julio sold can be found by evaluating $5 + 4d$. If $d = 3$, what is the value of the expression?

MA.5.A.6.5 Solve non-routine problems using various strategies including "solving a simpler problem" and "guess, check, and revise."

Problem Solving

Act It Out and Use Reasoning

A children's zoo displays birds in 3 different cages. The zoo has three kinds of birds. There are 36 birds in all. How many of each type of bird are in the zoo?

Use objects to show the birds and then use reasoning to solve the problem.

Hands-On
unit cubes

3 times as many canaries as parrots

24 parakeets

Guided Practice*

Do you know HOW?

Solve. You can use cubes to act out the problem.

1. The Rodriquez family is donating 25 baseball caps to a charity auction. There are 11 blue caps. There are 2 more white caps than green caps. How many of each color cap are they donating?

Do you UNDERSTAND?

2. In the example at the top, suppose there are 2 times as many canaries as parrots and the number of parakeets is the same. How many of each type of bird are in the zoo?

3. **Write a Problem** Write a real-world problem that can be solved by acting it out and using reasoning.

Independent Practice

In **4** and **5**, solve. Use cubes to act out the problems.

4. Mr. Niles has a box of accessories for clarinets. He has a total of 42 objects. He has 12 mouthpieces. He has four times as many reeds as neck straps. How many of each object does he have?

5. Sylvia has a jewelry collection of bracelets, necklaces, and earrings. She has 16 bracelets. The number of earrings is 2 times the number of necklaces. She has 43 pieces of jewelry in all. How many of each piece of jewelry does she have?

Stuck? Try this....

- What do I know?
- What am I asked to find?
- What diagram can I use to help understand the problem?
- Can I use addition, subtraction, multiplication, or division?
- Is all of my work correct?
- Did I answer the right question?
- Is my answer reasonable?

*For another example, see Set D on page 103.

Use objects and show what you know.
Let 36 cubes represent all the birds.
Use reasoning to make conclusions.

🟦🟦🟦🟦🟦🟦🟦🟦🟦🟦🟦🟦
🟦🟦🟦🟦🟦🟦🟦🟦🟦🟦🟦🟦
24 parakeets
🟦🟦🟦🟦🟦🟦🟦🟦🟦🟦🟦🟦
12 canaries and parrots

There are 24 parakeets and 36 birds
in all. That leaves a total of 12 canaries
and parrots.

Use 12 cubes. There are 3 times as many
canaries as parrots.

🟦🟦🟦🟦🟦🟦🟦🟦🟦

🟦🟦🟦

There are 24 parakeets, 9 canaries, and
3 parrots.
$24 + 9 + 3 = 36$, so the answer is correct.

In **6** through **8**, copy and complete the table at the right.

6. Brady joined the band. In Group 1, there are a total
of 44 students. There are 8 students who play the
oboe. Twice as many students play the flute as
those who play the clarinet. How many students
from Group 1 play each instrument?

7. There are 41 students in Group 2. Twice as many
students play the trumpet as play the trombone,
and 8 students play the saxophone. How many
students in Group 2 play each instrument?

Data	Instrument	Number of Students
	Group 1	44
	Oboe	8
	Clarinet	⬜
	Flute	⬜
	Group 2	41
	Saxophone	8
	Trumpet	⬜
	Trombone	⬜

8. Later, 7 students joined Group 2 and
1 student left to join Group 1. Some
students decided to play a different
instrument. Now 20 students play
trombone and 7 more students play
trumpet than play saxophone. How
many students play each instrument?

9. What is the perimeter of this figure?

Critical THINKING

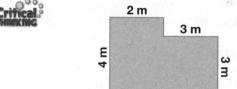

2 m
3 m
4 m
3 m

10. Reggie earned $360 in the summer. If he
earned $40 per week, how many weeks
did he work?

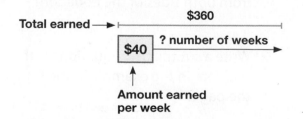

Total earned → $360
$40 ? number of weeks
Amount earned per week

11. The Garden Theater presented a play. A
total of 179 people attended in 3 days.
The first day, 58 people attended. On
the second day, 47 people attended.
How many attended on the third day?

179 people

58 people	47 people	x
1st day	2nd day	3rd day

MA.5.A.4.1 Use the properties of equality to solve numerical and real world situations.

Solving Addition and Subtraction Equations

How can you use addition and subtraction to solve equations?

In 2008, there were 91 women in Congress. How many women were serving in the U.S. Senate?

Members of U.S. Congress	
2008	
U.S. Senate	
Men	84
Women	
U.S. House of Representatives	
Men	365
Women	75

Other Examples

Addition Property of Equality:
You can add the same number to both sides of an equation and the sides remain equal.

Example:
$$9 - 4 = 5$$
$$9 - 4 + 2 = 5 + 2$$

Subtraction Property of Equality:
You can subtract the same number from both sides of an equation and the sides remain equal.

Example:
$$8 + 6 = 14$$
$$8 + 6 - 3 = 14 - 3$$

Operations that undo each other are inverse operations.
Addition and subtraction have an inverse relationship.

Guided Practice*

Do you know HOW?

In **1** and **2**, what would you do to get the variable by itself on one side of each equation?

1. $x - 45 = 90$ **2.** $n + 23.4 = 36.9$

In **3** through **6**, use inverse operations and a property of equality to solve these equations.

3. $x + 13 = 42$ **4.** $x - 12 = 37$

5. $a + 8 = 37$ **6.** $b - 9 = 25$

Do you UNDERSTAND?

7. What could you do to check the answer in the example at the top of the page?

8. When finding the number of women in the Senate, why must 75 be subtracted from both sides of the equation?

9. Write a subtraction equation for the problem in the example at the top of the page.

DIGITAL
Animated Glossary
www.pearsonsuccessnet.com

Since Congress includes both the Senate and the House, you can write an addition equation. An equation is <u>a number sentence that uses an equal sign to show that two expressions have the same value.</u>

91	
x	75

Let x = the number of women in the Senate.

Equation: x + 75 = 91.

To solve the equation, get the variable alone.

$$x + 75 = 91$$
$$x + 75 - 75 = 91 - 75$$
$$x = 91 - 75$$
$$x = 16$$

You can subtract 75 from both sides of the equation and the quantities on each side of the equal sign are still equal.

There were 16 women serving in the U.S. Senate in 2008.

Independent Practice

In **10** through **18**, solve each equation.

10. $d - 14 = 13$

11. $p + 31 = 52$

12. $c - 68 = 78$

13. $n + 70 = 265$

14. $y - 28 = 98$

15. $746 + t = 947$

16. $91 = 19 + m$

17. $75 = n - 39$

18. $k + 22 = 30$

Problem Solving

19. If there are 57 students in the school band and 29 of them are boys, how many girls are in the band?

20. Writing to Explain Why will the equations $x + 14 = 37$ and $x - 14 = 37$ have different solutions for x?

21. Cam has 73 crayons which is 18 more than the number of crayons Yun has. Draw a picture to show $y + 18 = 73$. Solve to find the number of crayons Yun has.

22. Mr. Kugel's class raised $213 from different class projects and collected $27 in donations. How much more money is needed to pay for a $500 class picnic?

23. **Think About the Process** Which operation would you use to solve the equation $x - 17 = 23$?

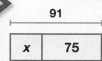

A Add 17.

C Multiply by 17.

B Subtract 17.

D Divide by 1.

24. Write and solve an equation to represent the diagram below.

645	
163	r

25. **Social Studies** The area of Lake Victoria in Africa is 26,828 square miles. The area of Lake Michigan in the U.S. is 22,539 square miles. Solve the equation $x + 22,539 = 26,828$ to find how many more square miles Lake Victoria covers than Lake Michigan.

MA.5.A.4.1 Use the
properties of equality to
solve numerical and real
world situations.

Solving Multiplication and Division Equations

How can you use multiplication and division to solve equations?

Keef's scoutmaster is buying model cars for his troop. The cars are sold by the case. How many cases should the scoutmaster buy for 32 boys?

4 cars in each case

Other Examples

Multiplication Property of Equality:
You can multiply both sides of an equation by the same nonzero number and the sides remain equal.

Example:

$$\frac{14}{2} = 7$$

$$\frac{14}{2} \times 2 = 7 \times 2$$

Division Property of Equality:
You can divide both sides of an equation by the same nonzero number and the sides remain equal.

Example:

$$6 \times 5 = 30$$

$$\frac{6 \times 5}{5} = \frac{30}{5}$$

Operations that undo each other are inverse operations. Multiplication and division have an inverse relationship.

Guided Practice*

Do you know HOW?

In **1** and **2**, what would you do to get each variable alone on one side of the equation?

1. $24n = 120$ **2.** $\frac{b}{7} = 42$

In **3** through **6**, use inverse operations and a property of equality to solve these equations.

3. $y \div 9 = 12$ **4.** $3m = 63$

5. $85 = 17r$ **6.** $24 = \frac{c}{3}$

Do you UNDERSTAND?

7. What could you do to check the answer in the example at the top of the page?

8. Write a division equation for the problem at the top of the page.

9. In the example above, if there were 6 cars in a case, how many cases would the scoutmaster need to buy to be sure every scout had a car?

Animated Glossary
www.pearsonsuccessnet.com

For another example, see Set E on page 103.

Let c = the number of cases needed.

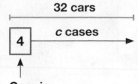

32 cars

4 c cases →

↑
Cars in each case

Since each case contains 4 cars, you can write the equation

$4c = 32$

To solve the equation, get the variable alone.

$4c = 32$

$\dfrac{4c}{4} = \dfrac{32}{4}$

$c = 8$

You can divide both sides of the equation by 4 and the quantities on each side of the equal sign are still equal.

Tip   *Remember that $\dfrac{4c}{4}$ is the same as $4 \times c \div 4$.*

The scoutmaster should buy 8 cases of cars.

Independent Practice

In **10** through **17**, solve each equation.

10. $14d = 56$

11. $\dfrac{c}{8} = 64$

12. $45y = 135$

13. $184 = 23p$

14. $\dfrac{m}{5} = 12$

15. $8 = \dfrac{k}{30}$

16. $72 = 12t$

17. $14 = \dfrac{w}{7}$

Problem Solving

18. Geometry Each side of a pentagon measures 11 inches. What is the perimeter of the pentagon?

19. Reasoning Randy divides 48 by 6 to solve an equation for y. One side of the equation is 48. Write the equation.

Critical THINKING

20. Martin is going on a 216-mile trip. If his car gets 24 miles per gallon, how many gallons of gas will he need for his trip?

21. Writing to Explain How could you use mental math to find m in the equation $279 \times m \div 279 = 72$?

22. Daria measured the length of three ants in science class. They were $\dfrac{2}{3}$ inch, $\dfrac{3}{5}$ inch, and $\dfrac{1}{4}$ inch. Which ant is the longest?

23. Think About the Process Which operation would you use to solve the equation $17x = 255$?

  A Add 17.   **C** Multiply by 17.

  B Subtract 17.   **D** Divide by 17.

24. Some giraffes at the Jacksonville Zoo and Gardens in Jacksonville, Florida, can grow to be 20 feet tall. Some fifth graders can be 5 feet tall. Solve $5x = 20$ to find how many times as tall as a fifth grader a giraffe is.

25. **Science** General Grant, a sequoia tree, is 273 feet tall. A typical red oak tree is about 70 feet tall. Solve the equation $70x = 280$ to find about how many times as tall the General Grant is as a typical red oak.

MA.5.A.4.1 Use the properties of equality to solve numerical and real world situations.

Draw a Picture and Write an Equation

At an art fair, Dean sold different types of paintings. The price of a portrait is $125 more than the price of a still-life painting. What is the price of a still-life painting?

Still Life
$?

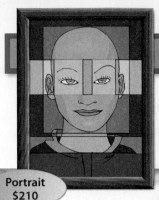

Portrait
$210

Landscape
$135

Another Example

Dean also sold 8 pen-and-ink sketches at the art fair. All the sketches were the same price. He made $192 on the sale of the sketches. What was the price of each sketch?

Read and Understand

What do you know?   Dean sold 8 sketches and made $192.

What are you trying to find?   The price of one sketch

Plan

What strategy will you use?   Write an equation. A diagram can help to picture how the information is related.

Let n = the price of one sketch.

| $192 |
| *n* | *n* | *n* | *n* | *n* | *n* | *n* | *n* |

$8 \times n = 192$
$(8 \times n) \div 8 = 192 \div 8$
$n = 24$

Divide both sides of the equation by 8 to get n alone on one side of the equation.

Each sketch sold for $24.

Explain It

1. **Reasonableness** Is $24 for each sketch a reasonable answer?

2. How does the diagram above show the information in the problem?

Choose a variable for the unknown quantity.

Let p = the price of a still-life painting.

Use a diagram to picture the relationship between the prices.

$210

p	$125

Write an equation.

$p + 125 = 210$

Solve the equation.

$$p + 125 = 210$$
$$p + 125 - 125 = 210 - 125$$
$$p = 85$$

Subtract 125 from both sides to get the variable alone.

The price of a still-life painting is $85.

Estimate to see if the answer makes sense.

Round 85 to 100.

$100 + 125 = 225$, which is close to 210.

The price of $85 is reasonable.

Guided Practice*

Do you know HOW?

1. Use the picture to write and solve an equation.

34

s	18

Do you UNDERSTAND?

2. **Write a Problem** Write a real-world problem that you can solve by drawing a picture and writing an addition or subtraction equation.

Independent Practice

In **3** through **5**, use each picture to write and solve each equation.

3. Alice read 5 more pages today than she did yesterday. Today she read 42 pages. How many pages did Alice read yesterday?

42 pages

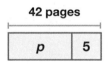

4. Dan biked 27 miles yesterday. If he biked 3 times as far as Joe, how far did Joe bike?

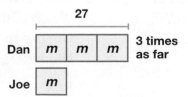

5. Max is saving $15 per month to buy a desk that costs $285. How many months will he need to save?

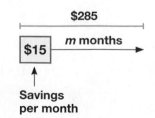

Savings per month

Stuck? Try this....

- What do I know?
- What am I asked to find?
- What diagram can I use to help understand the problem?
- Can I use addition, subtraction, multiplication, or division?
- Is all of my work correct?
- Did I answer the right question?
- Is my answer reasonable?

In **6** through **8**, draw a picture, and write and solve an equation for each problem.

6. Kieko and Linda sold a total of 124 calendars. Kieko sold 57 of them. How many calendars did Linda sell?

7. Carmen has saved $13 to buy a DVD that costs $29. How much more money does Carmen need to save?

8. Jonathan loaned his brother $22 and had $126 left. How much money did Jonathan have before he loaned the money?

9. **Writing to Explain** Caryn drew this picture and wrote this equation to represent the problem below.

A zoo has 19 more species of fish than birds. There are 152 species of fish. How many species of birds does the zoo have?

b

19	152

$b - 19 = 152$

Is Caryn correct? Explain your answer.

10. **Reasoning** A cashier has already checked out 21 customers. If she can check out 3 new customers every 6 minutes, how many minutes will it take her to check out the next 27 customers?

11. Orlando saved $520 in 1 year. He saved $330 in the last 4 months. Write and solve an equation to find how much Orlando saved in the first 8 months.

12. Dean also does abstract paintings. He charges $85 less than the price of a portrait. He charges $210 for a portrait. Write and solve an equation to find the price of one of Dean's abstract paintings.

13. **Science** A year on Earth is 365 days. A year on Mars is 687 days. Write and solve an equation to find how many days longer a year on Mars is than on Earth.

Think About the Process

14. A total of 44 adults are going on a field trip with the class. If 14 of the adults are men, how many are women? Which of the following equations gives the number of women?

A $14 + 44 = w$

B $w - 14 = 44$

C $14 + w = 44$

D $w - 44 = 14$

15. Tony is running a 10-kilometer race. He just reached the 4-kilometer marker. Which of the following equations can you use to find out how many more kilometers he needs to run?

F $k - 4 = 10$

G $4 + k = 10$

H $4 - k = 10$

I $10 + 4 = k$

Algebra Connections

Solution Pairs

Remember that an equation is a number sentence that uses an equal sign to show that two expressions have the same value.

When two variables occur in an equation, each variable can be replaced with a different number. When the two replacements make a true equation, the two replacements form a **solution pair**.

Example: Do $x = 12$ and $y = 8$ form a solution pair for $x = y + 4$?

Substitute the given values for x and y into the equation.

Replacing x with 12 and y with 8 gives $12 = 8 + 4$, or $12 = 12$. The equation is true.

So, $x = 12$ and $y = 8$ form a solution pair for $x = y + 4$.

For **1** through **15**, use the table of values at the right. For each equation, determine if the given replacements form a solution pair. Write yes or no.

1. $y + z = 10$

2. $b = x + 15$

3. $b = a + 15$

4. $a + x = 40$

5. $40 - c = x$

6. $c - x = 6$

7. $b - y = 43$

8. $b = 99 - z$

9. $60 - y = b$

10. $63 = b - c$

11. $20 + z = c$

12. $10 - y = z$

13. $20 = x + y$

14. $b + c = 58$

15. $a + b = 85$

Table of Values
$a = 30$
$b = 45$
$c = 18$
$x = 12$
$y = 8$
$z = 2$

For **16** and **17**, refer to the table at the right.

16. The cost of an adult ticket is equal to twice the cost of a child's ticket. So, $a = 2 \times c$. Find two different pairs of values for a and c to make the equation true.

17. An adult ticket costs $3 more than a student ticket. So $a = s + 3$. Find two different pairs of values for a and s to make the equation true.

Cost of Museum Tickets

Ticket	Price
Child	c
Adult	a
Student	s
Early Bird	e

1 Which of the following is a way to write 4^5? (4-1)

   A. 4×5

   B. $5 \times 5 \times 5 \times 5$

   C. $4 \times 4 \times 4 \times 4$

   D. $4 \times 4 \times 4 \times 4 \times 4$

2 What is the first step in evaluating the expression below? (4-2)

$100 - 2^3 \times (4 + 6)$

   F.   Multiply 2^3 by 4.

   G.   Add 4 and 6.

   H.   Evaluate 2^3.

   I.   Subtract 2^3 from 100.

3 The cost for n students to attend a workshop is $7n + 12$ dollars. What is the cost for 6 students to attend the workshop? (4-3)

   A. $25

   B. $36

   C. $54

   D. $156

4 An African elephant can eat up to 4,200 pounds of food in a week. You can find the number of pounds of food it can eat in a day by solving the equation $7n = 4,200$. What is the value of n? (4-6)

   F. $n = 700$

   G. $n = 600$

   H. $n = 70$

   I. $n = 60$

5 What step can be taken to get the x by itself on one side of the equation $x - 13 = 102$? (4-5)

   A.   Add 13 to both sides of the equation.

   B.   Subtract 13 from both sides of the equation.

   C.   Multiply both sides of the equation by 13.

   D.   Divide both sides of the equation by 13.

6 In one apartment building, people have a total of 16 dogs, cats, and birds. There are 8 dogs and three times as many cats as birds. How many cats are in the building? (4-4)

   F.   12

   G.   6

   H.   4

   I.   2

7 Lisa bought 5 boxes of black markers plus 4 single red markers. The total number of markers she bought is $5m + 4$, if m is the number of black markers in each box. What is the value of $5m + 4$ when $m = 6$? (4-3)

   A.   9

   B.   20

   C.   30

   D.   34

8 Which expression has a value of 3? (4-2)

  F. $12 + 6 \div 2 \times 3$

  G. $(12 - 6) \div 2 \times 3$

  H. $12 - 6 \div (2 \times 3)$

  I. $12 - (6 \div 2) \times 3$

9 On average, residents of the United Kingdom have 28 vacation days each year, 14 fewer than the average in Italy. The average number of vacation days in Italy can be found by solving the equation $n - 14 = 28$. What is the value of n? (4-5)

  A. $n = 2$

  B. $n = 14$

  C. $n = 42$

  D. $n = 49$

10 What step can be taken to get the variable m alone on one side of the equation $\frac{m}{5} = 25$? (4-6)

  F. Add 5 to each side of the equation.

  G. Subtract 5 from each sides of the equation.

  H. Multiply each side of the equation by 5.

  I. Divide each side of the equation by 5.

11 A museum is open for a total of 26 hours on Friday, Saturday, and Sunday. On Friday the museum is open for 8 hours. The museum is open for 2 hours more on Saturday than Sunday. How many hours is the museum open on Saturday? (4-4)

  A. 6 hours   **C.** 10 hours

  B. 8 hours   **D.** 12 hours

12 Alita sold bracelets she made for $3 each. She had total sales of $36. Which equation can be used to find n, the number of bracelets she sold? (4-7)

Cost of each bracelet

  F. $n + 3 = 36$

  G. $n - 3 = 36$

  H. $n \times 3 = 36$

  I. $n \div 3 = 36$

13 The number of square tiles on a patio is 9^2. What is the standard form of 9^2? (4-1)

14 THINK SOLVE EXPLAIN

Alberto chose a song for his recital that has 112 measures. The song is divided into 7 movements, or parts, each with the same number of measures. Draw a picture and write and solve an equation to help you find the number of measures in each movement. (4-7)

Set A, pages 82–83

Write 7^3 as multiplication and in standard form.

base → 7^3 ← exponent

Exponential notation: 7^3

As multiplication: $7 \times 7 \times 7$

Standard form: 343

Remember that the exponent tells how many times the base is used as a factor.

Write each as multiplication and in standard form.

1. 17^2 **2.** 10^5 **3.** 2^6 **4.** 5^4

Set B, pages 84–86

When evaluating an expression, you need to follow the order of operations.

Step 1 Compute inside parentheses.

Step 2 Evaluate terms with exponents.

Step 3 Multiply and divide from left to right.

Step 4 Add and subtract from left to right.

Evaluate $4 + 2^3 \times 3 + 7$.

$4 + \mathbf{2^3} \times 3 + 7$ ← Evaluate term with exponents.
$4 + \mathbf{8 \times 3} + 7$ ← Multiply.
$\mathbf{4 + 24 + 7}$ ← Add.
35

Remember that if you follow the order of operations you will compute correctly.

Evaluate.

1. $12 - 0 \times 6 \div 2$

2. $6 \times 3 \div (5 + 4)$

3. $5 + 3^2 - (7 - 3)$

4. $2^4 \div (4 + 4) + 9$

5. $4 + 6 - 2 \times 5$

Set C, pages 88–89

To evaluate an algebraic expression, replace the variable with the given value.

Evaluate $18 \div 6 + t$, for $t = 7$.

$18 \div 6 + t$

$18 \div 6 + 7$ ← Substitute the given value.

$3 + 7$ ← Apply order of operations.

10

Remember to replace the variable with the given value and follow the order of operations.

Evaluate for the given values.

1. $s - 20 \div 4; s = 8$

2. $2 \times p - 9; p = 8$

3. $(21 - s) \div 14; s = 7$

4. $35 - b^2; b = 5$

Set D, pages 90–91

Use objects to act out the problem and then use reasoning to solve.

A pet shop has a total of 19 dogs, cats, and ferrets. There are 4 ferrets and twice as many cats as dogs. How many of each kind of pet are in the shop?

Use 19 cubes to model the problem. Let 4 of the cubes represent ferrets. That leaves 15 cubes to represent the cats and dogs. Since $5 \times 2 = 10$ and $5 + 10 = 15$, there are 10 cats and 5 dogs.

Remember that acting out a problem with objects can help you reason through the problem.

Use objects to act out and solve.

1. Kerry has 12 paperweights in her collection. She has twice as many paperweights made of glass as of metal and 3 paperweights made of wood. How many paperweights made of each material does Kerry have?

Set E, pages 92–93, 94–95

Use the inverse operation to get the variable alone on one side of the equation.

Solve $x + 7 = 15$.   Solve $16x = 32$.

$$x + 7 = 15$$
$$x + 7 - 7 = 15 - 7$$
$$x = 8$$

$$16x = 32$$
$$\frac{16x}{16} = \frac{32}{16}$$
$$x = 2$$

Remember to use inverse operations to get the variable alone on one side of the equation.

Solve each equation.

1. $a - 17 = 9$ 2. $\frac{n}{4} = 21$

3. $34 + p = 59$ 4. $7 = \frac{k}{20}$

Set F, pages 96–98

The length of Wing Park Pool is 4 times as great as the length of Jamie's pool. The length of Wing Park Pool is 64 feet. What is the length of Jamie's pool?

Let p = the length of Jamie's pool.

64 feet

Wing Park Pool | p | p | p | p | 4 times as long

Jamie's Pool | p |

$$4 \times p = 64$$
$$(4 \times p) \div 4 = 64 \div 4$$
$$p = 16$$

The length of Jamie's pool is 16 feet.

Remember that drawing a picture can help you visualize a problem and write an equation to use to solve the problem.

Solve.

1. Tom had $70. Then he gave his sister $25. How much money does Tom have left?

2. A toy store has 5 times as many dolls as Mia. The store has 105 dolls. How many dolls does Mia have?

Equations and Graphs

1 Many cities in the United States are laid out like a coordinate grid. How can this be helpful when finding locations in cities such as Fort Lauderdale, Florida? You will find out in Lesson 5-1.

2 American manned space missions are launched from Kennedy Space Center near Orlando, Florida. How many hours have astronauts in the Space Shuttle program spent in space? You will find out in Lesson 5-6.

3

The Empire State Building is a famous landmark. Where is this landmark located? You will find out in Lesson 5-2.

Review What You Know!

Vocabulary

Choose the best term from the box.

> • squared   • cubed
> • variable   • equation

1. ___?___ is a name for a number to the second power.

2. A ___?___ represents an unknown quantity that can change.

3. ___?___ is a name for a number to the third power.

Expressions

Write a numerical expression for each word phrase.

4. The product of four times thirty

5. Seven more than three times ten

6. The sum of ninety and seventeen

7. The quotient of twenty-four divided by eight

Solving Equations

Solve each equation.

8. $62 = 39 + n$

9. $17f = 85$

10. $c - 50 = 27$

11. $6 = \frac{x}{3}$

Writing to Explain Write an answer to the question.

12. You know that $3 + 5 = 8$. Explain why $3 + 5 + 4 = 8 + 4$.

Topic Essential Questions

• How are points graphed?

• How are equations graphed and interpreted?

MA.5.G.5.1 Identify and plot ordered pairs on the first quadrant of the coordinate plane.

Ordered Pairs

How do you name a point on a coordinate grid?

A map shows the location of landmarks and has guides for finding the landmarks. In a similar way, a coordinate grid is used to graph and name the locations of points in a plane.

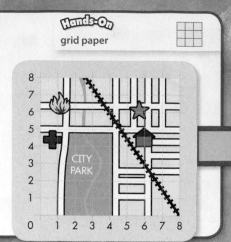

Another Example How do you graph a point on a coordinate grid?

Graph Point R at (4, 5).

Step 1

Draw and number the x-axis and y-axis on grid paper.

Step 2

Move 4 units to the right from 0. Then move 5 units up.

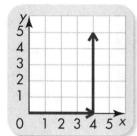

Step 3

Mark a point and label it R.

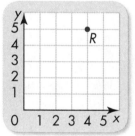

Explain It

1. Why is the order important when naming and graphing the coordinates of a point?

2. If the location of Point R changed to (6, 5), would it be to the right or to the left of its current position?

3. You have labeled the x-axis and y-axis on grid paper. You want to graph Point D at (0, 5). Do you move right zero units or move up zero units? Explain.

A coordinate grid has a horizontal *x*-axis and a vertical *y*-axis. The point at which the *x*-axis and *y*-axis intersect is called the origin.

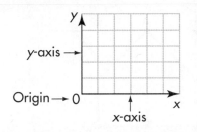

A point in a plane is named using an ordered pair of numbers. The first number, the *x*-coordinate, names the distance from the origin along the *x*-axis. The second number, the *y*-coordinate, names the distance from the origin along the *y*-axis.

A (1, 3)

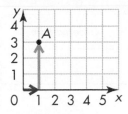

Guided Practice*

Do you know HOW?

In **1** and **2**, write each ordered pair. Use the grid at the right.

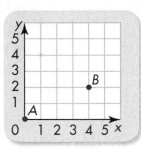

1. *A*

2. *B*

Graph and label each point on a grid.

3. *C* (1, 4)   **4.** *D* (5, 3)

Do you UNDERSTAND?

5. Using the example above, name the ordered pair for Point *B* if it is 3 units to the right of Point *A*.

6. What ordered pair names the origin of any coordinate grid?

7. Writing to Explain Describe how to locate Point *K* at (5, 3).

Independent Practice

In **8** through **13**, write each ordered pair. Use the grid at the right.

8. *T*   **9.** *X*

10. *Y*   **11.** *W*

12. *Z*   **13.** *S*

In **14** through **19**, graph and label each point on a grid.

14. *L* (2, 2)   **15.** *M* (0, 3)

16. *N* (1, 5)   **17.** *O* (5, 4)

18. *P* (4, 0)   **19.** *Q* (0, 0)

Animated Glossary, eTools
www.pearsonsuccessnet.com

*For another example, see Set A on page 124.

For **20** through **24**, complete the table. List the point and ordered pair for each vertex of the pentagon at the right.

	Point	Ordered Pair
20.		
21.		
22.		
23.		
24.		

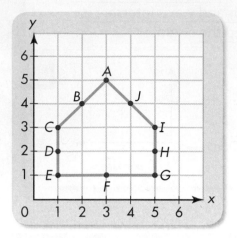

25. Use the coordinate grid from the last set of problems. Which of the following explains how to move from Point *B* to Point *H*?

    A Move right 3 units and down 2 units

    B Move left 2 units and up 1 unit

    C Move right 1 unit and down 2 units

    D Move right 2 units and down 3 units

26. Writing to Explain The streets on maps of many cities in the United States are laid out like a coordinate grid. How is this helpful when finding locations in cities such as Fort Lauderdale, Florida?

27. Algebra Write an equation to describe a rule for the table of values. Then complete the table.

x	y
3	1
6	2
12	4
9	■
■	5
24	■

28. A chess board is similar to a coordinate grid. The pieces that look like horses are knights. What letter-number combinations name the locations of the white knights?

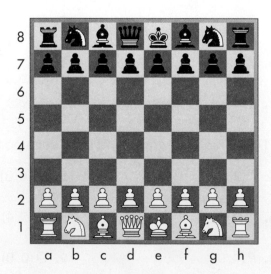

Mixed Problem Solving

Objects on Jupiter weigh about two and a half times as much as on Earth.

1. Look for a pattern to complete the table below and then graph the values on the coordinate grid.

Earth weight	50	60	70	▪	▪	100
Jupiter weight (approx.)	125	▪	175	200	225	▪

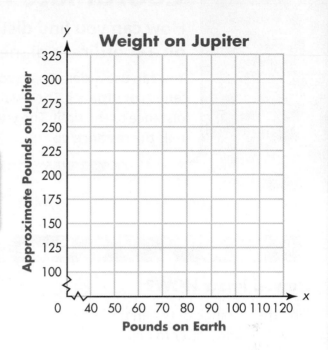

Weight on Jupiter

2. If a dog weighs 40 pounds on Earth, about how much would it weigh on Jupiter?

3. If Tyler weighs 120 pounds on Earth, about how much would he weigh on Jupiter?

. . . .

4. Complete this table using the graph that shows the Big Dipper.

Point	Ordered Pair
A	
B	
C	
D	
E	
F	
G	

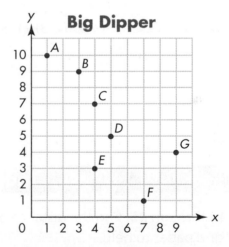

Big Dipper

5. If you were to move this drawing of the Big Dipper 3 units to the right on this grid, what would be the ordered pair for Point D?

6. **Strategy Focus** Examine the ordered pairs for Points C and E. How do you know that a vertical line can connect those two points? Explain how you decided.

MA.5.G.5.1 Identify and plot ordered pairs on the first quadrant of the coordinate plane.

Distances on a Coordinate Plane

Hands-On
grid paper

How can you find distances on a coordinate plane?

You can use ordered pairs to find length or distance. The *x*-value tells distance to the right. The *y*-value tells the distance up.

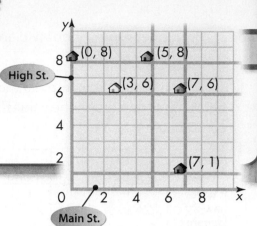

Guided Practice*

Do you know HOW?

Find the distance between the ordered pairs. Use grid paper to help.

1. (1, 3), (1, 8)

2. (2, 3), (12, 3)

3. (4, 3), (3, 3)

4. (2, 3), (2, 1)

5. (7, 15), (7, 2)

6. (7, 3), (1, 3)

7. (4, 4), (8, 4)

8. (35, 1), (12, 1)

Do you UNDERSTAND?

9. Writing to Explain If you are given two ordered pairs, how can you tell if they lie on a vertical line or on a horizontal line?

10. Which house did you start at if walking two blocks to the right and two blocks up brings you to another house?

11. What is the distance from the blue house to Main Street? to High Street?

Independent Practice

For **12** through **25**, find the distance between the ordered pairs. Use grid paper to help.

12. (2, 7), (6, 7)

13. (6, 7), (6, 4)

14. (6, 4), (6, 0)

15. (11, 8), (1, 8)

16. (8, 3), (8, 8)

17. (4, 9), (9, 9)

18. (0, 3), (1, 3)

19. (15, 6), (15, 12)

20. (5, 7), (5, 0)

21. (1, 9), (9, 9)

22. (10, 6), (4, 6)

23. (18, 10), (21, 10)

24. (14, 17), (12, 17)

25. (19, 23), (19, 18)

eTools
www.pearsonsuccessnet.com

*For another example, see Set B on page 124.

How far is the red house from the green house?

Compare the ordered pairs: (7, 1)
(7, 6)

The *x*-values are the same.

Because the points lie on a vertical line, you subtract the *y*-values to find the distance.

6 − 1 = 5

The distance between the red and green houses is 5 units.

How far is the blue house from the purple house?

Compare the ordered pairs: (0, 8)
(5, 8)

The *y*-values are the same.

Because the points lie on a horizontal line, you subtract the *x*-values to find the distance.

5 − 0 = 5

The distance between the purple and blue houses is 5 units.

Problem Solving

For **26** through **28**, use the coordinate grid at the right.

26. What two points have a vertical distance of 8 units between them?

27. What is the horizontal distance between Point *A* and Point *F*?

28. Is the horizontal distance between points *A* and *F* greater than or less than the vertical distance between Points *D* and *E*? Explain.

Critical THINKING

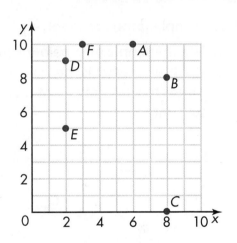

For **29** through **31**, use the map at the right.

29. About how many vertical blocks separate the New York Public Library and the Empire State Building?

30. About how many horizontal blocks separate the New York Public Library and Grand Central Terminal?

31. About how many total blocks would you walk from the Empire State Building to arrive at Grand Central Terminal?

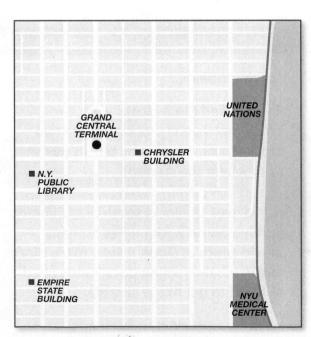

MA.5.A.6.5 Solve non-routine problems using various strategies including "solving a simpler problem" and "guess, check, and revise."

Problem Solving

Solve a Simpler Problem

If you are riding in a taxi, the shortest distance between two points is usually NOT a straight line.

Find the distance (the number of blocks) from school to the post office and then home. Arrows show one-way streets.

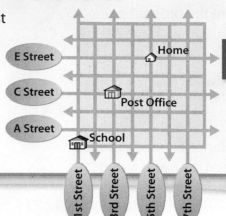

Guided Practice*

Do you know HOW?

Use a simpler problem to solve.

1. Use the simple map below. Following the streets, what is the least number of blocks to walk from Point A to Point B to Point C?

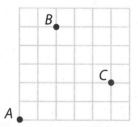

Do you UNDERSTAND?

2. Find another way to travel from school to the post office to home. Is the total distance you found the same as the total distance shown in the example above?

3. **Write a Problem** Write a problem in which you use a simpler problem to solve. Then answer the problem you wrote.

Independent Practice

Solve each problem.

4. Rosa walked three blocks west, two blocks north, one block east, and two blocks south. How many blocks was she from where she started?

5. Lionel lives 13 blocks south of the library. Randy's house is four times as many blocks south as Lionel's. How many blocks and in what direction does Randy need to travel to get to the library?

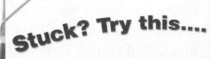

Stuck? Try this....

- What do I know?
- What diagram can I use to help understand the problem?
- Can I use addition, subtraction, multiplication, or division?
- Is all of my work correct?
- Did I answer the right question?
- Is my answer reasonable?

For another example, see Set C on page 124.

I can solve a simpler problem.

First, I'll find the distance from school to the post office.

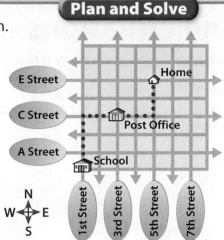

I can take 1st Street 3 blocks north. Then I can take C Street 2 blocks east and get to the post office.

3 + 2 = 5

That is 5 blocks.

Now I can go from the post office to home.

I can go 2 more blocks east on C Street. Then I can go 2 blocks north on 5th Street.

2 + 2 = 4

That is 4 more blocks.

5 + 4 = 9, so it is 9 blocks from school to home.

For **6** and **7**, use the map at the right.

6. How far is it from Walter's house to the park if each unit represents 1 block?

7. Nancy rode her bike from her house to Jerry's house, and then to the park. How many blocks did she ride her bike?

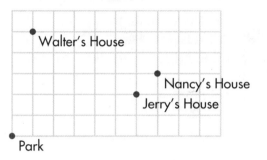

Use the map at the right for **8** through **10**. In the map, each side of a square equals 5 miles.

8. Estimate how many miles by highway it is from Smithberg to McAllen.

9. Estimate how many miles by highway it is from McAllen to Providence.

10. Estimate how many miles by highway it is from Smithberg to Providence.

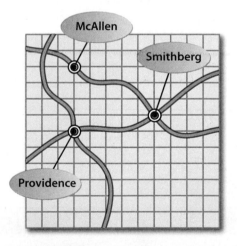

11. Hayley has set a goal to read all 26 books on the library's Best Books list. She plans to read 2 books each week. How long will it take Hayley to read all the books?

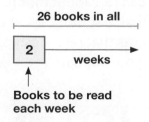

12. In a Double Dutch tournament, the winning team jumped 447 times in two minutes. The second place team jumped 375 times in two minutes. How many more jumps did the winning team make?

A   65 jumps   C   75 jumps

B   72 jumps   D   82 jumps

MA.5.A.4.2 Construct and describe a graph showing continuous data, such as a graph of a quantity that changes over time. Also MA.5.G.5.1.

Graphing Equations

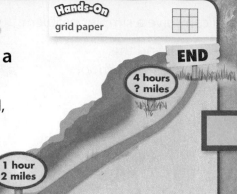

How do you graph an equation on a coordinate grid?

Amy can hike 2 miles in 1 hour. At that speed, how far would she hike in 4 hours?

An equation whose graph is a straight line is called a **linear equation**.

Another Example **How do you graph linear equations?**

Carl is four years older than Jamal. How can you graph this situation?

Step 1

Write an equation.

Carl is four years older than Jamal.

Carl's age = Jamal's age + 4
$$y \quad = \quad x \quad + 4$$

 Tip When making a table of values for a linear equation, use at least three values for x.

Step 2

Make a table of values.

Jamal x (years)	Carl y (years)
2	6
4	8
6	10

Step 3

Plot the ordered pairs and connect the points.

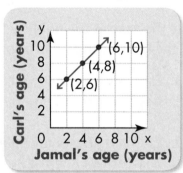

Guided Practice*

Do you know HOW?

In **1** through **4**, find the values of y when x = 2, 4, and 6. Then, name the ordered pairs.

1. $y = x + 3$

2. $y = 3x$

3. $y = x - 1$

4. $y = 4x$

For **5**, graph the equation.

5. $y = x + 4$

Do you UNDERSTAND?

6. **Reasonableness** Does the line for $y = x - 4$ include the point (4, 0)?

7. A lion can run about four times faster than a squirrel. What equation represents that relationship? How would you graph it?

Step 1	Step 2	Step 3

Step 1

Write an equation.

Amy hikes 2 miles each hour.

miles = 2 × hours

Let y be the number of miles and x be the number of hours.

$$y = 2x$$

Step 2

Make a table of x- and y-values to show how x and y relate and satisfy the equation.

$$y = 2x$$

x	y
1	2
2	4
3	6

Step 3

Label the axes on a coordinate grid. Plot the ordered pairs and connect the points to graph the equation.

Extend the line. The y-value when $x = 4$ shows that Amy hiked 8 miles.

Independent Practice

In **8** through **11**, name the ordered pairs. Let $x = 0$, 2, and 4.

8. $y = 6x$ **9.** $y = x + 3$ **10.** $y = x + 7$ **11.** $y = x - 0$

In **12** through **15**, make a table of values for each equation and then graph each equation. Use $x = 1$, 2, and 3.

12. $y = x - 1$ **13.** $y = 4x$ **14.** $y = x + 1$ **15.** $y = x$

Problem Solving

16. Reasoning If the points (1, 3), (1, 7), (1, 12), and (1, 25) were graphed, they would form a vertical line. Do you think the equation for this line would be $x = 1$ or $y = 1$? Explain.

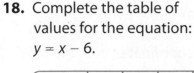

17. Writing to Explain How do you know that the point (4, 8) will appear on graphs for both of the equations $y = 2x$ and $y = x + 4$?

18. Complete the table of values for the equation: $y = x - 6$.

x	6	7		11
y	0		2	

19. Will the point (5, 10) be included on a graph for the equation $y = 2x$? Explain your answer.

THINK SOLVE EXPLAIN

20. Which ordered pair will be included on the graph for $y = 3 + x$?

A (13, 16) **C** (1, 3)

B (9, 6) **D** (9, 3)

MA.5.A.4.2 Construct and describe a graph showing continuous data, such as a graph of a quantity that changes over time. Also MA.5.G.5.1.

More Graphing Equations

Hands-On
grid paper

How do you graph an equation with more than one operation?

Salad costs $2 a pound. Jenna is buying 6 pounds for a luncheon. She has one coupon for $2 off. How much will she spend?

Let x equal the number of pounds of salad. Graph the equation $y = 2x - 2$.

Other Examples

Make a table of values to find three ordered pairs on the graph $y = 2x + 1$. Choose three values for x. Then, evaluate $2x + 1$ for each value of x.

y = 2x + 1	
x	y
1	3
2	5
3	7

← $y = (2 \times 1) + 1$

← $y = (2 \times 2) + 1$

← $y = (2 \times 3) + 1$

Graph the coordinates shown in the table.

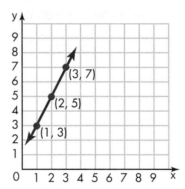

Three ordered pairs on the graph of $y = 2x + 1$ are (1, 3), (2, 5), and (3, 7).

Guided Practice*

Do you know HOW?

Complete the table.

1.

y = 3x + 1	
x	y
4	
6	
8	

2.

y = 2x − 2	
x	y
2	
4	
6	

Do you UNDERSTAND?

3. How much would Jenna pay for two lunches that cost $8 each if she uses her coupon?

4. Graph the coordinates from the table in Exercise 2 and draw the line.

eTools
www.pearsonsuccessnet.com

DIGITAL

*For another example, see Set D on page 125.

Make a table of x- and y-values. Use 2, 4, and 6 for the x-values. Use the equation $y = 2x - 2$ to find the y-values.

$y = 2x - 2$	
x	y
2	2
4	6
6	10

← $y = (2 \times 2) - 2$

← $y = (4 \times 2) - 2$

← $y = (6 \times 2) - 2$

Graph the coordinates shown in the table and draw the line.

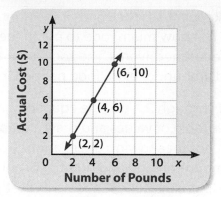

(6, 10)
(4, 6)
(2, 2)

Actual Cost ($)
Number of Pounds

Read the graph. Jenna will spend $10 with the coupon.

Independent Practice

For **5** through **16**, make a table of values for three ordered pairs on the graph of each equation. Then graph each equation.

5. $y = x + 3$

6. $y = 2x - 1$

7. $y = x + 1$

8. $y = x - 1$

9. $y = 3x - 3$

10. $y = 2x - 3$

11. $y = 2x + 1$

12. $y = 2x + 2$

13. $y = 2x + 3$

14. $y = 3x \div 3$

15. $y = 4x - 3$

16. $y = 6x \div 2$

Problem Solving

17. Geometry The U.S. five-dollar bill and ten-dollar bill are shown at the right. Are their shapes congruent? Explain.

18. When you divide a number by 8, can the remainder be 7? Explain. Give an example to support your explanation.

THINK
SOLVE
EXPLAIN

19. Algebra What number can be substituted in the box to make the equation below true?

$(6 - 3) \times 4 = 6 \times$ ▢

20. Corrine is packing books into boxes. Each box can hold 12 books. Copy and complete the table to the right.

Number of boxes (x)	Number of books (y)
1	12
2	▢
3	▢
4	▢

A zookeeper uses the chart at the right to figure out how much food to put in the pens of different herbivores. The zookeeper adds a fixed amount of extra food per pen.

For **21** through **23**, use the equation given to make a table of values and draw a graph in the first quadrant showing the relationship between the amount of food and number of animals. Let x = the number of animals, and let y = the total amount of food.

Data	Animal	Feed per Animal (lb)	Extra Feed per Pen (lb)
	Deer	3	1
	Sheep	4	3
	Goats	1	5
	Antelope	2	4
	Elk	7	3

21. antelope $y = 2x + 4$

22. deer $y = 3x + 1$

23. goat $y = x + 5$

24. 🔍 **Science** The Thrust SSC jet-car set a land speed record of 766 miles per hour. Starting at 0 miles per hour, the Thrust SSC's speed increased at an average speed of about 40 miles per hour each second. Use the graph to find the speed at 10 seconds and at 15 seconds.

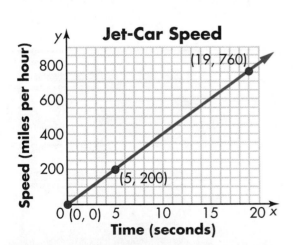

Jet-Car Speed

(19, 760)

(5, 200)

(0, 0)

Speed (miles per hour)

Time (seconds)

25. **Think** **About the Process** Look at the graph below. Point *T* is at (6, 4). Point *U* is at (1, 4). How can you find the number of units from Point *T* to Point *U*?

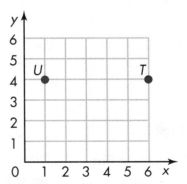

A Add 4 + 6

B Add 1 + 6

C Subtract 6 − 4

D Subtract 6 − 1

26. Explain why half of Region A is not larger than half of Region B.

THINK
SOLVE
EXPLAIN

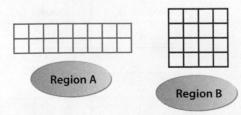

Region A

Region B

27. The numbers in the pattern below increase by the same amount each time. What are the next three numbers in this pattern?

1 3 5 7 ▢ ▢ ▢

F 9 11 13   **H** 8 13 21

G 6 7 9   **I** 7 8 9

Mixed Problem Solving

"The Star-Spangled Banner" was written by poet Francis Scott Key. Francis Scott Key wrote this poem during the British attack on Fort McHenry in 1814, during the War of 1812.

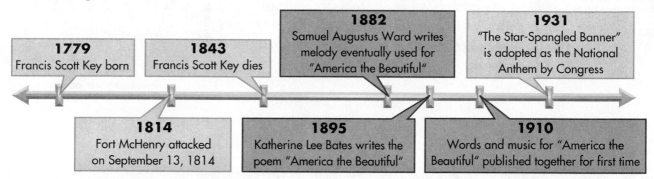

1779 Francis Scott Key born

1843 Francis Scott Key dies

1882 Samuel Augustus Ward writes melody eventually used for "America the Beautiful"

1931 "The Star-Spangled Banner" is adopted as the National Anthem by Congress

1814 Fort McHenry attacked on September 13, 1814

1895 Katherine Lee Bates writes the poem "America the Beautiful"

1910 Words and music for "America the Beautiful" published together for first time

1. Francis Scott Key was born in 1779 and lived until 1843. During his life, he worked as a lawyer in Washington, D.C., for many famous politicians. Solve the equation below to find how old Francis Scott Key was when he wrote "The Star-Spangled Banner."

   $1{,}779 + x = 1{,}814$

2. "The Star-Spangled Banner" was adopted as the National Anthem of the United States by Congress in 1931. Solve the equation below to find how many years after it was written Francis Scott Key's poem was made the National Anthem.

   $1{,}814 + x = 1{,}931$

3. "America the Beautiful" was written and composed by two different people. Katherine Lee Bates is the author of the poem, "America the Beautiful." The poem was published in 1895. Samuel Augustus Ward wrote the melody in 1882. The words and music were first published together in 1910. How many years passed between the publication of the poem and the publication of the words and music?

4. **Strategy Focus** Solve using the strategy *Write an Equation*.

   Katherine Lee Bates was inspired to write the poem "America the Beautiful" while atop Pikes Peak in Colorado. Pikes Peak is a mountain that rises 14,110 feet above sea level. One yard is equal to 3 feet. Which equation could you use to find how many yards, y, Pikes Peak is above sea level?

   A $y + 3 = 14{,}110$ **C** $y \times 3 = 14{,}110$

   B $y - 3 = 14{,}110$ **D** $y \div 3 = 14{,}110$

MA.5.G.5.1 Identify and plot ordered pairs on the first quadrant of the coordinate plane.
Also MA.5.A.4.2

Problem Solving

Writing to Explain

How do you write a good math explanation?

The graph shows a trip that Lynne took to the grocery store. Write a story about Lynne's trip that fits the data on the graph. Explain what happens at each point shown on the graph.

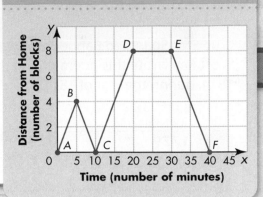

Lynne's Trip

Guided Practice*

Do you know HOW?

1. What ordered pair locates Point *B* on the graph? What do these coordinates represent?

2. What does Point *C* tell you about Lynne's location?

3. How can you explain what happened between Points *A* and *C*?

Do you UNDERSTAND?

4. Why does Point *B* represent half the distance to the store?

5. Why can you say Lynne shopped for 10 minutes?

6. **Write a Problem** Write a problem that uses data from the graph. Your problem should ask for an explanation as part of the solution.

Independent Practice

The graph shows what happened when Jim went biking.

7. What might have happened between Points *C* and *D*?

8. Between which two points did Jim bike the fastest? the slowest?

9. Write a story to fit the data on the graph. Tell what Jim and his friend might have been doing between each pair of data points.

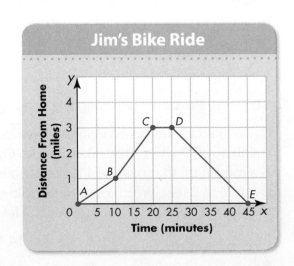

Jim's Bike Ride

For another example, see Set E on page 125.

Think I know Points *A*, *C*, and *F* all have a *y*-value of 0. So Lynne must have returned home once during her trip.

My written explanation should be correct, simple, complete, and easy to understand.

Lynne leaves home at Point *A* to go to the store. At Point *B*, she is halfway to the store but realizes she has forgotten her wallet. So she goes back home at Point *C*. After getting her wallet, Lynne walks to the store at Point *D*. She shops for 10 minutes, to Point *E*. Then Lynne walks home, arriving at Point *F*.

10. **Science** Scientists believe that the first dinosaurs lived on Earth about 230 million years ago. They believe dinosaurs became extinct about 65 million years ago. Write an equation and solve it to find out for about how many years dinosaurs roamed the Earth.

11. In July 2008, a wildfire near Yosemite National Park burned about 53 square miles of forest. If one square mile equals 640 acres, about how many acres of forest were burned?

The table at the right shows the amount of time that astronauts have spent in space during several space programs. Use the table for **12** and **13**.

12. Write and solve an equation to find the total number of hours, *h*, astronauts spent in space during the Gemini and Apollo space programs combined.

Critical THINKING

13. Explain how estimation can be used to determine if the total number of hours astronauts spent in space during the Space Shuttle program is more or less than the number of hours spent in the other programs combined.

THINK SOLVE EXPLAIN

Program	Years	Total Hours
Mercury	1959–1963	54
Gemini	1965–1966	970
Apollo	1968–1972	2,502
Skylab	1973–1974	4,105
Space Shuttle	1981–1995	12,407

Data

14. Students at Gifford Elementary collected stamps from various countries. The students collected 546 stamps from Africa, 132 from Europe, and 321 from North and South America. If a stamp album can hold 24 stamps on each page, how many pages will the stamps completely fill?

Use the grid below for **1** through **4**.

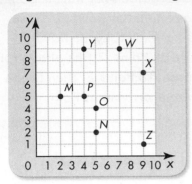

1. Which point is located at (5, 2)? (5-1)

  A. M

  B. N

  C. O

  D. P

2. What is the ordered pair for Point Y? (5-1)

  F. (7, 9)

  G. (9, 7)

  H. (9, 1)

  I. (4, 9)

3. What is the vertical distance between Point X and Point Z? (5-2)

  A. 9 units

  B. 7 units

  C. 6 units

  D. 1 unit

4. Which tells how to find the horizontal distance between Point M and Point P? (5-2)

  F. Subtract 5 − 2

  G. Subtract 4 − 2

  H. Subtract 5 − 4

  I. Subtract 2 − 0

Use the map below for **5** and **6**. Each square represents 1 city block.

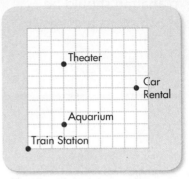

5. What is the least number of blocks to walk to get from the Train Station to the Aquarium and then to the Theater? (5-3)

  A. 10 blocks

  B. 11 blocks

  C. 12 blocks

  D. 13 blocks

6. Ali started at the theater. He walked to the car rental and then drove to the aquarium. If he took the shortest route, how far did Ali travel? (5-3)

  F. 5 blocks

  G. 8 blocks

  H. 17 blocks

  I. 20 blocks

7. Which ordered pair is on the graph for $y = 3x$? (5-4)

  A. (1, 3)

  B. (3, 1)

  C. (2, 5)

  D. (5, 2)

8 Martina drew the graph shown. Which equation did she graph? (5-4)

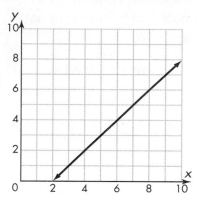

F. $y = x - 2$

G. $y = x - 1$

H. $y = x + 2$

I. $y = x + 1$

9 Which number completes the table of values for $y = 2x + 8$? (5-5)

x	y
1	10
2	12
3	

A. 4

B. 11

C. 13

D. 14

10 Which ordered pair is on the graph of the equation below? (5-5)

$$y = 4x - 5$$

F. (0, 0)

G. (5, 15)

H. (5, 0)

I. (0, 15)

11 If Daneesha walked five blocks north, then three blocks east, then five blocks south, how far was she, in blocks, from where she started? (5-3)

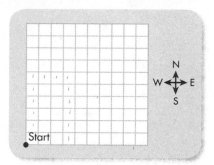

12 The graph shows a red-tailed hawk hunting for prey. Explain what could have happened between Point C and Point D. (5-6)

THINK
SOLVE
EXPLAIN

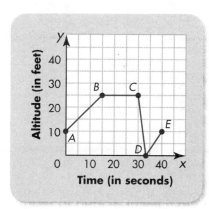

Set A, pages 106–107

What ordered pair names Point *A*?

Start at the origin. The *x*-coordinate is the horizontal distance along the *x*-axis. The *y*-coordinate is the vertical distance along the *y*-axis.

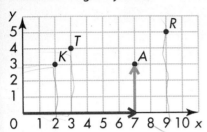

Point *A* is at (7, 3).

Remember to first find the *x*-coordinate. Then find the *y*-coordinate. Write the coordinates in (*x, y*) order.

1. Which point is located at (9, 5)?

2. Which point is located at (2, 3)?

3. What ordered pair names Point *T*?

Set B, pages 110–111

What is the length of line segment *AB*?

Because the points lie on a vertical line, you can subtract the *y*-values to find the distance.

Line segment *AB* is 6 − 4 = 2 units.

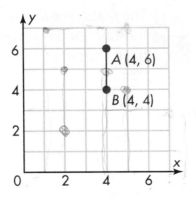

Remember that if the *y*-values are the same, the line is horizontal.

Find the distance between the ordered pairs.

1. (5, 8), (1, 8)   2. (4, 3), (10, 3)

3. (5, 4), (4, 4)   4. (2, 5), (2, 2)

Set C, pages 112–113

Find the shortest driving distance from school to the park and then home.

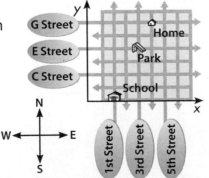

School to park: Go 4 blocks north on 1st Street and 2 blocks east on E Street: 6 blocks.

Park to home: Go north 2 more blocks on 3rd Street and 1 block east on G Street: 3 blocks.

The shortest distance is 6 + 3 = 9 blocks.

Remember that arrows show one-way streets.

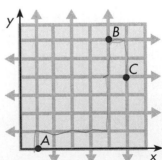

1. Suppose you walk from Point *A* to Point *B*. Then you walk from Point *B* to Point *C*. What is the least number of blocks you could walk?

Set D, pages 114–115, 116–118

Graph the equation $y = 3x - 2$.

First make a table of values.

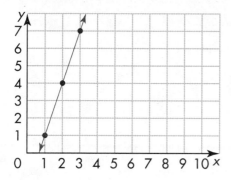

$y = 3x - 2$	
x	y
1	1
2	4
3	7

← $y = (3 \times 1) - 2$
← $y = (3 \times 2) - 2$
← $y = (3 \times 3) - 2$

Use the table to plot the ordered pairs. Then draw a line to connect the points.

Remember to find at least three coordinates.

1. Copy and complete the table.

$y = 8x \div 4$	
x	y
1	
2	
3	

2. Copy the grid below. Use the table in Exercise 1 to plot the ordered pairs and complete the graph.

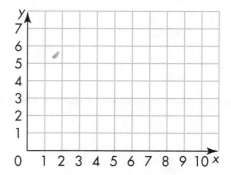

Set E, pages 120–121

The graph shows sales of a new video game. Write a story about the first 3 days of the sale.

New Video Game

Remember that a written explanation should be correct, simple, complete, and easy to understand.

Use the questions to help you complete a story about the graph.

1. What happens to sales on Days 4 and 5?

2. What happens on Day 6?

3. How might you explain what happened on Day 7?

Sales of a new video game rise during the first 3 days. Sales increase from 4 games on Day 1 to 12 games on Day 3.

Topic 6

Adding and Subtracting Decimals

1 The world's largest aloha shirt measures more than 4 meters around the chest. What is the actual measure of this part of the shirt? You will find out in Lesson 6-1.

2 One of the smallest dinosaurs was Compsognathus. How long was this dinosaur? You will find out in Lesson 6-9.

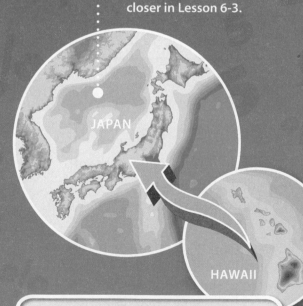

Review What You Know!

③ The bones in a human's leg are not the same length. Do you know the difference in the length of the bones? You will find out in Lesson 6-8.

④ Did you know that Hawaii is moving closer to Japan every year? Find out how much closer in Lesson 6-3.

JAPAN

HAWAII

Vocabulary

Choose the best term from the box.

- difference   • sum
- Associative Property of Addition
- Commutative Property of Addition

1. Using the __?__ allows you to add two or more numbers in any order.

2. The __?__ is the answer to a subtraction problem.

3. The answer to an addition problem is called the __?__.

Whole Number Place Value

Tell the place value of the underlined digit.

4. 1,402   5. 512   6. 10,368

7. 4,941   8. 5,577   9. 12,306

Rounding Whole Numbers

Round each number to the nearest hundred.

10. 748   11. 293   12. 139

Round each number to the nearest thousand.

13. 3,857   14. 2,587   15. 2,345

Adding and Subtracting

Add or subtract.

16. 6,709 + 313   17. 654 − 85

18. **Writing to Explain** How do you know that 65 + (21 + 3) is equal to (65 + 21) + 3 without finding the sums?

Topic Essential Questions

- How can sums and differences of decimals be estimated?

- What are standard procedures for adding and subtracting decimals?

MA.5.A.2.3 Make reasonable estimates of fraction and decimal sums and differences, and use techniques for rounding.

Rounding Decimals

How can you round decimals?

Rounding <u>replaces one number with another number that tells about how many or how much.</u> Round 2.36 to the nearest tenth.

Think Is 2.36 closer to 2.3 or 2.4?

Another Example **How do you round to the nearest whole number?**

Round 3.2 to the nearest whole number.

Think Is 3.2 closer to 3 or 4?

Step 1

Find the rounding place. Look at the digit to the right of the rounding place.

3.<u>2</u>

Step 2

If the digit is 5 or greater, add 1 to the rounding digit. If the digit is less than 5, leave the rounding digit alone.

Since 2 < 5, leave 3 the same.

Step 3

Drop the digits to the right of the decimal point. Drop the decimal point.

3.2 rounds to 3

Guided Practice*

Do you know HOW?

In **1** through **6**, round each number to the place of the underlined digit.

1. 1<u>6</u>.5

2. 5<u>6</u>.1

3. 1.<u>3</u>2

4. 42.7<u>8</u>

5. 1.6<u>5</u>2

6. 582.0<u>4</u>

Do you UNDERSTAND?

7. To round 74.58 to the nearest tenth, which digit do you look at? What is 74.58 rounded to the nearest tenth?

8. A car-rental service charges customers for the number of miles they travel, rounded to the nearest whole mile. George travels 40.8 miles. For how many miles will he be charged? Explain.

Animated Glossary
www.pearsonsuccessnet.com

Step 1	Step 2	Step 3
Find the rounding place. Look at the digit to the right of the rounding place.	If the digit is 5 or greater, add 1 to the rounding digit. If the digit is less than 5, leave the rounding digit alone.	Drop the digits to the right of the rounding digit.
2.3̲6	Since 6 > 5, add 1 to the 3.	2.36 rounds to 2.4

Independent Practice

In **9** through **16**, round each decimal to the nearest whole number.

9. 6.7   **10.** 4.5   **11.** 12.1   **12.** 57.3

13. 34.731   **14.** 215.39   **15.** 30.923   **16.** 1.0869

In **17** through **24**, round each number to the place of the underlined digit.

17. 7.1̲58   **18.** 0.7̲58   **19.** 6.4̲382   **20.** 0.472̲3

21. 84.7̲32   **22.** 7.382̲9   **23.** 5.02̲8   **24.** 23.009̲1

Problem Solving

25. The world's largest aloha shirt measures 4.26 meters around the chest. Round 4.26 to the nearest whole number and to the nearest tenths place.

26. Writing to Explain In the final 3 quarters of a basketball game, a team scored 17, 25, and 13 points. Their final score was 75. Explain how to find how many points the team scored in the first quarter.

Critical THINKING

27. An African Watusi steer's horn measures 95.25 centimeters around. What is 95.25 when rounded to the nearest tenth? nearest whole number? nearest ten?

28. Science The picture at the right shows the length of an average American alligator. What is the length of the alligator rounded to the nearest tenth?

4.39 meters

A 4.0 meters   **B** 4.3 meters   **C** 3 meters   **D** 4.4 meters

MA.5.A.6.5 Solve non-routine problems using various strategies including "solving a simpler problem" and "guess, check, and revise."

Problem Solving

Look for a Pattern

There are patterns in decimal number charts. Continue the pattern to label the other squares.

0.01	0.02	0.03					0.08		0.1
				0.15	0.16			0.19	
								0.29	
	0.32		0.34			0.37			

Another Example

In this decimal number chart, what are the patterns in the diagonals?

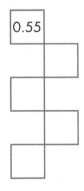

Using the same system as above, you could fill in the diagonals of a decimal number chart.

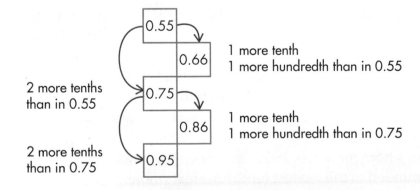

0.55

0.66 — 1 more tenth
1 more hundredth than in 0.55

2 more tenths than in 0.55 — 0.75

0.86 — 1 more tenth
1 more hundredth than in 0.75

2 more tenths than in 0.75 — 0.95

Explain It

1. If the grid in Another Example above were extended by 2 cells in the same design, what decimals would be used to complete the grid?

What are the missing decimals?

0.01

As you work with vertical columns, you will see the tenths increase by 1 and the hundredths stay the same as you move down.

0.01
0.11
0.21
0.31

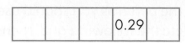

What are the missing decimals?

			0.29

Moving from left to right, tenths are the same in each row except for the last number; the hundredths increase by 1.

0.26	0.27	0.28	0.29	0.30

Guided Practice*

Do you know HOW?

In **1** and **2**, determine the patterns, and then complete the grids.

1.

0.42

2.

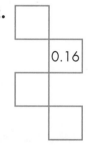

Do you UNDERSTAND?

3. In a completed decimal chart, look at the first row, which begins with 0.01, 0.02…. If Rene were to create a thousandths chart, what two numbers would immediately follow 0.001?

4. Write a Problem Write a real-world problem that you could solve by looking for a pattern.

Independent Practice

In **5** and **6**, determine the patterns, and then complete the grids.

5.

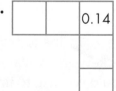

6.

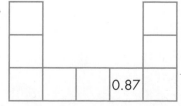

Stuck? Try this….

- What do I know?
- What am I asked to find?
- What diagram can I use to help understand the problem?
- Can I use addition, subtraction, multiplication, or division?
- Is all of my work correct?
- Did I answer the right question?
- Is my answer reasonable?

*For another example, see Set B on page 156.

7. Describe the patterns you should use to complete the following grid, then complete it.

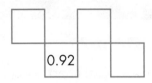

8. Determine the patterns, and then complete the grid.

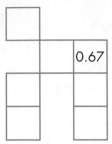

9. Determine the patterns, and then complete the grid.

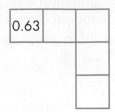

10. What is the missing number in the grid?

	0.27	0.28	0.29

11. Drake drew a grid of five cells in a row. The number 0.75 was in the middle cell. What did Drake's grid look like?

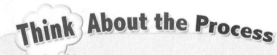

12. Determine a pattern, and then complete the grid.

0.004	0.005	

13. Juan and his family went to a movie. They bought 2 adult tickets for $8 apiece and 3 student tickets for $5 apiece. They paid with two $20 bills. How much change did they get?

14. **Science** The greatest distance of Mercury from Earth is 136,000,000 miles. The greatest distance of Mars from Earth is 248,000,000 miles. Write these numbers in expanded form.

Think About the Process

Critical THINKING

15. Ms. Bates bought three items that cost $37, $35, and $19, and gave the clerk $100. Which expression shows how to find the amount of change she would get from $100?

  A $37 + $35 + $19 + $100

  B $100 − $37

  C $100 − ($37 + $35 + $19)

  D $100 + $37 + $35 − $19

16. If 100 people are waiting in line to buy tickets and only 53 tickets are available, which expression would you use to find how many people won't be able to buy tickets?

  F 100 + 53

  G 100 − 53

  H 100 × 53

  I 53 + 53

Algebra Connections

Number Patterns

The following numbers form a pattern.

3 7 11 15 19 …

In this case the pattern is a simple one. The pattern is add 4.

Some patterns are more complicated. Look at the following pattern.

20 24 30 34 40 44 50 …

In this case, the pattern is add 4, add 6.

Example:

What are the next two numbers in the pattern?

24 29 28 33 32 37 36 …

Think The first number is increased by 5. The next number is decreased by 1. I see that the pattern continues.

24   29   28   33   32   37   36 …
   +5   −1   +5   −1   +5   −1

To find the next two numbers, add 5, and then subtract 1. The next two numbers are 41 and 40.

Look for a pattern. Find the next two numbers.

1. 9 18 27 36 45 …

2. 90 80 70 60 50 …

3. 2 102 202 302 …

4. 26 46 66 86 …

5. 20 31 42 53 64 …

6. 100 92 84 76 68 …

7. 1 3 9 27 …

8. 800 400 200 100 …

9. 20 21 19 20 18 19 17 …

10. 10 11 21 22 32 33 …

11. 25 32 28 35 31 38

12. 5 15 10 20 15 25 20

13. The following numbers are called Fibonacci numbers.

1 1 2 3 5 8 13 21 34 55 …

Explain how you could find the next two numbers.

14. Write a Problem Make up a number pattern that involves two operations.

MA.5.A.2.3 Make reasonable estimates of fraction and decimal sums and differences, and use techniques for rounding.

Estimating Sums and Differences of Decimals

How do you estimate when you add and subtract decimals?

In Beijing, China, it rained 5.82 inches in the first half of the year. In the second half of the year, it rained 18.63 inches. Estimate the rainfall for the whole year.

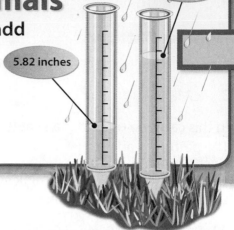

5.82 inches

18.63 inches

Guided Practice*

Do you know HOW?

In **1** through **4**, estimate each sum or difference.

1. 0.72 + 0.56

2. 18.54 − 1.99

3.   13.94
   +   4.72

4.   47.31
   − 11.25

Do you UNDERSTAND?

5. Explain why 1.4 and 0.75 both round to 1.

6. Reasonableness In the example above, explain why 2.5 inches is NOT a reasonable estimate of the rainfall for the whole year.

Independent Practice

In **7** through **22**, round to the nearest whole number to estimate each sum or difference.

 You can write rounded numbers in vertical format before adding or subtracting.

7. 9.6 + 3.27

8. 9.51 + 8.61

9. 7.11 + 0.15

10. 1.45 + 6.85

11. 18.85 − 6.8

12. 4.312 − 1.285

13. 31.12 − 4.86

14. 0.663 − 0.34

15.   82.43
   −   3.90

16.   5.78
   − 3.86

17.   63.93
   +   3.31

18.   3.736
   + 0.81

19.   2.1
   + 7.5

20.   3.45
   − 2.44

21.   19.060
   + 1.991

22.   4.84
   + 0.735

For another example, see Set C on page 156.

Estimate 5.82 + 18.63.

Round each decimal to the nearest whole number. Then add.

$$5.82 \longrightarrow 6$$
$$+ \; 18.63 \longrightarrow + \; 19$$
$$\overline{ \; 25}$$

About 25 inches of rain fell in Beijing.

In August, 6.7 inches of rain fell in Beijing. In September, it rained 2.3 inches. About how much more did it rain in August than in September?

$$6.7 \longrightarrow 7$$
$$- \; 2.3 \longrightarrow - \; 2$$
$$\overline{ \; 5}$$

Round each decimal to the nearest whole number. Then subtract the rounded numbers.

It rained about 5 inches more in August.

Problem Solving

In **23** and **24**, use the table at the right.

23. The table shows the weight of each type of vegetable Vanessa bought to make a large salad for her family picnic. About how much more did the cucumbers weigh than the lettuce?

24. About how much did the vegetables weigh in all?

Vegetable	Weight (pounds)
	2.0
	2.63
	1.25
	3.5

25. **Science** Hawaii is moving toward Japan at a rate of approximately 2.8 inches per year. About how much closer will Hawaii be to Japan in 3 years?

26. Writing to Explain The length of a dog run is equal to twice its width, and the perimeter is 60 feet. What are the length and width? Show your work and explain how you found your answer.

Critical THINKING

> Perimeter = distance around a figure

27. Neil is installing 38 square yards of carpet. He uses 12.2 square yards in one room and 10.5 square yards in another room. About how many square yards of carpet does he have left?

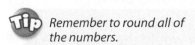

Remember to round all of the numbers.

Lesson

6-4

MA.5.A.2.1 Represent addition and subtraction of decimals and fractions with like and unlike denominators using models, place value or properties.

Modeling Addition and Subtraction of Decimals

Hands-On
grid paper

How do you add decimals using grids?

Use the table at the right to find the total monthly cost of using the dishwasher and the DVD player.

Device	Cost/month
DVD player	$0.40
Microwave oven	$3.57
Ceiling light	$0.89
Dishwasher	$0.85

Another Example How do you subtract decimals with grids?

Find the difference between the cost per month to run the microwave oven and the ceiling light.

Use hundredths grids to subtract 3.57 − 0.89.

Step 1 Shade three grids and 57 squares to show 3.57.

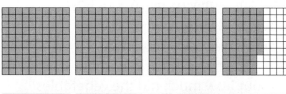

Step 2 Cross out 8 columns and 9 squares of the shaded grid to show 0.89 being subtracted from 3.57.

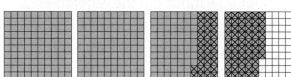

Count the squares that are shaded but not crossed out to find the difference.
3.57 − 0.89 = 2.68

Explain It

1. **Reasonableness** How could you use the grids to check your answer above?

2. How would the grid above be different if the cost per month to run the microwave were $2.57?

Use hundredths grids to add $0.85 + $0.40.

It costs $0.85 to use the dishwasher per month.

Shade 85 squares to show $0.85.

It costs $0.40 to use the DVD player per month.

Use a different color and shade 40 more squares to show $0.40. Count all of the shaded squares to find the sum.

$0.85 + $0.40 = $1.25

The monthly cost of using the dishwasher and DVD player is $1.25.

Guided Practice*

Do you know HOW?

In **1** through **6**, use hundredths grids to add or subtract.

1. $1.22 + 0.34$

2. $0.63 + 0.41$

3. $2.73 - 0.94$

4. $\$1.38 - \$0.73$

5. $0.47 - 0.21$

6. $2.02 + 0.8$

Do you UNDERSTAND?

7. If you were to shade 40 squares first, and then shade 85 more, would the answer be the same as shading 85 squares and then 40 more?

8. Show the difference between the monthly cost of using the DVD player and the dishwasher.

Independent Practice

In **9** through **18**, add or subtract. Use hundredths grids to help.

9. $0.1 + 0.73$

10. $\$0.37 + \$0.47$

11. $1.2 + 0.56$

12. $\$1.33 - \$0.35$
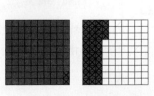

13. $3.0 - 1.47$
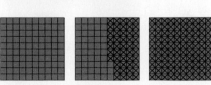

14. $\$1.11 + \$0.89$

eTools
www.pearsonsuccessnet.com

15. $2.23 - 1.8$

16. $0.4 - 0.21$

17. $0.58 + 2.4$

18. $1.31 - 0.55$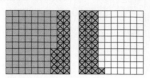

Problem Solving

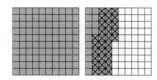

19. Writing to Explain How is adding $4.56 + 2.31$ similar to adding $\$2.31 + \$4.56$?

20. Do you think the difference of $1.4 - 0.95$ is less than one or greater than one? Explain.

THINK
SOLVE
EXPLAIN

21. Number Sense Is the sum of $0.46 + 0.25$ less than or greater than one? Explain.

22. Estimation Estimate to decide if the sum of $314 + 175$ is more or less than 600.

23. Which expression is represented by the model below?

A $2.00 + 0.31$ **C** $1.76 - 1.45$

B $1.76 - 0.31$ **D** $1.45 - 0.31$

24. Which expression shows 2^3?

F $2 + 2 + 2$

G $2 \times 2 \times 2$

H $2 + 3$

I 2×3

25. **Think About the Process** Which expression can be used to find the perimeter of the pool shown to the right? Remember, perimeter = the distance around a figure.

A $50 + 25$ **C** $50 + 50 + 25 + 25$

B $25 + 25 + 25 + 25$ **D** $50 + 50 + 50 + 50$

length = 50 meters

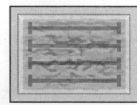

width = 25 meters

26. Write the number sentence that is shown by the hundredths grids to the right.

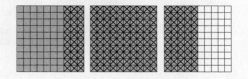

Going Digital

Reasonableness of Differences

Estimate 4.72 − 2.85. Use a calculator to subtract. Then explain whether or not the sum you found is reasonable.

Step 1   Estimate 4.72 − 2.85.

$$5 - 3 = 2$$

Step 2   Use a calculator to subtract.

Press: 4.72 [−] 2.85 [ENTER =]

Display: 1.87

Step 3   Explain whether or not the difference is reasonable.

Since 1.87 is close to the estimate of 2, the difference is reasonable.

Press (Clear) before starting a new problem.

Estimate 7.51 − 6.49 and use a calculator to subtract. Explain the difference between the estimation and the calculator result.

The estimated difference is 2, and the calculator result is 1.02. The two answers have a difference of about 1, because the first number rounded up and the second number rounded down.

Practice

Estimate each difference. Find the difference on a calculator. Then explain whether or not the difference is reasonable.

1. 28.34 − 7.85   **2.** 6.86 − 2.18   **3.** 5.2 − 0.74

4. 1.73 − 0.8   **5.** 14.97 − 12.39   **6.** 9.05 − 5.92

7. 2.4 − 0.56   **8.** 65.47 − 38.19   **9.** 16.15 − 3.9

10. 3.7 − 1.2   **11.** 2.82 − 1.21   **12.** 5.76 − 3.21

13. 8.47 − 7.08   **14.** 6.59 − 6.03   **15.** 8.88 − 3.84

MA.5.A.2.1 Represent addition and subtraction of decimals and fractions with like and unlike denominators using models, place value or properties.

Adding Decimals Using Place Value

Hands-On
Place-value blocks

How can you use place value to add decimals?

Mr. Chin used 1.58 gallons of gas to drive on Saturday and 2.75 gallons to drive on Sunday. How many gallons of gas did Mr. Chin use in all?

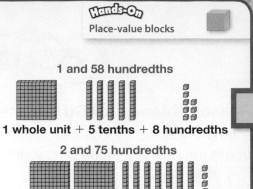

1 and 58 hundredths

1 whole unit + 5 tenths + 8 hundredths

2 and 75 hundredths

2 whole units + 7 tenths + 5 hundredths

Guided Practice*

Do you know HOW?

Find the sum.

1. 1.75 + 1.66

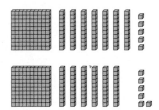

Do you UNDERSTAND?

2. In the example above, why can you regroup 13 hundredths as 1 tenth and 3 hundredths?

3. Reasonableness Kit says that the sum of 2.75 and 3.25 is 6. Is she right? Explain why or why not.

Independent Practice

Leveled Practice In **4** and **5**, use the models to find each sum.

4. 1.64 + 2.35

5. 0.56 + 1.57

In **6** through **13**, use place-value blocks to find each sum.

6. 0.56 + 3.97   **7.** 2.81 + 3.18   **8.** 1.17 + 5.59   **9.** 5.49 + 6.09

10. 2.87   **11.** 8.44   **12.** 2.98   **13.** 5.19
    + 2.13   + 0.86   + 7.06   + 2.09

DIGITAL
eTools
www.pearsonsuccessnet.com

For another example, see Set E on page 157.

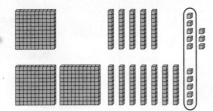

You can add decimal place values and regroup as with whole numbers. Start with the least place value, hundredths.

8 hundredths + 5 hundredths = 13 hundredths. Regroup 13 hundredths as 1 tenth and 3 hundredths.

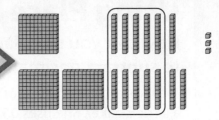

Add the digits in the tenths place. Remember to include the tenth you regrouped.

5 tenths + 7 tenths + 1 tenth = 13 tenths. Regroup 13 tenths as 1 whole and 3 tenths.

Then add the whole numbers: 1 + 2 + 1 = 4

So, 1.58 + 2.75 = 4.33 gallons of gas.

Problem Solving

The table shows world records for men's 100-meter swimming events. Use the table to answer **14** and **15**.

14. What was the combined record time for freestyle and backstroke in August 2008?

15. What was the combined record time for breaststroke and butterfly in August 2008?

Data	Swim stroke	Record time (August 2008) (in seconds)
	100 m freestyle	47.05
	100 m backstroke	52.54
	100 m breaststroke	58.91
	100 m butterfly	50.58

16. John has a fever. His temperature is 3.7°C above normal. Normal body temperature is 36.8°C. What is John's temperature?

A 40.5°C

B 39.5°C

C 33.1°C

D 73.8°C

17. Which is the standard form for 9^3?

F $9 \times 9 \times 9$

G 9×3

H 729

I 27

18. Reasonableness Claire flew to the Olympic Games in Beijing, China. There were 312 passengers on her flight and there were no empty seats. There were 39 rows of seats and each row had the same number of seats. Claire said there were 10 seats in each row. Is her answer reasonable? Explain why or why not.

Critical THINKING

19. Claire's family has tickets to 12 Olympic events. Three events are for swimming. Four events are for track and field. Five events are for gymnastics. In simplest form, what fraction of the events are swimming events? Explain how you found your answer.

THINK SOLVE EXPLAIN

Lesson
6-6

MA.5.A.2.1 Represent addition and subtraction of decimals and fractions with like and unlike denominators using models, place value or properties.

Subtracting Decimals Using Place Value

Hands-On
base-ten blocks

How can you use place value to subtract decimals?

A chemist has 1.55 liters of an acid in a large beaker. She uses 0.78 liter of the acid in an experiment. How many liters of acid are left in the beaker?

1 and 55 hundredths = 1 whole unit, 5 tenths, and 5 hundredths

---

Guided Practice*

Do you know HOW?

In **1** and **2**, use a model to find the difference.

1. 2.69 − 1.45

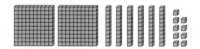

2. 2.27 − 1.38

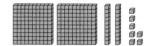

Do you UNDERSTAND?

3. Reasoning Why can you regroup 55 hundredths as 4 tenths and 15 hundredths?

4. For Exercise **1**, why do you not have to regroup to do the subtraction?

5. For Exercise **2**, Cole regrouped 2.27 as 1 whole, 12 tenths, and 17 hundredths. What did Cole do wrong?

Independent Practice

Leveled Practice In **6** and **7**, use the models to find each difference.

6. 2.36 − 0.95

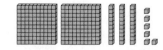

7. 2.15 − 1.59

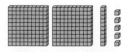

In **8** through **15**, use place-value blocks to find each difference.

8. 5.66 − 4.95   **9.** 4.87 − 2.13   **10.** 6.45 − 4.75   **11.** 2.25 − 0.79

12.   7.39   **13.**   3.44   **14.**   7.98   **15.**   6.19
      − 1.98   − 0.86   − 5.06   − 5.43

eTools
www.pearsonsuccessnet.com

For another example, see Set F on page 158.

You can regroup to subtract decimals in the same way you regroup to subtract with whole numbers. Start with the least place value, hundredths.

1 and 55 hundredths can be regrouped as 1 whole, 4 tenths, and 15 hundredths. 8 hundredths can then be subtracted from 15 hundredths to leave 7 hundredths.

Then regroup the ones to subtract tenths.

1 and 4 tenths can be regrouped as zero and 14 tenths. 7 tenths can then be subtracted from 14 tenths to leave 7 tenths.

So, 1.55 − 0.78 = 0.77. There is 0.77 liter of acid left in the beaker.

Problem Solving

The table shows some typical wingspans for birds you might see in Florida. Use the table to answer **16** and **17**.

16. 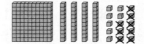 **Science** How much greater is the wingspan of a white pelican than that of a red-tailed hawk?

17. 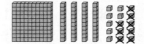 **Science** How much shorter is the wingspan of a red-tailed hawk than that of an osprey?

Wingspans of Some Florida Birds	
Bird	**Wingspan (in feet)**
Red-tailed hawk	4.17
White pelican	9.00
Night heron	3.66
Laughing gulls	3.34
Osprey	4.83

18. Heather's suitcase weighed 21.00 pounds. After she took out her shoes, it weighed 20.08 pounds. How much do Heather's shoes weigh?

   A 41.08 pounds

   B 21.08 pounds

   C 9.20 pounds

   D 0.92 pound

19. **Algebra** Darcy took 43 photographs. Rich took x photographs. Together they took 116 photographs. Which equation can you use to find the number of photographs, x, that Rich took?

   F $43 + 116 = x$

   G $43 + x = 116$

   H $116 + x = 43$

   I $x − 43 = 116$

20. An inch is 2.54 centimeters. A foot is 30.48 centimeters. How many centimeters long is a computer keyboard that is 1 foot 1 inch long?

21. **Writing to Explain** Is 6 a reasonable estimate for finding the difference between 9.59 and 2.17? Explain why or why not.

MA.5.A.2.2 Add and subtract fractions and decimals fluently and verify the reasonableness of results, including in problem situations.

Adding Decimals

How can you add decimals?

What was the combined time for the first two legs of the relay race?

Choose an Operation Add to join groups.

Find 21.49 + 21.59.

Estimate: 21 + 22 = 43

Swimmers	Times in Seconds
Caleb	21.49
Bradley	21.59
Vick	20.35
Matthew	19.03

Guided Practice*

Do you know HOW?

In **1** through **6**, find each sum.

1. 0.82 + 4.21

2. 9.1 + 7.21

3. 9.7 + 0.24

4. 3.28 + 6.09

5. 0.26 + 8.3

6. 4.98 + 3.02

Do you UNDERSTAND?

7. Reasonableness How do you know the total time for the first two legs of the race is reasonable?

8. Writing to Explain How is finding $4.25 + $3.50 like finding 4.25 + 3.5? How is it different?

Independent Practice

In **9** through **26**, find each sum. Use estimation to check your answers for reasonableness.

9. 1.03
   + 0.36

10. 6.9
   + 2.8

11. 45.09
   + 2.005

12. 2.02
   + 0.78

13. 13.094
   + 4.903

14. 356.2
   + 12.45

15. 4.298
   + 0.65

16. 9.001
   + 1.999

17. $8.23
   + $64.10

18. $44.00
   + $91.46

19. 17.49
   + 9.0

20. 42.89
   + 8.2

21. $271.90 + $34.22

22. 658.2 + 0

23. 0.922 + 6.4

24. 8.02 + 9.07

25. 13.9 + 0.16

26. 0.868 + 15.973

Step 1	Step 2	Step 3

Step 1

Write the numbers. Line up the decimal points.

```
  21.49
+ 21.59
```

Step 2

First, add the hundredths. Regroup if necessary.

```
     1
  21.49
+ 21.59
      8
```

Step 3

Add the tenths, ones, and tens. The decimal point in the sum is aligned with the decimal point in the addends. Check the sum with your estimate.

```
   1 1
  21.49
+ 21.59
  43.08
```

The total time for the first two legs of the race was 43.08 seconds.

Problem Solving

27. A balloon mural of the Chicago skyline measures 17.6 meters on two sides and 26.21 meters on the other two sides. What is the perimeter?

    A 38.81 meters   **B** 48.21 meters   **C** 55.74 meters   **D** 87.62 meters

28. Writing to Explain Juan adds 3.8 + 4.6 and gets a sum of 84. Is his answer correct? Tell how you know.

Critical
THINKING

29. At a flower shop, Teri sees that roses are $3 each, carnations are $4 for 3 flowers, and tulips are $4 for 4 flowers. She buys 3 roses and 3 carnations. She has $20. How much change does Teri get back?

30. Think About the Process Jamie earned $27 taking care of a neighbor's dog for one week. She spent $19.95 on a new DVD. Later, she earned $15 for raking leaves. Which expression shows how to find the money Jamie has left?

    F $27 + $19.95 + $15   **H** $27 − $19.95 + $15

    G $19.95 − $15 + $27   **I** $27 − $19.95 − $15

31. Which two cities had the greatest combined rainfall for the period given?

    A Caribou and Boise

    B Tampa and Macon

    C Macon and Boise

    D Caribou and Tampa

City	Rainfall amount in a typical year (in inches)
Macon, GA	45
Boise, ID	12.19
Caribou, ME	37.44
Tampa, FL	46.70

32. What is the total yearly rainfall for all four cities in the table?

33. Which city gets less than 40 inches of rain but more than 35 inches of rain?

MA.5.A.2.2 Add and subtract fractions and decimals fluently and verify the reasonableness of results, including in problem situations.

Subtracting Decimals

How can you subtract decimals?

What is the difference in the wingspans of the two butterflies?

Choose an Operation
Subtract to find the difference.

Find 5.92 − 4.37.
Estimate: 6 − 4 = 2

4.37 cm

5.92 cm

Other Examples

Using 0 as a placeholder

Find 49.59 − 7.9.

$$\begin{array}{r} \overset{8}{4}\,\overset{15}{9}.\,\overset{}{5}\,9 \\ -\ \ 7.\,9\,0 \\ \hline 4\,1.\,6\,9 \end{array}$$

Annex a 0 as a placeholder to show hundredths.

Using 0 as a placeholder

Find 24.6 − 8.27.

$$\begin{array}{r} \overset{1}{2}\,\overset{14}{4}.\,\overset{5}{6}\,\overset{10}{0} \\ -\ \ 8.\,2\,7 \\ \hline 1\,6.\,3\,3 \end{array}$$

Annex a 0 as a placeholder to show hundredths.

Subtracting Money

Find $26.32 − $5.75.

$$\begin{array}{r} \$2\,\overset{5}{6}.\,\overset{\overset{12}{2}}{3}\,\overset{12}{2} \\ -\ \ \ 5.\,7\,5 \\ \hline \$2\,0.\,5\,7 \end{array}$$

Guided Practice*

Do you know HOW?

In **1** through **8**, find each difference.

1. $\begin{array}{r} 16.82 \\ -\ \ 5.21 \\ \hline \end{array}$

2. $\begin{array}{r} 7.21 \\ -\ \ 6.1 \\ \hline \end{array}$

3. $\begin{array}{r} 23.06 \\ -\ \ 8.24 \\ \hline \end{array}$

4. $\begin{array}{r} \$4.08 \\ -\ \ 2.12 \\ \hline \end{array}$

5. 56.8 − 2.765

6. $43.80 − $16.00

7. 22.4 − 10.7

8. $36.40 − $21.16

Do you UNDERSTAND?

9. Reasonableness Explain why 1.55 centimeters is a reasonable answer for the difference in the wingspans of the two butterflies.

10. In the other examples above, is the value of 7.9 changed when you annex a zero after 7.9? Why or why not?

11. Writing to Explain How is finding 9.12 − 4.8 similar to finding $9.12 − $4.80? How is it different?

Step 1

Write the numbers, lining up the decimal points.

```
  5. 9 2
- 4. 3 7
```

Step 2

Subtract the hundredths. Regroup if needed.

```
      8 12
  5. 9̶ 2̶
- 4. 3 7
        5
```

Step 3

Subtract the tenths and ones. Bring down the decimal point.

```
      8 12
  5. 9̶ 2̶
- 4. 3 7
  1. 5 5
```

The difference is reasonable since the estimate was 2.

The difference in the wingspans is 1.55 centimeters.

Independent Practice

In **12** through **23**, find each difference. Use estimation to check your answers for reasonableness.

12.
```
  7.8
- 4.9
```

13.
```
  $20.60
- $14.35
```

14.
```
  43.905
-  7.526
```

15.
```
  65.29
- 28.038
```

16. 15.03 − 4.121

17. 13.9 − 3.8

18. 65.18 − 12.005

19. $52.02 − $0.83

20. 7.094 − 3.657

21. 34.49 − 12.619

22. 85.22 − 43.548

23. $10.05 − $4.50

Problem Solving

24. Why is it necessary to line up decimal points when subtracting decimals?

THINK
SOLVE
EXPLAIN

25. Reasonableness Sue subtracted 2.9 from 20.9 and got 1.8. Explain why this is not reasonable.

Critical
THINKING

26. **Social Studies** The pyramid of Khafre measures 143.5 meters high. The pyramid of Menkaure measures 65.5 meters high. What is the difference in the heights of these two pyramids?

A 68.8 meters

C 78 meters

B 69.3 meters

D 212.3 meters

27. An average person's upper leg bone measures 19.88 inches and the lower leg bone measures 16.94 inches. How much longer is the upper leg bone than the lower leg bone?

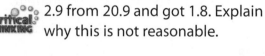

| upper leg bone | 19.88 inches |
| lower leg bone | ? | 16.94 inches |

Khafre
143.5 meters

Menkaure
65.5 meters

MA.5.A.2.2 Add and subtract fractions and decimals fluently and verify the reasonableness of results, including in problem situations.

More Adding and Subtracting Decimals

How can you add and subtract decimals?

Samir rented 1 recently released movie and 1 documentary. He used the coupon. How much did Samir's movie rental cost?

$1.50 OFF ANY TWO RENTALS

Movie Rental Rates

Recent Releases	$3.95
Documentaries	$2.49
Classics	$1.79

Guided Practice*

Do you know HOW?

In **1** through **6**, add or subtract.

1. 8.9
    + 6.83

2. 4.79
    + 23.25

3. 6.26 + 3.7

4. 5.25 − 2.8

5. 7.5 − (2.5 + 2.1)

6. 1.99 + 3.5 − 1.8

Do you UNDERSTAND?

7. Kit says that the answer in Exercise 4 is 4.97. What did Kit do wrong?

8. How are adding and subtracting decimals similar to and different from adding and subtracting whole numbers?

Independent Practice

For **9** through **25**, add or subtract. Estimate to check the reasonableness of your answer.

9. 7.23
    + 0.88

10. 48.61
    − 0.76

11. 27.58
    + 70.06

12. 15.19
    − 3.28

13. 14.06
    − 9.98

14. 15.22
    + 53.99

15. 19.25
    − 7.52

16. 59.31
    + 3.69

17. 10 − (4.5 + 3.1)

18. 7.89 + 4.5 − 3.87

19. 75 − (22.5 + 21.78)

20. 90 − (25.45 + 2.10)

21. 49.99 + 3.50 − 18

22. 63.4 − (6.25 + 1.25)

23. 19.29 + 2.71 − 3.32

24. 16 − (5.86 + 4.95)

25. 93 − (52.06 + 21.6)

*For another example, see Set I on page 159.

Step 1

First find the cost of the two movies at the regular price.

? Regular price	
$3.95	$2.49

$$\begin{array}{r} \$3.95 \\ +\ \ 2.49 \\ \hline \$6.44 \end{array}$$

The regular price is $6.44.

Step 2

Then subtract the amount of the coupon.

$6.44	
?	$1.50

$$\begin{array}{r} \$6.44 \\ -\ \ 1.50 \\ \hline \$4.94 \end{array}$$

Samir's movies cost $4.94 to rent.

Problem Solving

26. **Science** One of the largest dinosaurs ever found, the *Puertasaurus*, measured 39.92 meters long. One of the smallest dinosaurs, the *Compsognathus*, measured 1.43 meters long. What was the difference in the length of these dinosaurs?

27. The gold medalist for the 100-meter race at the Beijing Olympics set a new world record in August 2008, running the race in 9.69 seconds. The gold medalist in the 1908 Olympics held in London ran the 100-meter race in 10.80 seconds. How many seconds faster is the 2008 world record than the 1908 Olympic time?

1908	10.80	
2008	9.69	?

28. **Geometry** Susannah bought a rectangular rug for her room. The rug is 6 feet wide and 8 feet long. Her room is square, 10 feet on each side. How much greater is the perimeter of her room than the perimeter of the rug?

A 100 feet   **C** 40 feet

B 48 feet   **D** 12 feet

Use the simple map shown on the graph for **29.**

29. The map shows Mei and Patti's neighborhood.

a Mei lives in the Hillcrest Apartments. What ordered pair names where Mei lives?

b Patti lives at (2, 7). In which apartment does Patti live?

c Explain how Mei can take the bus to Sunnyview. What is the least number of blocks she could travel?

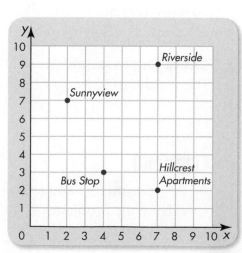

MA.5.A.2.2 Add and subtract fractions and decimals fluently and verify the reasonableness of results, including in problem situations.

Problem Solving

Multiple-Step Problems

Monica wants to buy all of the fruit shown on this sign. She has coupons for $0.45 off the cost of one pint of blueberries, and $0.35 off one watermelon. What will Monica's total cost be after the discounts?

FRESH FRUIT TODAY

(3 pounds) $1.29

(1 pint) $3.29

(2 pounds) $0.92

(each) $5.65

Another Example

A children's news and talk show is broadcast for 2 hours each weekday. On Saturday and Sunday, the show is an hour longer than during the week. How many hours is this show broadcast each week?

What is one hidden question?

How many hours of the show are broadcast during weekdays?

? total hours

| 2 | 2 | 2 | 2 | 2 |

↑
Hours per weekday

$5 \times 2 = 10$

The show is on for 10 hours during weekdays.

What is another hidden question?

How many hours of the show are broadcast during the weekend?

? total hours

| 3 | 3 |

↑
Hours per weekend day

$2 \times 3 = 6$

The show is on for 6 hours during the weekend.

Add the number of weekday and weekend hours.

10 weekday hours + 6 weekend hours = 16 hours
The show is on for 16 hours each week.

Check for reasonableness: I can estimate 2 hours × 7 days = 14 hours. This is close to 16 hours.

Explain It

1. Why do you find and answer the hidden questions before solving the problem?

What do I know?

Monica wants to buy the fruit with prices shown on a store sign. She has coupons for $0.45 and $0.35 off the price of one pint of blueberries and one watermelon.

What am I asked to find?

The cost of all the fruit after the discount

Find and answer the hidden question or questions.

1. How much does the fruit cost?

? total cost

$1.29	$3.29	$0.92	$5.65

$1.29 + $3.29 + $0.92 + $5.65 = $11.15

2. How much are the coupons worth?

? total saved

$0.45	$0.35

$$\begin{array}{r} \$0.45 \\ + \$0.35 \\ \hline \$0.80 \end{array}$$

Subtract the total saved from the cost of the fruit.
$11.15 − $0.80 = $10.35

Monica will pay $10.35 for the fruit after the discount.

Guided Practice*

Do you know HOW?

Solve.

1. Nate has a $5 bill and a $10 bill. He spends $2.50 for a smoothie and $2 for a muffin. How much money does he have left?

Do you UNDERSTAND?

2. What are the hidden questions and answers for Problem 1?

3. Write a Problem Write a real-world multiple-step problem that can be solved using addition and subtraction.

Independent Practice

In **4** through **6**, write and answer the hidden question or questions. Then solve.

4. Elias saved $30 in July, $21 in August, and $50 in September. He spent $17.75 on movies and $26.25 on gas. How much money does Elias have left?

5. Paige takes riding lessons 5 days per week for 2 hours each day. Maggie takes guitar lessons twice a week for 2.5 hours each day, and piano lessons three days per week for 1 hour each day. Which girl spends more hours on lessons? How many more hours?

6. Lonny planted 15 roses, 12 geraniums, and 6 daisies. His dog digs up 4 roses and 2 daisies. How many flowers are left planted?

Stuck? Try this....

- What do I know?
- What am I asked to find?
- What diagram can I use to help understand the problem?
- Can I use addition, subtraction, multiplication, or division?
- Is all of my work correct?
- Did I answer the right question?
- Is my answer reasonable?

For **7** and **8**, write and answer the hidden question or questions. Then solve.

Driving Log		
	Business	**Personal Use**
Monday	48 miles	11 miles
Tuesday	59 miles	8 miles
Wednesday	78 miles	28 miles

7. At the right is a driving log that Mr. Smith kept for the last three days of his trip. How many more miles did he drive for business than for personal use?

Salad Inventory	
Macaroni Salad	11 pounds
Pasta Salad	22 pounds
Potato Salad	15 pounds

8. The table at the right shows the amount of salad a deli had on Monday morning. During the morning, the deli sold 5 pounds of macaroni salad, 16 pounds of pasta salad, and 14 pounds of potato salad. How many total pounds of salad did the deli have left Monday afternoon?

9. At the craft festival, Tuan spent $12 for food, $19.50 for a small painting, and $6 for a straw hat. Tuan had $4 left. How much did Tuan spend on the small painting and the hat together? Draw a picture and write an equation to solve.

10. Look for a pattern, and then describe it. What are the next three missing numbers?

0.39	0.45	0.51			

11. **Writing to Explain** Pull-over shirts cost $24.95 each. Describe how to estimate the cost of 4 shirts. What is the estimate?

Think About the Process

12. A men's store has 63 blue oxford shirts and 44 tan oxford shirts. The same store has 39 red rugby shirts. Which hidden question needs to be answered to find the difference between the number of oxford shirts and rugby shirts?

   A How many oxford shirts does the store have?

   B How many blue and red shirts does the store have?

   C How many total shirts does the store have?

   D Why does the store sell oxford shirts?

13. Rita budgeted $250 to refurnish her home. She spent $156 on two rugs and $205 on a new lamp. Rita wants to know how much more money she'll need. Which expression can be evaluated to answer this hidden question: How much has Rita spent on the rugs and the lamp?

   F $156 + $205

   G $250 − $156

   H $156 + $250

   I $250 + $205

Adding Decimals

Use ⚙ tools

Place-Value Blocks

Use the Place-Value Blocks eTool to add 1.46 + 0.285.

Step 1 ▢ Go to the Place-Value Blocks eTool. Use the pull-down menu at the top of the page to select Large as the unit block. Select the two-part workspace icon. Click on the large cube, which represents one whole, and then click in the top part of the workspace. In the same way as above, show 4 flat place-value blocks and 6 long place-value blocks. The odometer should read 1.460.

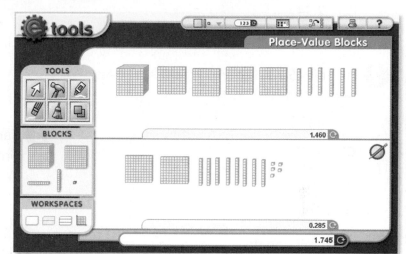

Step 2 Show 0.285 in the bottom part of the workspace, using the small cube for thousandths. The odometer for the bottom workspace should read 0.285.

Step 3 🖊 ↗ Use the arrow tool to select the 5 thousandths in the bottom part of the workspace and move them to the top. Move the 8 hundredths so they are next to the 4 hundredths in the top. Click on the glue icon, and then click on a long block. This will change 10 hundredths to 1 tenth. Move the remaining 2 tenths to the top space and look at the blocks to find the sum. 1.46 + 0.285 = 1.745.

Practice

Use the Place-Value Blocks eTool to find each sum.

1. 1.728 + 0.154   **2.** 0.375 + 0.29   **3.** 0.569 + 0.253   **4.** 0.86 + 0.649

5. 1.649 + 0.123   **6.** 1.223 + 0.789   **7.** 0.123 + 1.223   **8.** 0.789 + 1.649

9. 1.518 + 0.456   **10.** 1.527 + 0.912   **11.** 0.456 + 1.527   **12.** 0.912 + 1.518

13. 1.312 + 0.708   **14.** 1.630 + 0.815   **15.** 1.847 + 0.217   **16.** 1.309 + 0.219

1 What is 2.934 rounded to the nearest hundredth? (6-1)

A. 2.90

B. 2.93

C. 2.94

D. 3.00

2 What is 45.7001 rounded to the nearest whole number? (6-1)

F. 46

G. 45.7

H. 46.7

I. 47

3 What missing decimal goes in square *T* of the decimal number chart? (6-2)

0.01	0.02	0.03		
0.11		0.13	0.14	*T*
0.21			0.24	0.25

A. 0.04

B. 0.05

C. 0.15

D. 0.5

4 Lee's turtle has a shell that is 14.229 centimeters long. Ty's turtle has a shell that is 12.14 centimeters long. Which is the best estimate of the difference in length between the turtles' shells? (6-3)

F. About 1 centimeter

G. About 2 centimeters

H. About 3 centimeters

I. About 4 centimeters

5 Samantha rode her bicycle 6.79 miles on Saturday and 8.21 miles on Sunday. Which is the best estimate of the total miles she rode on the weekend? (6-3)

A. 15 miles

B. 16 miles

C. 17 miles

D. 20 miles

6 Larry spent $1.89 on a bottle of paint and $0.45 on a sponge brush. What was the total amount he spent? (6-4)

F. $2.34

G. $1.34

H. $1.32

I. $1.24

7 Kimmy is using place-value blocks to add 5.69 + 7.85. Which describes the first step in solving the problem? (6-5)

A. Add 5 + 7

B. Add 9 hundredths + 5 hundredths

C. Add 6 tenths + 8 tenths

D. Regroup 1 tenth as 10 hundredths

8 Eduardo is training for a swim meet. He swam his first lap in 26.56 seconds and his second lap in 26.97 seconds. What is his combined time for the first two laps? (6-7)

F. 50.03 seconds

G. 52.53 seconds

H. 53.43 seconds

I. 53.53 seconds

9 The Thomas Jefferson Memorial is on 18.36 acres of land, and the Franklin Delano Roosevelt Memorial is on 7.5 acres of land. On how many more acres of land is the Jefferson Memorial than the Roosevelt Memorial? (6-8)

A. 9.86

B. 10.86

C. 11.31

D. 17.61

10 Parker had a batting average of .287, and Keenan had an average of .301. How much higher was Keenan's batting average than Parker's? (6-8)

F. .256

G. .14

H. .023

I. .014

11 Monica bought a skirt for $15 and a hat for $12. Which is a way to find how much change she would get from $40? (6-10)

A. Add 40 to the difference of 15 and 12

B. Add 12 to the difference of 40 and 15

C. Subtract the sum of 15 and 12 from 40

D. Subtract 15 from the sum of 12 and 40

12 Casey's goal is to do 15 hours of volunteer work each week. On Monday, he spent 4.5 hours working at the animal shelter and 2 hours at the recycling center. How many more hours should Casey volunteer in order to meet his goal? (6-10)

F. 8.5 hours

G. 8 hours

H. 7.5 hours

I. 7 hours

13 What is 7.25 + 7.69 − 5.25? (6-9)

14 Liz is using place-value blocks to subtract 2.29 − 1.56. Explain how she can use the place-value block model below to find the difference. (6-6)

Set A, pages 128–129

Round 12.087 to the place of the underlined digit.

12.0<u>8</u>7   Look at the digit following the underlined digit. Look at 7.

            Round to the next greater number of hundredths because 7 > 5.

12.087 is about 12.09.

Round 9.073 to the place of the underlined digit.

<u>9</u>.073   Look at the digit following the underlined digit. Look at 0.

            Since 0 < 5 the digit in the ones place remains the same.

9.073 is about 9.

Remember that rounding a number means replacing it with a number that tells about how much or how many.

Round each number to the place of the underlined digit.

1. 10.<u>2</u>45   2. 7<u>3</u>.4

3. 9.1<u>4</u>5   4. 3.<u>9</u>99

5. 6.79<u>0</u>1   6. 13.0<u>2</u>3

7. 99.10<u>2</u>9   8. 45.<u>3</u>98

9. 0.1<u>5</u>3   10. 0.6<u>2</u>5

11. <u>8</u>.978   12. 5.<u>7</u>39

Set B, pages 130–132

Margaret drew a grid of six cells from a decimal number chart. What are the next two numbers?

| 0.73 | 0.74 | 0.75 | 0.76 | | |

Pattern: Moving from left to right, the hundredths increase by 0.01. The next two numbers are 0.77 and 0.78.

| 0.73 | 0.74 | 0.75 | 0.76 | 0.77 | 0.78 |

Remember that decimal number charts have patterns.

Copy and complete the grids.

1.

0.31
0.41
0.51

2.

0.03	
	0.14
	0.24
0.33	

Set C, pages 134–135

Estimate 23.64 + 7.36.

Round each decimal to the nearest whole number. Then add.

23.64 rounds to 24.
7.36 rounds to 7.

24 + 7 = 31

Remember to compare the digit in the tenths place to 5 when you round to the nearest whole number.

Estimate each answer.

1. 19.35 + 8.74   2. 12.3 − 9.7

3.
$$\begin{array}{r} 14.04 \\ +9.33 \\ \hline \end{array}$$

4.
$$\begin{array}{r} 7.48 \\ -3.92 \\ \hline \end{array}$$

Set D, pages 136–138

Use hundredths grids to subtract 1.86 − 0.95.

Shade one whole grid and 86 squares to show 1.86.

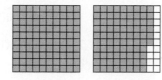

To subtract 0.95, cross out 95 shaded squares on the grids.

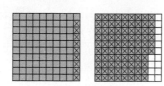

Count the squares that are shaded but not crossed out.

1.86 − 0.95 = 0.91

Remember when adding decimals, shade the first number in one color and then continue on shading the second number with another color.

1. 0.02 + 0.89

2. 0.67 − 0.31

3. 0.34 + 0.34

4. 0.81 − 0.78

Set E, pages 140–141

Use place-value models to add 2.35 + 0.89.

Step 1 Add the hundredths. Regroup if you can.

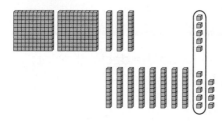

5 hundredths
+ 9 hundredths

14 hundredths, or
1 tenth and
4 hundredths

Step 2 Add the tenths. Regroup if you can.

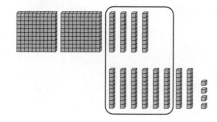

3 tenths
8 tenths
+ 1 tenth

12 tenths, or
1 and 2 tenths

Step 3 Add the whole numbers.

2 + 1 = 3

2.35 + 0.89 = 3.24

Remember to regroup as with whole numbers. 10 hundredths = 1 tenth.
10 tenths = 1 whole.

In **1** and **2**, use the models to find each sum.

1.   1.29
      + 1.75

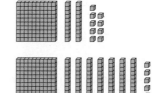

2.   0.57
      + 1.54

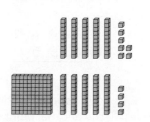

In **3** and **4**, use place-value blocks to find each sum.

3. 1.19 + 2.29

4. 5.47 + 0.89

Set F, pages 142–143

Use place-value models to subtract 1.25 − 0.69.

 Step 1 Regroup 1 tenth to make 15 hundredths.

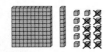

Step 2 Subtract hundredths.

15 hundredths − 9 hundredths = 6 hundredths

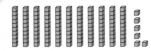

Step 3 Regroup 1 whole to make 11 tenths.

Step 4 Subtract tenths.
11 tenths − 6 tenths = 5 tenths

1.25 − 0.69 = 0.56

Remember to regroup as with whole numbers. 1 tenth = 10 hundredths. 1 whole = 10 tenths.

In **1** and **2**, use a model to find the difference.

1. 1.32
    − 0.89

2. 2.45
    − 1.56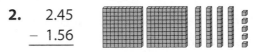

In **3** and **4**, use place-value blocks to find each difference.

3. 2.32 − 0.75

4. 4.69 − 3.98

Set G, pages 144–145

Find 9.326 + 2.95.

Estimate: 9 + 3 = 12

Step 1 Write the numbers. Line up the decimal points. Annex zeros to show place value and to act as placeholders.

```
  9. 3 2 6
+ 2. 9 5 0
```

Step 2 Add as you would whole numbers. Bring the decimal point down into the answer.

```
      1
  9. 3 2 6
+ 2. 9 5 0
-----------
 12. 2 7 6
```

The sum 12.276 is reasonable because it is close to the estimate, 12.

Remember to line up the decimal points before you add.

Find each sum.

1. 3.77 + 4.66

2. 12.68 + 31.919

3. 6.142 + 1.322

4. 67.8 + 14.755

5. 7.029 + 48.7

6. 10.93 + 0.967

7. 1.47 + 1.80

8. 125.9 + 6.777

Set H, pages 146–147

Find 7.83 − 3.147.

Estimate: 8 − 3 = 5.

Step 1 Write the numbers. Line up the decimal points. Annex zeros to show place value.

$$\begin{array}{r} 7.\ 8\ 3\ 0 \\ -\ 3.\ 1\ 4\ 7 \\ \hline \end{array}$$

Step 2 Subtract as you would whole numbers. Bring the decimal point down into the answer.

$$\begin{array}{r} {}^{7}\ {}^{12}\ {}^{10} \\ 7.\ \cancel{8}\ \cancel{3}\ \cancel{0} \\ -\ 3.\ 1\ 4\ 7 \\ \hline 4.\ 6\ 8\ 3 \end{array}$$

The difference 4.683 is reasonable because it is close to the estimate, 5.

Remember that you can add to check.

Find each difference.

1. 9.21 − 1.72

2. 15.51 − 11.302

3. 5.7 − 0.623

4. 16.209 − 14.5

5. 17.099 − 9.7

Set I, pages 148–149

Use order of operations to solve multiple-step problems involving decimals.
Solve 15 − (3.5 + 5.95)

Step 1 3.5 + 5.95 = 9.45

Step 2 15 − 9.45 = 5.55

So, 15 − (3.5 + 5.95) = 5.55

Remember to align decimals on the decimal point when adding or subtracting.

1. 12 − (4.15 + 3.68)

2. (5.75 + 12.32) − 6.75

3. (3.15 − 1.87) + 5.63

4. (5.45 − 3.98) + 8

Set J, pages 150–152

Gene wants to buy a catcher's mitt for $52.00 and baseball shoes for $95.75. He has a coupon for $8.50 off the price of the catcher's mitt. How much money will Gene owe for his total purchase?

Find and answer the hidden question.

How much will Gene have to pay for the mitt?

$52.00		
$8.50	? cost after coupon	

$52.00 − $8.50 = $43.50

Add the discounted price of the mitt to the price of the shoes to find the total amount Gene owes.
$43.50 + $95.75 = $139.25

Gene will pay $139.25 for his purchase.

Remember to look for the hidden question or questions first.

Answer the hidden question. Then solve.

1. Pedro earned money doing different jobs for neighbors. He kept a table of what he earned. If Pedro bought a magazine subscription for $16.95, how much money did he have left?

Job	Earnings
Mowing lawn	$13.50
Raking leaves	$11.00
Walking dogs	$14.75

Topic 7

Adding and Subtracting Fractions with Like Denominators

1 The ghost crab is one of many kinds of crabs that live in Florida coastal waters. When do ghost crabs feed? You will find out in Lesson 7-8.

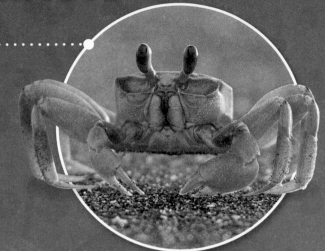

2 How can you find the fraction of children that are boys on the spinning swing ride? You will find out in Lesson 7-9.

Review What You Know!

3 Is the number of feet for the height of the world's largest pencil a prime or composite number? You will find out in Lesson 7-2.

4 Totems like this one can be divided into equal parts to show images. How can the parts that show the images as in this totem be compared? You will find out in Lesson 7-9.

Vocabulary

Choose the best term from the box.

- denominator
- factor
- improper fraction
- numerator

1. In the fraction $\frac{2}{3}$, the number 2 is the _?_ of the fraction and 3 is the _?_ of the fraction.

2. A fraction whose numerator is greater than or equal to its denominator is called a(n) _?_ .

Equivalent Fractions

Write the missing values to show pairs of equivalent fractions.

3. $\frac{2}{3} = \frac{?}{6}$ **4.** $\frac{?}{4} = \frac{3}{12}$

5. $\frac{6}{5} = \frac{?}{10}$ **6.** $\frac{1}{2} = \frac{50}{?}$

7. $\frac{1}{5} = \frac{?}{20}$ **8.** $\frac{3}{?} = \frac{30}{100}$

Models for Fractions

Tell what fraction is represented by each model.

9.

10.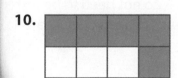

11. Writing to Explain Draw two ways to model $\frac{5}{6}$. Explain why there can be more than one way to model a fraction.

Topic Essential Questions

- What does it mean to add and subtract fractions with like denominators?
- What is a standard procedure for adding and subtracting fractions with like denominators?
- How can fractions be added and subtracted on a number line?

MA.5.A.6.1 Identify and relate prime and composite numbers, factors and multiples within the context of fractions.

Understanding Factors

How can you find all the factors of a number?

Three possible arrays of 12 buttons are shown. The arrays can help find all the factors of 12. The factors of 12 are 1, 2, 3, 4, 6, and 12.

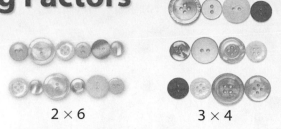

2×6 3×4

1×12

Another Example **How can you use divisibility rules to find factors?**

A factor pair is a pair of whole numbers whose product equals a given whole number. A factor pair for 12 is 3 and 4.

Find all the factor pairs of 32. Then list all the factors of 32.

Try	Is It a Factor?	Factor Pair
1	Yes, 1 is a factor of every whole number.	1 and 32
2	Yes, because 32 is even.	2 and 16
3	No; $3 + 2 = 5$, and 32 is not divisible by 3.	
4	Yes; 32 is divisible by 4.	4 and 8
5	No, because 32 does not end in 0 or 5.	
6	No, because 32 is not divisible by both 2 and 3.	
7	No.	
8	Yes; 32 is divisible by 8.	4 and 8

Numbers greater than 8 do not need to be tested because starting with 8, the factor pairs repeat. The factors of 32 are 1, 2, 4, 8, 16, and 32.

Explain It

1. Why is it helpful to know the divisibility rules?

2. If 15 and 14 are factors of a number, what are four other numbers that will be factors of the same number? Explain.

Arrays can help you find all the factors of a number. However, an easier way is to use divisibility rules.

A whole number is <u>divisible</u> by another when the quotient is a whole number and the remainder is 0.

Divisibility Rules

A number is divisible by

2 → If the number is even.

3 → If the sum of the digits of the number is divisible by 3.

4 → If the last two digits are divisible by 4.

5 → If the last digit is 0 or 5.

6 → If the number is divisible by BOTH 2 and 3.

9 → If the sum of the digits is divisible by 9.

10 → If the last digit is 0.

Guided Practice*

Do you know HOW?

In **1** through **4**, list all the factors of each number.

1. 25   **2.** 42

3. 36   **4.** 18

Do you UNDERSTAND?

5. What factor pair does every number have?

6. List the possible arrays you can arrange 18 buttons in.

Independent Practice

In **7** through **12**, name two different factor pairs of the given number.

7. 30   **8.** 32   **9.** 36

10. 40   **11.** 42   **12.** 39

In **13** through **24**, list all the factors of each number.

13. 45   **14.** 48   **15.** 50

16. 54   **17.** 60   **18.** 70

19. 84   **20.** 98   **21.** 108

22. 114   **23.** 8   **24.** 55

DIGITAL

Animated Glossary
www.pearsonsuccessnet.com

25. A restaurant wall was divided into 4 equal parts as shown. What fraction of the wall is the

  a mirror?

  b paneling?

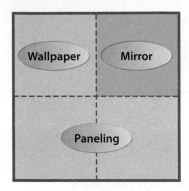

26. A museum has 80 African baskets. Which list of factor pairs shows all the possible arrangements of baskets into equal rows? Assume that an arrangement such as 4 × 20 is the same as 20 × 4.

  A 1 × 80; 4 × 20; 8 × 10

  B 1 × 80; 2 × 40; 4 × 20; 5 × 16; 8 × 10

  C 2 × 40; 5 × 16; 8 × 10

  D 2 × 40; 4 × 20; 5 × 16; 8 × 10

27. The list shows all the factors for which number?

        4, 8, 14, 7, 2, 1, 56, 28

  F 9

  G 28

  H 56

  I 112

28. Name a fraction and a decimal for the shaded part of the figure below.

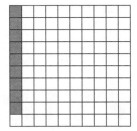

29. How can you tell if 189 is divisible by 3 without doing the division?

Critical
THINKING

30. Name the fraction and decimal at *F*.

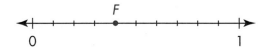

31. **Think About the Process** The town meeting hall was set up in 18 rows with 15 chairs in each row. There were also 10 chairs at the speakers' table. Which expression shows how many chairs were in the meeting hall?

  A (18 + 15) + 10

  B (15 × 10) + 18

  C (18 × 15) + 10

  D (10 × 15) × 18

32. **Writing to Explain** List the factors of 24. Then list the factors of 16. How are the factors the same and how are they different?

33. Pull-over shirts cost $19.95 each and one pair of jeans costs $24.25. What is an estimate for the cost of both items?

Algebra Connections

Find a Rule

Remember that tables can be used to show relationships between pairs of numbers.

Number of Feet	1	2	3	4
Number of Inches	12	24	36	48

If you know a length in feet, you can multiply by 12 to find the length in inches. When you know a length in inches, you can divide by 12 to find the length in feet.

Example:
What rule connects the number of hours to the number of days? Find the missing numbers.

Number of Days	1	2	3	4	■	■
Number of Hours	24	48	72	96	120	240

Rule:
Divide the number of hours by 24 to find the number of days.

120 ÷ 24 = 5. So, 120 hours = 5 days.
240 ÷ 24 = 10. So, 240 hours = 10 days.

For **1** through **7**, find a rule. Then find the missing numbers in each table.

1.

Quarters	4	8	12	16	20	60
Dollars	1	2	3	4	■	■

2.

Apples	30	35	40	45	50	75
Baskets	6	7	8	9	■	■

3.

Loaves	1	2	3	4	5	9
Slices	20	40	60	80	■	■

4.

Cups	3	4	5	6	7	10
Fluid Ounces	24	32	40	48	■	■

5.

Marbles	Bags
50	1
100	2
150	3
200	■
450	■

6.

Tomatoes	Containers
30	2
45	3
60	4
75	5
120	■

7.

Yards	Inches
1	36
2	72
3	108
4	144
10	■

MA.5.A.6.1 Identify and relate prime and composite numbers, factors and multiples within the context of fractions.

Prime and Composite Numbers

What are prime and composite numbers?

Every whole number greater than 1 is either a prime number or a composite number. A prime number has exactly two factors, 1 and itself. A composite number has more than two factors.

$1 \times 3 = 3$

$1 \times 8 = 8$

$2 \times 4 = 8$

Another Example **What is another way to find out if a number is prime or composite?**

Eratosthenes was born in Cyrene (now Libya) about 230 B.C. He developed a method for deciding if a number is prime. It is called the Sieve of Eratosthenes because it "strains out" prime numbers from other numbers.

Use a number chart to find all the prime numbers between 1 and 60.

Cross out 1. It is neither prime nor composite.

Circle 2, the least prime number. Cross out every second number after 2.

Circle 3, the next prime number. Cross out every third number after 3 (even if it has already been crossed out).

Circle 5, and repeat the process.

Circle 7, and repeat the process.

Continue the process for 11, 13, and so on.

The numbers left are prime.

Explain It

1. What are the first 10 prime numbers? How do you know?

2. Why is 1 not a prime number?

Prime or Composite?

Is 27 a prime number or a composite number?

You can use divisibility rules to help you decide.

Since 27 is an odd number it is not divisible by 2.

Since the sum of the digits is $2 + 7 = 9$, then 27 is divisible by 3. So, 27 also has factors of 3 and 9.

So, 27 is composite.

Is 11 prime or composite?

Since 11 is an odd number, it is NOT divisible by 2.

It is also NOT divisible by 3, 4, 5, 6, 7, 8, 9, or 10.

So, 11 is prime.

Guided Practice*

Do you know HOW?

For **1** through **4**, use divisibility rules to help you decide whether the number is prime or composite.

1. 71

2. 63

3. 86

4. 97

Do you UNDERSTAND?

5. Is every even number greater than 2 a composite number? Explain.

6. Which of the first ten prime numbers are even numbers?

Independent Practice

For **7** through **14**, use divisibility rules to help you decide whether the number is prime or composite.

7. 106

8. 93

9. 87

10. 103

11. 83

12. 77

13. 89

14. 287

For **15** through **17**, list all of the factors for each number. Then tell if the number is prime or composite. Circle the factors that are prime.

	Number	Factors	Prime or Composite
15.	24		
16.	43		
17.	65		

DIGITAL

Animated Glossary
www.pearsonsuccessnet.co

*For another example, see Set B on page 194.

18. Name two decimals shown by the model below.

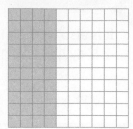

19. Which number has the digit 6 in the ten-thousands place?

    A 6,147,218   **C** 642,180

    B 1,562,803   **D** 16,095

20. **Science** An emperor penguin can grow to be about 45 inches tall. A king penguin can grow to be about 3 feet tall. Which penguin grows to be taller? About how much taller?

21. **Critical THINKING** Twin primes are two prime numbers with a difference of 2. The prime numbers 5 and 3 are twin primes because 5 − 3 = 2. Which of the following pairs of numbers are NOT twin primes?

    F 41 and 43

    G 59 and 61

    H 71 and 73

    I 109 and 111

22. **Think About the Process** Every Sunday Jay walks 6 blocks one way to his grandmother's house for lunch. After lunch, he walks 2 blocks farther to the park. He then walks home on the same exact route. Which shows how to find the number of blocks Jay walks in 4 weeks?

    A $(6 + 2) \times (4 + 6)$

    B $6 \times (2 \times 4)$

    C $6 \times 2 \times 2$

    D $(6 + 2) \times 2 \times 4$

23. **Algebra** If n is a prime factor of both 15 and 50, what is the value of n?

24. The world's largest pencil is 65 feet tall. Is 65 a prime number or a composite number?

25. **Reasonableness** Shirley multiplied 379×8 and got 3,032. Use estimation to check the reasonableness of her answer.

26. **Writing to Explain** Red-tailed hawks can be found in Florida and can dive at a speed of more than 120 miles per hour. Explain how you know that 120 is a composite number.

27. Which pair of compatible numbers would be best to estimate the sum of 249 and 752?

    F 200 and 700   **H** 300 and 800

    G 250 and 750   **I** 400 and 700

28. Jonah said that 143 is prime because it is not divisible by any numbers from 2 through 10. Is he correct? Explain.

29. Which of the following is a composite number?

    A 13   **C** 93

    B 37   **D** 101

Divisibility Rules

Use 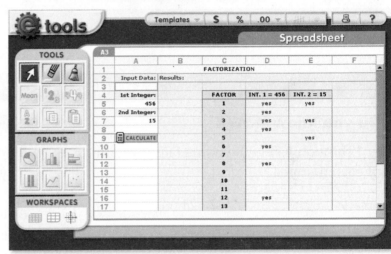 tools
Spreadsheet/Data/Grapher

If the sum of the digits of a number is divisible by 3, is the number divisible by 3? If the sum of the digits of a number is divisible by 9, is the number divisible by 9?

Step 1 Go to the Spreadsheet/ Data/Grapher eTool. Choose *Factorization* from the Templates pull-down menu at the top of the page. To test a number, enter 456 under *1st Integer* and press Enter. Add the digits in 456 mentally. The sum is $4 + 5 + 6 = 15$. Enter 15 under *2nd Integer* and press Enter. Click Calculate. The *yes* next to 3 in the Integer 1 column means that 456 is divisible by 3. The *yes* next to 3 in the Integer 2 column means that 15 is divisible by 3. So, both 456 and 15 are divisible by 3. The blanks next to 9 mean that neither 456 nor 15 is divisible by 9.

Step 2 Enter 837 under *1st Integer*. The sum of the digits in 837 is $8 + 3 + 7 = 18$. Enter 18 under *2nd Integer*. The results show that both 837 and 18 are divisible by 3 and by 9.

Practice

Copy and complete the table.

Number	Sum of Digits	Sum Divisible by 3?	Sum Divisible by 9?	Number Divisible by 3?	Number Divisible by 9?
984	21	yes	no	yes	no
371	11				
585					
714					

Finding Prime Factors

How can you write a number as a product of prime factors?

Every composite number can be written as a product of prime numbers. This product is the prime factorization of the number. A factor tree is a diagram that shows the prime factorization of a composite number.

Find the prime factorization of 48.

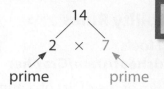

Guided Practice*

Do you know HOW?

In **1** through **4**, find the prime factorization of each number.

1. 9 **2.** 21

3. 12 **4.** 18

Do you UNDERSTAND?

5. Which property of multiplication tells you that $2 \times 3 \times 2 = 2 \times 2 \times 3$?

6. In the example above, if you selected 6 and 8 for the first factors, would the prime factors be different?

Independent Practice

In **7** through **9**, complete each factor tree.

7.
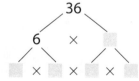

8.
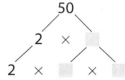

9.
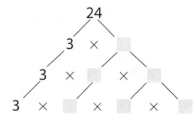

In **10** through **21**, find the prime factorization of each composite number, using exponents when possible. If the number is prime, write *prime*.

10. 20	**11.** 13	**12.** 22	**13.** 26
14. 30	**15.** 54	**16.** 48	**17.** 37
18. 93	**19.** 84	**20.** 75	**21.** 304

Animated Glossary
www.pearsonsuccessnet.com

For another example, see Set C on page 194.

Step 1

Use a factor tree to write 48 as the product of any two factors.

4 and 12 are not prime.

Step 2

Continue the process. Any factor that is not a prime is broken down further.

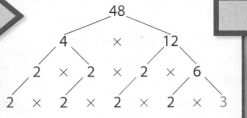

Step 3

Write the prime factors in order from least to greatest.

So, $48 = 2 \times 2 \times 2 \times 2 \times 3$.

Using exponents, you can write $2 \times 2 \times 2 \times 2$ as 2^4.

So, $48 = 2^4 \times 3$.

Problem Solving

22. Reasoning What is the least whole number that has 2 different prime factors?

23. How do you know immediately that 2,056 is not a prime number?

24. Writing to Explain How do you know when a factor tree is complete?

25. Evaluate $11.4 - n$ when $n = 5$, $n = 6.5$, and $n = 10$.

26. Geometry Draw a net that could be used to build a cube.

27. Tanya is packing her collection of snow globes in a crate with sections. The case is 2 sections high, 4 sections long, and 2 sections wide. How many globes can fit in the crate?

28. As of 2008, the Kingda Ka is the fastest and tallest roller coaster in the world. Its maximum height is 456 feet, and its top speed is 128 miles per hour. What is the prime factorization of 128?

A $2^2 \times 4^4$ **C** 2^7

B 2^6 **D** $2 \times 2 \times 4 \times 8$

29. Marcia's birthday is in December on a day that is a prime number. Which date could it be?

F December 4   **H** December 27

G December 15   **I** December 31

30. From a catalog, Stephen ordered 3 pounds of oranges at $2 per pound, and 4 pounds of pears at $3 per pound. He had to pay $6.25 for shipping. What was his total cost?

31. There are 63 couples lined up for an egg-tossing contest. Each couple will get one egg. There are 12 eggs in a dozen, and eggs come in cartons of one dozen. How many cartons of eggs are needed for the contest?

Critical THINKING

Lesson

7-4

MA.5.A.6.1 Identify and relate prime and composite numbers, factors and multiples within the context of fractions.

Common Factors and Greatest Common Factor

How can you find the greatest common factor?

A pet store has goldfish and angelfish that have to be put into the fewest number of glass containers. Each container must contain the same number of fish, and each must contain all goldfish or all angelfish.

20 angelfish

30 goldfish

Another Example How can you use prime factorization to find the GCF of two numbers?

Step 1 Find the prime factors of each number.

Step 2 List the prime factors of each number.

24: 2 × 2 × 2 × 3
18: 2 × 3 × 3

$$24$$
4   ×   6
2 × 2 × 2 × 3

$$18$$
2   ×   9
2 × 3 × 3

Step 3 Circle the prime factors that both numbers share. Here they share the numbers 2 and 3.

24: ②× 2 × 2 ×③
18: ②× 3 ×③

Step 4 Multiply the common factors. 2 × 3 = 6

So, the GCF of 18 and 24 is 6.

Guided Practice*

Do you know HOW?

For **1** through **4**, find the GCF of each pair of numbers.

1. 9 and 12   **2.** 20 and 45

3. 7 and 28   **4.** 18 and 32

Do you UNDERSTAND?

5. If two numbers are prime, what is their GCF?

6. Writing to Explain In the example above, how would the GCF change if there were 40 goldfish?

Animated Glossary
www.pearsonsuccessnet.com

DIGITAL

Find the greatest common factor (GCF) of 20 and 30 to find the greatest number of fish that could be put into each container.

If a number is a factor of two numbers, it is called a common factor.

The greatest common factor (GCF) of two numbers is the greatest number that is a factor of both numbers.

One Way

To find the greatest common factor of 20 and 30, you can list all the factors of each number and circle all the common factors.

20: 1, 2, 4, 5, 10, 20
30: 1, 2, 3, 5, 6, 10, 15, 30

The GCF of 20 and 30 is 10.

So, the store can put 10 fish in each container.

Independent Practice

In **7** through **18**, find the GCF of each number using prime factorization or a list of factors.

7. 20 and 35

8. 16 and 18

9. 15 and 6

10. 24 and 36

11. 48 and 30

12. 22 and 77

13. 100 and 96

14. 60 and 32

15. 90 and 81

16. 72 and 27

17. 11 and 15

18. 14 and 21

Problem Solving

19. Rick Hansen set a record by wheelchair. He wheeled his wheelchair across 4 continents and 34 countries. What is the GCF of 4 and 34?

A 1   **B** 2   **C** 4   **D** 17

20. Which list shows all the common factors of 36 and 54?

F 1, 2, 3, 6   **H** 1, 2, 3, 6, 9, 18

G 1, 2, 3, 6, 9   **I** 1, 2, 3, 6, 9, 12, 18

21. If you buy a television for $486, including tax, and are allowed to pay for it in 6 equal payments, how much will each payment be?

22. How many factor pairs does 40 have? List them.

THINK
SOLVE
EXPLAIN

The Venn diagram at the right shows the common factors and the GCF of 30 and 42.

23. What does each region of the diagram show?

24. Use a Venn diagram to show the common factors of 48 and 72. What is the GCF?

Factors of 30		Factors of 42
5	1	7
10	2	14
15	3	21
30	6	42

MA.5.A.6.1 Identify and relate prime and composite numbers, factors and multiples within the context of fractions.

Fractions in Simplest Form

How can you write a fraction in simplest form?

A stained glass window has 20 panes. Out of 20 sections, 12 are yellow. So $\frac{12}{20}$ of the panes are yellow. Notice how the picture also shows that $\frac{3}{5}$ are yellow.

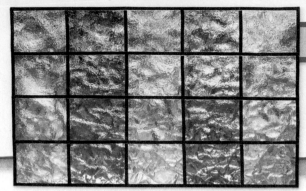

Another Example How can you use the GCF to find the simplest form of a fraction?

There are 36 students in the fifth-grade class. Twenty-seven will go to the mathematics competition. What is the simplest form of the fraction of the class going to the competition?

A $\frac{1}{9}$　　　**B** $\frac{2}{5}$　　　**C** $\frac{3}{4}$　　　**D** $\frac{7}{8}$

Factors of 27: 1, 3, 9, 27

Factors of 36: 1, 2, 3, 4, 6, 9, 18, 36.

The GCF of 27 and 36 is 9.

Then, divide the numerator and denominator by the GCF.

$$\frac{27 \div 9}{36 \div 9} = \frac{3}{4}$$

The simplest form of $\frac{27}{36}$ is $\frac{3}{4}$.

The correct choice is **C**.

Explain It

1. In finding the simplest form in Another Example, do you get the same answer if you list factor pairs? Explain.

2. John said that he divided the numerator and denominator of $\frac{18}{54}$ by 2, so $\frac{9}{27}$ is the simplest form of the fraction. Do you agree? Explain.

A fraction is in simplest form when its numerator and denominator have no common factor other than 1.

To write $\frac{12}{20}$ in simplest form, find a common factor of the numerator and the denominator. Since 12 and 20 are even numbers, they have 2 as a common factor.

Divide both 12 and 20 by 2.

$$\frac{12 \div 2}{20 \div 2} = \frac{6}{10}$$

Both 6 and 10 are even. Divide both by 2.

$$\frac{6 \div 2}{10 \div 2} = \frac{3}{5}$$

Since 3 and 5 have no common factor other than 1, you know that $\frac{3}{5}$ is in simplest form.

Guided Practice*

Do you know HOW?

In **1** through **6**, write each fraction in simplest form.

1. $\frac{16}{32}$ 2. $\frac{10}{14}$

3. $\frac{28}{35}$ 4. $\frac{16}{20}$

5. $\frac{30}{40}$ 6. $\frac{10}{15}$

Do you UNDERSTAND?

7. In the stained glass window pattern above, what fraction in simplest form names the green tiles?

8. **Writing to Explain** Why is it easier to divide the numerator and denominator by the GCF rather than any other factor?

Independent Practice

For **9** through **32**, write each fraction in simplest form.

9. $\frac{300}{400}$ 10. $\frac{55}{60}$ 11. $\frac{3}{6}$ 12. $\frac{75}{100}$

13. $\frac{14}{21}$ 14. $\frac{4}{12}$ 15. $\frac{42}{48}$ 16. $\frac{63}{70}$

17. $\frac{18}{21}$ 18. $\frac{20}{50}$ 19. $\frac{6}{42}$ 20. $\frac{15}{25}$

21. $\frac{9}{81}$ 22. $\frac{12}{100}$ 23. $\frac{7}{21}$ 24. $\frac{16}{30}$

25. $\frac{62}{100}$ 26. $\frac{16}{18}$ 27. $\frac{28}{42}$ 28. $\frac{32}{80}$

29. $\frac{40}{80}$ 30. $\frac{800}{1,000}$ 31. $\frac{60}{80}$ 32. $\frac{8}{100}$

DIGITAL   Animated Glossary
www.pearsonsuccessnet.com

33. Write a fraction in simplest form that shows the shaded part of the figure.

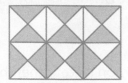

34. Mrs. Lok is planning a 600-mile trip. Her car has an 18-gallon gas tank and gets 29 miles per gallon. Will 1 tank full of gas be enough for the trip?

35. THINK SOLVE EXPLAIN Explain how you know that $\frac{55}{80}$ is not in simplest form.

36. If 4 T-shirts cost $68, what is the cost of 1 T-shirt?

37. Critical THINKING Can you assume that any fraction is in simplest form if either the numerator or denominator is a prime number?

38. A store manager wants to give away the last 84 samples of hand cream. She counts 26 customers in the store. She will give each customer the same number of free samples. How many free samples will each customer get?

39. 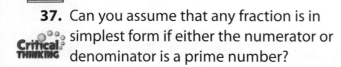 **Science** Mayflies can live at the bottom of lakes for 2 to 3 years before they become winged adults. Mayflies are between $\frac{4}{10}$ inch and 1.6 inches long. What is $\frac{4}{10}$ expressed in simplest form?

A $\frac{1}{6}$ **C** $\frac{2}{5}$

B $\frac{1}{4}$ **D** $\frac{8}{20}$

40. Reasoning Use divisibility rules to find one number that satisfies each of the given conditions.

a A number greater than 75 that is divisible by 2 and 5

b A three-digit number divisible by 3, 5, and 6

41. **Think** About the Process Rita sells birdhouses for $10 each. She uses $3\frac{1}{2}$ feet of wood for each birdhouse. Which operation would she use to find how much money she will receive if she sells 14 birdhouses?

F Multiplication

G Division

H Addition

I Subtraction

42. **Think** About the Process A parking garage has 4 levels with 28 spaces on each level. If 52 spaces are occupied, which of the following shows a way to find the number of spaces that are unoccupied?

A Add 28 to the product of 52 and 4.

B Add 52 to the product of 28 and 4.

C Subtract 28 from the product of 52 and 4.

D Subtract 52 from the product of 4 and 28.

Mixed Problem Solving

The Earth's climates are divided into three major climate zones. These zones are called the polar, temperate, and tropical zones. Temperatures and precipitation within these zones are affected by many factors including latitude, elevation, and closeness to bodies of water.

Most of the United States falls in the temperate zone. Hawaii and parts of Florida and Texas are in the tropical zone, and parts of Alaska are in the polar zone. Climates vary greatly within each zone.

1. The Hoh Rain Forest in Washington is one of the few temperate rain forests in North America. How many feet of rain fell in the Hoh Rain Forest in 1987? Round to the nearest foot.

Record Annual Rainfall	
Hoh Rain Forest	190 inches, 1987
Mount Waialeale	683 inches, 1982
Death Valley	5 inches, 1983

1 foot = 12 inches

2. Mount Waialeale in Hawaii is considered to be one of the rainiest spots on Earth. The average annual rainfall is over 460 inches. However, a record annual amount occurred in 1982. How many feet of rain fell on Mount Waialeale in 1982? Round to the nearest foot.

3. Death Valley in California is the hottest and driest spot in North America. Four mountain ranges lie between Death Valley and the Pacific Ocean, creating a drying effect. How many times as great as the record annual rainfall in Death Valley is the record annual rainfall at Hoh Rain Forest?

4. The National Weather Service began keeping weather records at Death Valley in 1911. For the first 65 years, the average annual rainfall was 1.6 inches. For the following 30 years, the average increased to 2.5 inches. How much did the average annual rainfall increase from the first 65-year period to the following 30-year period?

5. Elevations in Death Valley National Park range from 282 feet below sea level to 11,049 feet above sea level. Temperatures drop 3° to 5° Fahrenheit for every thousand vertical feet rise in elevation. If a hiker starts at an elevation of 3,000 feet above sea level and climbs to an elevation of 6,000 feet, how many degrees would the temperature be expected to drop?

MA.5.A.2.1 Represent addition and subtraction of decimals and fractions with like and unlike denominators using models, place value or properties.

Modeling Addition of Fractions

Hands-On
fraction strips

$\frac{1}{8}$

How can you use fraction strips to add fractions?

Ten whitewater rafting teams are racing downriver. Two teams have red rafts and one team has a blue raft. What fraction of the rafts are either red or blue?

Choose an Operation Add the fraction of the total rafts that are red to the fraction of the total rafts that are blue.

Guided Practice*

Do you know HOW?

In **1** through **6**, use fraction strips to add fractions. Simplify, if possible.

1. $\frac{1}{3} + \frac{1}{3}$ **2.** $\frac{1}{6} + \frac{1}{6}$

3. $\frac{2}{5} + \frac{1}{5}$ **4.** $\frac{2}{6} + \frac{2}{6}$

5. $\frac{1}{4} + \frac{2}{4}$ **6.** $\frac{1}{5} + \frac{3}{5}$

Do you UNDERSTAND?

7. In the problem above, what fraction of the rafts are yellow? What two fractions would you add to find the part of the rafts that are either red or yellow?

8. What two fractions are being added below? What is the sum?

| $\frac{1}{6}$ | $\frac{1}{6}$ | | $\frac{1}{6}$ | $\frac{1}{6}$ | $\frac{1}{6}$ |

Independent Practice

In **9** through **23**, find each sum. Simplify, if possible. You may use fraction strips.

9. $\frac{1}{3} + \frac{1}{3}$

10. $\frac{4}{10} + \frac{1}{10}$

11. $\frac{2}{12} + \frac{4}{12}$

12. $\frac{1}{6} + \frac{2}{6} + \frac{3}{6}$

13. $\frac{3}{12} + \frac{4}{12}$

14. $\frac{4}{10} + \frac{3}{10}$

15. $\frac{5}{8} + \frac{1}{8}$

16. $\frac{3}{4} + \frac{1}{4}$

17. $\frac{4}{12} + \frac{2}{12}$

18. $\frac{1}{4} + \frac{1}{4}$

19. $\frac{2}{10} + \frac{3}{10}$

20. $\frac{1}{10} + \frac{2}{10} + \frac{1}{10}$

21. $\frac{4}{6} + \frac{1}{6}$

22. $\frac{2}{3} + \frac{1}{3}$

23. $\frac{1}{8} + \frac{5}{8} + \frac{1}{8}$

DIGITAL   eTools
www.pearsonsuccessnet.com

$\frac{2}{10}$ of the rafts are red and $\frac{1}{10}$ of the rafts are blue. Use two $\frac{1}{10}$ strips to show $\frac{2}{10}$ and one $\frac{1}{10}$ strip to show $\frac{1}{10}$.

Three $\frac{1}{10}$ strips are needed.

Add the numerators. Write the sum over the common denominator.

$$\frac{2}{10} + \frac{1}{10} = \frac{3}{10}$$

Three out of ten or $\frac{3}{10}$ of the total rafts are either red or blue.

Problem Solving

24. **Draw a Picture** A pizza is divided into 6 equal pieces. Draw a picture to show that $\frac{1}{6} + \frac{2}{6} = \frac{3}{6}$ or $\frac{1}{2}$.

25. Tomika has 2 cats. Fluffy weighs 8.625 pounds and Prince weighs 11.25 pounds. How much do the cats weigh together?

26. **Reasoning** Suppose two different fractions with the same denominators are both less than 1. Can their sum equal 1? Can their sum be greater than 1?

27. A chicken farm produces an average of 1,848 eggs per week. There are 12 eggs in a dozen. How many dozen eggs does the farm produce in an average week?

28. **Writing to Explain** Sophia walked $\frac{1}{4}$ of a mile to Sheila's house, and they both walked $\frac{2}{4}$ of a mile to the pool. How far did Sophia walk? Explain how you found your answer.

29. **Estimation** Pencils come 20 to a package, 48 packages to a carton, and 12 cartons to a case. About how many pencils are in a case?

30. **Algebra** Find the missing value in the equation.

$$\frac{1}{10} + \frac{\blacksquare}{10} + \frac{3}{10} = \frac{9}{10}$$

    A 2   **C** 4

    B 3   **D** 5

31. **Think About the Process** Maribel had 8 stickers. She bought 4 more. Then she gave her sister 5 stickers.

What numerical expression shows how many stickers Maribel has now?

    F $(8 + 4) - 5$ **H** $8 - (4 + 5)$

    G $(8 \times 4) \div 5$ **I** $8 - (4 - 5)$

32. **Number Sense** When does the sum of two fractions equal 1?

Critical THINKING

MA.5.A.2.2 Add and subtract fractions and decimals fluently and verify the reasonableness of results, including in problem situations.

Adding Fractions with Like Denominators

How can you add fractions with like denominators?

The table shows the results of a fifth-grade class survey. What fraction of the class chose soccer or basketball as their favorite sport?

Choose an Operation Add the fractions for soccer and basketball to find the results.

Favorite Sport	
	$\frac{4}{20}$
	$\frac{3}{20}$
	$\frac{6}{20}$
	$\frac{7}{20}$

Guided Practice*

Do you know HOW?

For **1** through **6**, add the fractions. Simplify, if possible.

1. $\frac{2}{4} + \frac{1}{4}$ 2. $\frac{3}{9} + \frac{6}{9}$

3. $\frac{2}{12} + \frac{4}{12}$ 4. $\frac{1}{10} + \frac{4}{10}$

5. $\frac{3}{15} + \frac{7}{15}$ 6. $\frac{9}{20} + \frac{6}{20}$

Do you UNDERSTAND?

For **7** and **8**, add the fractions. Simplify, if possible.

7. In the survey above, what do the numerators stand for? The denominators?

8. Using the survey above, what fraction of the class chose either roller skating or biking?

Independent Practice

In **9** through **26**, add the fractions. Simplify, if possible.

9. $\frac{2}{6} + \frac{2}{6}$ 10. $\frac{3}{25} + \frac{2}{25}$ 11. $\frac{1}{7} + \frac{4}{7}$

12. $\frac{5}{11} + \frac{6}{11}$ 13. $\frac{2}{13} + \frac{5}{13}$ 14. $\frac{2}{9} + \frac{4}{9}$

15. $\frac{3}{18} + \frac{6}{18}$ 16. $\frac{7}{30} + \frac{8}{30}$ 17. $\frac{2}{8} + \frac{4}{8}$

18. $\frac{3}{16} + \frac{5}{16}$ 19. $\frac{2}{12} + \frac{6}{12}$ 20. $\frac{3}{20} + \frac{1}{20} + \frac{1}{20}$

21. $\frac{4}{25} + \frac{5}{25}$ 22. $\frac{5}{16} + \frac{1}{16}$ 23. $\frac{3}{6} + \frac{1}{6}$

24. $\frac{3}{8} + \frac{3}{8}$ 25. $\frac{7}{50} + \frac{3}{50}$ 26. $\frac{25}{100} + \frac{75}{100}$

*For another example, see Set G on page 196.

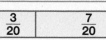

Step 1	Step 2	Step 3

Step 1

?

| $\frac{3}{20}$ | $\frac{7}{20}$ |

Write the sum of the fractions.

$$\frac{3}{20} + \frac{7}{20}$$

Step 2

Add the numerators. Write the sum over the common denominator.

$$\frac{3}{20} + \frac{7}{20} = \frac{10}{20}$$

Step 3

Write the sum in simplest form, if possible.

$$\frac{10 \div 10}{20 \div 10} = \frac{1}{2}$$

One half $\left(\frac{1}{2}\right)$ of the students chose soccer or basketball as their favorite sport.

Problem Solving

27. Maria swam a race in 20.12 seconds. Erika swam the race in 22.5 seconds. What is the difference in their times?

  A 2.43 seconds

  B 2.4 seconds

  C 2.38 seconds

  D 1.56 seconds

28. Geometry Perimeter is the distance around the outside of any polygon. If a side of a square is $\frac{1}{2}$ foot long, what is the perimeter of the square?

$\frac{1}{2}$ foot

29. THINK SOLVE EXPLAIN Using the survey in the example at the top of the page, find two activities that have a sum of $\frac{9}{20}$. Explain.

30. Reasoning If a painter poured $\frac{1}{4}$ gallon of yellow paint and $\frac{1}{4}$ gallon of red paint into a bucket, how much paint is in the bucket? What color did the painter make?

31. Reasoning Critical THINKING One brand of socks is on sale at 3 pairs for $6. Another brand is on sale at 5 pairs for $9. Which is the better buy?

32. Michael's family lives at 13450 Oak Street. What is the expanded form of 13,450?

33. Algebra Find the missing numerator in each equation.

  a $\frac{4}{9} + \frac{\blacksquare}{9} = \frac{8}{9}$ **c** $\frac{2}{7} + \frac{\blacksquare}{7} = \frac{5}{7}$

  b $\frac{\blacksquare}{10} + \frac{3}{10} = \frac{9}{10}$ **d** $\frac{4}{12} + \frac{\blacksquare}{12} = \frac{7}{12}$

34. Jorgé bought $\frac{3}{8}$ of a yard of fabric. He already had $\frac{1}{8}$ of a yard of the same cloth. What are 3 equivalent fractions for how much fabric Jorgé has now?

MA.5.A.2.1 Represent addition and subtraction of decimals and fractions with like and unlike denominators using models, place value or properties.

Modeling Subtraction of Fractions

Hands-On fraction strips $\frac{1}{8}$

How can you use fraction strips to subtract fractions?

A garden plot is divided into twelve equal sections. If two sections are used to grow hot peppers, what fraction is left to grow other crops?

Choose an Operation Take away a part from the whole to find the difference.

Guided Practice*

Do you know HOW?

For **1** through **6**, use fraction strips to subtract. Simplify, if possible.

1. $\frac{4}{4} - \frac{1}{4}$ 2. $\frac{4}{5} - \frac{2}{5}$

3. $\frac{7}{8} - \frac{5}{8}$ 4. $\frac{9}{10} - \frac{3}{10}$

5. $\frac{7}{12} - \frac{3}{12}$ 6. $\frac{7}{8} - \frac{1}{8}$

Do you UNDERSTAND?

7. In the problem above, what part of the garden is represented by each fraction strip?

8. In the example above, if 4 plots are used to grow hot peppers, what fraction is left to grow other crops? How did you find your answer?

Independent Practice

In **9** through **26**, use fraction strips to subtract. Simplify, if possible.

9. $\frac{2}{3} - \frac{1}{3}$ 10. $\frac{3}{5} - \frac{2}{5}$ 11. $\frac{6}{10} - \frac{2}{10}$

12. $\frac{11}{12} - \frac{5}{12}$ 13. $\frac{2}{2} - \frac{1}{2}$ 14. $\frac{3}{4} - \frac{1}{4}$

15. $\frac{5}{6} - \frac{2}{6}$ 16. $\frac{6}{8} - \frac{2}{8}$ 17. $\frac{4}{12} - \frac{1}{12}$

18. $\frac{4}{6} - \frac{1}{6}$ 19. $\frac{5}{8} - \frac{2}{8}$ 20. $\frac{7}{10} - \frac{4}{10}$

21. $\frac{8}{10} - \frac{2}{10}$ 22. $\frac{3}{5} - \frac{1}{5}$ 23. $\frac{5}{6} - \frac{4}{6}$

24. $\frac{4}{5} - \frac{4}{5}$ 25. $\frac{8}{10} - \frac{4}{10}$ 26. $\frac{1}{3} - \frac{1}{3}$

eTools
www.pearsonsuccessnet.com

DIGITAL

*For another example, see Set H on page 196.

Use twelve $\frac{1}{12}$ fraction strips to represent the whole garden.

Take two strips away.

Ten strips are left. So $\frac{10}{12}$ of the garden is used for other crops.

Write the part taken away over the common denominator. Subtract the numerators.

$$\frac{12}{12} - \frac{2}{12} = \frac{10}{12}$$

Write in simplest form, if possible.

$$\frac{10}{12} = \frac{5}{6}$$

Problem Solving

27. Draw a Picture Draw a model of the garden plot according to the data table below. The plot is divided into 12 sections. What fraction of the plot will be flowers?

Class Garden Plot

Crop	Number of Sections
Strawberries	1
Hot Peppers	2
Corn	2
Tomatoes	4
Flowers	the rest

28. Number Sense A quilt is divided into 8 equal panels. Seven panels are blue. Two blue panels are removed to be repaired. Which equation shows the blue part of the quilt that remains after two parts are removed?

A $\frac{7}{8} - \frac{2}{8} = \frac{5}{16}$ **C** $\frac{7}{8} - \frac{2}{8} = \frac{5}{8}$

B $\frac{1}{8} - \frac{6}{8} = \frac{3}{8}$ **D** $\frac{7}{8} - \frac{2}{8} = \frac{9}{16}$

29. What fraction of the circle is the orange part? What fraction of the circle is not orange?

30. Clare had $\frac{5}{6}$ of a pound of almonds. She used $\frac{3}{6}$ of a pound to make a cake. How many pounds of almonds were left? Simplify, if possible.

31. **Science** To avoid predators, ghost crabs usually stay in burrows during the day and feed mostly at night. Suppose a ghost crab eats $\frac{1}{8}$ of its food before 10:00 P.M. By midnight, it has eaten $\frac{5}{8}$ of its food. How much of its food did it eat between 10:00 P.M. and midnight?

MA.5.A.2.2 Add and subtract fractions and decimals fluently and verify the reasonableness of results, including in problem situations.

Subtracting Fractions with Like Denominators

How do you subtract fractions when the denominators are the same?

A recipe for pancakes calls for $\frac{7}{8}$ of a cup of milk. Lori only has $\frac{3}{8}$ of a cup. How much more milk does she need to make the pancakes?

Choose an Operation Subtract the fractions to find the difference.

$\frac{3}{8}$ cup

Guided Practice*

Do you know HOW?

For **1** through **6**, subtract the fractions. Simplify, if possible.

1. $\frac{2}{3} - \frac{1}{3}$ 2. $\frac{3}{4} - \frac{2}{4}$

3. $\frac{5}{6} - \frac{2}{6}$ 4. $\frac{9}{12} - \frac{3}{12}$

5. $\frac{7}{8} - \frac{3}{8}$ 6. $\frac{7}{10} - \frac{1}{10}$

Do you UNDERSTAND?

7. **Writing to Explain** A pancake recipe calls for $\frac{3}{5}$ cup of flour and Lori has 1 cup. Does she have enough flour to make 2 batches of pancakes? Explain.

8. In the example above, if Lori's neighbor gave her $\frac{6}{8}$ cup of milk, would she then have enough milk to make her recipe?

Independent Practice

In **9** through **29**, subtract the fractions. Simplify, if possible.

9. $\frac{11}{12} - \frac{1}{12}$ 10. $\frac{3}{15} - \frac{1}{15}$ 11. $\frac{6}{18} - \frac{4}{18}$

12. $\frac{4}{4} - \frac{1}{4} - \frac{1}{4}$ 13. $\frac{5}{9} - \frac{2}{9}$ 14. $\frac{8}{100} - \frac{3}{100}$

15. $\frac{5}{6} - \frac{1}{6}$ 16. $\frac{5}{8} - \frac{2}{8} - \frac{3}{8}$ 17. $\frac{11}{15} - \frac{8}{15}$

18. $\frac{12}{20} - \frac{10}{20}$ 19. $\frac{9}{12} - \frac{8}{12}$ 20. $\frac{15}{16} - \frac{7}{16} - \frac{3}{16}$

21. $\frac{8}{10} - \frac{5}{10}$ 22. $\frac{7}{16} - \frac{4}{16}$ 23. $\frac{3}{8} - \frac{1}{8}$

24. $\frac{9}{20} - \frac{5}{20}$ 25. $\frac{20}{25} - \frac{10}{25}$ 26. $\frac{9}{16} - \frac{8}{16}$

27. $\frac{300}{1,000} - \frac{100}{1,000}$ 28. $\frac{9}{75} - \frac{4}{75}$ 29. $\frac{4}{9} - \frac{1}{9}$

*For another example, see Set I on page 197.

Step 1	Step 2	Step 3

Step 1

$\frac{7}{8}$ cup

$\frac{3}{8}$ cup	?

Write the difference of the fractions.

$\frac{7}{8} - \frac{3}{8}$

Step 2

Subtract the numerators. Write the difference over the common denominator.

$\frac{7}{8} - \frac{3}{8} = \frac{4}{8}$

Step 3

Write the difference in simplest form, if possible.

$\frac{4}{8} = \frac{1}{2}$

Lori needs another $\frac{1}{2}$ cup of milk to make pancakes.

Problem Solving

30. The Screaming Eagle roller coaster has $\frac{9}{12}$ of the cars full. What fraction of the cars are empty?

    A $\frac{9}{12}$ **C** $\frac{1}{3}$

    B $\frac{4}{12}$ **D** $\frac{1}{4}$

31. 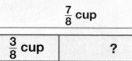 **Science** A giraffe's neck is approximately $\frac{1}{3}$ of its height. What fraction of the giraffe's height is not the neck?

    F 30 **H** $\frac{1}{2}$

    G $\frac{2}{3}$ **I** $\frac{1}{3}$

32. There are 20 colored marbles in a bag: $\frac{10}{20}$ of the marbles are green, $\frac{3}{20}$ yellow, and $\frac{7}{20}$ blue. Emmanuel has already picked $\frac{2}{20}$ of the marbles. What fraction of marbles are left in the bag?

33. **Writing to Explain** Chris mowed $\frac{1}{4}$ of the yard in the morning and $\frac{2}{4}$ before football practice. How much of the yard does Chris have left to mow that night? Explain how you found your answer.

34. If $\frac{17}{50}$ of the children on a spinning swing ride are girls, what fraction of the children on the ride are boys?

35. Micah is thinking of a 2-digit number. It is a multiple of 6 and 12. It is a factor of 108. The sum of its digits is 9. What number is Micah thinking of?

36. The totem shown at the right is divided into equal parts that represent different animals. How much more of the totem is devoted to bears than to whales? Write your answer as a fraction.

Critical THINKING

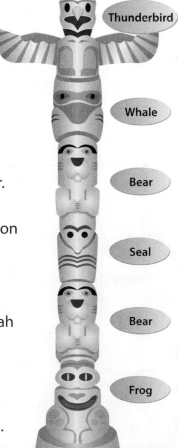

Thunderbird

Whale

Bear

Seal

Bear

Frog

MA.5.A.2.1 Represent addition and subtraction of decimals and fractions with like and unlike denominators using models, place value or properties.

Adding and Subtracting on the Number Line

How do you use a number line to solve fraction problems?

Mark starts to ride his bike to Juan's house.

After $\frac{3}{10}$ mile, he gets a flat tire and must walk $\frac{6}{10}$ mile.

What is the distance from Mark's house to Juan's house?

Choose an Operation Add to find the total distance.

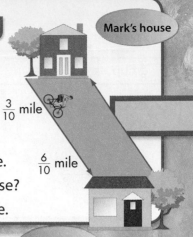

Mark's house

$\frac{3}{10}$ mile

$\frac{6}{10}$ mile

Juan's house

Another Example How do you subtract fractions on a number line?

A board is $\frac{11}{12}$ foot in length. Then $\frac{5}{12}$ foot is cut from the board. How long is the remaining board?

Step 1

Draw a number line for twelfths.

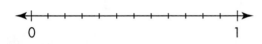

0   1

Step 2

Start at $\frac{11}{12}$. Move 5 spaces to the left to show subtracting $\frac{5}{12}$.

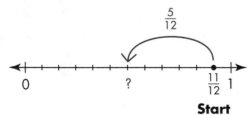

$\frac{5}{12}$

0   ? $\frac{11}{12}$ 1

Start

Step 3

The ending point is $\frac{6}{12}$ or $\frac{1}{2}$. The equation shown on the number line is $\frac{11}{12} - \frac{5}{12} = \frac{1}{2}$.

The remaining board is $\frac{1}{2}$ foot long.

Explain It

1. Explain how you can find $\frac{5}{12} - \frac{1}{12}$ on the number line above.

What You Show

Draw a number line for tenths. Start at 0. Move 3 spaces to show adding $\frac{3}{10}$. Then move 6 more spaces to show adding $\frac{6}{10}$.

Think What fraction names the ending point on the number line?

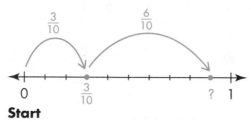

The equation shown on the number line is $\frac{3}{10} + \frac{6}{10} = \frac{9}{10}$.

What You Write

Find $\frac{3}{10} + \frac{6}{10}$.

Add the numerators.

$$\frac{3}{10} + \frac{6}{10} = \frac{9}{10}$$

The distance from Mark's house to Juan's house is $\frac{9}{10}$ mile.

Guided Practice*

Do you know HOW?

For **1** and **2**, write the equation shown on the number line. Write your answer. Simplify, if possible.

1.

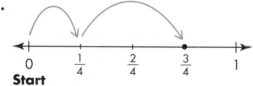

2.

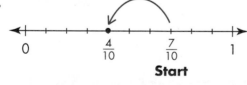

Do you UNDERSTAND?

3. Writing to Explain In the example above, how is the denominator illustrated on the number line? The numerator?

4. In the example above, if the distance between the houses were $\frac{4}{12}$ of a mile, how far would Mark have to go if he wanted to walk from his house to Juan's and then back home?

5. Draw a number line to represent $\frac{3}{12} + \frac{5}{12}$. Write the sum in simplest form.

Independent Practice

In **6** through **9** write the equation shown by each number line. Write your answer. Simplify, if possible.

Tip *Arrows to the right show addition. Arrows to the left show subtraction.*

6.

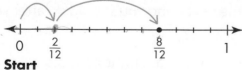

7.

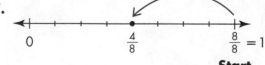

8.

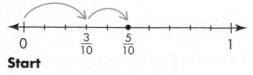

9.

For another example, see Set J on page 197.

Lesson 7-10   187

Independent Practice

For **10** through **15**, find each answer and simplify, if possible.
Remember that you can draw or use a number line.

10. $\frac{3}{8} + \frac{4}{8}$

11. $\frac{7}{10} - \frac{3}{10}$

12. $\frac{1}{12} + \frac{3}{12}$

13. $\frac{1}{4} + \frac{1}{4} + \frac{1}{4}$

14. $\frac{9}{20} - \frac{2}{20} + \frac{5}{20}$

15. $\frac{4}{16} + \frac{8}{16} - \frac{2}{16}$

Problem Solving

16. Algebra Find the missing numerator in each equation.

a $\frac{\blacksquare}{5} + \frac{2}{5} = \frac{4}{5}$

b $\frac{8}{10} - \frac{\blacksquare}{10} = \frac{3}{10}$

c $\frac{3}{12} + \frac{\blacksquare}{12} = \frac{11}{12}$

17. Luis filled his gallon fish tank before vacation. When he came back, only $\frac{5}{8}$ of the water remained. How much water evaporated? Use a number line to show how you found your answer.

18. A box of fruit contains 6 peaches, 5 bananas, 13 strawberries, and 3 plums. What fraction of the fruit in the box is either peaches or plums?

A $\frac{9}{27}$

B $\frac{9}{26}$

C $\frac{9}{21}$

D $\frac{9}{18}$

19. Rodolfo and Aarron are having a turtle race. Rodolfo's turtle reached the finish line, while Aarron's turtle crawled $\frac{4}{7}$ of the way, and then stopped for a nap. Show the turtles' finishing positions on a number line. How much farther did Aarron's turtle have to go to finish? Be sure to label your answer.

20. Estimation Ethan started his hike at the trailhead, has reached the picnic area, and is headed toward the lookout tower. According to the map, how much farther does Ethan have to hike? Estimate the distance.

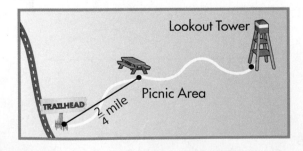

21. Number Sense If you are asked to find $6{,}427 \div 52$, how do you know the quotient is greater than 100 before you actually divide?

Critical THINKING

22. **Think About the Process** You want to show $\frac{7}{8} - \frac{2}{8} = \frac{5}{8}$ on a number line. What is the next thing you should do after you locate $\frac{7}{8}$?

F Move to the right 2 spaces.

G Move to the left 2 spaces.

H Mark the ending point $\frac{5}{8}$.

I Locate $\frac{2}{8}$ on the line.

Algebra Connections

Fractions and Equations

Remember that an equation uses an equal sign to show that two expressions have the same value.

$\frac{1}{3} + \frac{1}{3} = \frac{2}{3}$

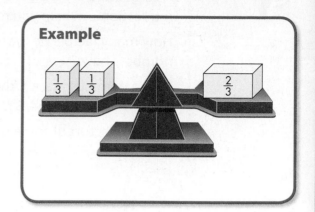

Example

In **1** through **12**, complete each equation by filling in the missing value(s). Check your answers by making sure the expressions in the equations are equal to each other.

1. $\frac{3}{8} + \frac{\blacksquare}{\blacksquare} = \frac{5}{8}$

2. $\frac{\blacksquare}{\blacksquare} - \frac{1}{15} = \frac{1}{15}$

3. $\frac{9}{\blacksquare} + \frac{4}{\blacksquare} = \frac{13}{18}$

4. $\frac{8}{10} - \frac{3}{\blacksquare} = \frac{5}{\blacksquare}$

5. $\frac{\blacksquare}{4} + \frac{\blacksquare}{4} = \frac{3}{4}$

6. $\frac{5}{6} - \frac{\blacksquare}{\blacksquare} = \frac{2}{6}$

7. $\frac{\blacksquare}{\blacksquare} - \frac{7}{12} = \frac{3}{12}$

8. $\frac{5}{16} + \frac{\blacksquare}{\blacksquare} = \frac{11}{16}$

9. $\frac{1}{2} - \frac{\blacksquare}{\blacksquare} = 0$

10. $\frac{4}{9} + \frac{\blacksquare}{\blacksquare} = \frac{7}{9}$

11. $\frac{1}{4} + \frac{\blacksquare}{\blacksquare} + \frac{1}{4} = \frac{3}{4}$

12. $\frac{8}{10} - \frac{\blacksquare}{\blacksquare} - \frac{1}{10} = \frac{6}{10}$

. . . .

For **13** through **18**, use the number line below to write and solve each equation. Simplify, if possible. The distance between the labels that are next to each other represent twelfths.

```
0  A  B  C  D  E  F  G  H  I  J  K  1
```

Example: $B + B = \frac{2}{12} + \frac{2}{12} = \frac{4}{12} = \frac{1}{3}$

13. $A + A = \blacksquare$

14. $K - A = \blacksquare$

15. $B + D = \blacksquare$

16. $F - B = \blacksquare$

17. $H + A = \blacksquare$

18. $I - C = \blacksquare$

19. Write a word problem using one of the equations in **13** through **18**.

MA.5.A.6.5 Solve non-routine problems using various strategies including "solving a simpler problem" and "guess, check, and revise."

Make and Test Conjectures

A conjecture is <u>a generalization that you think is true</u>. A question can help you make a conjecture.

How many factors do perfect square numbers have?

16 is a perfect square. Other perfect squares are: 4, 9, 25, 36, 49, 64, 81, 100.

Find the factors of some perfect squares.

Guided Practice*

Do you know HOW?

Test these conjectures. Explain whether they are correct or incorrect.

1. The difference of two odd numbers is always even.

2. All composite numbers are divisible by 2.

Do you UNDERSTAND?

3. How can you test or check a conjecture to see if it is correct?

4. **Write a Problem** Write a conjecture about the sum of three odd numbers. Then test your conjecture.

Independent Practice

In **5** through **9**, test these conjectures. Explain whether they are correct or incorrect.

5. Composite numbers have an even number of factors.

6. The product of two prime numbers is never an even number.

7. All multiples of 6 end in 0, 2, 4, 6, or 8.

8. The sum of any two perfect squares is an even number.

9. A GCF cannot always be found for a set of whole numbers.

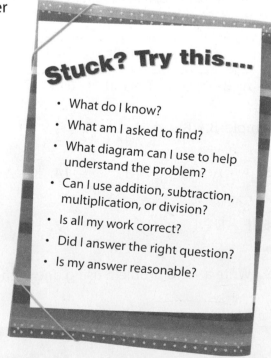

Stuck? Try this....

- What do I know?
- What am I asked to find?
- What diagram can I use to help understand the problem?
- Can I use addition, subtraction, multiplication, or division?
- Is all my work correct?
- Did I answer the right question?
- Is my answer reasonable?

Try several cases to help you make a conjecture.

Factors of 4: 1, 2, 4
3 factors

Factors of 9: 1, 3, 9
3 factors

Make a Conjecture
All perfect square numbers have exactly 3 factors.

Test Your Conjecture
Find the factors of other perfect squares.

16: 1, 2, 4, 8, 16
5 factors

25: 1, 5, 25
3 factors

36: 1, 2, 3, 4, 6, 9, 12, 18, 36
9 factors

The conjecture is not right. Use reasoning to make another conjecture.

Make a Conjecture
All perfect squares have an odd number of factors.

Test Your Conjecture
100: 1, 2, 4, 5, 10, 20, 25, 50, 100
9 factors

The conjecture works for the numbers tested.

In **10** through **13**, make a conjecture about each of the following. Then test your conjecture.

10. Adding two odd numbers.

11. Multiplying two odd numbers.

12. Adding an even number and an odd number.

13. Multiplying an even number and an odd number.

14. Writing to Explain How can you test the following conjecture: All fractions have an equivalent fraction.

15. Geometry A rectangular patio is 7 feet long and 5 feet wide. What is the area of the patio?

16. Algebra Hector deposits $153.32 into his savings account, raising the balance to $3,126.70. Use an algebraic equation to find how much was in Hector's account before the deposit.

17. Leela is making jumps on her skateboard at the skateboard park. One ramp is 2.75 feet tall. Another ramp is 3.5 feet taller. How tall, in feet, is the taller ramp?

18. Sekino is going skiing in the mountains. When he left his home, the temperature was 25° Celsius. When he arrived at the ski lodge, it was 5° Celsius. What was the difference in temperature?

19. Which fraction is equivalent to $\frac{3}{4}$?

A $\frac{8}{12}$ B $\frac{12}{16}$ C $\frac{16}{20}$ D $\frac{7}{8}$

1 The I-95 interstate highway crosses 16 states, the most of any interstate. What is the prime factorization of 16? (7-3)

   A. $8 \times 8 = 8^2$

   B. $4 \times 4 = 4^2$

   C. $2 \times 2 \times 2 = 2^3$

   D. $2 \times 2 \times 2 \times 2 = 2^4$

2 On Friday, $\frac{3}{12}$ of the students in class were absent. What fraction of the students attended class? (7-8)

   F. $\frac{12}{12}$

   G. $\frac{9}{12}$

   H. $\frac{8}{12}$

   I. $\frac{3}{12}$

3 Rick made a paper football that was $\frac{7}{8}$ inch long. Carly made one $\frac{5}{8}$ inch long. How many inches longer is Rick's paper football than Carly's? (7-9)

   A. $\frac{1}{4}$ inch

   B. $\frac{1}{2}$ inch

   C. $\frac{3}{4}$ inch

   D. $\frac{3}{2}$ inches

4 Which of the following numbers is prime? (7-2)

   F. 14

   G. 19

   H. 27

   I. 39

5 Which equation is represented on the number line below? (7-10)

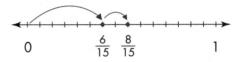

   A. $\frac{6}{15} - \frac{2}{15} = \frac{4}{15}$

   B. $\frac{6}{15} + \frac{2}{15} = \frac{8}{15}$

   C. $\frac{6}{6} + \frac{2}{2} = \frac{8}{8}$

   D. $\frac{15}{15} - \frac{8}{15} = \frac{7}{15}$

6 Manny used the computer for $\frac{2}{10}$ of his time before school, and $\frac{3}{10}$ of his time after school. Which of the following can be used to find how much of his time was spent on the computer? (7-7)

   F. Add $10 + 10$, and write the sum over $2 + 3$ to get $\frac{20}{5}$. Simplify $\frac{20}{5}$ to $\frac{4}{1}$.

   G. Add $2 + 3$, and write the sum over $10 + 10$ to get $\frac{5}{20}$. Simplify $\frac{5}{20}$ to $\frac{1}{5}$.

   H. Add $2 + 3$, and write the sum over 10 to get $\frac{5}{10}$. Simplify $\frac{5}{10}$ to $\frac{1}{2}$.

   I. Add $2 + 3$ and write the sum over $10 - 10$ to get $\frac{5}{0}$.

7 The table shows waterfowl that Hong counted at the lake. What fraction of the waterfowl listed are mallards? (7-5)

Waterfowl Type	Number
Canadian geese	5
Cranes	3
Mallards	12

A. $\frac{3}{5}$

B. $\frac{8}{12}$

C. $\frac{3}{2}$

D. $\frac{5}{3}$

8 Which of the following lists all the common factors of 45 and 60? (7-4)

F. 1, 3, 5

G. 1, 3, 5, 15

H. 1, 2, 3, 5

I. 1, 15

9 The average length of an adult Rough Green snake is $\frac{16}{18}$ yard. For an Eastern Garter snake it is $\frac{13}{18}$ yard. How much longer is a Rough Green snake than an Eastern Garter snake? (7-9)

A. $\frac{1}{9}$ yard

B. $\frac{1}{6}$ yard

C. $\frac{5}{18}$ yard

D. $\frac{1}{2}$ yard

10 Max is earning money to pay for his new trumpet. He earned $\frac{3}{10}$ of the money he needed last week and $\frac{1}{10}$ of the money this week. What fraction of the money has he earned? (7-6)

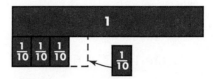

F. $\frac{4}{20}$

G. $\frac{1}{5}$

H. $\frac{2}{5}$

I. $\frac{3}{5}$

11 The numbers 1, 2, 4, 8, and 16 are all of the factors for which number? (7-1)

12 Aaron made a conjecture that any number ending in zero will be divisible by 4. Test his conjecture. Explain whether it is correct or incorrect. (7-11)

THINK
SOLVE
EXPLAIN

Set A, pages 162–164

List the factors of 12.

Factors are numbers you multiply to give a particular product. Two factors form a factor pair.

Shown below are factor pairs for 12.

$1 \times 12 = 12,$
$2 \times 6 = 12,$
$3 \times 4 = 12$

The factors of 12 are 1, 2, 3, 4, 6, and 12.

Remember that you can use divisibility rules to help find factors.

List the factors of each number.

1. 15   **2.** 20

3. 24   **4.** 36

5. 70   **6.** 80

7. 85   **8.** 98

Set B, pages 166–168

Is 6 a prime or composite number?

A prime number is a whole number that has exactly two factors, 1 and itself. A composite number is a number that is not prime; it has factors other than 1 and itself.

Factors of 6: 1 and 6, and 2 and 3

The number 6 is composite.

Remember that a prime number is a whole number greater than 1 that has exactly two factors, 1 and itself.

Classify each number as prime or composite.

1. 11   **2.** 15

3. 18   **4.** 19

5. 27   **6.** 33

Set C, pages 170–171

Use a factor tree to find the prime factorization of 56.

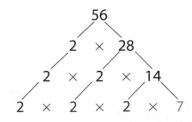

So, $56 = 2 \times 2 \times 2 \times 7$.

Using exponents, you can write the prime factorization of 56 as $2^3 \times 7$.

Remember to order the factors from least to greatest when you write the prime factorization of a number.

Find the prime factorization of each composite number. Use exponents when possible. If the number is prime, write *prime*.

1. 40   **2.** 32

3. 18   **4.** 17

5. 100   **6.** 60

Set D, pages 172–173

What is the greatest common factor of 10 and 35?

Common factors are factors shared by a group of numbers. The greatest common factor (GCF) is the greatest factor shared by a group of numbers.

List factors for 10 and 35.

10: 1, 2, 5, 10

35: 1, 5, 7, 35

Circle common factors.

10: 1, 2, 5, 10

35: 1, 5, 7, 35

Common factors of 10 and 35 are 1 and 5.
The GCF of 10 and 35 is 5.

Remember to use divisibility rules to help you find factors of a number.

Find the GCF for each pair of numbers.

1. 15, 45   **2.** 60, 80

3. 12, 14   **4.** 24, 56

5. 24, 36   **6.** 21, 30

7. 27, 45   **8.** 12, 18

9. 16, 32   **10.** 18, 27

11. Number Sense What is the greatest common factor of 25 and 75?

Set E, pages 174–176

Write $\frac{15}{18}$ in simplest form.

To express a fraction in simplest form, divide the numerator and denominator by the greatest common factor.

List factors of 15 and 18.

15: 1, 3, 5, 15

18: 1, 2, 3, 6, 9, 18

Circle common factors.

15: 1, 3, 5, 15

18: 1, 2, 3, 6, 9, 18

The GCF of 15 and 18 is 3.

Use the GCF to simplify the fraction.

$\frac{15 \div 3}{18 \div 3} = \frac{5}{6}$

Remember that the simplest form can also be found by dividing by common factors until the common factor is 1.

Write each fraction in simplest form.

1. $\frac{8}{12}$ **2.** $\frac{10}{18}$

3. $\frac{40}{50}$ **4.** $\frac{30}{75}$

5. $\frac{2}{16}$ **6.** $\frac{5}{15}$

7. $\frac{14}{20}$ **8.** $\frac{10}{25}$

9. $\frac{36}{100}$ **10.** $\frac{450}{1,000}$

11. Which fraction is NOT in simplest form?

A $\frac{3}{5}$ **C** $\frac{3}{9}$

B $\frac{3}{7}$ **D** $\frac{3}{11}$

Set F, pages 178–179

While Ricardo's family was bird watching, they spotted eight loons. There were five in the water, one in the air, and two walking on land. What fraction of the loons did they see in the water or on land?

Add the fraction of the total loons that were in the water to the fraction of the total loons that were on land. Use fraction strips.

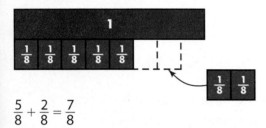

$$\frac{5}{8} + \frac{2}{8} = \frac{7}{8}$$

Remember that you can use fraction strips to model addition of fractions.

Add. Simplify if possible.

1. $\frac{2}{4} + \frac{2}{4}$

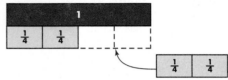

2. $\frac{3}{6} + \frac{2}{6}$

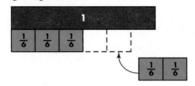

Set G, pages 180–181

Add $\frac{4}{15} + \frac{5}{15}$. Write in simplest form.

Step 1

Add the numerators; keep the denominator.
$$\frac{4}{15} + \frac{5}{15} = \frac{9}{15}$$

Step 2

Simplify the sum if possible.
$$\frac{9 \div 3}{15 \div 3} = \frac{3}{5}$$

Remember to add the numerators when denominators are the same.

Add. Simplify if possible.

1. $\frac{2}{5} + \frac{2}{5}$ 2. $\frac{10}{20} + \frac{5}{20}$

3. $\frac{3}{8} + \frac{4}{8}$ 4. $\frac{2}{15} + \frac{10}{15}$

Set H, pages 182–183

Use fraction strips to subtract $\frac{5}{8} - \frac{2}{8}$.

Use five $\frac{1}{8}$ strips to model $\frac{5}{8}$. Take two strips away.

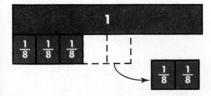

Three strips are left.

$$\frac{5}{8} - \frac{2}{8} = \frac{3}{8}$$

Remember that you can use fraction strips to model subtraction of fractions.

Subtract. Simplify if possible.

1. $\frac{3}{3} - \frac{1}{3}$

2. $\frac{3}{4} - \frac{2}{4}$

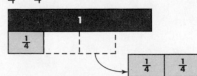

Set I, pages 184–185

Subtract $\frac{7}{8} - \frac{5}{8}$. Write in simplest form.

Step 1

Subtract the numerators; keep the denominator.

$\frac{7}{8} - \frac{5}{8} = \frac{2}{8}$

Step 2

Simplify the difference if possible.

$\frac{2 \div 2}{8 \div 2} = \frac{1}{4}$

Remember that you can subtract the numerators when the denominators are the same.

Subtract the fractions. Write in simplest form, if possible.

1. $\frac{7}{10} - \frac{1}{10}$ 2. $\frac{10}{15} - \frac{3}{15}$

3. $\frac{9}{16} - \frac{4}{16}$ 4. $\frac{11}{20} - \frac{4}{20}$

5. $\frac{4}{8} - \frac{2}{8}$ 6. $\frac{20}{24} - \frac{13}{24}$

Set J, pages 186–188

Find the sum or difference shown on the number line. Write in simplest form, if possible.

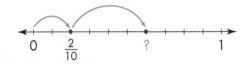

$\frac{2}{10} + \frac{4}{10} = \frac{6}{10} = \frac{3}{5}$

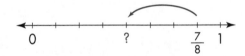

$\frac{7}{8} - \frac{3}{8} = \frac{4}{8} = \frac{1}{2}$

Remember when adding or subtracting fractions with like denominators on a number line, the denominator does not change.

Find the sum or difference shown on the number line. Write in simplest form, if possible.

1.

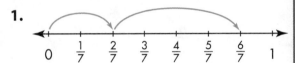

2.

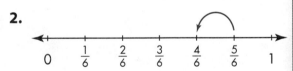

Set K, pages 190–191

A conjecture is a generalization that you think is true.

Make a Conjecture The product of two odd numbers is an odd number.

Test your conjecture.

$3 \times 3 = 9$ $5 \times 7 = 35$

$9 \times 9 = 81$ $11 \times 13 = 143$

The conjecture works for the numbers tested.

Remember to try several cases to test a conjecture. Explain whether these conjectures are correct or incorrect.

1. If a number is divisible by 8, it is also divisible by 2 and 4.

2. The difference of two odd numbers is always odd.

3. The product of two prime numbers is always composite.

Adding and Subtracting Fractions with Unlike Denominators

1 How long is the hiking trail around Mirror Lake in Yosemite National Park? You will find out in Lesson 8-4.

2 Coral reef formations near the coasts of Florida are very large. About what fraction of the ocean floor is covered by coral reefs? You will find out in Lesson 8-2.

3

How many chemical elements are named for women scientists? You will find out in Lesson 8-3.

4

Native Americans have made baskets, like the ones shown below, since the early 1900s. What is the length of each side of a triangle on a basket like this one? You will find out in Lesson 8-3.

Topic Essential Questions

- What does it mean to add and subtract fractions with unlike denominators?
- What is a standard procedure for adding and subtracting fractions with unlike denominators?

Vocabulary

Choose the best term from the box.

> • divisible   • simplest form
> • common factor
> • greatest common factor (GCF)

1. A number that is a factor of two or more numbers is a __?__.

2. The greatest number that is a factor of two or more numbers is the __?__.

3. A fraction in which the greatest common factor of the numerator and denominator is 1 is in __?__.

Finding Multiples

Write three multiples for each number.

4. 5   **5.** 7   **6.** 9

Simplest Form

Write each fraction in simplest form.

7. $\frac{9}{12}$ **8.** $\frac{10}{15}$ **9.** $\frac{10}{50}$

Adding Fractions

Add. Simplify, if possible.

10. $\frac{5}{10} + \frac{3}{10}$ **11.** $\frac{2}{9} + \frac{5}{9}$

12. $\frac{5}{12} + \frac{3}{12}$ **13.** $\frac{2}{5} + \frac{3}{5}$

14. Writing to Explain How do you add two fractions that have a common denominator?

MA.5.A.6.1 Identify and relate prime and composite numbers, factors and multiples within the context of fractions.

Common Multiples and Least Common Multiple

How do you find the least common multiple?

Loren is buying fish fillets and buns for the soccer team dinner. What is the smallest number of fish fillets and buns she can buy to have the same number of each?

Guided Practice*

Do you know HOW?

In **1** through **6**, find the LCM of each pair of numbers.

1. 2 and 4
   2: 2, 4, 6, 8, . . .
   4: 4, 8, 12, 16, . . .

2. 3 and 4
   3: 3, 6, 9, 12, 15, . . .
   4: 4, 8, 12, 16, . . .

3. 3 and 7

4. 8 and 15

5. 12 and 9

6. 6 and 18

Do you UNDERSTAND?

7. In the example above, why is 24 the LCM of 6 and 8?

8. How many packages of each does Loren need to buy to have 24 fish fillets and 24 buns?

Independent Practice

Leveled Practice In **9** through **27**, find the LCM of each pair of numbers.

9. 2 and 4
   2: 2, 4, . . .
   4: 4, 8, . . .

10. 2 and 3
   2: 2, 4, 6, 8, . . .
   3: 3, 6, 9, 12, . . .

11. 5 and 6
   5: 5, 10, 15, 20, 25, 30, 35, 40, . . .
   6: 6, 12, 18, 24, 30, 36, 42, . . .

12. 3 and 5

13. 6 and 8

14. 4 and 5

15. 3 and 10

16. 4 and 9

17. 8 and 20

18. 6 and 9

19. 10 and 12

20. 8 and 12

21. 4 and 6

22. 8 and 16

23. 12 and 16

24. 8 and 9

25. 4 and 12

26. 5 and 10

27. 14 and 21

Animated Glossary
www.pearsonsuccessnet.com

*For another example, see Set A on page 218.

Find the common multiples of 6 and 8.

Remember that a multiple of a number is a product of a given whole number and another whole number.

A **common multiple** is <u>a number that is a multiple of two or more numbers.</u>

List the multiples of 6 and 8.

6: 6, 12, 18, 24, 30, 36, 42, 48, 54, …

8: 8, 16, 24, 32, 40, 48, 56, …

Two common multiples of 6 and 8 are 24 and 48.

Find the least common multiple of 6 and 8.

A **least common multiple (LCM)** is <u>the least number that is a multiple of both numbers.</u>

Both 24 and 48 are common multiples of 6 and 8. So, the LCM of 6 and 8 is 24.

Loren will need to buy 24 fish fillets and 24 buns.

Problem Solving

28. Pecans are sold in 6-ounce cans, almonds in 9-ounce cans, and peanuts in 12-ounce cans. What is the least number of ounces you can buy to have equal amounts of pecans, almonds, and peanuts?

29. Writing to Explain Can you always find the LCM for two numbers by multiplying them together? Why or why not?

Critical THINKING

30. Number Sense The batting averages of three players are .261, .267, .264. Write the averages in order from least to greatest. Use <.

31. A cell phone call costs $0.07 per minute for the first 25 minutes and $0.10 per minute for each additional minute. How much would a 47-minute call cost?

32. a Peter is distributing pamphlets about dog care and samples of dog biscuits. The dog biscuits come in packages of 12 and the pamphlets are in packages of 20. What is the smallest number of samples and pamphlets he needs to distribute without having any left over?

b How many packages of dog biscuits and pamphlets will Peter need?

33. Katie bought dinner at 5 different restaurants. Each dinner cost between $12 and $24. What is a reasonable total cost for all 5 dinners?

A Less than $60

B More than $150

C Between $24 and $60

D Between $60 and $120

34. Julie drank $\frac{2}{3}$ cup of cranberry juice. Her brother said she drank $\frac{4}{6}$ cup of juice. Is her brother correct? Explain your answer.

THINK SOLVE EXPLAIN

35. A factory whistle blows every 30 minutes. The clock tower chimes every 15 minutes. If they both sounded at 1:00 P.M., at what time will they both sound at the same time again?

MA.5.A.2.1 Represent addition and subtraction of decimals and fractions with like and unlike denominators using models, place value or properties.

Finding Common Denominators

How can you find a common denominator for fractions with unlike denominators?

Tyrone divided a rectangle into thirds. Sally divided a rectangle of the same size into fourths. How could you divide a rectangle of the same size so that you see both thirds and fourths?

Thirds   **Fourths**

Another Example How can you use multiples to find a common denominator?

Find a common denominator for $\frac{7}{12}$ and $\frac{5}{6}$. Then rename each fraction.

One Way

Multiply the denominators: $12 \times 6 = 72$. Rename each fraction to have a common denominator of 72.

$$\frac{7}{12} = \frac{7 \times 6}{12 \times 6} = \frac{42}{72} \qquad \frac{5}{6} = \frac{5 \times 12}{6 \times 12} = \frac{60}{72}$$

So, $\frac{42}{72}$ and $\frac{60}{72}$.

Another Way

Check to see if one denominator is a multiple of the other: 12 is a multiple of 6.

$$\frac{5}{6} = \frac{5 \times 2}{6 \times 2} = \frac{10}{12}$$

So, $\frac{7}{12}$ and $\frac{10}{12}$.

Guided Practice*

Do you know HOW?

In **1** through **4**, find a common denominator for each pair of fractions.

1. $\frac{2}{3}$ and $\frac{3}{4}$ **2.** $\frac{1}{6}$ and $\frac{1}{3}$

3. $\frac{3}{8}$ and $\frac{2}{3}$ **4.** $\frac{3}{7}$ and $\frac{1}{2}$

In **5** and **6**, find a common denominator for each pair of fractions. Then rename each fraction.

5. $\frac{1}{5}$ and $\frac{3}{10}$ **6.** $\frac{1}{2}$ and $\frac{2}{5}$

Do you UNDERSTAND?

7. How many twelfths are in each $\frac{1}{3}$ section of Tyrone's rectangle, and how many twelfths are in each $\frac{1}{4}$ section of Sally's rectangle?

8. Writing to Explain Is the product of two denominators always a common denominator? Give an example in your explanation.

Animated Glossary
www.pearsonsuccessnet.com

The rectangle below was divided into thirds and fourths.

Twelfths

The rectangle is divided into 12 equal parts. Each part is $\frac{1}{12}$.

The fractions $\frac{1}{3}$ and $\frac{1}{4}$ can be renamed.

$$\frac{1}{3} = \frac{4}{12} \qquad \frac{1}{4} = \frac{3}{12}$$

Fractions that have the same denominator, such as $\frac{4}{12}$ and $\frac{3}{12}$, are said to have a **common denominator**.

Independent Practice

For **9** through **12**, find a common denominator for each pair of fractions.

9. $\frac{4}{5}$ and $\frac{3}{8}$ **10.** $\frac{1}{2}$ and $\frac{2}{3}$ **11.** $\frac{4}{5}$ and $\frac{3}{20}$ **12.** $\frac{3}{5}$ and $\frac{1}{2}$

For **13** through **16**, find a common denominator for each pair of fractions. Then rename each fraction.

13. $\frac{2}{5}$ and $\frac{1}{6}$ **14.** $\frac{1}{3}$ and $\frac{4}{5}$ **15.** $\frac{5}{8}$ and $\frac{3}{4}$ **16.** $\frac{3}{10}$ and $\frac{3}{8}$

Problem Solving

17. 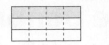 **Science** Coral reefs cover less than $\frac{1}{500}$ of the ocean floor, but they contain more than $\frac{1}{4}$ of all marine life. Which is a common denominator for $\frac{1}{500}$ and $\frac{1}{4}$?

    A 2   **B** 100   **C** 125   **D** 500

18. Marlee is taking a class to improve her reading. She began reading a book on Monday and completed 3 pages. On Tuesday she read 6 pages, on Wednesday 12 pages. If this pattern continues, how many pages will Marlee read on Friday?

For **19** and **20**, use the table at the right.

19. Number Sense Mr. Paulsen rides a motorcycle. It will take $2\frac{1}{2}$ gallons of gasoline to fill his tank. He has $10 to spend on gasoline. Does he have enough money to fill his tank? Explain.

Critical THINKING

Gasoline Prices	
Grade	**Price (per gallon)**
Regular	$4.199
Premium	$4.409
Diesel	$5.019

20. What is the price of premium gasoline rounded to the nearest dollar? Rounded to the nearest dime? Rounded to the nearest penny?

MA.5.A.2.1 Represent addition and subtraction of decimals and fractions with like and unlike denominators using models, place value or properties.
Also MA.5.A.2.2

Adding Fractions with Unlike Denominators

How can you add fractions with unlike denominators?

Alex rode his scooter from his house to the park. Later, he rode from the park to baseball practice. How far did Alex ride?

Choose an Operation Add to find the total distance Alex rode his scooter.

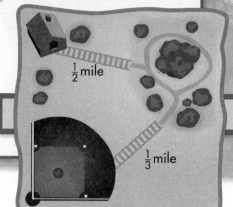

$\frac{1}{2}$ mile

$\frac{1}{3}$ mile

Guided Practice*

Do you know HOW?

In **1** through **4**, find each sum. Simplify, if necessary.

1.
$$\frac{1}{2} = \frac{9}{18}$$
$$+ \frac{2}{9} = \frac{4}{18}$$
_____

2.
$$\frac{2}{6} = \frac{8}{24}$$
$$+ \frac{3}{8} = \frac{9}{24}$$
_____

3. $\frac{1}{4} + \frac{7}{10}$

4. $\frac{5}{12} + \frac{1}{8}$

Do you UNDERSTAND?

5. **Writing to Explain** In the example above, would you get the same sum if you used 12 as the common denominator?

6. In the example above, if the park were $\frac{2}{5}$ mile from baseball practice, how far would Alex ride his scooter?

Independent Practice

Leveled Practice In **7** through **22**, find each sum. Simplify, if necessary.

7.
$$\frac{1}{9} = \frac{\ }{18}$$
$$+ \frac{5}{6} = \frac{\ }{18}$$
_____

8.
$$\frac{1}{12} = \frac{\ }{12}$$
$$+ \frac{2}{3} = \frac{\ }{12}$$
_____

9.
$$\frac{1}{3} = \frac{\ }{15}$$
$$+ \frac{1}{5} = \frac{\ }{15}$$
_____

10.
$$\frac{1}{8} = \frac{\ }{56}$$
$$+ \frac{3}{7} = \frac{\ }{56}$$
_____

11. $\frac{2}{9} + \frac{2}{3}$

12. $\frac{5}{8} + \frac{1}{6}$

13. $\frac{3}{20} + \frac{2}{5}$

14. $\frac{1}{6} + \frac{3}{10}$

15. $\frac{7}{8} + \frac{1}{12}$

16. $\frac{11}{16} + \frac{1}{4}$

17. $\frac{5}{16} + \frac{3}{8}$

18. $\frac{7}{12} + \frac{3}{16}$

19. $\frac{1}{2} + \frac{1}{8} + \frac{1}{8}$

20. $\frac{1}{9} + \frac{1}{6} + \frac{4}{9}$

21. $\frac{1}{4} + \frac{1}{3} + \frac{1}{4}$

22. $\frac{1}{5} + \frac{1}{4} + \frac{2}{5}$

*For another example, see Set C on page 218.

Step 1

Change the fractions to equivalent fractions with a common, or like, denominator.

The least common denominator (LCD) of two fractions is the least common multiple of the denominators.

Multiples of 2: 2, 4, 6, 8, 10, 12, . . .

Multiples of 3: 3, 6, 9, 12, . . .

The LCM is 6, so the LCD is 6.

Step 2

Write the equivalent fractions.

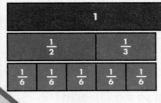

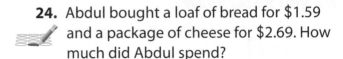

$$\overset{\times 3}{\frac{1}{2}} = \frac{3}{6} \qquad \overset{\times 2}{\frac{1}{3}} = \frac{2}{6}$$

Step 3

Add. Simplify if necessary.

$$\frac{1}{2} = \frac{3}{6}$$
$$+ \frac{1}{3} = \frac{2}{6}$$
$$\overline{\frac{5}{6}}$$

Alex rode his scooter $\frac{5}{6}$ mile.

Problem Solving

23. Cindy added $\frac{5}{8}$ cup of water to $\frac{1}{4}$ cup of juice concentrate. How much juice did Cindy make?

24. Abdul bought a loaf of bread for $1.59 and a package of cheese for $2.69. How much did Abdul spend?

25. Mr. Perez is building a fence. He wants to bolt together 2 boards. One is $\frac{3}{4}$ inch thick and the other is $\frac{1}{8}$ inch thick. What will be the total thickness of the 2 boards?

26. **Science** About $\frac{1}{10}$ of the bones in your body are in your skull. Your hands have about $\frac{1}{4}$ of the bones in your body. What fraction of the bones in your body are in your hands and skull?

27. **Social Studies** Native Americans made baskets like this in the 1900s. If two sides of the triangle shown on the basket each measure $\frac{1}{4}$ inch, and the third side measures $\frac{3}{8}$ inch, what is the perimeter of the triangle?

28. A girls' club sold hats to raise money. **Critical THINKING** They ordered 500 hats that cost $5.15 each. They sold the hats for $18.50 each. All the hats were sold. Which expression shows how to find the amount of money the club made after expenses?

A $500 \times (18.50 + 5.15)$

B $(500 \times 18.50) + (500 \times 5.15)$

C $(500 \times 5.15) - (500 \times 18.50)$

D $500 \times (18.50 - 5.15)$

29. **Science** In all, 36 chemical elements were named after people or places. Of these, 2 were named for women scientists, and 25 were named for places. What fraction of these 36 elements were named for women and places? Write your answer in simplest form.

Lesson
8-4

MA.5.A.2.1 Represent
addition and subtraction of
decimals and fractions with
like and unlike denominators
using models, place value or
properties.
Also MA.5.A.2.2

Subtracting Fractions with Unlike Denominators

How can you subtract fractions with unlike denominators?

Linda used $\frac{1}{4}$ yard of the fabric she bought for a sewing project. How much fabric did she have left?

Choose an Operation Subtract to find how much fabric was left.

$\frac{2}{3}$ yard

Guided Practice*

Do you know HOW?

In **1** through **4**, find each difference. Simplify, if necessary.

1.
$$\frac{5}{6} = \frac{5}{6}$$
$$-\frac{1}{2} = \frac{3}{6}$$

2.
$$\frac{4}{7} = \frac{12}{21}$$
$$-\frac{1}{3} = \frac{7}{21}$$

3. $\frac{1}{2} - \frac{3}{10}$

4. $\frac{7}{8} - \frac{1}{3}$

Do you UNDERSTAND?

5. In the example above, is it possible to use a common denominator greater than 12 and get the correct answer? Why or why not?

6. In the example above, if Linda had started with one yard of fabric and used $\frac{5}{8}$ of a yard, how much fabric would be left?

Independent Practice

Leveled Practice In **7** through **24**, find each difference. Simplify, if necessary.

7.
$$\frac{1}{3} = \frac{\blacksquare}{6}$$
$$-\frac{1}{6} = \frac{\blacksquare}{6}$$

8.
$$\frac{2}{3} = \frac{\blacksquare}{12}$$
$$-\frac{5}{12} = \frac{\blacksquare}{12}$$

9.
$$\frac{3}{5} = \frac{\blacksquare}{15}$$
$$-\frac{1}{3} = \frac{\blacksquare}{15}$$

10.
$$\frac{2}{9} = \frac{\blacksquare}{72}$$
$$-\frac{1}{8} = \frac{\blacksquare}{72}$$

11.
$$\frac{1}{4} = \frac{\blacksquare}{8}$$
$$-\frac{1}{8} = \frac{\blacksquare}{8}$$

12.
$$\frac{2}{3} = \frac{\blacksquare}{6}$$
$$-\frac{1}{2} = \frac{\blacksquare}{6}$$

13.
$$\frac{3}{4} = \frac{\blacksquare}{8}$$
$$-\frac{3}{8} = \frac{\blacksquare}{8}$$

14.
$$\frac{5}{6} = \frac{\blacksquare}{6}$$
$$-\frac{1}{3} = \frac{\blacksquare}{6}$$

15. $\frac{5}{8} - \frac{1}{4}$

16. $\frac{9}{16} - \frac{3}{8}$

17. $\frac{1}{5} - \frac{1}{7}$

18. $\frac{7}{10} - \frac{2}{4}$

19. $\frac{5}{6} - \frac{3}{4}$

20. $\frac{2}{3} - \frac{5}{9}$

21. $\frac{4}{5} - \frac{1}{4}$

22. $\frac{5}{8} - \frac{7}{12}$

23. $\frac{6}{7} - \frac{1}{2}$

24. $\frac{5}{12} - \frac{4}{16}$

For another example, see Set C on page 218.

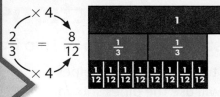

Step 1

Change the fractions to equivalent fractions with a common denominator.

Find the LCM of the denominators

Multiples of 3:
3, 6, 9, 12, . . .

Multiples of 4:
4, 8, 12, . . .

The LCM is 12, so the LCD is 12.

Step 2

Write the equivalent fractions.

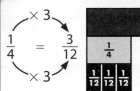

$$\frac{2}{3} = \frac{8}{12}$$

$$\frac{1}{4} = \frac{3}{12}$$

Step 3

Subtract. Simplify if necessary.

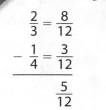

$$\frac{2}{3} = \frac{8}{12}$$
$$-\frac{1}{4} = \frac{3}{12}$$
$$\overline{\frac{5}{12}}$$

Linda has $\frac{5}{12}$ yard of fabric left.

Problem Solving

25. Write a number sentence to name the difference between Point *A* and Point *B*.

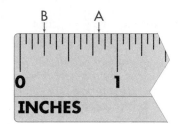

26. Geometry Find the perimeter of the figure below.

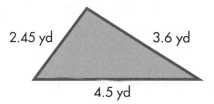

2.45 yd   3.6 yd

4.5 yd

27. Estimation Roy earned $72.50, $59, and $41.75 in tips when waiting tables last weekend. About how much did Roy earn in tips?

28. Mariko's social studies class lasts $\frac{5}{6}$ of an hour. Only $\frac{3}{12}$ of an hour has gone by. What fraction of an hour remains of Mariko's social studies class?

29. Writing to Explain Why do fractions need to have a common denominator before you add or subtract them?

30. Number Sense What is the greatest common multiple of 3 and 4?

Critical THINKING

The hiking trail around Mirror Lake in Yosemite National Park is 5 miles long. Use the table for **31** and **32**.

31. What fraction more of the trail did Jon hike than Andrea?

32. What fraction more of the trail did Callie hike than Jon?

Hiker	Fraction of Trail Hiked
Andrea	$\frac{2}{5}$
Jon	$\frac{1}{2}$
Callie	$\frac{4}{5}$

Data

MA5.A.2.3 Make reasonable estimates of fraction and decimal sums and differences, and use techniques for rounding.

Estimating Sums and Differences of Fractions

How can you estimate the sum of two fractions?

Mr. Frish is welding together 2 copper pipes to repair a leak. He will use the pipes shown. About how long will the welded pipes be?

Choose an Operation Add to find the sum. Estimate $\frac{1}{6} + \frac{5}{12}$ to find about how long the combined pipes will be.

$\frac{5}{12}$ foot long

$\frac{1}{6}$ foot long

Another Example How can you estimate the difference of two fractions?

Estimate $\frac{15}{16} - \frac{1}{8}$.

Step 1

Replace each fraction with the nearest half or whole. A number line can make it easy to decide if each fraction is closest to 0, $\frac{1}{2}$, or 1.

$\frac{15}{16}$ is between $\frac{1}{2}$ and 1, but is closer to 1.

$\frac{1}{8}$ is between 0 and $\frac{1}{2}$, but is closer to 0.

Step 2

Subtract to find the estimate.

A good estimate of $\frac{15}{16} - \frac{1}{8}$ is $1 - 0$, or 1.

 You can use the symbol $\approx$ to show an estimate. The symbol $\approx$ means "approximately equal to."

So, $\frac{15}{16} - \frac{1}{8} \approx 1$.

Guided Practice*

Do you know HOW?

For **1** through **3**, use a number line to tell if each fraction is closest to 0, $\frac{1}{2}$, or 1.

1. $\frac{9}{10}$ **2.** $\frac{2}{5}$ **3.** $\frac{1}{8}$

For **4** through **7**, estimate each sum or difference by replacing each fraction with 0, $\frac{1}{2}$, or 1.

4. $\frac{9}{10} + \frac{5}{6}$ **5.** $\frac{11}{12} - \frac{5}{6}$

6. $\frac{2}{3} - \frac{1}{8}$ **7.** $\frac{5}{9} + \frac{5}{6}$

Do you UNDERSTAND?

8. Writing to Explain In the problem above, would you get the same estimate if Mr. Frish's pipes measured $\frac{2}{6}$ foot and $\frac{7}{12}$ foot?

9. Number Sense Nalini says that if the denominator is more than twice the numerator, the fraction can always be replaced with 0. Is she correct? Give an example in your explanation.

Replace each fraction with the nearest half or whole. A number line can make it easy to decide if each fraction is closest to 0, $\frac{1}{2}$, or 1.

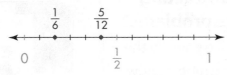

$\frac{1}{6}$ is between 0 and $\frac{1}{2}$, but is closer to 0. Replace $\frac{1}{6}$ with 0.

$\frac{5}{12}$ is also between 0 and $\frac{1}{2}$, but is closer to $\frac{1}{2}$. Replace $\frac{5}{12}$ with $\frac{1}{2}$.

Add to find the estimate.

A good estimate of $\frac{1}{6} + \frac{5}{12}$ is $0 + \frac{1}{2}$, or $\frac{1}{2}$.

So the welded pipes will be about $\frac{1}{2}$ foot long.

Since both addends are less than $\frac{1}{2}$, it is reasonable that the sum is less than 1.

Independent Practice

For **10** through **14**, use a number line to tell if each fraction is closest to 0, $\frac{1}{2}$, or 1.

10. $\frac{11}{12}$ **11.** $\frac{2}{5}$ **12.** $\frac{7}{12}$ **13.** $\frac{2}{9}$ **14.** $\frac{2}{7}$

For **15** through **18**, estimate each sum or difference by replacing each fraction with 0, $\frac{1}{2}$, or 1. You may draw or use number lines to help.

15. $\frac{11}{18} - \frac{2}{9}$ **16.** $\frac{1}{16} + \frac{2}{15}$ **17.** $\frac{7}{10} + \frac{1}{3}$ **18.** $\frac{19}{20} - \frac{9}{16}$

Problem Solving

19. Estimation The Annual Mug Race is the longest river sailboat race in the world. The event is run along the St. Johns River, which is 310 miles long. About how many times as long as the race is the river?

The Annual Mug Race is 42 miles long.

20. Katie made a bag of trail mix with $\frac{1}{2}$ cup of raisins, $\frac{3}{5}$ cup of banana chips, and $\frac{3}{8}$ cup of peanuts. About how much trail mix did Katie make?

21. Kim has a fever. Her temperature is 100.5°F. Normal body temperature is 98.6°F. How much above the normal temperature is Kim's fever?

22. Which fraction below is NOT equal to $\frac{1}{2}$?

   A $\frac{8}{16}$ **C** $\frac{25}{50}$

   B $\frac{9}{18}$ **D** $\frac{8}{15}$

23. Number Sense How would you replace $\frac{27}{50}$ with the nearest half or whole without using a number line? Explain.

Critical THINKING

MA.5.A.2.2 Add and subtract fractions and decimals fluently and verify the reasonableness of results, including in problem situations.

More Adding and Subtracting Fractions

How can adding and subtracting fractions help you solve problems?

Kayla had $\frac{9}{10}$ gallon of paint. She painted the ceilings in her bedroom and bathroom. How much paint does she have left after painting the two ceilings?

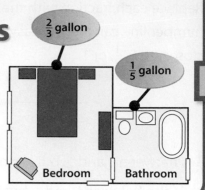

$\frac{2}{3}$ gallon

$\frac{1}{5}$ gallon

Bedroom   Bathroom

Guided Practice*

Do you know HOW?

For **1** through **6**, find the sum or difference. Simplify, if possible.

1. $\frac{1}{15}$
$+\ \frac{1}{6}$

2. $\frac{7}{16}$
$-\ \frac{1}{4}$

3. $\frac{25}{50} - \frac{2}{4}$

4. $\frac{2}{5} + \left(\frac{7}{10} - \frac{4}{10}\right)$

5. $\frac{7}{8} - \frac{3}{6}$

6. $\frac{7}{8} + \left(\frac{4}{8} - \frac{2}{4}\right)$

Do you UNDERSTAND?

7. Choose an Operation In the example at the top, how much more paint did Kayla use to paint the bedroom ceiling than the bathroom ceiling?

8. Writing to Explain For Exercise 5, Kevin estimated the difference of $\frac{7}{8} - \frac{3}{6}$ to be 0. Is his estimate reasonable? Explain.

Independent Practice

For **9** through **24**, find the sum or difference. Simplify, if possible.

9. $\frac{4}{50}$
$+\ \frac{3}{5}$

10. $\frac{2}{3}$
$-\ \frac{7}{12}$

11. $\frac{9}{10}$
$+\ \frac{2}{100}$

12. $\frac{4}{9}$
$+\ \frac{1}{4}$

13. $\frac{13}{15} - \frac{1}{3}$

14. $\frac{7}{16} + \frac{3}{8}$

15. $\frac{5}{7} - \frac{1}{2}$

16. $\frac{5}{6} - \frac{5}{18}$

17. $\frac{1}{12} + \frac{7}{8}$

18. $\frac{2}{75} + \frac{13}{15}$

19. $\frac{8}{25} - \frac{9}{75}$

20. $\frac{3}{50} + \frac{7}{10}$

21. $\left(\frac{7}{8} + \frac{1}{12}\right) - \frac{1}{2}$

22. $\left(\frac{11}{18} - \frac{4}{9}\right) + \frac{1}{6}$

23. $\left(\frac{9}{16} + \frac{1}{4}\right) - \frac{5}{8}$

24. $\frac{2}{3} + \left(\frac{5}{12} - \frac{1}{6}\right)$

For another example, see Set E on page 219.

Add to find out how much paint Kayla used for the two ceilings.

To add, write each fraction using the LCD, 15, as the denominator.

$$\frac{2}{3} = \frac{10}{15}$$
$$+ \frac{1}{5} = \frac{3}{15}$$
$$\overline{\qquad \frac{13}{15}}$$

Kayla used $\frac{13}{15}$ gallon of paint.

Subtract the amount of paint Kayla used from the amount she started with.

To subtract, write each fraction using the LCD, 30, as the denominator.

$$\frac{9}{10} = \frac{27}{30}$$
$$- \frac{13}{15} = \frac{26}{30}$$
$$\overline{\qquad \frac{1}{30}}$$

Kayla has $\frac{1}{30}$ gallon of paint left.

Problem Solving

25. Stefan's sculpture is $\frac{7}{12}$ foot tall. He attaches it to a base that is $\frac{1}{3}$ foot tall. How tall, in feet, is the sculpture with the base?

26. Tara made a snack mix with $\frac{3}{4}$ cup of rice crackers and $\frac{2}{3}$ cup of pretzels. She then ate $\frac{5}{8}$ cup of the mix for lunch. How much of the snack mix is left?

27. Writing to Explain Charlie's goal is to use less than 50 gallons of water per day. His water bill for the month showed that he used 1,524 gallons of water in 30 days. Did Charlie meet his goal this month? Explain how you decided.

28. Number Sense Jereen spent $\frac{1}{4}$ hour on homework after school, another $\frac{1}{2}$ hour after she got home, and a final $\frac{1}{3}$ hour after dinner. Did she spend more or less than 1 hour on homework in all? Explain.

Critical THINKING

29. Herb's Bakery electric bill for the month was $112.59. The gas bill for the month was $215.35. What was the bakery's total energy bill for the month?

30. **Science** A cat's heart beats about 130 beats per minute. A kitten's heartbeat can be as fast as 240 beats per minute. How many times does a kitten's heart beat in one half-hour?

31. Use the map. Which ordered pair tells the location of the concert hall?

   A (2, 9)

   B (2, 3)

   C (4, 6)

   D (6, 4)

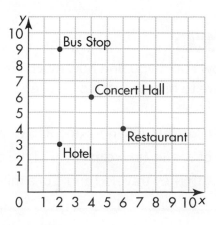

MA.5.A.2.2 Add and subtract fractions and decimals fluently and verify the reasonableness of results, including in problem situations.

Draw a Picture and Write an Equation

Brad and his father hiked three trails. The Gadsen Trail is $\frac{9}{10}$ of a mile, the Rosebriar Trail is $\frac{1}{2}$ of a mile, and the Eureka Trail is $\frac{3}{5}$ of a mile. How far did they walk in all?

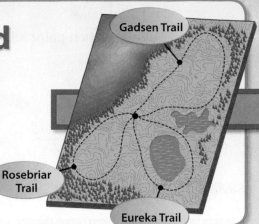

Another Example Sandra and Ron are hiking a trail. They have already hiked $\frac{1}{10}$ of a mile. How much farther do they have to travel to reach the $\frac{3}{4}$-mile mark?

Let x = how much farther they have to travel

$$\frac{3}{4} - \frac{1}{10} = x$$

	$\frac{3}{4}$ of a mile in all
$\frac{1}{10}$	x

Find common denominators.

$$\frac{3}{4} = \frac{15}{20} \qquad \frac{1}{10} = \frac{2}{20}$$

Write an equation and subtract the fractions.

$$\frac{15}{20} - \frac{2}{20} = x$$

$$x = \frac{13}{20}$$

Sandra and Ron need to hike $\frac{13}{20}$ of a mile farther to reach the $\frac{3}{4}$-mile mark.

Explain It

1. How could you find how much farther Sandra and Ron will have to hike to reach one mile?

2. **Reasoning** If Sandra and Ron turn around and hike back $\frac{1}{10}$ of a mile, how can you find the difference between the length they traveled and $\frac{3}{4}$ of a mile?

What do I know? Brad and his father hiked 3 trails.

Gadsen Trail $= \frac{9}{10}$ mi

Rosebriar Trail $= \frac{1}{2}$ mi

Eureka Trail $= \frac{3}{5}$ mi

What am I asked to find? How far did Brad and his father walk in all?

Let x = total miles hiked

$\frac{9}{10} = \frac{9}{10}$

$\frac{1}{2} = \frac{5}{10}$

$\frac{3}{5} = \frac{6}{10}$

	x miles in all	
$\frac{9}{10}$	$\frac{5}{10}$	$\frac{6}{10}$

Write an equation and add the fractions.

$x = \frac{9}{10} + \frac{5}{10} + \frac{6}{10} = \frac{20}{10}$ or 2 miles

Brad and his father walked 2 miles in all.

Guided Practice*

Do you know HOW?

Draw a picture and write an equation to solve.

1. Hannah ran $\frac{1}{3}$ of a mile. David ran $\frac{1}{6}$ of a mile. How much farther did Hannah run than David?

Do you UNDERSTAND?

2. **Writing to Explain** If you were asked to find how far Brad and his father walked on the Rosebriar and Eureka Trails alone, would the common denominator be different?

3. **Write a Problem** Write a problem that you can solve by drawing a picture and writing an equation.

Independent Practice

Draw a picture and write an equation to solve.

4. Steve connected a wire extension that is $\frac{3}{8}$ foot long to another wire that is $\frac{1}{2}$ foot long. How long is the wire with the extension?

	x foot	
$\frac{3}{8}$	$\frac{1}{2}$

Stuck? Try this....

- What do I know?
- What diagram can I use to help understand the problem?
- Can I use addition, subtraction, multiplication, or division?
- Is all of my work correct?
- Did I answer the right question?
- Is my answer reasonable?

5. The smallest female spider measures about $\frac{1}{2}$ millimeter (mm) in length. The smallest male spider measures about $\frac{2}{5}$ mm in length. How much longer is the female spider than the male spider?

$\frac{1}{2}$ mm long	
$\frac{2}{5}$	x

6. A recipe calls for 3 times as many carrots as peas. If Carmen used 2 cups of peas, how many cups of carrots will she use?

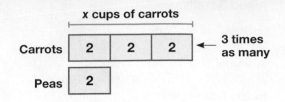

7. Felix bought $\frac{5}{6}$ pound of peanuts. He ate $\frac{3}{4}$ pound of the peanuts with his friends. How much did Felix have left?

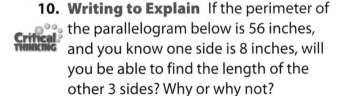

8. Geometry Jack's dog has a rectangular pen. The length is two feet longer than the width. The width is 6 feet. What is the perimeter of the pen?

9. Terrence has 8 comic books and 4 detective books. His sister says $\frac{2}{3}$ of his books are comic books. Terrence says that $\frac{8}{12}$ of his books are comic books. Who is correct? Explain your answer.

THINK
SOLVE
EXPLAIN

10. Writing to Explain If the perimeter of the parallelogram below is 56 inches, and you know one side is 8 inches, will you be able to find the length of the other 3 sides? Why or why not?

Critical
THINKING

8 inches

11. A banana bread recipe calls for $\frac{3}{4}$ cup of mashed bananas and $\frac{1}{8}$ cup of walnuts. Draw a picture and write an equation to find the total amount of bananas and walnuts added to the recipe.

Think About the Process

12. Four relay team members run an equal part of an 8-mile race. Which equation shows how far each member runs?

A $4 + 2 = 6$ **C** $2 + 2 + 2 = 6$

B $8 \div 4 = 2$ **D** $8 + 4 = 12$

13. At an automobile dealership, there are 3 green cars, 4 blue cars, and 4 silver cars. Which equation tells how many cars are not silver?

F $4 - 3 = 1$ **H** $3 + 4 + 4 = 11$

G $11 - 4 = 7$ **I** $7 \times 4 = 28$

Algebra Connections

Equations with Fractions

Remember that you can evaluate an algebraic expression by substituting a value of the variable and simplifying.

Evaluate each equation for $v = \frac{1}{4}$ to determine whether it is true.

1. $\frac{2}{3} + v = \frac{3}{7}$

2. $v + \frac{1}{2} = \frac{3}{4}$

3. $v - \frac{1}{5} = \frac{1}{20}$

4. $\frac{1}{4} + v = \frac{3}{16}$

5. $\frac{4}{5} - v = \frac{2}{3}$

6. $\frac{3}{4} - v = \frac{1}{2}$

7. $\frac{3}{10} + v = \frac{11}{20}$

8. $v + \frac{1}{6} = \frac{5}{12}$

9. $\frac{1}{3} + v = \frac{1}{2}$

10. $v - \frac{1}{4} = 0$

11. $v - \frac{1}{8} = \frac{1}{8}$

12. $v + \frac{2}{5} = \frac{7}{8}$

> **Example:** If $m = \frac{2}{5}$, which of the three equations listed below are true?
>
> $\frac{1}{2} + m = 1; m + \frac{3}{5} = 1; \frac{4}{9} - m = \frac{1}{2}$
>
> **Think** *How can I check to see if each equation is true?*
>
> Substitute $\frac{2}{5}$ for m in each equation.
>
> $\frac{1}{2} + \frac{2}{5} = \frac{5}{10} + \frac{4}{10} = \frac{9}{10} \neq 1$
>
> $\frac{2}{5} + \frac{3}{5} = 1$
>
> $\frac{4}{9} - \frac{2}{5} = \frac{20}{45} - \frac{18}{45} = \frac{2}{45} \neq \frac{1}{2}$
>
> The only true equation is $m + \frac{3}{5} = 1$.

· ·

13. It rained $\frac{2}{3}$ inch on Saturday. Find the total amount of rain, t, for the weekend if it rained $\frac{1}{4}$ inch on Sunday. Write and solve an equation to find the answer.

14. Jill walked $\frac{1}{3}$ mile less than Romero walked. If w equals how far Romero walked, which expression describes how far Jill walked?

A $\frac{1}{3} - w$ **C** $w - \frac{1}{3}$

B $\frac{1}{3} + w$ **D** $\frac{1}{3} + w$

15. **Write a Problem** Write a real-world problem using the equation $n = \frac{3}{8} - \frac{1}{6}$.

1 Darrell bought $\frac{1}{4}$ pound of American cheese and $\frac{1}{8}$ pound of Swiss cheese at the deli. Which picture models how much cheese Darrell bought? (8-7)

A.

$\frac{1}{4}$	
$\frac{1}{8}$	x

B.

$\frac{1}{4}$		
$\frac{1}{8}$	$\frac{1}{8}$	x

C.

$\frac{1}{8}$	
$\frac{1}{4}$	x

D.

x	
$\frac{1}{4}$	$\frac{1}{8}$

2 Replace each addend with 0, $\frac{1}{2}$, or 1. What is the estimate of the sum of $\frac{5}{8} + \frac{8}{9}$? (8-5)

F. $\frac{1}{2} + 1 = 1\frac{1}{2}$

G. $0 + 1 = 1$

H. $\frac{1}{2} + \frac{1}{2} = 1$

I. $1 + 1 = 2$

3 Which of the following pairs of numbers has a least common multiple of 24? (8-1)

A. 4 and 6

B. 3 and 8

C. 2 and 12

D. 3 and 6

4 In music, a sixteenth note often receives $\frac{1}{4}$ of a beat and an eighth note often receives $\frac{1}{2}$ of a beat. What fraction of a beat would a sixteenth note and an eighth note receive together? (8-3)

F. $\frac{3}{4}$

G. $\frac{3}{8}$

H. $\frac{3}{16}$

I. $\frac{1}{4}$

5 The table lists sizes of packages of school supplies. What is the smallest number of pencils and erasers that Mrs. Deng can buy so that she will have the same number of each? (8-1)

Item	Number in Package
Paper	50
Pencils	12
Erasers	10

A. 24

B. 30

C. 60

D. 120

6 Which renames $\frac{5}{12}$ and $\frac{3}{8}$ using a common denominator? (8-2)

F. $\frac{5}{12}$ and $\frac{3}{12}$

G. $\frac{10}{16}$ and $\frac{6}{16}$

H. $\frac{10}{24}$ and $\frac{12}{24}$

I. $\frac{10}{24}$ and $\frac{9}{24}$

7 Teri and her friends bought a party-size sandwich that was $\frac{7}{9}$ yard long. They ate $\frac{2}{3}$ of a yard. What part of a yard was left? (8-4)

  A. $\frac{5}{6}$ yard

  B. $\frac{5}{9}$ yard

  C. $\frac{1}{9}$ yard

  D. $\frac{1}{18}$ yard

8 Which of the following is NOT a common denominator for $\frac{1}{3}$ and $\frac{5}{6}$? (8-2)

  F. 24

  G. 18

  H. 9

  I. 6

9 Sandra drove for $\frac{1}{3}$ hour to get to the store. Then she drove $\frac{1}{5}$ hour to get to the library. What fraction of an hour did Sandra drive in all? (8-6)

  A. $\frac{2}{8}$ hour

  B. $\frac{1}{4}$ hour

  C. $\frac{1}{2}$ hour

  D. $\frac{8}{15}$ hour

10 A green snake is $\frac{8}{9}$ yard long. A garter snake is $\frac{13}{18}$ yard long. How much longer is the green snake than the garter? (8-4)

  F. $\frac{1}{6}$ yard

  G. $\frac{4}{18}$ yard

  H. $\frac{5}{18}$ yard

  I. $\frac{5}{9}$ yard

11 Of the balls shown, $\frac{1}{3}$ are basketballs and $\frac{1}{15}$ are soccer balls. What fraction of the balls are either basketballs or soccer balls? (8-3)

  A. $\frac{1}{9}$

  B. $\frac{2}{15}$

  C. $\frac{1}{5}$

  D. $\frac{2}{5}$

12 Benjamin and his sister shared a large sandwich. Benjamin ate $\frac{3}{5}$ of the sandwich and his sister ate $\frac{1}{7}$ of the sandwich. What is the best estimate of how much more Benjamin ate than his sister? (8-5)

  F. $\frac{1}{2} - 0 = \frac{1}{2}$

  G. $\frac{1}{2} - \frac{1}{2} = 0$

  H. $1 - \frac{1}{2} = \frac{1}{2}$

  I. $1 - 0 = 1$

13 What number is the least common multiple of 6 and 10? (8-1)

14 Rhys is kayaking down a $\frac{4}{5}$-mile stream. He has already traveled $\frac{1}{4}$ of a mile. How much farther does he need to travel? Draw a picture and write an equation to solve. (8-7)

THINK SOLVE EXPLAIN

Set A, pages 200–201

Find the least common multiple (LCM) of 9 and 12.

Make a list of the common multiples of each number.

Multiples of 9: 9, 18, 27, 36, 45, …

Multiple of 12: 12, 24, 36, 48, …

Identify the least number that is a multiple of both 9 and 12.

The least common multiple of 9 and 12 is 36.

Remember that the least common multiple of two numbers is the least number that is a multiple of both of the numbers.

1. 3 and 5   **2.** 4 and 6

3. 5 and 9   **4.** 6 and 10

5. 8 and 12   **6.** 8 and 3

7. 10 and 4   **8.** 6 and 9

Set B, pages 202–203

Find a common denominator for $\frac{4}{9}$ and $\frac{1}{3}$. Then rename the fractions to have that common denominator.

Step 1   Multiply the denominators:

$9 \times 3 = 27$, so 27 is a common denominator.

Step 2   Rename the fractions:

$\frac{4}{9} \times \frac{3}{3} = \frac{12}{27}$ $\frac{1}{3} \times \frac{9}{9} = \frac{9}{27}$

So, $\frac{12}{27}$ and $\frac{9}{27}$.

Remember you can check to see if one denominator is a multiple of the other. Since 9 is a multiple of 3, another common denominator of $\frac{4}{9}$ and $\frac{1}{3}$ is 9.

1. $\frac{3}{5}$ and $\frac{7}{10}$

2. $\frac{5}{6}$ and $\frac{7}{18}$

3. $\frac{3}{7}$ and $\frac{1}{4}$

4. $\frac{4}{9}$ and $\frac{3}{5}$

Set C, pages 204–205, 206–207

Find $\frac{5}{6} - \frac{3}{4}$.

Step 1   Find the least common multiple (LCM) of 6 and 4.
The LCM is 12, so the least common denominator (LCD) is 12.

Step 2   Use the LCD to write equivalent fractions.

$\frac{5}{6} = \frac{5 \times 2}{6 \times 2} = \frac{10}{12}$ $\frac{3}{4} = \frac{3 \times 3}{4 \times 3} = \frac{9}{12}$

Step 3   Subtract the equivalent fractions. Simplify, if possible.

$\frac{10}{12} - \frac{9}{12} = \frac{1}{12}$

Remember to multiply the numerator and denominator by the same number when writing equivalent fractions.

1. $\frac{2}{5} + \frac{3}{10}$ **2.** $\frac{1}{9} + \frac{5}{6}$

3. $\frac{3}{4} - \frac{5}{12}$ **4.** $\frac{7}{8} - \frac{2}{3}$

5. $\frac{5}{16} - \frac{1}{8}$ **6.** $\frac{7}{10} - \frac{1}{6}$

7. $\frac{9}{25} + \frac{1}{3}$ **8.** $\frac{1}{4} + \frac{3}{8}$

9. $\frac{4}{5} - \frac{1}{3}$ **10.** $\frac{5}{8} - \frac{1}{2}$

11. $\frac{1}{6} + \frac{1}{2} + \frac{1}{6}$ **12.** $\frac{7}{100} + \frac{4}{50} + \frac{3}{25}$

Set D, pages 208–209

Estimate $\frac{7}{12} - \frac{1}{8}$.

Estimate the difference by replacing each fraction with 0, $\frac{1}{2}$ or 1.

Step 1 $\frac{7}{12}$ is close to $\frac{6}{12}$. Round $\frac{7}{12}$ to $\frac{1}{2}$.

Step 2 $\frac{1}{8}$ is close to 0. Round $\frac{1}{8}$ to 0.

Step 3 $\frac{1}{2} - 0 = \frac{1}{2}$

$\frac{7}{12} - \frac{1}{8}$ is about $\frac{1}{2}$.

Remember that you can use a number line to replace fractions with the nearest half or whole.

Estimate each sum or difference.

1. $\frac{2}{3} + \frac{5}{6}$ 2. $\frac{7}{8} - \frac{5}{12}$
3. $\frac{1}{8} + \frac{1}{16}$ 4. $\frac{5}{8} - \frac{1}{6}$

Set E, pages 210–211

Find $\left(\frac{1}{5} + \frac{1}{2}\right) - \frac{2}{3}$.

Step 1 Add $\frac{1}{5} + \frac{1}{2}$.

• Find a common denominator: $5 \times 2 = 10$

• Rename each fraction and add:
$\frac{1}{5} = \frac{2}{10}$ $\frac{1}{2} = \frac{5}{10}$
$\frac{2}{10} + \frac{5}{10} = \frac{7}{10}$ Simplify if necessary.

Step 2 Subtract $\frac{7}{10} - \frac{2}{3}$.

• Find a common denominator: $10 \times 3 = 30$

• Rename each fraction and subtract:
$\frac{7}{10} = \frac{21}{30}$ $\frac{2}{3} = \frac{20}{30}$
$\frac{21}{30} - \frac{20}{30} = \frac{1}{30}$ Simplify if necessary.

Remember if one denominator is a multiple of the others, it is the LCD.

Add or subtract to evaluate.

1. $\left(\frac{3}{5} + \frac{1}{10}\right) - \frac{3}{8}$
2. $\left(\frac{5}{6} - \frac{7}{18}\right) + \frac{1}{3}$
3. $\left(\frac{3}{4} + \frac{1}{12}\right) - \frac{2}{3}$
4. $\left(\frac{4}{9} - \frac{3}{18}\right) + \frac{1}{6}$

Set F, pages 212–214

Tina and Andy are building a model airplane. Tina built $\frac{1}{3}$ of the model, and Andy built $\frac{1}{5}$. How much more has Tina built than Andy?

| Tina | $\frac{1}{3}$ | |
| Andy | $\frac{1}{5}$ | x |

Find a common denominator and subtract.

$\frac{1}{3} = \frac{5}{15}$ $\frac{1}{5} = \frac{3}{15}$ So, $x = \frac{5}{15} - \frac{3}{15} = \frac{2}{15}$

Tina built $\frac{2}{15}$ more of the model than Andy.

Remember to use a picture to help you write an equation.

1. Bonnie ran $\frac{1}{4}$ of a mile. Olga ran $\frac{1}{8}$ of a mile. How much farther did Bonnie run than Olga?

2. Linda's plant was $\frac{9}{12}$ foot tall. Macy's plant was $\frac{2}{3}$ foot tall. How much taller is Linda's plant than Macy's?

Adding and Subtracting Mixed Numbers

1

This Parson's chameleon can extend its tongue up to $1\frac{1}{2}$ times the length of its body. What is the total length of the chameleon when its tongue is fully extended? You will find out in Lesson 9-3.

2

How much smaller is the bumblebee bat than the Etruscan pygmy shrew? You will find out in Lesson 9-4.

Review What You Know!

 **3**

The world's smallest horse is named Thumbelina. How much shorter is Thumbelina than the next shortest horse? You will find out in Lesson 9-4.

4

How can you write the height of the *Long Term Parking Sculpture* in France as a mixed number and an improper fraction? You will find out in Lesson 9-1.

Vocabulary

Choose the best term from the box.

- least common multiple (LCM)
- common multiple
- least common denominator (LCD)
- prime factorization

1. Writing a number as the product of prime numbers is called __?__ .

2. A __?__ is a number that is a multiple of two or more numbers.

3. The number 12 is the __?__ of 3, 4, and 6.

Comparing Fractions

Compare. Write >, <, or = for each ◯.

4. $\frac{5}{25} \bigcirc \frac{2}{5}$

5. $\frac{12}{27} \bigcirc \frac{6}{9}$

6. $\frac{11}{16} \bigcirc \frac{2}{8}$

7. $\frac{2}{7} \bigcirc \frac{1}{5}$

Fractions in Simplest Form

Write each fraction in simplest form.

8. $\frac{6}{18}$

9. $\frac{12}{22}$

10. $\frac{15}{25}$

11. $\frac{8}{26}$

12. $\frac{14}{35}$

13. $\frac{4}{18}$

Writing to Explain Write an answer for each question.

14. How do you know when a fraction is in simplest form?

15. How can the greatest common factor help you write a fraction in simplest form?

Topic Essential Questions

- What does it mean to add and subtract mixed numbers?

- What is a standard procedure for adding and subtracting mixed numbers?

MA.5.A.2.1 Represent addition and subtraction of decimals and fractions with like and unlike denominators using models, place value or properties.

Mixed Numbers and Improper Fractions

How can you change a mixed number to an improper fraction?

Jill has measured $2\frac{1}{4}$ cups of flour. The number $2\frac{1}{4}$ is a mixed number. It has a whole-number part and a fractional part. Write $2\frac{1}{4}$ as an improper fraction.

FLOUR

$2\frac{1}{4}$ cups of flour

Another Example How can you change an improper fraction to a mixed number?

Write $\frac{10}{3}$ as a mixed number. Simplify if possible.

One Way

Use a model.

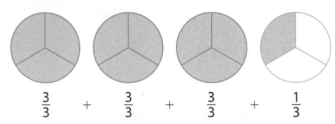

$\frac{3}{3}$ + $\frac{3}{3}$ + $\frac{3}{3}$ + $\frac{1}{3}$

There are 3 wholes shaded and $\frac{1}{3}$ of another circle shaded.

So, $\frac{10}{3} = 3\frac{1}{3}$.

Another Way

You can think of fractions as division. So, use division.

Divide the numerator by the denominator.

Write the remainder as a fraction.
Put the remainder over the divisor.

$$3\overline{)10} \quad \begin{array}{r} 3\frac{1}{3} \\ -9 \\ \hline 1 \end{array}$$

So, $\frac{10}{3} = 3\frac{1}{3}$.

Explain It

1. Why can you divide the numerator by the denominator?

2. When the remainder was rewritten as a fraction in Another Way, why wasn't the fraction rewritten in simplest form?

One Way

Use fraction strips to model $2\frac{1}{4}$. An **improper fraction** is a fraction whose numerator is greater than or equal to its denominator.

1			
$\frac{1}{4}$	$\frac{1}{4}$	$\frac{1}{4}$	$\frac{1}{4}$
$\frac{1}{4}$	$\frac{1}{4}$	$\frac{1}{4}$	$\frac{1}{4}$
$\frac{1}{4}$			

There are 9 fourths in $2\frac{1}{4}$.

So, $2\frac{1}{4} = \frac{9}{4}$.

Another Way

Use the method below to write $2\frac{1}{4}$ as an improper fraction.

- Multiply the denominator of the fraction by the whole number. $2 \times 4 = 8$.
- Add the product to the numerator of the fraction to get the new numerator. $8 + 1 = 9$
- Keep the same denominator. $\frac{9}{4}$

So, $2\frac{1}{4} = \frac{9}{4}$.

Guided Practice*

Do you know HOW?

For **1** through **3**, write each as an improper fraction.

1. $3\frac{1}{4}$
2. $9\frac{1}{10}$
3. $5\frac{3}{4}$

For **4** through **6**, write each as a mixed number. Simplify if possible.

4. $\frac{3}{2}$
5. $\frac{15}{6}$
6. $\frac{14}{3}$

Do you UNDERSTAND?

7. **Writing to Explain** In the example at the top, why is $2 + \frac{1}{4} = \frac{8}{4} + \frac{1}{4}$?

   Tip As an improper fraction $2 = \frac{2}{1}$.

8. For a recipe, Jill will need $4\frac{1}{2}$ cups flour. Write $4\frac{1}{2}$ as an improper fraction.

Independent Practice

Leveled Practice In **9** and **10**, write a mixed number and an improper fraction for the shaded portion of each model.

9.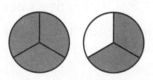

10.

In **11** through **18**, write each mixed number as an improper fraction and each improper fraction as a mixed number in simplest form.

11. $4\frac{1}{2}$
12. $\frac{13}{7}$
13. $4\frac{9}{10}$
14. $5\frac{1}{8}$

15. $\frac{22}{6}$
16. $\frac{25}{10}$
17. $8\frac{2}{3}$
18. $\frac{37}{9}$

Animated Glossary
www.pearsonsuccessnet.com

For another example, see Set A on page 240.

19. The *Long Term Parking Sculpture* in France contains 60 cars embedded in concrete. Write your answers in simplest form.

65.6 feet

   a How tall is the sculpture expressed as a mixed number?

   b How tall is the sculpture expressed as an improper fraction?

20. Sam's four packages weigh 0.9 pound, 0.03 pound, 1.8 pounds, and 0.14 pound.

   a Write the weights from least to greatest.

   b What is the total weight of Sam's packages?

For **21** through **23**, use the table at the right.

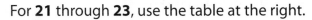

21. Sarah is making costumes for the school play. Write the amount of material for a peasant blouse as a mixed number.

22. Which costume requires the most fabric?

23. Which costume requires the least fabric?

24. Which property tells you that $7 \times 1 = 7$?

25. What is the value of the underlined digit in 423,1<u>4</u>8,675? Write your answer in word form.

Costume Shopping List	
Costume	**Yards**
Peasant skirt	$\frac{12}{3}$
Peasant vest	$\frac{9}{8}$
Peasant blouse	$\frac{9}{4}$
Noble's cloak	$\frac{31}{8}$

26. **Science** Sam collects Florida horse conch shells. If $\frac{9}{13}$ of his shell collection are brown shells and $\frac{2}{13}$ of his shell collection are white shells, what fraction of his collection is a color other than brown or white?

   A $\frac{11}{13}$ **C** $\frac{7}{13}$

   B $\frac{9}{13}$ **D** $\frac{2}{13}$

28. Missy says that $\frac{5}{5}$ is an improper fraction. Is she correct? Explain.

THINK
SOLVE
EXPLAIN

27. **Think** About the Process Which describes a way to change $4\frac{2}{3}$ into an improper fraction?

   F Multiply 4 by 3. Then, add 2. Write that number as a numerator over a denominator of 3.

   G Multiply 4 by 2. Then, add 3. Write that number as a numerator over a denominator of 3.

   H Add 4 and $\frac{2}{3}$.

   I Divide 4 by $\frac{2}{3}$.

Skills Review Write each phrase as an algebraic expression.

1. 7 less than a number x

2. 5 times a number p

3. 4 times a number m, minus 3 times a number k

4. 8 plus two times a number j

Use the properties of operations to fill in the blanks in each expression.

5. $28 \times 5 = 5 \times$ ▨

6. $12 \times 25 \times 32 = 12 \times$ ▨ $\times 25 \times 32$

7. $7 + (30 + 15) = (7 + 30) +$ ▨

8. $23 + 8 = 23 + 8 +$ ▨

Evaluate each expression for $x = 3$ and $y = 5$.

9. $5x + 8$

10. $(10 - y)(10)$

11. $10y + 23$

12. Write an algebraic expression for the value of y that explains the relationship between x and y. Then finish the table.

x	7	8	9	10	11
y	17	19	21	▨	▨

Error Search Find each answer that is not correct. Write it correctly and explain the error.

13. $8 + 2 \times 6 = 60$

14. $8 \times 0 + (4 \times 1) = 4$

15. $4(24) = 4(6) + 4(4)$

16. $32 + 73 = (30 + 70) + (2 + 3)$

17. $58(40) = 50(40) \times 8(40)$

18. $4(51 + 32) = 4(80) + 4(3)$

Number Sense

Insert parentheses to make each sentence true.

19. $3 \times 8 + 3 \times 2 = 66$

20. $2 \times 5 + 4 - 8 = 10$

21. $15 - 2 \times 3 + 5^2 = 64$

22. $4x - 5 = 4x - 20$

23. $6 + 8 - 3 \times 7 = 41$

24. $4 + 4 \times 3 + 5 = 29$

25. $3^2 - 8 \times 0 = 9$

26. $80 \div 2 \times 2 + 2 \times 3 = 26$

27. $25 - 10 + 3 \div 2 + 4 = 3$

MA.5.A.2.1 Represent addition and subtraction of decimals and fractions with like and unlike denominators using models, place value or properties.

Modeling Addition and Subtraction of Mixed Numbers

Hands-On fraction strips

$\frac{1}{8}$

How can you model addition of mixed numbers?

Bill has 2 boards he will use to make picture frames. What is the total length of the boards Bill has to make picture frames?

Choose an Operation Add to find the total length.

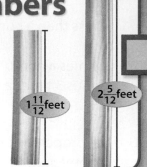

$1\frac{11}{12}$ feet

$2\frac{5}{12}$ feet

Another Example How can you model subtraction of mixed numbers?

Find $2\frac{5}{12} - 1\frac{11}{12}$.

Step 1

Model the number you are subtracting from, $2\frac{5}{12}$.

If the fraction you will be subtracting is greater than the fraction of the number you model, rename 1 whole.

Since $\frac{11}{12} > \frac{5}{12}$, rename 1 whole as $\frac{12}{12}$.

Step 2

Use your renamed model to cross out the number that you are subtracting, $1\frac{11}{12}$.

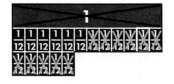

There are $\frac{6}{12}$ left.

So, $2\frac{5}{12} - 1\frac{11}{12} = \frac{6}{12}$.

Simplify: $\frac{6}{12} = \frac{1}{2}$

Explain It

1. In the example above, why is $2\frac{5}{12}$ renamed as $1\frac{17}{12}$?

Guided Practice*

Do you know HOW?

Use fraction strips to find each sum or difference. Simplify, if possible.

1. $1\frac{2}{5} + 2\frac{4}{5}$
2. $4\frac{1}{4} - 3\frac{3}{4}$
3. $5\frac{3}{6} - 2\frac{5}{6}$
4. $3\frac{1}{3} + 2\frac{2}{3}$

Do you UNDERSTAND?

5. How is renaming to add mixed numbers different from regrouping to add whole numbers?

6. **Number Sense** When adding two mixed numbers is it always necessary to rename the fractional sum? Explain.

For another example, see Set B on page 240.

Model the addends and add the fractional parts.

$2\frac{5}{12}$

$+ 1\frac{11}{12}$
_____
$\frac{16}{12}$

Rename $\frac{16}{12}$ as $1\frac{4}{12}$.

Now add the whole numbers, including the renamed fraction.

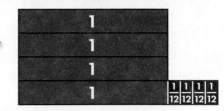

$2 + 1 + 1 = 4$

So, $2\frac{5}{12} + 1\frac{11}{12} = 4\frac{4}{12}$.

Simplify: $4\frac{4}{12} = 4\frac{1}{3}$

The total length of the boards is $4\frac{1}{3}$ feet.

Independent Practice

In **7** and **8**, use each model to find the sum or difference. Simplify if possible.

7. Charles used $1\frac{2}{3}$ cups of walnuts and $2\frac{2}{3}$ cups of cranberries to make breakfast bread. How many cups of walnuts and cranberries did he use in all?

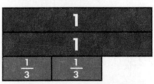

8. Terrell ran to his friend's apartment in $2\frac{5}{6}$ minutes. It took Terrell $4\frac{1}{6}$ minutes to go back home. How much more time did Terrell take to get home?

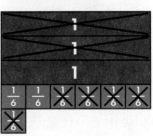

In **9** through **16**, use fraction strips to find each sum or difference. Simplify if possible.

9. $2\frac{3}{5} + 1\frac{3}{5}$ **10.** $4\frac{5}{12} + 1\frac{7}{12}$ **11.** $4\frac{9}{10} + 3\frac{7}{10}$ **12.** $5\frac{3}{4} + 2\frac{3}{4}$

13. $9\frac{1}{6} - 4\frac{5}{6}$ **14.** $12\frac{3}{8} - 9\frac{5}{8}$ **15.** $8\frac{1}{3} - 7\frac{2}{3}$ **16.** $13\frac{7}{9} - 10\frac{8}{9}$

For **17** and **18**, use fraction strips to solve. Simplify, if possible.

17. Kit said, "On summer vacation, I spent $2\frac{4}{7}$ weeks with my grandma and $1\frac{6}{7}$ weeks with my aunt."

    a How many weeks is that in all?

    b How many weeks longer did Kit spend with her grandmother than with her aunt?

18. Hannah used $1\frac{2}{3}$ gallons of white paint for the ceiling and $3\frac{2}{3}$ gallons of green paint for the walls of her kitchen.

    a How much paint did Hannah use in all?

    b How much more green paint did Hannah use than white paint?

For **19** and **20**, use the map at the right.

19. What ordered pair tells the location of the stadium?

20. **Think** **About the Process** Ben walked from the restaurant to the bus stop. Then he took the bus to the stadium. If he took the shortest route, how many blocks did Ben travel?

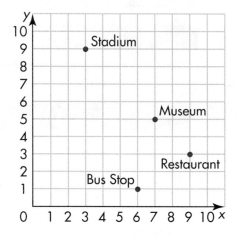

21. What is the value of the underlined digit in 6.2<u>7</u>5?

    A 7 ones   **B** 7 tenths   **C** 7 hundredths   **D** 7 thousandths

For **22** and **23**, use the table at the right.

22. **Science** How many inches longer is a Hercules beetle than a ladybug?

23. What is the difference between the largest and the smallest stag beetles?

Beetles by Length	
Beetle	**Length in inches**
Hercules beetle	$6\frac{3}{4}$
Ladybug	$\frac{1}{4}$
Stag beetle	$1\frac{1}{8}$ to $2\frac{4}{8}$

24. Raoul's heart beats about 72 times each minute. How many times does his heart beat in 15 minutes?

25. Nicole, Tasha, Maria, and Joan ran a relay race. Nicole ran the first leg of the race in $1\frac{13}{15}$ minutes. Tasha ran the second leg in $2\frac{1}{15}$ minutes. Maria ran the third leg in $1\frac{7}{15}$ minutes. Joan ran the last leg in $2\frac{2}{15}$ minutes to finish the race.

    a Reasoning How can you find how much faster Maria ran than Joan?

    b The team wanted to run the race in less than six minutes. Did they meet their goal? Explain.

Mixed Problem Solving

The human body is very complex. Two systems of the human body are the muscular and circulatory systems.

1. An average ten-year-old weighs about $86\frac{1}{2}$ pounds and has muscles that weigh about $34\frac{1}{5}$ pounds. Find the difference between these two weights.

2. Use the information given in Exercise 1. About how much do the muscles of two average ten-year-olds weigh? Write your answer as a mixed number.

3. Your body temperature can change from hour to hour. Tony's temperature was 98.6°F at 2 P.M. His temperature increased 0.6°F during the first hour, 0.2°F the second hour, and 0.1°F during the third hour. It decreased 0.8°F during the fourth hour. What was Tony's temperature at 6 P.M.?

4. The circulatory system includes the heart, the blood, and the blood vessels. A person is born with about 0.25 liter of blood. An adult has about 5 liters of blood. What is the difference between the amount of blood an adult has and the amount of blood a newborn baby has?

In **5** and **6**, use the following information.

The left ventricle of an average person can pump about 315 liters of blood in 1 hour.

5. Estimate to find about how many liters of blood the left ventricle can pump in 1 minute. Hint: There are 60 minutes in an hour.

6. The left ventricle pumps blood away from the heart into your body's largest artery, the aorta. About how much blood is pumped into the aorta in 10 minutes?

  A 5 liters   **C** 50 liters

  B 10 liters   **D** 500 liters

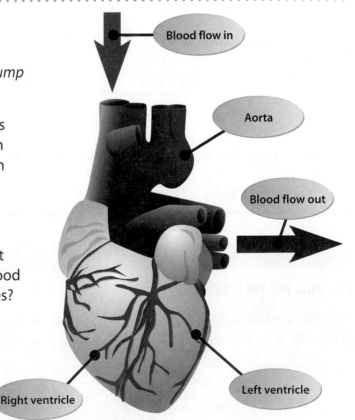

MA.5.A.2.2 Add and subtract fractions and decimals fluently and verify the reasonableness of results, including in problem situations.
Also MA.5.A.2.3

Adding Mixed Numbers

How can you add mixed numbers?

Rhoda mixes sand with $2\frac{2}{3}$ cups of potting mixture to prepare soil for her cactus plants. After mixing them together, how many cups of soil does Rhoda have?

Choose an Operation Add to find the total amount of soil.

$1\frac{1}{2}$ cups

Another Example How can you check for reasonableness?

You just found that the sum of $2\frac{2}{3}$ and $1\frac{1}{2}$ is $4\frac{1}{6}$. You can use estimation to check that a sum is reasonable.

Estimate $2\frac{2}{3} + 1\frac{1}{2}$.

A number line can help you replace mixed numbers with the nearest one-half or whole unit.

$2\frac{2}{3}$ is closer to $2\frac{1}{2}$ than to 2 or 3.

$1\frac{1}{2}$ is halfway between 1 and 2.

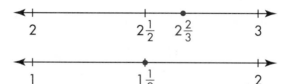

Add: $2\frac{1}{2} + 1\frac{1}{2} = 4$

Since $2\frac{2}{3}$ was replaced with $2\frac{1}{2}$, the answer will be greater than the estimate.

The actual sum, $4\frac{1}{6}$, is reasonable because it is close to the estimate, 4.

Guided Practice*

Do you know HOW?

Estimate and then find each sum. Check for reasonableness.

1. $1\frac{7}{8} = 1\frac{\square}{8}$
   $+ 1\frac{1}{4} = 1\frac{\square}{8}$

2. $2\frac{2}{5} = 2\frac{\square}{30}$
   $+ 5\frac{5}{6} = 5\frac{\square}{30}$

3. $4\frac{1}{9} + 1\frac{1}{3}$

4. $6\frac{5}{12} + 4\frac{5}{8}$

Do you UNDERSTAND?

5. **Reasoning** How is adding mixed numbers like adding fractions and whole numbers?

6. **Writing to Explain** Kyle used 9 as an estimate for $3\frac{1}{6} + 5\frac{7}{8}$. He added and got $9\frac{1}{24}$ for the actual sum. Is his answer reasonable?

*For another example, see Set C on page 240.

Step 1

Find $2\frac{2}{3} + 1\frac{1}{2}$.

Write equivalent fractions with the least common denominator.

$2\frac{2}{3} = 2\frac{4}{6}$

$+ 1\frac{1}{2} = 1\frac{3}{6}$
_____

Step 2

Add the fractions.

$2\frac{2}{3} = 2\frac{4}{6}$

$+ 1\frac{1}{2} = 1\frac{3}{6}$
_____
$\frac{7}{6}$

Step 3

Add the whole numbers. Simplify the sum if possible.

$2\frac{2}{3} = 2\frac{4}{6}$

$+ 1\frac{1}{2} = 1\frac{3}{6}$
_____
$3\frac{7}{6}$

$3\frac{7}{6} = 4\frac{1}{6}$

Rhoda prepared $4\frac{1}{6}$ cups of soil.

Independent Practice

Leveled Practice For **7** through **18**, estimate and then find each sum. Check for reasonableness.

7. $3\frac{1}{6} = 3\frac{}{6}$

$+ 5\frac{2}{3} = 5\frac{}{6}$
_____

8. $11\frac{1}{2} = 11\frac{}{10}$

$+ 10\frac{3}{5} = 10\frac{}{10}$
_____

9. $9\frac{3}{16}$

$+ 7\frac{5}{8}$
_____

10. $5\frac{6}{7}$

$+ 8\frac{1}{7}$
_____

11. $4\frac{1}{10} + 6\frac{1}{2}$

12. $9\frac{7}{12} + 4\frac{3}{4}$

13. $5 + 3\frac{1}{8}$

14. $8\frac{3}{4} + 7\frac{3}{4}$

15. $2\frac{3}{4} + 7\frac{3}{5}$

16. $3\frac{8}{9} + 8\frac{1}{2}$

17. $1\frac{7}{12} + 2\frac{3}{8}$

18. $3\frac{11}{12} + 9\frac{1}{16}$

Problem Solving

19. Arnie skated $1\frac{3}{4}$ miles from home to the lake, then went $1\frac{1}{3}$ miles around the lake, and then back home. How many miles did he skate?

 A $2\frac{1}{12}$ miles

 B $3\frac{1}{12}$ miles

 C $4\frac{5}{6}$ miles

 D $4\frac{5}{12}$ miles

20. a Use the map below to find the distance from the start of the trail to the end.

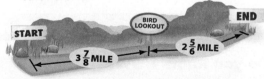

 b Louise walked from the start of the trail to the bird lookout and back. **Critical THINKING** Did she walk more or less than if she had walked from the start of the trail to the end?

21. The length of a male Parson's chameleon can be up to $23\frac{1}{2}$ inches. It can extend its tongue up to $35\frac{1}{4}$ inches to catch its food. What is the total length of a male Parson's chameleon when its tongue is fully extended?

Lesson 9-4

MA.5.A.2.2 Add and subtract fractions and decimals fluently and verify the reasonableness of results, including in problem situations. Also **MA.5.A.2.3**

Subtracting Mixed Numbers

How can you subtract mixed numbers?

A golf ball measures about $1\frac{2}{3}$ inches across the center. What is the difference between the distance across the center of the hole and the golf ball?

Choose an Operation Subtract to find the difference.

$4\frac{1}{4}$ inches

Another Example **How can you check for reasonableness?**

You just found that the difference of $4\frac{1}{4}$ and $1\frac{2}{3}$ is $2\frac{7}{12}$. You can use estimation to check that a difference is reasonable.

Estimate $4\frac{1}{4} - 1\frac{2}{3}$.

$4\frac{1}{4}$ is close to 4.
Replace $4\frac{1}{4}$ with 4.

$1\frac{2}{3}$ is closer to 2 than to 1.

Subtract: $4 - 2 = 2$.

The actual difference, $2\frac{7}{12}$, is reasonable because it is close to the estimate, 2.

Guided Practice*

Do you know HOW?

Estimate and then find each difference.
Check for reasonableness.

1. $\begin{array}{l} 7\frac{2}{3} = 7\frac{\boxed{}}{6} = 6\frac{\boxed{}}{6} \\ -\ 3\frac{5}{6} = 3\frac{\boxed{}}{6} = 3\frac{\boxed{}}{6} \\ \hline \end{array}$

2. $\begin{array}{l} 5\ \ = \ \ \boxed{}\frac{\boxed{}}{4} \\ -\ 2\frac{3}{4} = \ \ 2\frac{3}{4} \\ \hline \end{array}$

3. $6\frac{3}{10} - 1\frac{4}{5}$

4. $9\frac{1}{3} - 4\frac{3}{4}$

Do you UNDERSTAND?

5. In Exercise 2, why do you need to rename the 5?

6. **Reasonableness** Could two golf balls fall into the hole at the same time? Explain your reasoning.

---

232   *For another example, see Set D on page 241.*

Write equivalent fractions with the least common denominator.

$$4\frac{1}{4} = 4\frac{3}{12}$$

$$- 1\frac{2}{3} = 1\frac{8}{12}$$

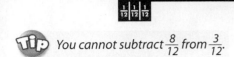

Tip You cannot subtract $\frac{8}{12}$ from $\frac{3}{12}$.

Rename $4\frac{3}{12}$ to show more twelfths.

$$4\frac{3}{12} = 3\frac{15}{12}$$

$$- 1\frac{8}{12} = 1\frac{8}{12}$$

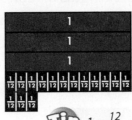

Tip $1 = \frac{12}{12}$

Subtract the fractions. Then subtract the whole numbers. Simplify, if possible.

$$4\frac{1}{4} = 4\frac{3}{12} = 3\frac{15}{12}$$

$$- 1\frac{2}{3} = 1\frac{8}{12} = 1\frac{8}{12}$$

$$2\frac{7}{12}$$

The hole is $2\frac{7}{12}$ inches wider.

Independent Practice

Leveled Practice For **7** through **18**, estimate and then find each difference. Check for reasonableness.

7. $8\frac{1}{4} = 8\frac{}{8} = 7\frac{}{8}$

$- 2\frac{7}{8} = 2\frac{}{8} = 2\frac{}{8}$

8. $3\frac{1}{2} = 3\frac{}{6}$

$- 1\frac{1}{3} = 1\frac{}{6}$

9. $4\frac{1}{8}$

$- 1\frac{1}{2}$

10. 6

$- 2\frac{4}{5}$

11. $6\frac{1}{3} - 5\frac{2}{3}$

12. $9\frac{1}{2} - 6\frac{3}{4}$

13. $8\frac{3}{16} - 3\frac{5}{8}$

14. $7\frac{1}{2} - \frac{7}{10}$

15. $15\frac{1}{6} - 4\frac{3}{8}$

16. $13\frac{1}{12} - 8\frac{1}{4}$

17. $6\frac{1}{3} - 2\frac{3}{5}$

18. $10\frac{5}{12} - 4\frac{7}{8}$

Problem Solving

19. The average weight of a basketball is $21\frac{1}{10}$ ounces. The average weight of a baseball is $5\frac{1}{4}$ ounces. How many more ounces does the basketball weigh?

20. As of 2008, the world's shortest horse is Thumbelina. She is $17\frac{1}{4}$ inches tall. The second shortest horse, Black Beauty, is $18\frac{1}{2}$ inches tall. How much shorter is Thumbelina than Black Beauty?

21. The smallest mammals on Earth are the bumblebee bat and the Etruscan pygmy shrew. A length of a bumblebee bat is $1\frac{9}{50}$ inches. A length of an Etruscan pygmy shrew is $1\frac{21}{50}$ inches. How much smaller is the bat than the shrew?

22. Writing to Explain How are the parallelogram and the rectangle alike? How are they different?

Critical THINKING

MA.5.A.2.2 Add and subtract fractions and decimals fluently and verify the reasonableness of results, including in problem situations.

More Adding and Subtracting Mixed Numbers

How can adding and subtracting mixed numbers help you solve problems?

Clarisse has two lengths of fabric to make covers for a sofa and chair. The covers require $9\frac{2}{3}$ yards of fabric. How much fabric will Clarisse have left over?

$7\frac{5}{6}$ yards

$5\frac{3}{4}$ yards

Guided Practice*

Do you know HOW?

1. $5\frac{1}{9}$
   $- 2\frac{2}{3}$

2. $2\frac{1}{4}$
   $+ 8\frac{2}{3}$

3. $6\frac{7}{25}$
   $- 3\frac{9}{50}$

For **4** through **7**, simplify each expression.

4. $\left(12\frac{1}{6} - 6\frac{5}{12}\right) + 1\frac{1}{4}$

5. $\left(7\frac{2}{3} + 3\frac{4}{5}\right) - 1\frac{4}{15}$

6. $6\frac{1}{4} + \left(2\frac{1}{3} - 1\frac{5}{8}\right)$

7. $8\frac{2}{5} - \left(3\frac{2}{3} + 2\frac{3}{5}\right)$

Do you UNDERSTAND?

8. **Think About the Process** In the example above, why do you add before you subtract to solve the problem?

9. **Writing to Explain** In the example above, does Clarisse have enough fabric left over to make two cushions that each use $2\frac{1}{3}$ yards of fabric? Explain.

Independent Practice

10. $9\frac{1}{3}$
    $- 4\frac{1}{6}$

11. $12\frac{1}{4}$
    $- 9\frac{3}{5}$

12. $6\frac{3}{5}$
    $+ 1\frac{3}{25}$

13. $3\frac{4}{9}$
    $+ 2\frac{2}{3}$

14. $5\frac{31}{75}$
    $- 3\frac{2}{25}$

15. $7\frac{1}{5}$
    $+ 4\frac{5}{6}$

16. $15\frac{4}{7}$
    $- 6\frac{3}{4}$

17. $8\frac{1}{4}$
    $- 5\frac{5}{12}$

18. $11\frac{7}{8}$
    $+ 3\frac{9}{24}$

19. $9\frac{3}{10}$
    $+ 5\frac{1}{2}$

In **20** through **25**, simplify each expression.

20. $\left(2\frac{5}{8} + 2\frac{1}{2}\right) - 4\frac{2}{3}$

21. $\left(5\frac{3}{4} + 1\frac{5}{6}\right) - 6\frac{7}{12}$

22. $4\frac{3}{5} + \left(8\frac{1}{5} - 7\frac{3}{10}\right)$

23. $\left(13 - 10\frac{1}{3}\right) + 2\frac{2}{3}$

24. $9\frac{9}{1,000} - 5\frac{9}{100}$

25. $2\frac{13}{20} + 11\frac{13}{25}$

*For another example, see Set E on page 241.

Add to find out how much fabric Clarisse has in all.

$$5\frac{3}{4} = 5\frac{9}{12}$$
$$+\ 7\frac{5}{6} = 7\frac{10}{12}$$
$$\overline{\qquad\qquad 12\frac{19}{12} = 13\frac{7}{12}}$$

Clarisse has $13\frac{7}{12}$ yards of fabric in all.

Subtract the amount she will use, $9\frac{2}{3}$ yards, from the total length of fabric.

$$13\frac{7}{12} = 12\frac{19}{12}$$
$$-\ \ \ 9\frac{2}{3} = \ \ 9\frac{8}{12}$$
$$\overline{\qquad\qquad\ \ \ 3\frac{11}{12}}$$

Clarisse will have $3\frac{11}{12}$ yards of fabric left over.

Problem Solving

For **26** and **27**, use the number line to estimate to the nearest $\frac{1}{2}$ or whole.

1   $1\frac{1}{2}$ 2 $2\frac{1}{2}$ 3

26. Estimate the sum of $2\frac{3}{8} + 1\frac{1}{12}$.

27. Estimate the difference of $2\frac{1}{8} - 1\frac{9}{10}$.

28. Which is 6.245 rounded to the nearest hundredth?

   A 6.0   **C** 6.24

   B 6.2   **D** 6.25

29. Which number is NOT a common factor of 24 and 36?

   F 4   **H** 9

   G 6   **I** 12

For **30** through **32**, use the table. Simplify answers, if possible.

Frog Species	Body Length (cm)	Maximum Jump (cm)
Bullfrog	$20\frac{3}{10}$	$213\frac{1}{2}$
Leopard frog	$12\frac{1}{2}$	$162\frac{1}{2}$
South African sharp-nosed frog	$7\frac{3}{5}$	$334\frac{2}{5}$

30. **Science** How much longer is the maximum jump of a South African sharp-nosed frog than the maximum jump of a leopard frog?

31. Rounded to the nearest whole number, how many centimeters long is a bullfrog?

32. **Writing to Explain** Which frog can leap about 10 times its body length? Explain how you found your answer.

Critical THINKING

MA.5.A.2.2 Add and subtract fractions and decimals fluently and verify the reasonableness of results, including in problem situations.

Draw a Picture and Write an Equation

Yori has two dog-sitting jobs. Each day she walks $\frac{3}{10}$ of a mile to get to her first job. Then she walks to her second job. How far is it from Yori's first job to her second job?

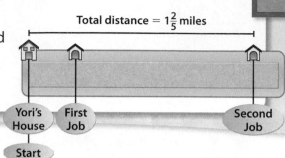

Total distance = $1\frac{2}{5}$ miles

Yori's House · First Job · Second Job

Start

Guided Practice*

Do you know HOW?

Copy and finish drawing the picture. Write an equation and solve.

1. Dwayne has a dog-walking job. He walks a collie $1\frac{9}{10}$ miles and a schnauzer $2\frac{3}{4}$ miles. What is the total distance he walks for his job?

d total distance

Do you UNDERSTAND?

2. What phrase from Exercise 1 gives you a clue that you will use addition in your drawing to solve the problem?

3. **Write a Problem** Write a real-world problem that uses addition or subtraction of fractions with like denominators and that can be solved by drawing a picture and writing an equation.

Independent Practice

In **4** through **6**, draw a picture and write an equation. Then solve.

4. If Jessie hikes all 3 trails, how far will she hike?

5. Kent only wants to hike Wing Trail. How much farther will Jessie hike than Kent?

Trails and Distances

- Wing Trail $2\frac{3}{4}$ mi
- Sunset Trail $1\frac{7}{8}$ mi
- Ridge Trail $1\frac{1}{3}$ mi

Stuck? Try this....

- What do I know?
- What am I asked to find?
- What diagram can I use to help understand the problem?
- Can I use addition, subtraction, multiplication, or division?
- Is all of my work correct?
- Did I answer the right question?
- Is my answer reasonable?

*For another example, see Set F on page 241.

What do I know?

Yori walks $\frac{3}{10}$ of a mile to her first job. At her second job she will have walked a total of $1\frac{2}{5}$ miles.

What am I asked to find?

The distance from the first to the second job

Draw a Picture

$1\frac{2}{5}$ miles

$\frac{3}{10}$	d miles

Write an Equation

Let d = the distance from first to second job

$$\frac{3}{10} + d = 1\frac{2}{5} \quad \text{or} \quad 1\frac{2}{5} - \frac{3}{10} = d$$

$$1\frac{2}{5} - \frac{3}{10} = 1\frac{4}{10} - \frac{3}{10} = 1\frac{1}{10}$$

$$d = 1\frac{1}{10} \text{ miles}$$

It is $1\frac{1}{10}$ miles from Yori's first job to her second job.

---

6. Renee mixed red, white, and yellow paint. She used $1\frac{2}{3}$ gallons of red paint, $5\frac{5}{6}$ gallons of white paint, and $2\frac{1}{2}$ gallons of yellow. How many gallons of paint did Renee mix in all?

7. Katya needs $2\frac{5}{6}$ yards of satin fabric. She has $\frac{3}{4}$ of a yard now. How much more fabric does Katya need to buy?

8. Number Sense Give an example of when the sum of two fractions equals 1 whole.

9. Parker's dad drove $2\frac{1}{3}$ miles from the start of a construction zone. He stopped to read this road sign. How far will Parker's dad have driven when he reaches the end of the construction zone?

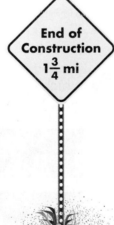

End of Construction $1\frac{3}{4}$ mi

10. Writing to Explain Gene says that the two circles below show the same amount. Do you agree? Write a good math explanation to support your decision.

11. Writing to Explain In many cases, a baby's weight at birth is equal to one half his or her weight at age one. Explain how to estimate the weight of a baby at birth if this baby weighs 18 pounds at age one.

12. Last year, Mr. Kline's fifth-grade class planted a longleaf pine sapling that was $1\frac{5}{12}$ feet tall. Now the sapling is $3\frac{1}{4}$ feet tall. How many feet did the sapling grow from last year?

A $1\frac{1}{2}$ feet   **B** $1\frac{5}{6}$ feet   **C** $2\frac{1}{2}$ feet   **D** $3\frac{3}{12}$ feet

Which improper fraction does the model show? (9-1)

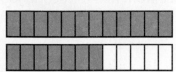

A. $\frac{12}{19}$

B. $\frac{12}{15}$

C. $\frac{15}{12}$

D. $\frac{19}{12}$

② Yao drank $\frac{11}{4}$ bottles of water during a soccer game. What is this number expressed as a mixed number? (9-1)

F. $3\frac{1}{4}$

G. $2\frac{3}{4}$

H. $2\frac{1}{2}$

I. $2\frac{1}{4}$

③ Which expression does the model show? (9-2)

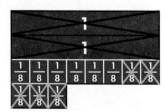

A. $3\frac{3}{8} + \frac{5}{8}$

B. $3\frac{3}{8} + 2\frac{5}{8}$

C. $3\frac{3}{8} - 2\frac{5}{8}$

D. $3\frac{3}{8} - \frac{5}{8}$

④ Marie needs $2\frac{1}{4}$ yards of fabric. She already has $1\frac{3}{8}$ yards. How many more yards of fabric does she need? (9-4)

F. $\frac{1}{8}$ yard

G. $\frac{3}{4}$ yard

H. $\frac{7}{8}$ yard

I. $1\frac{7}{8}$ yards

⑤ Mary weighed $7\frac{1}{2}$ pounds when she was born. What number makes the statement true? (9-1)

$$7\frac{1}{2} = \frac{\blacksquare}{2}$$

A. 15

B. 14

C. 9

D. 8

⑥ Which expression does the model show? (9-2)

F. $\frac{4}{5} + \frac{3}{5}$

G. $\frac{5}{5} + \frac{5}{5}$

H. $3 + \frac{1}{5}$

I. $1\frac{4}{5} + 2\frac{3}{5}$

7 Rick made a paper football that was $1\frac{1}{6}$ inches long. Carly made one $\frac{5}{6}$ of an inch long. How much longer was Rick's paper football than Carly's? (9-4)

A. $\frac{1}{6}$ inch

B. $\frac{1}{3}$ inch

C. $\frac{2}{3}$ inch

D. $\frac{5}{6}$ inch

8 The Jacobys went on a 600-mile trip. On the first day they drove $5\frac{2}{3}$ hours and on the second day they drove $4\frac{3}{5}$ hours. How many hours did they drive during the first two days? (9-3)

F. $10\frac{4}{15}$ hours

G. 10 hours

H. $9\frac{19}{30}$ hours

I. $9\frac{4}{15}$ hours

9 Which equation does NOT match the picture? (9-6)

	x	
$2\frac{7}{8}$		$4\frac{5}{6}$

A. $x - 2\frac{7}{8} = 4\frac{5}{6}$

B. $x = 2\frac{7}{8} + 4\frac{5}{6}$

C. $x = 4\frac{5}{6} - 2\frac{7}{8}$

D. $x - 4\frac{5}{6} = 2\frac{7}{8}$

10 What is the sum of $4\frac{1}{6} + 3\frac{1}{5}$? (9-3)

F. $7\frac{1}{15}$

G. $7\frac{2}{11}$

H. $7\frac{11}{60}$

I. $7\frac{11}{30}$

11 What is the sum of $1\frac{7}{8} + 2\frac{3}{8}$? (9-2)

A. $3\frac{1}{4}$

B. $3\frac{1}{2}$

C. $4\frac{1}{8}$

D. $4\frac{1}{4}$

12 Dawson says that when you simplify the expression $\left(2\frac{4}{10} + 8\frac{4}{5}\right) - 3\frac{1}{5}$ you get a whole number. What whole number do you get? (9-5)

13 The main ingredients for Kayla's banana bread recipe are $2\frac{1}{3}$ cups of flour, $\frac{3}{4}$ cup of sugar, and $1\frac{1}{2}$ cups of mashed bananas. How many more cups of dry ingredients (flour and sugar) than wet ingredients (bananas) go into Kayla's banana bread? Explain. (9-5)

THINK
SOLVE
EXPLAIN

Set A, pages 222–224

Write the improper fraction and mixed number.

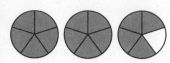

There are 2 wholes shaded and $\frac{4}{5}$ of 1 whole shaded. You can see that this is $2\frac{4}{5}$ or $\frac{14}{5}$. You can also follow the steps below to write $2\frac{4}{5}$ as an improper fraction.

Step 1

Multiply the denominator of the fraction by the whole number.
$2 \times 5 = 10$

Step 2

Add the numerator of the fraction to the product of the denominator and the whole number.
$10 + 4 = 14$

Step 3

Write the fraction using the same denominator. $\frac{14}{5}$

So, $2\frac{4}{5} = \frac{14}{5}$.

Remember that an improper fraction and a mixed number can represent the same value.

Write each mixed number as an improper fraction.

1. $3\frac{1}{2}$ **2.** $2\frac{2}{3}$ **3.** $5\frac{1}{6}$

4. $3\frac{4}{5}$ **5.** $1\frac{1}{5}$ **6.** $9\frac{7}{8}$

Write each improper fraction as a mixed number in simplest form.

7. $\frac{4}{3}$ **8.** $\frac{3}{2}$ **9.** $\frac{6}{4}$

10. $\frac{12}{9}$ **11.** $\frac{31}{7}$ **12.** $\frac{46}{5}$

Set B, pages 226–228

Find $2\frac{1}{6} - 1\frac{5}{6}$.

Step 1 Model the number you are subtracting from and rename 1 whole if necessary to subtract.

Step 2 Use your renamed model to cross out the number you are subtracting.

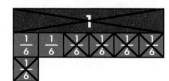

$2\frac{1}{6} - 1\frac{5}{6} = \frac{2}{6}$

Step 3 Write the answer in simplest form: $\frac{2}{6} = \frac{1}{3}$

Remember that when you use a model to add mixed numbers, you should rename improper fractions in the sum.

Use a model to find each sum or difference. Simplify if possible.

1. $2\frac{1}{4} + 3\frac{3}{4}$ **2.** $6\frac{2}{3} + 5\frac{2}{3}$

3. $7\frac{5}{9} + 8\frac{7}{9}$ **4.** $12\frac{1}{4} - 7\frac{2}{4}$

5. $15\frac{3}{5} - 3\frac{4}{5}$ **6.** $5\frac{5}{8} - 3\frac{1}{8}$

Set C, pages 230–231

Find $1\frac{5}{6} + 2\frac{3}{8}$.

$1\frac{5}{6} = 1\frac{20}{24}$

$+ 2\frac{3}{8} = 2\frac{9}{24}$

$\overline{ 3\frac{29}{24} = 4\frac{5}{24}}$

Step 1 Write equivalent fractions with the LCD.

Step 2 Add the fractions.

Step 3 Add the whole numbers. Rename improper fractions and simplify the sum, if possible.

Remember that mixed numbers are added the same way whole numbers and fractions are added.

1. $5\frac{1}{2} + 2\frac{1}{8}$ **2.** $3\frac{1}{4} + 1\frac{5}{6}$

3. $5\frac{7}{10} + 4\frac{2}{5}$ **4.** $7\frac{3}{5} + 6\frac{2}{3}$

5. $8\frac{5}{9} + 9\frac{1}{3}$ **6.** $2\frac{5}{12} + 3\frac{3}{4}$

Set D, pages 232–233

Find $5\frac{1}{5} - 3\frac{1}{2}$.

$$5\frac{1}{5} = 5\frac{2}{10} = 4\frac{12}{10}$$
$$-\,3\frac{1}{2} = 3\frac{5}{10} = 3\frac{5}{10}$$
$$\overline{\qquad\qquad\quad 1\frac{7}{10}}$$

Step 1 Write equivalent fractions with the LCD.

Step 2 Rename $5\frac{2}{10}$ to show more tenths.

Step 3 Subtract the fractions. Subtract the whole numbers. Simplify the difference.

Remember that subtracting mixed numbers may require renaming.

1. $7\frac{5}{6} - 3\frac{2}{3}$ 2. $2\frac{3}{5} - 1\frac{1}{2}$

3. $5\frac{2}{3} - 4\frac{5}{6}$ 4. $9 - 3\frac{3}{8}$

5. $3\frac{1}{9} - 1\frac{1}{3}$ 6. $6\frac{1}{4} - 3\frac{2}{5}$

7. $9\frac{1}{4} - 2\frac{5}{8}$ 8. $4 - 1\frac{2}{5}$

Set E, pages 234–235

Gil has two lengths of wallpaper, $2\frac{3}{4}$ yards and $1\frac{7}{8}$ yards long. He used some and now has $1\frac{5}{6}$ yards left over. How many yards of wallpaper did Gil use?

Step 1 Add to find the total amount of wallpaper Gil has.

$$2\frac{3}{4} = 2\frac{18}{24}$$
$$+\,1\frac{7}{8} = 1\frac{21}{24}$$
$$\overline{\qquad\quad 4\frac{5}{8}}$$

Step 2 Subtract to find the amount of wallpaper Gil used.

$$4\frac{5}{8} = 4\frac{15}{24}$$
$$-\,1\frac{5}{6} = 1\frac{20}{24}$$
$$\overline{\qquad\quad 2\frac{19}{24}}$$

Gill used $2\frac{19}{24}$ yards of wallpaper.

Remember when you add or subtract mixed numbers, rename the fractional part to have a common denominator.

Simplify each expression.

1. $\left(2\frac{1}{6} + 3\frac{3}{4}\right) - 1\frac{5}{12}$

2. $\left(4\frac{4}{5} + 7\frac{1}{3}\right) - 1\frac{7}{15}$

3. $\left(8\frac{3}{8} - 4\frac{5}{6}\right) + 1\frac{11}{24}$

4. $2\frac{9}{25} + 2\frac{9}{50} + 2\frac{1}{100}$

Set F, pages 236–237

Draw a picture, write an equation, and solve.

Johanna will need milk to make two different recipes. In one recipe, she will need $1\frac{5}{8}$ cups, and in the other recipe she will need $1\frac{7}{8}$ cups. How many cups of milk will Johanna need in all?

Draw a picture.

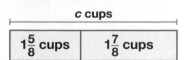

Write an equation and solve.

Let c = cups $1\frac{5}{8} + 1\frac{7}{8} = c$ $c = 3\frac{1}{2}$ cups

Johanna needs $3\frac{1}{2}$ cups of milk in all.

Remember to draw a picture and write an equation to solve.

1. Jonathan bicycled $1\frac{6}{15}$ miles from his house to the park. From there he went $\frac{2}{10}$ mile to the bookstore. Finally, he went $\frac{4}{10}$ mile to the grocery store. How far did he ride his bicycle?

2. A $6\frac{1}{4}$-inch length is cut from a ribbon that is $19\frac{1}{2}$ inches long. How much ribbon is left?

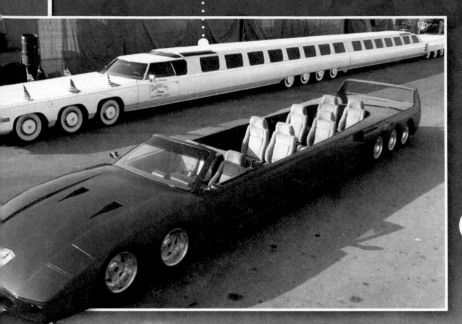

Units of Length

1 As of 2008, the largest car ever built included a swimming pool inside! It is the white car, shown here. About how many feet long is this car? You will find out in Lesson 10-4.

2 The smallest post office in the United States is located in Ochopee, Florida. What are the dimensions of this post office? You will find out in Lesson 10-2.

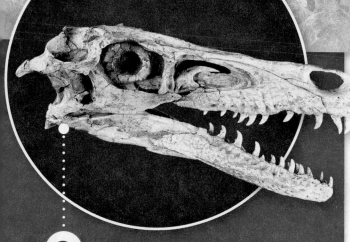

3 About how long is this dinosaur skull bone in millimeters? You will find out in Lesson 10-4.

4 The lighthouse in Yokohama, Japan, is known as the tallest lighthouse in the world. How many yards tall is this lighthouse? You will find out in Lesson 10-2.

Vocabulary

Choose the best term from the box.

- length
- mixed number
- prime number
- composite number

1. A _?_ is a whole number and a fraction.

2. _?_ is the measure of how long something is.

3. A _?_ is a whole number greater than 1 that has exactly two factors, itself and 1.

Multiplying by 10 and 100

Find each product.

4. 6×10 5. 6×100

6. 4×100 7. 4×10

8. 120×10 9. 100×100

10. 671×100 11. 43×10

12. 50×100 13. $2,311 \times 10$

Comparing

Write $<$, $=$, or $>$ for each $\bigcirc$.

14. $2^2 + 1$ $\bigcirc$ 10

15. 0.01 $\bigcirc$ 0.001

16. $50 - 6$ $\bigcirc$ $50 - 2 \times 3$

17. 7×3 $\bigcirc$ 2^4

18. $1,000$ $\bigcirc$ 10×10

19. **Writing to Explain** Which is greater, $\frac{1}{5}$ or $\frac{3}{8}$? Explain what steps you took to find the solution.

Topic Essential Questions

- What are customary measurement units for length and how are they related?

- What are metric measurement units for length and how are they related?

MA.5.G.5.3 Solve problems requiring attention to approximation, selection of appropriate measuring tools, and precision of measurement.
Also MA.5.G.5.2

Using Customary Units of Length

How can you use fractions to measure more precisely?

Since an inch (in.) is divided into equal parts, you can use fractions to measure lengths. All measurements are approximations. What is the length of the DVD case to the nearest $\frac{1}{8}$ inch?

Hands-On
inch ruler

Other Examples

The length of a notebook is about 1 foot (ft).	The length of a baseball bat is about 1 yard (yd).	The length of 1 mile (mi) is about four times around the track.
Almost 1 foot		
1 ft = 12 in.	1 yd = 36 in. 1 yd = 3 ft	1 mi = 5,280 ft 1 mi = 1,760 yd

---

Guided Practice*

Do you know HOW?

For **1** and **2**, measure each segment to the nearest inch, $\frac{1}{2}$ inch, $\frac{1}{4}$ inch, and $\frac{1}{8}$ inch.

1.

2.

Do you UNDERSTAND?

3. In the example above, why isn't the measurement of the DVD case 8 inches to the nearest inch?

4. Writing to Explain Which is a more precise measurement, to the nearest $\frac{1}{2}$ inch or to the nearest $\frac{1}{8}$ inch? Explain.

Independent Practice

In **5** through **7**, use a ruler to measure each object to the nearest inch, $\frac{1}{2}$ inch, $\frac{1}{4}$ inch, and $\frac{1}{8}$ inch.

5.

6.

7.

The smaller the units used for measuring, the more precise the measurement. You can use a ruler to find the length to the nearest inch, $\frac{1}{2}$ inch, $\frac{1}{4}$ inch, and $\frac{1}{8}$ inch.

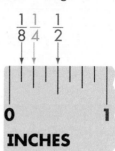

INCHES

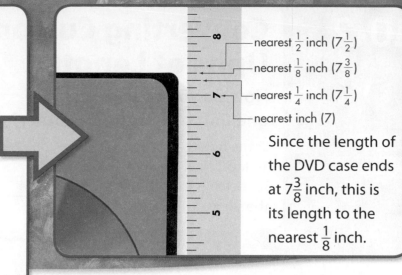

nearest $\frac{1}{2}$ inch ($7\frac{1}{2}$)
nearest $\frac{1}{8}$ inch ($7\frac{3}{8}$)
nearest $\frac{1}{4}$ inch ($7\frac{1}{4}$)
nearest inch (7)

Since the length of the DVD case ends at $7\frac{3}{8}$ inch, this is its length to the nearest $\frac{1}{8}$ inch.

Independent Practice

For **8** through **11**, choose the most appropriate unit to measure the length of each. Write in., ft, yd, or mi.

8. pencil

9. floor

10. road

11. lawn

Problem Solving

12. Which line segment measures about $2\frac{1}{2}$ inches long?

A ├────────────────┤

B ├──────────┤

C ├──────────────────────┤

D ├────────────────┤

13. **Think** **About the Process** Mae spent $12 on a new purse, $6 on lunch, and $14 for a book. She had $12 when she got home. Which expression shows how much money Mae started with?

F $12 - 12 + 6 + 14$

G $(2 \times 12) + 14 + 6$

H $12 - 6 - (14 + 12)$

I $2 \times (12 + 12) - 14$

14. **Writing to Explain** When you measure the length of an object, will your measurement ever be exact? Explain.

Critical THINKING

15. Jan has $49 to spend on poster board. If each poster board costs $3, how many poster boards can she buy?

16. The measure of the length of a paper clip to the nearest inch, $\frac{1}{2}$ inch, and $\frac{1}{4}$ inch is 2 inches. How is this possible?

17. Fifteen pounds of meat cost $26.85. Is it reasonable to say that the price per pound is $11? Explain.

THINK SOLVE EXPLAIN

DIGITAL

Animated Glossary, eTools
www.pearsonsuccessnet.com

Lesson

10-2

MA.5.G.5.2 Compare, contrast, and convert units of measure within the same dimension (length, mass, or time) to solve problems.

Converting Customary Units of Length

How do you change from one unit of length to another?

1 foot (ft) = 12 inches (in.)
1 yard (yd) = 3 ft = 36 in.
1 mile (mi) = 1,760 yd = 5,280 ft

Some frogs can jump 11 feet. What are some other ways to describe the same distance?

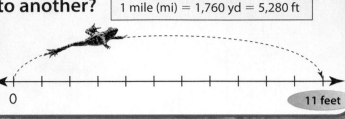

0

11 feet

Another Example How do you compare customary units of length?

Compare lengths. Write >, <, or = for $\bigcirc$: 14 yd $\bigcirc$ 41 ft

One Way

Convert the larger unit to the smaller unit and compare.

Convert: 1 yd = 3 ft
So, 14 yd = 14 × 3 ft
= 42 ft

Compare: 42 > 41
So, 14 yd > 41 ft

Another Way

Convert the smaller unit to the larger unit and compare.

Convert: 3 ft = 1 yd
So, 41 ft = $\frac{41}{3}$ yd
= $13\frac{2}{3}$ yd

Compare: 14 > $13\frac{2}{3}$
So, 14 yd > 41 ft

Guided Practice*

Do you know HOW?

In **1** through **5**, convert each unit of length.

1. 9 ft = ⬛ yd

2. 288 in. = ⬛ yd

3. 5 ft = ⬛ in.

4. 8 ft 7 in. = ⬛ in.

5. 219 in. = ⬛ ft ⬛ in. or ⬛ ft

For **6** and **7**, compare lengths. Write >, <, or = for each $\bigcirc$.

6. 64 in. $\bigcirc$ 2 yd

7. 29 yd $\bigcirc$ 87 ft

Do you UNDERSTAND?

8. If you want to convert yards to feet, what operation would you use?

9. If you want to convert feet to miles, what operation would you use?

10. **Writing to Explain** In the example at the top, explain how you could use a mixed number to write 11 feet as an equivalent measure in yards.

To change larger units to smaller units, multiply.

11 ft = ▮ in.

Think 1 foot = 12 inches.

	11 ft									
12 in.	12 in.	12 in.	12 in.	12 in.	12 in.	12 in.	12 in.	12 in.	12 in.	12 in.

↑
1 ft

Find 11 × 12.

11 × 12 = 132

11 feet = 132 inches

To change smaller units to larger units, divide.

11 ft = ▮ yd ▮ ft

Think 3 feet = 1 yard.

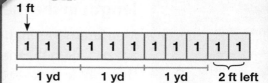

1 ft
↓

1	1	1	1	1	1	1	1	1	1	1

1 yd   1 yd   1 yd   2 ft left

Find 11 ÷ 3.

11 ÷ 3 = 3 R2

11 feet = 3 yards, 2 feet

Independent Practice

In **11** through **22**, convert each unit of length.

Tip *You may need to make two conversions.*

11. 3 yd = ▮ in.

12. 24 ft = ▮ yd

13. 2 mi = ▮ ft

14. 56 ft = ▮ yd ▮ ft

15. 12 ft 7 in. = ▮ in.

16. 6 in. = ▮ ft

17. 4 yd = ▮ in.

18. 10 yd = ▮ in.

19. 18 ft = ▮ in.

20. 2 mi = ▮ yd

21. 5,280 ft = ▮ mi

22. 15 yd 6 ft = ▮ ft

For **23** through **25**, compare lengths. Write >, <, or = for each ◯.

23. 100 ft ◯ 3 yd

24. 74 in. ◯ 2 yd 2 in.

25. 5,200 ft 145 in. ◯ 1 mi 40 in.

Problem Solving

26. The lighthouse in Yokohama, Japan, is known as the tallest in the world. It is 348 feet tall. How many yards tall is this lighthouse?

27. **Critical THINKING** The dimensions of the nation's smallest post office are 8 ft 4 in. × 7 ft 3 in. Why would you use the measurement 8 ft 4 in. instead of 7 ft 16 in?

28. Ariana had 144 peaches. She has to pack 9 boxes with an equal number of peaches. How many peaches should she pack in each box?

144 peaches

?	?	?	?	?	?	?	?	?

↑
Peaches per box

29. The New York City Marathon is 26 miles, 385 yards. How many feet is this?

    A 5,306 ft   **B** 45,760 ft   **C** 138,435 ft   **D** 1,647,360 ft

Lesson
10-3

MA.5.G.5.3 Solve problems
requiring attention to
approximation, selection
of appropriate measuring
tools, and precision of
measurement.
Also MA.5.G.5.2

Using Metric Units of Length

Hands-On
centimeter ruler

What units are used to measure length in the metric system?

Measurements in the metric system are based on the meter. The chart at the right lists other commonly used metric units and their equivalents.

Metric Equivalents

1 centimeter = 10 millimeters (mm)
1 meter (m) = 100 centimeters (cm)
1 meter = 1,000 millimeters
1,000 meters = 1 kilometer (km)

Another Example How do you measure length using metric units?

CM 1 2 3 4 5 6 7 8 9 10 11 12 13 14 15

To the nearest centimeter: 12 cm   To the nearest millimeter: 118 mm

Guided Practice*

Do you know HOW?

1. Which unit would be most appropriate to measure the length of a kitchen?

2. Measure this segment to the nearest centimeter and nearest millimeter.

Do you UNDERSTAND?

3. In Another Example, which is the more precise measurement, to the nearest centimeter or to the nearest millimeter?

4. **Writing to Explain** Why is the millimeter not an appropriate unit to measure the distance across a town?

Independent Practice

For **5** through **7**, write mm, cm, m, or km as the most appropriate unit.

5. Thickness of a fingernail   6. Length of a picnic table   7. Length of a road

In **8** through **13**, measure each segment to the nearest centimeter and to the nearest millimeter.

8. ├─────────────┤   9. ├────────┤   10. ├──────┤

11. ├────┤   12. ├─────┤   13. ├────────┤

248   *For another example, see Set C on page 256.*

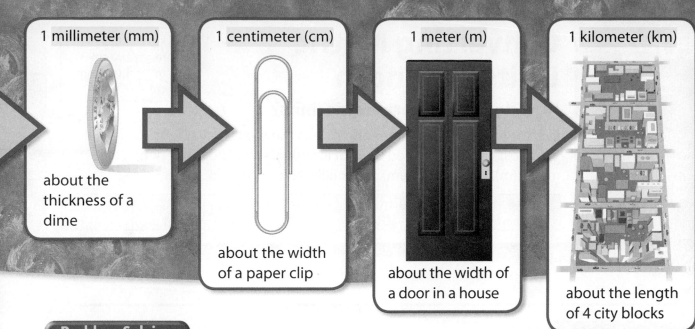

1 millimeter (mm)	1 centimeter (cm)	1 meter (m)	1 kilometer (km)
about the thickness of a dime	about the width of a paper clip	about the width of a door in a house	about the length of 4 city blocks

Problem Solving

14. Which object is 65 millimeters wide?

A

B

C
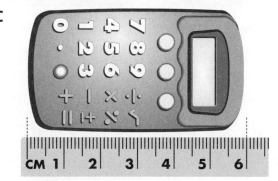

D

15. Writing to Explain Darcy is estimating how much fabric she will need to make a new jacket. Is estimating reasonable in this situation? Why or why not?

Critical THINKING

16. Dana ordered 1 medium cheese pizza with 8 slices. She ate 2 slices. Write 2 equivalent fractions to show the part of the pizza Dana did NOT eat.

17. Choose from the measures listed below to determine the most appropriate lengths.

40 mm	2 m
18 cm	200 km

a The distance between two cities

b The length of a bicycle

c The length of a drinking straw

d The length of a caterpillar

18. If a measuring cup has $\frac{1}{4}$ cup milk in it, what decimal represents the amount of milk needed to finish filling the cup?

MA.5.G.5.2 Compare, contrast, and convert units of measure within the same dimension (length, mass, or time) to solve problems.

Converting Metric Units of Length

1 km	= 1,000 m
1 m	= 100 cm
1 m	= 1,000 mm
1 cm	= 10 mm

How do you convert metric units?

Every metric unit is 10 times as much as the next smaller unit. The most commonly used units of length are the kilometer (km), meter (m), centimeter (cm), and millimeter (mm).

1 kilometer 1,000 m	1 hectometer 100 m	1 dekameter 10 m	1 meter 1 m	1 decimeter 0.1 m	1 centimeter 0.01 m	1 millimeter 0.001 m

---

Another Example **How do you compare metric units?**

Compare lengths. Write >, <, or = for ◯ : 12 m ◯ 800 cm

One Way

Convert the larger unit to the smaller unit and compare.

Convert: 1 m = 100 cm
So, 12 m = 12 × 100
= 1,200 cm

Compare: 1,200 > 800
So, 12 m > 800 cm

Another Way

Convert the smaller unit to the larger unit and compare.

Convert: 100 cm = 1 m
So, 800 cm = 800 ÷ 100
= 8 m

Compare: 12 > 8
So, 12 m > 800 cm

Guided Practice*

Do you know HOW?

In **1** and **2**, convert each unit of length.

1. 800 cm = ▮ m   **2.** 58 m = ▮ mm

Compare lengths. Write >, <, or = for ◯.

3. 9,000 m ◯ 20 km

Do you UNDERSTAND?

4. Writing to Explain To find the number of meters in one kilometer, why do you multiply 1 × 1,000?

5. Number Sense Convert 12.5 centimeters to millimeters. Explain.

Independent Practice

In **6** through **11**, convert each unit of length.

6. 75 cm = ▮ mm   **7.** 120,000,000 mm = ▮ km   **8.** 121 km = ▮ cm

9. 17,000 m = ▮ km   **10.** 48,000 mm = ▮ m   **11.** 4 km = ▮ m

For another example, see Set D on page 257.

The distance between two highway markers is 3 kilometers. How many meters is this?

$$3 \text{ km} = \boxed{} \text{ m}$$

To change from larger units to smaller units, multiply.

(Think) 1 km = 1,000 m

Find 3 × 1,000.

3 km = 3,000 m

The distance between a kitchen and living room is 1,200 centimeters. How many meters is this?

$$1,200 \text{ cm} = \boxed{} \text{ m}$$

To change from smaller units to larger units, divide.

(Think) 100 cm = 1 m

Find 1,200 ÷ 100.

1,200 cm = 12 m

For **12** through **17**, compare lengths. Write >, <, or = for each ◯.

12. 25,365 cm ◯ 30 m

13. 36 km ◯ 36,000 m

14. 1,200 mm ◯ 12 m

15. 52,800 cm ◯ 1 km

16. 7,500,000 m ◯ 750 km

17. 800 m ◯ 799,999 mm

Problem Solving

For **18**, use the photo at the right.

18. About how many millimeters long is this dinosaur skull bone?

19. What is the equivalent length of the bumblebee bat in centimeters?

- **A** 0.03
- **B** 13
- **C** 3
- **D** 300

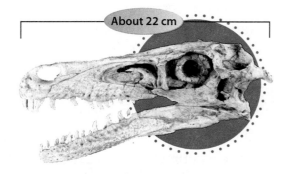

About 22 cm

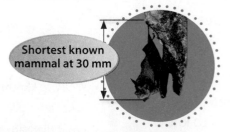

Shortest known mammal at 30 mm

20. A new pencil was 18 cm long. Now it measures 12.7 cm. How many centimeters of the pencil have been used?

21. Estimation As of 2008, the longest car ever built was 30.5 meters long. A meter is a little longer than a yard. Estimate the length of this car in feet.

22. (Think About the Process) There are 16 seats in each row of a theater. There are 32 rows in all. Which expression would you use to find the number of seats in the theater?

- **F** 16 + 32
- **G** 32 ÷ 16
- **H** 32 × 16
- **I** 332 − 16

23. Writing to Explain Which fraction is

greater: $\frac{7}{8}$ or $\frac{9}{12}$? Explain how you know.

MA.5.A.6.5 Solve non-routine problems using various strategies including "solving a simpler problem" and "guess, check, and revise."

Problem Solving

Draw a Picture and Make an Organized List

The Diaz family has 12 one-foot sections of fence to build a rectangular kennel for their dog. They want the kennel to have a perimeter of 12 feet, and have the greatest possible area. What should the dimensions of the kennel be?

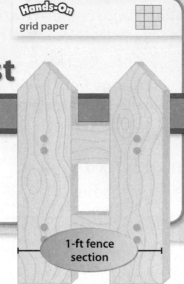

1-ft fence section

Guided Practice*

Do you know HOW?

Draw a picture and make a list to solve.

1. Ali has 18 meters of fence to enclose her garden. She wants this garden to have a rectangular shape with the greatest possible area. What should the dimensions of Ali's garden be?

Do you UNDERSTAND?

2. How can drawing a picture and making an organized list help you solve some problems?

3. **Write a Problem** Write a real-world problem that can be solved by drawing a picture and making a list.

Independent Practice

4. Julie will be making a quilt. If she wants the quilt to have a perimeter of 30 feet, and cover the greatest area possible, what should its dimensions be? Draw a picture and make a list to solve.

5. Eric painted a square picture that has an area of 400 square centimeters. To frame it, he needs to know the perimeter. What is the perimeter of Eric's picture?

6. A rectangle is 4 inches long and 3 inches wide. If the dimensions of the rectangle are doubled, how will the area change?

Critical THINKING

A The area will double.

B The area will be 3 times greater.

C The area will be 4 times greater.

D The area will be 5 times greater.

Stuck? Try this....

- What do I know?
- What am I asked to find?
- What diagram can I use to help understand the problem?
- Can I use addition, subtraction, multiplication, or division?
- Is all of my work correct?
- Did I answer the right question?
- Is my answer reasonable?

*For another example, see Set E on page 257.

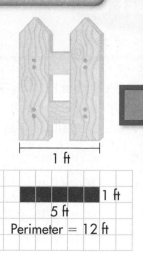

The length of the kennel cannot be longer than 5 feet because the perimeter needs to be 12 feet.

I can draw a picture on grid paper to show this.

The area is $5 \times 1 = 5$ ft².

1 ft

5 ft
1 ft
Perimeter = 12 ft

I can draw more pictures and make a list of all possible dimensions and areas.

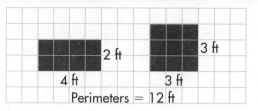

2 ft   3 ft
4 ft   3 ft
Perimeters = 12 ft

$$5 \times 1 = 5 \text{ ft}^2 \qquad 4 \times 2 = 8 \text{ ft}^2$$
$$3 \times 3 = 9 \text{ ft}^2$$

The dimensions of the kennel should be 3 ft wide × 3 ft long.

7. Mary is designing a geometric picture that will be put on a banner. The picture has a square with an area of 25 square inches. What are the dimensions of the square?

8. Beth's rectangular garden is 6 feet × 3 feet. She wants to plant 6 flowers per square foot.

   a How many flowers will she plant?

   b How can you check your answer?

9. The length of a rectangular sandbox is 8 feet. The area of the sandbox is 40 square feet. If the length of the box is extended 2 more feet, how many feet does the width of the box need to be to have a final area of 60 square feet?

10. Rocio finished 21 pages of a scrapbook in 3 days. On Monday, she finished half as many pages as on Tuesday. On Wednesday, Rocio finished twice as many pages as on Tuesday. How many pages did Rocio finish each day?

11. Robert has $107.56 in his savings account. He withdraws $30.60. Draw a picture and write an equation that can be solved to find Robert's new balance. Let b = Robert's new balance.

12. **Writing to Explain** Maria says that rectangles with the same perimeter can have different areas. Is Maria correct? Use a drawing to support your explanation.

13. Suppose you want to buy 12 comic books. The store sells small and large comics and is having a special. You have $24. Do you have enough money to buy 12 small books? Explain.

3 small for $6

4 large for $12

1 Use an inch ruler. Which is the measure of the segment to the nearest $\frac{1}{8}$ inch? (10-1)

A. 1 inch

B. $1\frac{1}{8}$ inches

C. $1\frac{2}{8}$ inches

D. $1\frac{3}{8}$ inches

2 Which of the following is true? (10-4)

F. 100 cm < 500 mm

G. 100 cm > 3 m

H. 100 cm > 1 km

I. 100 cm = 1 m

3 Which is the *least* precise measure? (10-1)

A. To the nearest inch

B. To the nearest $\frac{1}{2}$ inch

C. To the nearest $\frac{1}{4}$ inch

D. To the nearest $\frac{1}{8}$ inch

4 Which unit is most appropriate to measure the length of a house? (10-3)

F. Kilometer

G. Meter

H. Centimeter

I. Millimeter

5 The tail of a Boeing 747 airplane is 63 feet 8 inches tall. How many inches tall is the tail? (10-2)

A. 77 inches

B. 720 inches

C. 728 inches

D. 764 inches

6 Each 5 centimeters that an archaeologist digs is called a spit. How many millimeters are in a spit? (10-4)

F. $\frac{1}{2}$ millimeter

G. 10 millimeters

H. 50 millimeters

I. 500 millimeters

7 Use an inch ruler to measure. Which is closest to the height of the treble clef shown? (10-1)

A. $\frac{1}{4}$ inch

B. $\frac{3}{4}$ inch

C. $\frac{5}{6}$ inch

D. $\frac{7}{8}$ inch

8 A ship is 180 meters in length. How would you find how many centimeters are equal to 180 meters? (10-4)

F. 180×10

G. $180 \div 10$

H. 180×100

I. $180 \div 100$

9 Use a centimeter ruler. Which piece of yarn has a length of 6 centimeters? (10-3)

A.

B.

C.

D.

10 Which inequality is NOT true? (10-2)

F. 3 ft 11 in. < 1 yd 1 ft

G. 75 in. > 2 yd

H. 1 yd 9 ft > 4 yd

I. 3 yd 8 in. < 12 ft 4 in.

11 In Florida, any boat less than 12 feet will have a registration fee of $7.25. Boats larger than 12 feet will have a higher registration fee. If a boat is 152 inches in length, will the registration fee be $7.25? (10-2)

A. Yes, because 152 inches = 11 feet and 11 < 12.

B. Yes, because 12 feet = 1,200 inches and 152 < 1,200.

C. No, because 152 inches = 15.2 feet and 15.2 > 12.

D. No, because 12 feet = 144 inches and 144 < 152.

12 A mosaic is a piece of art made by putting together small pieces of glass. Maria uses 1-inch-square glass pieces to make a rectangular mosaic having an area of 10 square inches. Which of the following could be the perimeter of Maria's mosaic? (10-5)

F. 10 inches

G. 14 inches

H. 20 inches

I. 24 inches

13 Which is equivalent to the distance Jake swam? (10-4)

Student	Distance Swam
Alex	1 km 200 m
Santo	1,100 m
Jake	1,300 m
Savannah	1 km 500 m

A. 130 km

B. 13 km

C. 1 km 3,000 m

D. 1 km 300 m

14 Liam's thumb measures 4 centimeters. How many millimeters is this? (10-4)

15 THINK SOLVE EXPLAIN Mr. Santiago is building a rectangular fence for a garden with a perimeter of 14 meters. Use grid paper to draw a picture and make an organized list of all of the possible area models for the garden. What is the greatest possible area for the garden? (10-5)

Set A, pages 244–245

Find the length to the nearest inch, $\frac{1}{2}$ inch, $\frac{1}{4}$ inch, and $\frac{1}{8}$ inch.

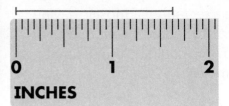

INCHES

To the nearest

inch: 2 in. $\frac{1}{2}$ inch: $1\frac{1}{2}$ in.

$\frac{1}{4}$ inch: $1\frac{3}{4}$ in. $\frac{1}{8}$ inch: $1\frac{5}{8}$ in.

Remember to write your measurements in fractions using simplest form. Use a ruler.

1. Find the length to the nearest $\frac{1}{4}$ inch and $\frac{1}{2}$ inch.

2. Find the length to the nearest inch and $\frac{1}{8}$ inch.

Set B, pages 246–247

Convert 3 yards to inches.

 1 yard = 36 inches.
To change larger units to smaller units, multiply.

$3 \times 36 = 108$

So, 3 yards = 108 inches.

| 1 foot (ft) = 12 inches (in.) |
| 1 yard (yd) = 3 ft = 36 in. |
| 1 mile (mi) = 1,760 yd = 5,280 ft |

Remember to multiply when changing larger units to smaller units and to divide when changing smaller units to larger units.

1. 2 ft = ___ in.   2. 48 in. = ___ ft

3. 12 ft = ___ yd   4. 5 ft = ___ in.

5. 5 yd = ___ ft   6. 84 in. = ___ ft

Compare. Write >, <, or = for each ◯.

7. 7 yd ◯ 50 ft   8. 212 in. ◯ 2 yd

9. 4 ft 8 in. ◯ 1 yd 2 ft 1 in.

Set C, pages 248–249

Choose a reasonable metric unit for the length of a driveway.

| A small stamp is 25 mm long and 15 mm wide. |
| A piece of chalk is about 1 cm thick. |
| A fast walker can walk 1 km in 10 minutes. |

The meter is the most reasonable unit.

Remember the shortest to longest units of length are millimeter (mm), centimeter (cm), meter (m), and kilometer (km).

Write mm, cm, m, or km as the most appropriate unit.

1. length of a calculator

2. distance from Chicago to Daytona Beach

Set D, pages 250–251

Convert 2 meters to centimeters.

1 km	= 1,000 m
1 m	= 100 cm
1 m	= 1,000 mm
1 cm	= 10 mm

 Think 1 meter = 100 centimeters.
To change larger units to smaller units, multiply.

$2 \times 100 = 200$

So, 2 meters = 200 centimeters.

Convert 3,000 meters to kilometers.

 Think 1 kilometer = 1,000 meters.
To change smaller units to larger units, divide.

$3,000 \div 1,000 = 3$

So, 3,000 meters = 3 kilometers.

Remember to convert to the same unit of measure before comparing two lengths.

Convert.

1. 5 m = ▢ cm   **2.** 2 km = ▢ m

3. 2 km = ▢ cm   **4.** 20 m = ▢ mm

5. 6 m = ▢ mm   **6.** 10 cm = ▢ mm

7. 2,000 mm = ▢ m

8. 9,000 m = ▢ km

Compare. Write >, <, or = for each ◯.

9. 1,000 cm ◯ 1 m

10. 90 mm ◯ 9 cm

11. 3 km ◯ 6,000 m

12. 1,000,000 cm ◯ 8 km

Set E, pages 252–253

When you are asked to draw a picture and make a list to solve a problem, follow these steps:

Step 1 Read and understand the problem.

Step 2 Make a plan by creating a list of possible solutions.

Step 3 Test each of the items in your list to find a solution.

Step 4 Look back and check your work.

Remember that drawing a picture can help you make a list.

1. Cristina has 16 square feet of material to make a rectangular quilt. She wants the quilt to have the least possible (minimum) perimeter. If Cristina uses all 16 square feet, what dimensions should she use for the quilt?

2. Ricardo is making a photo collage from small photos of himself and his friends. He printed each photo as a 1-inch × 1-inch square. He wants the perimeter to be 16 inches and have the greatest possible area. What should the dimensions of the collage be?

Units of Weight, Mass, and Time

1 Diving for lobsters is popular in Key West, Florida. Lobsters typically weigh between 1 and 20 pounds. How many ounces did the heaviest lobster ever recorded weigh? You will find out in Lesson 11-2.

2 How could an ancient Mayan pyramid be a type of calendar? You will find out in Lesson 11-5.

Review What You Know!

3 The ENIAC was built in 1946 and is known as the first computer ever built. It weighed 30 tons. What unit of weight is used to weigh most computers today? You will find out in Lesson 11-1.

4 How does the clock tower Big Ben signal when the British Parliament in London is in session? You will find out in Lesson 11-5.

Vocabulary

Choose the best term from the box.

- customary
- metric
- A.M.
- P.M.

1. A meter is a unit of length in the __?__ system of measurement.

2. A foot is a unit of length in the __?__ system of measurement.

3. Time between midnight and noon is referred to by the abbreviation __?__ .

Multiplication

Find each product.

4. 60×6 5. 24×3

6. 16×7 7. 12×16

8. 100×34 9. 10×6

Division

Find each quotient.

10. $144 \div 16$ 11. $56 \div 7$

12. $1,000 \div 100$ 13. $176 \div 16$

14. $3,600 \div 60$ 15. $120 \div 24$

Elapsed Time

Find each elapsed time.

16. Start: 4:25 P.M.   17. Start: 10:30 P.M.
    Finish: 5:10 P.M.   Finish: 12:15 A.M.

18. **Writing to Explain** Is the elapsed time between 11:40 A.M. and 2:20 P.M. more or less than 3 hours? Explain.

Topic Essential Questions

- What are measurement units for weight and mass, and how are they related?

- What units are used to represent and describe amounts of time?

MA.5.G.5.3 Solve problems requiring attention to approximation, selection of appropriate measuring tools, and precision of measurement.
Also MA.5.G.5.2

Customary Units of Weight

What are customary units of weight?

Weight is <u>how heavy something is</u>. Below are some customary units for measuring weight.

How much does a peach weigh?

1 ounce (oz)   1 pound (lb)

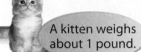

1 ton (T)

A key weighs about 1 ounce.

A kitten weighs about 1 pound.

A giraffe weighs about 1 ton.

Guided Practice*

Do you know HOW?

For **1** through **4**, give the best unit to measure the weight of each item.

1.

slice of bread

2.

sheep

3.

helicopter

4.

bicycle

Do you UNDERSTAND?

5. **Writing to Explain** How can you tell that the weight of the peach is NOT 8 ounces?

6. If you placed 3 keys on the same pan with the peach, how many ounces would be needed to balance the keys and the peach?

7. Mrs. Geiger needs 2 apples. How can she use a balance to measure the weight of 2 apples?

Independent Practice

For **8** through **19**, choose the most appropriate unit to measure the weight of each item.

Tip *Think of a familiar object that weighs one pound, one ounce, or one ton. Use that object to estimate the weight of other objects measured with the same unit.*

8. bulldozer

9. orange

10. pencil

11. greeting card

12. paper clip

13. canoe

14. ocean liner

15. football player

16. cell phone

17. car

18. fork

19. bag of potatoes

Animated Glossary
www.pearsonsuccessnet.com

For another example, see Set A on page 274.

Step 1

Choose the appropriate unit to measure:

A peach weighs less than a pound.

So, the best unit would be the ounce.

Step 2

Estimate:

Think A key weighs about one ounce. How many keys would weigh the same as a peach?

About 8 keys would weigh the same.

A peach weighs about 8 ounces.

Step 3

Measure:

Place the peach on one pan of the balance. Place an ounce weight on the other pan. Add ounce weights until the balance is level, and count the ounce weights.

To the nearest ounce, the peach weighs 7 ounces.

Problem Solving

20. One of the first computers built weighed 30 tons. What would be an appropriate unit of weight to measure the weight of most desktop computers today?

22. Which is a greater number, the number of pounds a rooster weighs or the number of ounces the same rooster weighs?

For **23** through **26**, use the table at the right.

23. How many ounces do two dozen medium apples weigh?

24. Estimate the weight of one apple.

25. Do five dozen large watermelons weigh more or less than 1,000 pounds?

26. How many pounds do three dozen bananas weigh?

27. Which is a good estimate for the weight of a bicycle?

    A 30 ounces   C 30 pounds

    B 3 pounds   D 3,000 ounces

21. **Estimation** Use the height of the box **Critical THINKING** shown below to estimate the length and width of the bottom of the box.

25 cm

Fruit	Weight of One Dozen
(apple)	72 ounces
(banana)	3 pounds
(watermelon)	264 pounds

MA.5.G.5.2 Compare, contrast, and convert units of measure within the same dimension (length, mass, or time) to solve problems.

Converting Customary Units of Weight

1 ton (T) = 2,000 pounds (lb)
1 pound (lb) = 16 ounces (oz)

How can you convert units of weight?

An adult African elephant might weigh 5 tons. A baby African elephant might weigh 250 pounds. How many pounds does the adult elephant weigh? How can you convert 250 pounds to tons?

about 250 pounds

about 5 tons

Another Example How do you compare customary units of weight?

Compare. Write >, <, or = for $\bigcirc$: 7 lb $\bigcirc$ 100 oz.

One Way

Convert the larger unit to the smaller unit and compare.

Convert: 1 lb = 16 oz
So, 7 lb = 7 × 16
= 112 oz

Compare: 112 > 100
So, 7 lb > 100 oz.

Another Way

Convert the smaller unit to the larger unit and compare.

Convert: 16 oz = 1 lb
So, 100 oz = 100 ÷ 16
= $6\frac{1}{4}$ lb

Compare: 7 > $6\frac{1}{4}$
So, 7 lb > 100 oz.

Guided Practice*

Do you know HOW?

In **1** through **4**, convert each unit of weight.

1. 2,000 lb = ▮ T
2. 48 oz = ▮ lb

3. $\frac{1}{2}$ lb = ▮ oz
4. 16,000 lb = ▮ T

For **5** through **8**, compare. Write >, <, or = for each $\bigcirc$.

5. 33 oz $\bigcirc$ 2 lb
6. 2 T $\bigcirc$ 4,500 lb

7. 4 lb $\bigcirc$ 64 oz
8. 1 T $\bigcirc$ 1,999 lb

Do you UNDERSTAND?

9. **Writing to Explain** When you convert 16 pounds to ounces, do you multiply or divide? Explain.

10. Estimate the number of tons in 10,145 pounds.

11. An adult giraffe can weigh up to 3,000 pounds. Does an adult giraffe or an adult elephant weigh more?

*For another example, see Set B on page 274.

To convert from larger units to smaller units, multiply.

5 T = ▢ lb

Think 1 T = 2,000 lb

5 T

2,000 lb	2,000 lb	2,000 lb	2,000 lb	2,000 lb

Find 5 × 2,000.

5 × 2,000 = 10,000

5 T = 10,000 lb

To convert from smaller units to larger units, divide.

250 lb = ▢ T   **Think** 2,000 lb = 1 T

? T → | 250 lb |

1 T → | 2,000 lb |

Find $\frac{250}{2,000}$.   **Think** 250 divided by 2,000

$\frac{250 \div 250}{2,000 \div 250} = \frac{1}{8}$

So, 250 lb = $\frac{1}{8}$ T.

Independent Practice

In **12** through **20**, convert each unit of weight. Some of your answers will be fractions.

12. 64 oz = ▢ lb

13. 5 T = ▢ lb

14. 6,000 lb = ▢ T

15. 240 oz = ▢ lb

16. 8 T = ▢ lb

17. 8 lb = ▢ oz

18. 8 oz = ▢ lb

19. 1,000 lb = ▢ T

20. 1 T = ▢ oz

For **21** through **23**, compare. Write >, <, or = for each ◯.

21. 5,000 lb ◯ 3 T

22. 24 lb ◯ 124 oz

23. 32,000 oz ◯ 1 T

Problem Solving

24. Writing to Explain The world's heaviest lobster weighed 44 pounds, 6 ounces. How many ounces did the lobster weigh? Describe the steps you took to find your answer.

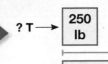

25. What is the greatest common factor of 36 and 63?

A 5   C 8

B 6   D 9

In **26** through **28**, use the table at the right to compare the weights of the animals. Write >, <, or = for each ◯.

26. 4 sheep ◯ 6 chimpanzees

27. 1 horse ◯ 4 dolphins

28. 20 chimpanzees ◯ 1 horse

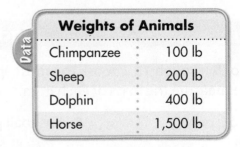

Weights of Animals

Chimpanzee	100 lb
Sheep	200 lb
Dolphin	400 lb
Horse	1,500 lb

29. How many ounces are equal to $1\frac{1}{2}$ pounds?

MA.5.G.5.3 Solve problems requiring attention to approximation, selection of appropriate measuring tools, and precision of measurement.
Also MA.5.G.5.2

Metric Units of Mass

What are metric units of mass?

Mass is the amount of matter that something contains.

What is the mass of a red brick?

1 gram (g)

1 kilogram (kg)

The mass of a red brick is?

A dollar bill has a mass of about 1 gram (g).

A cantaloupe has a mass of about 1 kilogram (kg).

Other Examples

Weight and mass are different.

The **weight** of an object changes depending on gravity.

The weight of the red brick on the Moon is not the same as its weight on Earth.

The **mass** of an object always stays the same.

The mass of the red brick on the Moon is the same as its mass on Earth.

Guided Practice

Do you know HOW?

For **1** and **2**, choose the most appropriate unit to measure the mass of each.

1.

hamster

2.

gorilla

Do you UNDERSTAND?

3. Which number would be less, the mass of a grapefruit in grams or the mass of the same grapefruit in kilograms?

4. How many cantaloupes would be needed to have the same mass as two red bricks?

Independent Practice

For **5** through **12**, choose the most appropriate unit to measure the mass of each item.

5. pencil　　　**6.** baseball player　　　**7.** baseball　　　**8.** honeydew melon

Animated Glossary
www.pearsonsuccessnet.com

DIGITAL

For another example, see Set C on page 274.

Step 1

Choose the appropriate unit to measure:

A brick has a greater mass than a cantaloupe.

So, the best unit would be the kilogram.

Step 2

Estimate:

 Think A cantaloupe has a mass of about one kilogram. How many cantaloupes would have the same mass as a red brick?

About 3 cantaloupes would have the same mass.

The brick has a mass of about 3 kilograms.

Step 3

Measure:

Place the brick on one pan of the balance. Add kilograms to the other pan until the balance is level. Count the kilograms.

To the nearest kilogram, the brick has a mass of 3 kilograms.

9. strawberry

10. penguin

11. sailboat

12. dragonfly

Problem Solving

For **13** through **15**, use the table at the right.

13. Order the coins from least mass to greatest mass.

14. A dollar bill has a mass of about 1 gram. About how many dollar bills have the same mass as a nickel?

15. There are 40 nickels in a roll of nickels. What is the total mass of the nickels in one roll?

 Find the mass of 4 nickels and multiply by 10.

Coin	Mass
	2.500 grams
	5.000 grams
	2.268 grams
	5.670 grams

16. Writing to Explain Mandy says that she has a mass of 32 kg on Earth. What is her mass on the Moon? Explain.

17. **Critical THINKING** Which number is greater, the mass of a carrot in grams or the mass of the same carrot in kilograms?

18. Use the bar diagram below. José needs $78 for a present. He has already saved $33. How much more does he need to save?

$78 in all

?	$33

19. What is a good estimate for the mass of an American saddlebred horse?

A 5 kg   **C** 500 kg

B 50 kg   **D** 5,000 kg

MA.5.G.5.2 Compare, contrast, and convert units of measure within the same dimension (length, mass, or time) to solve problems.

Converting Metric Units of Mass

How do you convert metric units of mass?

The three most commonly used units of mass are the milligram (mg), the gram (g), and the kilogram (kg).

about 5 g

1,000 mg = 1 g
1,000 g = 1 kg

100 kg

Guided Practice*

Do you know HOW?

In **1** through **3**, convert each unit of mass.

1. 925 g = ▢ mg

2. 19,000 g = ▢ kg

3. 1,000,000 mg = ▢ kg

For **4** and **5**, compare. Write >, <, or = for each ◯.

4. 7,000 mg ◯ 7,000 g

5. 100 kg ◯ 10,000 g

Do you UNDERSTAND?

6. How does what you know about the relationship between meters and millimeters help you understand the relationship between grams and milligrams?

7. Writing to Explain Which has the greater mass: 1 kg or 137,000 mg? Explain how you made your comparison.

8. If you need to convert kilograms to grams, what operation would you use?

Independent Practice

In **9** through **17**, convert each unit of mass.

9. 17,000 g = ▢ kg

10. 18 kg = ▢ g

11. 420,000 mg = ▢ g

12. 276 g = ▢ mg

13. 438 kg = ▢ g

14. 43,000 mg = ▢ g

15. 238,000 g = ▢ kg

16. 3,000,000 mg = ▢ kg

17. 22 kg = ▢ g

In **18** through **23**, compare. Write >, <, or = for each ◯.

18. 2,000 g ◯ 3 kg

19. 4 kg ◯ 4,000 g

20. 10,000 mg ◯ 13 g

21. 9,000 g ◯ 8 kg

22. 7 kg ◯ 7,000 g

23. 8,000 g ◯ 5 kg

For another example, see Set D on page 275.

From Grams to Milligrams

$$600 \text{ g} = \blacksquare \text{ mg}$$

To change from a larger unit to a smaller unit, multiply.

Think 1 g = 1,000 mg

Find 600 × 1,000.

600 g = 600,000 mg

From Grams to Kilograms

$$13,000 \text{ g} = \blacksquare \text{ kg}$$

To change from a smaller unit to a larger unit, divide.

Think 1,000 g = 1 kg

Find 13,000 ÷ 1,000.

13,000 g = 13 kg

Problem Solving

24. Number Sense Terri is beginning a science experiment in the lab. The instructions call for 227 mg of potassium. What is the difference between this amount and 1 gram?

25. Sheryl has a recipe for pasta with vegetables. The recipe calls for 130 grams of vegetables and twice as much pasta as vegetables. What is the mass in grams of the pasta needed for the recipe?

26. Writing to Explain How is converting grams to milligrams similar to converting pounds to ounces? How is it different?

Critical THINKING

27. If a man weighs 198 pounds on Earth, his mass on Earth is 90 kilograms.

  a What is this man's weight on the Moon?

  b What is his mass on the Moon? Explain.

28. Hummingbirds found in North America weigh about 3 grams. How many milligrams is this?

29. Think About the Process Two months out of the 12 months of the year begin with the letter *A*. In simplest form, what fraction of the months begin with the letter *A*?

  A $\frac{2}{12}$

  B $\frac{10}{12}$

  C $\frac{2}{6}$

  D $\frac{1}{6}$

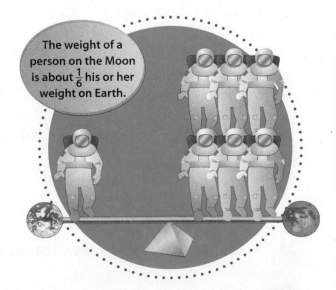

The weight of a person on the Moon is about $\frac{1}{6}$ his or her weight on Earth.

MA.5.G.5.2 Compare, contrast, and convert units of measure within the same dimension (length, mass, or time) to solve problems.

Units of Time

How do you compare units of time?

On her birthday, Kara calculated that she was 108 months old. Her friend Jordan has the same birthday. If Jordan turned 8 years old, who is older, Kara or Jordan?

You can convert different units of time in order to compare them.

Units of Time	
1 minute	= 60 seconds
1 hour	= 60 minutes
1 day	= 24 hours
1 week	= 7 days
1 month	= about 4 weeks
1 year	= 52 weeks
1 year	= 12 months
1 year	= 365 days
1 leap year	= 366 days
1 decade	= 10 years
1 century	= 100 years
1 millennium	= 1,000 years

Guided Practice*

Do you know HOW?

For **1** through **4**, compare. Write >, <, or = for each ◯. Use the table above to help.

1. 9 months ◯ 27 weeks

2. 17 years ◯ 2 decades

3. 5 minutes ◯ 300 seconds

4. 44 months ◯ 3 years

Do you UNDERSTAND?

5. **Writing to Explain** How can you tell which is longer, 63 hours or 3 days?

6. Do you multiply or divide if you want to change months to years?

7. How many years old is Kara?

Independent Practice

For **8** through **16**, compare. Write >, <, or = for each ◯.

8. 35 weeks ◯ 340 days

9. 7 days ◯ 120 hours

10. 2 years ◯ 730 days

11. 40 hours ◯ 2 days

12. 8 weeks ◯ 56 days

13. 12 months ◯ 40 weeks

14. 3 weeks ◯ 1 month

15. 1 day ◯ 25 hours

16. 10 decades ◯ 1 century

For **17** through **25**, convert each unit of time.

17. 6 days = ▨ hours

18. 2 years = ▨ months

19. 6 minutes = ▨ seconds

20. 3 decades = ▨ years

21. 4 hours = ▨ minutes

22. 4 centuries = ▨ years

23. 36 months = ▨ years

24. 104 weeks = ▨ years

25. 5,000 years = ▨ millennia

*For another example, see Set E on page 275.

Step 1

Change 8 years to months.

1 year = 12 months

To find the number of months in 8 years, multiply.

8 × 12 = 96

So, 8 years = 96 months.

Step 2

Compare the amounts.

Kara's age   Jordan's age

108 months ◯ 8 years

108 months ⊘ 96 months

So, Kara is older than Jordan.

Problem Solving

26. Estimation About how many minutes does it take you to do your homework? How many seconds is this?

27. Trish is going to camp for 2 months. Which is greater than 2 months?

     A 35 days   **C** 6 weeks

     B 40 days   **D** 10 weeks

28. Reasoning Gina has 3 yards of fabric. **Critical THINKING** She needs to cut 8 pieces, each 1 foot long. Does she have enough fabric? Explain.

29. A girl from England set a world record by sneezing 978 days in a row. About how many weeks did she sneeze in a row?

30. **Social Studies** The clock tower Big Ben is part of Westminster Palace. The light above the clock is turned on when the British Parliament is in session. If the light was on for $10\frac{1}{2}$ hours, how many minutes was Parliament in session?

31. A theater has 358 seats on the main level and 122 seats in the balcony. If there are 6 shows per day, how many people can see the show each day?

32. **Social Studies** It is believed that the Mayan pyramid of Kukulkan in Mexico was used as a calendar. It has 4 stairways leading to the top platform. Including one extra step at the top, it has a total of 365 steps, one for each day of the year. How many steps are in each stairway?

Each stairway has the same number of steps.

MA.5.A.6.5 Solve non-routine problems using various strategies including "solving a simpler problem" and "guess, check, and revise."

Problem Solving

Make a Table

An airline schedules flights to leave from Washington, D.C., to Boston every 45 minutes beginning at 1:25 P.M. The last flight departs at 8:10 P.M. Flights departing before 3:00 P.M. have flight times of 1 hour 20 minutes. Flights departing after 3:00 P.M. have flight times of 1 hour 25 minutes. Which flight would arrive in Boston the closest to 6 P.M.?

WASHINGTON, D.C. TO BOSTON	
DEPARTURES	**ARRIVALS**
1:25 P.M.	2:45 P.M.
2:10 P.M.	

Guided Practice*

Do you know HOW?

1. Make a table to solve the problem.

   The temperature in Cody's backyard was 86°F at 6 P.M. If the temperature dropped 2 degrees each hour until midnight, what was the temperature at midnight?

Do you UNDERSTAND?

2. In the example above, what are the headings for the table on page 271?

3. **Write a Problem** Write a real-world problem that can be solved using the table from the example above.

Independent Practice

For **4** and **5**, make a table to solve each problem.

4. Mark is recording the sunrise times this month. The Sun rose at 5:18 A.M. the first day of the month. Mark noticed that the Sun rose 1 minute later each day, except for every third day when it rose 2 minutes later. Copy and continue the table below to find the sunrise time for the 15th day of the month.

Day of Month	Sunrise
1	5:18 A.M.
2	5:19 A.M.
3	5:21 A.M.
4	5:22 A.M.
5	5:23 A.M.

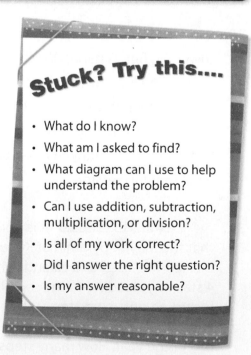

Stuck? Try this....

- What do I know?
- What am I asked to find?
- What diagram can I use to help understand the problem?
- Can I use addition, subtraction, multiplication, or division?
- Is all of my work correct?
- Did I answer the right question?
- Is my answer reasonable?

What do I know?

- First flight leaves at 1:25 P.M.
- Flights depart every 45 minutes.
- Flights departing before 3 P.M. take 1 hour 20 minutes.
- Flights departing after 3 P.M. take 1 hour 25 minutes.

What am I asked to find?

Which flight arrives in Boston the closest to 6:00 P.M.

Make a table of departure and arrival times.

Departures	Flight Times	Arrivals
1:25 P.M.	(1 h 20 min)	2:45 P.M.
2:10 P.M.	(1 h 20 min)	3:30 P.M.
2:55 P.M.	(1 h 20 min)	4:15 P.M.
3:40 P.M.	(1 h 25 min)	5:05 P.M.
4:25 P.M.	(1 h 25 min)	5:50 P.M.
5:10 P.M.	(1 h 25 min)	6:35 P.M.

The flight departing at 4:25 P.M. arrives the closest to 6:00 P.M.

5. Ernie's oven takes 2 minutes to heat to 100°F. Then, the oven heats an additional 50°F with each additional minute. How many minutes will it take the oven to heat to 350°F? To 400°F?

6. THINK SOLVE EXPLAIN Delia's play rehearsal was 23 minutes longer than usual. Usually rehearsal lasts 2 hours 30 minutes. If her rehearsal started at 3:30 P.M., what time did it end? Explain how you found your answer.

7. Critical THINKING Santino took a survey of his 21 classmates. He asked them how many minutes they spent on the telephone one night. His survey results are shown below.

20	35	0	65	30	45	50
10	25	60	45	15	20	40
0	40	25	30	0	25	20

a How could Santino organize the survey data so that it would be easier to analyze?

b Make an organized list of the survey data.

8. Angelo earns $8.00 per hour delivering pizzas in the summer. His weekly schedule is shown below. How much does Angelo earn each week delivering pizzas?

Friday	5:00 P.M. to 9:00 P.M.
Saturday	11:00 A.M. to 7:00 P.M.
Sunday	1:00 P.M. to 6:00 P.M.

A $128.00 C $144.00

B $136.00 D $152.00

For **9** and **10**, use the table at the right.

9. Toby wants to take the train from Greenleaf to Main in as little time as possible. Which train should he take?

10. How many minutes does Train C take to go from Newtown to Main?

Train	A	B	C
Greenleaf	6:40	7:10	7:30
Newtown	---	7:20	7:40
Fort Young	7:00	---	8:10
Castle Point	---	---	---
Main	7:20	7:47	8:30

1 Which inequality is NOT true? (11-4)

  A. 100 mg < 10 g

  B. 2,000 kg > 2,000 g

  C. 1,000,500 mg > 1 kg

  D. 600 g > 6 kg

2 Which of these units would best measure the weight of a large catfish? (11-1)

  F. Tons

  G. Ounces

  H. Pounds

  I. Inches

3 Which is the most appropriate unit to measure the mass of a tennis ball? (11-3)

  A. Grams

  B. Kilograms

  C. Meters

  D. Kilometers

4 The nutrition label on a carton of soy milk says that one glass contains 7 grams of protein. How many milligrams of protein does one glass contain? (11-4)

  F. 7 milligrams

  G. 70 milligrams

  H. 700 milligrams

  I. 7,000 milligrams

5 Which unit would best measure the weight of a small pair of scissors? (11-1)

  A. Pounds

  B. Ounces

  C. Tons

  D. Feet

6 It takes a guinea pig about 68 days to develop completely before it is born. Which amount of time is greater than 68 days? (11-5)

  F. 1 month

  G. 1,200 hours

  H. 9 weeks

  I. 10 weeks

7 A centennial celebration is a celebration that happens every century. How many years are there between centennial celebrations? (11-5)

  A. 10 years

  B. 100 years

  C. 1,000 years

  D. 10,000 years

8 The next total solar eclipse that will be visible in the United States will be on August 21, 2017. It will last 160 seconds. Which symbol makes the comparison true? (11-5)

160 seconds ◯ 3 minutes

  F. <

  G. >

  H. =

  I. ×

9 On average, the temperature inside a car parked in the sun will rise 16°F every 25 minutes. Geraldo's car is parked in the sun and has a temperature of 79°F at 12:30 P.M. Make a table to find the expected time for his car to reach 127°F. (11-6)

  A. 12:55 P.M.

  B. 1:20 P.M.

  C. 1:40 P.M.

  D. 1:45 P.M.

10 Which of the following can be used to find how many kilograms of sweet potatoes the recipe calls for? (11-4)

Soup Recipe
1 onion
2,000 grams sweet potatoes
3 liters water
15 milliliters chicken stock

  F. 1,000 ÷ 2,000

  G. 2,000 ÷ 1,000

  H. 2,000 × 1,000

  I. 2,000 × 100

11 Recently, the largest watermelon on record weighed 269 pounds. How many ounces did it weigh? (11-2)

  A. 16 ounces

  B. 32 ounces

  C. 2,096 ounces

  D. 4,304 ounces

12 Ten bales of cotton weigh about 5,000 pounds. Which comparison is true? (11-2)

  F. 5,000 pounds < 10,000 ounces

  G. 5,000 pounds = 3 tons

  H. 5,000 pounds < 3 tons

  I. 5,000 pounds > 3 tons

13 What is a good estimate for the mass of a quarter? (11-3)

  A. 6,000 grams

  B. 600 grams

  C. 60 grams

  D. 6 grams

14 How many seconds are there in two hours? (11-5)

15 Mackenzie arrived at the train station at 7:05 A.M. The first train she saw arrived at the station at 7:10 A.M. Trains arrived at the station every 20 minutes. Make a table to find how many trains arrived by 8:30 A.M. Explain how making a table can help you find your answer. (11-6)

THINK
SOLVE
EXPLAIN

Set A, pages 260–261

Which is the best unit to measure the weight of a pear?

A key weighs about 1 ounce (oz). A kitten weighs about 1 pound (lb). A giraffe weighs about 1 ton (T).

Most pears weigh less than a pound.

So, the best unit to use would be the ounce.

Remember to use benchmark weights to compare.

Choose the best unit to measure the weight of each item. Write oz, lb, or T.

1. whale   **2.** apple

3. cat   **4.** baseball

5. box of   **6.** truck
     books

Set B, pages 262–263

Convert 6 pounds to ounces.

Think   1 pound = 16 ounces.
To change larger units to smaller units, multiply.

$6 \times 16 = 96$

So, 6 pounds = 96 ounces.

To compare customary units, convert one of the units first, so that you can compare like units.

Remember that there are 16 ounces in one pound, and there are 2,000 pounds in one ton.

Complete.

1. 2 lb = ▢ oz   **2.** 48 oz = ▢ lb

3. 4,000 lb = ▢ T   **4.** 6 T = ▢ lb

5. 7 lb ◯ 70 oz   **6.** 6,000 oz ◯ 3 T

7. How many ounces are equivalent to one fourth of one ton?

Set C, pages 264–265

What is the most appropriate unit to measure the mass of a cell phone?

A dollar bill has a mass of about 1 gram (g).
A cantaloupe has a mass of about 1 kilogram (kg).

You can measure the mass of a cell phone on a balance.

1 kilogram is too large for a cell phone.
So, the gram would be a better unit to use.

Remember that weight depends on gravity. Mass always stays the same.

Choose the most appropriate unit, gram or kilogram, to measure the mass of each item.

1. crayon   **2.** watermelon

3. carrot   **4.** wallet

5. bicycle   **6.** table

7. penny   **8.** paper clip

Set D, pages 266–267

Convert 6 kilograms (kg) to grams (g).

 Think 1 kilogram = 1,000 grams.
To change larger units to smaller units, multiply.

6 × 1,000 = 6,000

So, 6 kg = 6,000 g.

Remember that to compare metric units, convert one of the units first, so that you can compare like units.

Complete.

1. 30 kg = ▢ g   **2.** 3,000 mg = ▢ g

3. 5,000 g = ▢ kg   **4.** 17 g = ▢ mg

Set E, pages 268–269

Which is longer, 12 years or 120 months?

Convert 12 years to months.

Since 1 year = 12 months, multiply the number of years by 12.

12 years × 12 = 144 months;
144 months > 120 months

So, 12 years > 120 months.

Remember that you can use a conversion table to help you convert and compare units of time.

Compare. Write >, <, or = in each ◯.

1. 36 months ◯ 104 weeks

2. 33 years ◯ 3 decades

3. 90 minutes ◯ 540 seconds

4. 5 centuries ◯ 5,000 years

Set F, pages 270–271

Mark is training for a race. For every 4 minutes he runs, he walks for 5 minutes. Yesterday, he walked for 35 minutes. How many minutes did he run?

A table can help you organize the information. To make a table, follow these steps:

Step 1 Set up the table with the correct labels.

Step 2 Enter known data into the table.

Step 3 Look for a pattern. Extend the table.

Step 4 Find the answer in the table.

Remember to read the problem carefully and make sure the information in your table is correct.

1. Katie is on a softball team. For every 10 minutes she practices fielding, she takes 5 minutes of batting practice. Yesterday, she took 20 minutes of batting practice. How many minutes did she practice fielding? Make a table to show how you found the answer.

Minutes Running	4	8	12	16	20	24	28
Minutes Walking	5	10	15	20	25	30	35

Mark ran for 28 minutes.

Topic 12

Measurements of Two-Dimensional Shapes

1 Mechanics put buses on parallelogram lifts in order to work underneath them. What is the area of the parallelogram shape that is used to hold up a bus? You will find out in Lesson 12-3.

2 How much area is needed to create a living chessboard? You will find out in Lesson 12-2.

3 Cowboys on cattle drives in the 1800s were called to dinner by the ringing of a triangular bell. What is the area of a triangular dinner bell? You will find out in Lesson 12-4.

4 What kinds of angles are formed by the handles of the world's largest basket? You will find out in Lesson 12-1.

Topic Essential Questions

- How can the measure of an angle be found?

- How can areas of common shapes be found?

Vocabulary

Choose the best term from the box.

> - square
> - line segment
> - angle
> - line
> - ray

1. A(n) ___?___ is part of a(n) ___?___ that has one endpoint and extends forever in one direction.

2. A(n) ___?___ has two endpoints.

3. Two rays that have the same endpoint form a(n) ___?___ .

Area

Find the area of each figure in square units.

| A | | B | |
| C | | | D |

4. Figure A   5. Figure B

6. Figure C   7. Figure D

Perimeter

8. Find the perimeter of the figure.

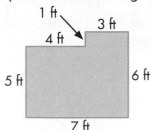

1 ft
3 ft
4 ft
5 ft
6 ft
7 ft

9. **Writing to Explain** How is perimeter different from area?

MA.5.G.5.3 Solve problems requiring attention to approximation, selection of appropriate measuring tools, and precision of measurement.

Measuring Angles

Hands-On
protractor

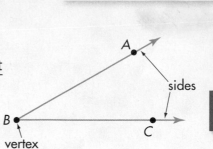

How can you measure an angle?

An angle is formed by two rays that have the same endpoint. The common endpoint is called the vertex (plural: vertices).

Angle *ABC* is shown above to the right. We write this as ∠*ABC*. It can also be named ∠*CBA* or just ∠*B*.

Another Example How can you classify angles?

An acute angle has a measure between 0° and 90°.

A right angle has a measure of 90°.

An obtuse angle has a measure between 90° and 180°.

A straight angle has a measure of 180°.

Guided Practice*

Do you know HOW?

In **1** and **2**, measure and classify each angle.

1.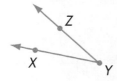

2.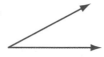

3. **Reasoning** Give three different names for this angle. Identify the vertex and sides.

Do you UNDERSTAND?

4. In the figure below, how many angles are formed? What are their measures? Are the angles acute, right, or obtuse?

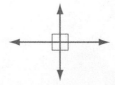

5. Draw an obtuse angle. Label it with 3 points and the angle measure.

Animated Glossary, eTools
www.pearsonsuccessnet.com

*For another example, see Set A on page 294.

To measure an angle

You use a protractor to measure and draw angles. Angles are measured in degrees. It takes 90° to fill a square corner.

Place the protractor's center on the angle's vertex. Place the 0° mark on one side of the angle. Read the measure where the other side of the angle crosses the protractor.

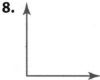

The measure of ∠PQR is 56°.

To draw an angle of 140°

Draw $\overrightarrow{TU}$. Be sure to label the endpoint T. Place the protractor's center on T. Line up $\overrightarrow{TU}$ with the 0° mark. Place a point at 140°. Label it W. Draw $\overrightarrow{TW}$.

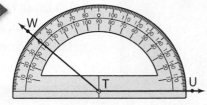

The measure of ∠WTU is 140°.

Independent Practice

In **6** through **8**, classify each angle as acute, right, obtuse, or straight. Then measure each angle.

6.

7.

8.

In **9** through **12**, draw the angles with a protractor. Classify the angles as acute, right, or obtuse.

9. 35°   **10.** 110°   **11.** 90°   **12.** 76°

Problem Solving

13. Reasoning If $\overrightarrow{CB}$ is perpendicular to $\overrightarrow{CD}$, then ∠BCD is

    A An acute angle.   **C** An obtuse angle.

    B A right angle.   **D** A straight angle.

14. For his graduation, John received the same amount of money from each of his 10 friends, plus $20 from his brother. If John received a total of $120, how much did each friend give him?

15. Angles can be found on the world's largest basket. What kind of angle is ∠ADC? ∠CBD? ∠ADB?

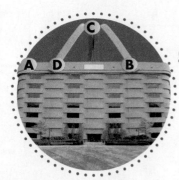

16. Writing to Explain Carlos says that two times the measure of an acute angle will always equal the measure of an obtuse angle. Is he right? Give examples to explain your answer.

Lesson
12-2

MA.5.G.5.4 Derive and
apply formulas for areas of
parallelograms, triangles,
and trapezoids from the
area of a rectangle.

Area of Rectangles

How can you measure the area of a rectangle?

The area of a figure is <u>the amount of surface it covers</u>. Tessa is covering a bulletin board with fabric. The board is 4 feet high and 5 feet long. How much fabric does she need?

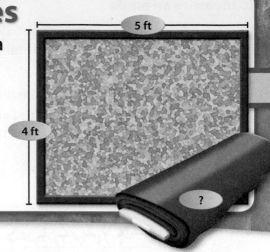

Guided Practice*

Do you know HOW?

In **1** and **2**, find the area of each rectangle.

1.
11 cm
15 cm

2.
20 in.
6 in.

Do you UNDERSTAND?

3. Find the area and perimeter of a square measuring 4 inches on each side. Compare the answers. What is the same? What is different?

4. Tessa wants to cover another bulletin board with fabric. That bulletin board has a base of 9 feet and a height of 4 feet. How much fabric will she need?

Independent Practice

In **5** through **10**, find the area of each rectangle.

5.
5 in.
18 in.

6.
5 mi
2 mi

7.
10 in.
20 in.

8.
22 cm
22 cm

9.
11 ft
2 ft

10.
9 mi
16 mi

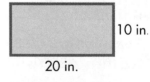
Animated Glossary
www.pearsonsuccessnet.com

*For another example, see Set B on page 294.

One Way

Draw a picture on graph paper. Then count the squares covered by the drawing.

There are 20 squares.

$A = 20$ ft²

"ft²" is read as "square feet."

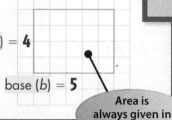

height (h) = **4**

base (b) = **5**

Area is always given in square units.

Tessa needs 20 square feet of fabric.

Another Way

Use a formula. The formula for finding the area of a rectangle is $A = b \times h$.

$A = b \times h$ ← **Think** b is the base and h is the height.

$A = 5 \times 4$

$A = 20$ ft²

Tessa needs 20 square feet of fabric.

Problem Solving

11. Flags come in many sizes. Copy the table below and fill in the areas for the rectangular flags. Then use your completed table for **12** and **13**.

Flag Size	Flag Area
4 in. × 6 in.	
12 in. × 18 in.	
2 ft × 3 ft	
3 ft × 5 ft	
4 ft × 6 ft	

Data

12. Which flag is larger, the one with an area of 216 square inches or the one with an area of 6 square feet?

13. Writing to Explain The 4 ft × 6 ft flag has a solid red rectangular area that covers 8 square feet of the flag. What fraction of the flag's total area is this red area? Explain.

14. Reasoning Can the distance from your house to your school be measured in square miles? Explain.

Critical THINKING

15. Suppose the measure of a side of a square is s. Write a formula to find the area of a square.

Critical THINKING

16. Hayley wants to plant ivy in her back yard, which is 24 feet by 6 feet. Each square foot of ivy will cost $2. How much will it cost, in dollars, to plant enough ivy to cover the yard?

17. Suppose that a square on a living chessboard measures 4 ft × 4 ft. How much area does the whole board cover?

A   72 ft²

B   256 ft²

C   512 ft²

D   1,024 ft²

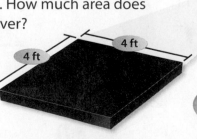

4 ft
4 ft

A living chessboard has 64 squares.

12-3

MA.5.G.5.4 Derive and apply formulas for areas of parallelograms, triangles, and trapezoids from the area of a rectangle.

Area of Parallelograms

How can finding the area of a rectangle help you find the area of a parallelogram?

Southwestern rugs often have parallelograms as part of the design. The base of this parallelogram is 6 cm. The height is 5 cm. What is its area?

$h = 5$ cm $b = 6$ cm

Guided Practice*

Do you know HOW?

In **1** and **2**, find the area of each parallelogram.

1.

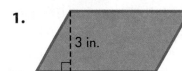

3 in.

6 in.

2.

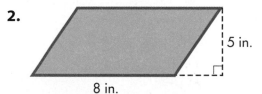

5 in.

8 in.

Do you UNDERSTAND?

3. In the example above, why is the shaded triangle that is cut off a right triangle?

4. **Writing to Explain** Can the length of a side of a parallelogram equal the height of a parallelogram? Explain.

5. What is the area of a parallelogram with a height of 13 yards and a base of 4 yards?

Independent Practice

For **6** through **12**, find the area of each parallelogram.

6.

3 cm

3 cm

7.

7 ft

9 ft

8.

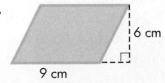

6 cm

9 cm

9.

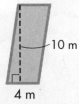

4 in.

2 in.

10.

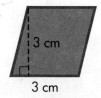

10 m

4 m

11.

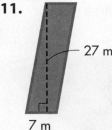

27 m

7 m

12.

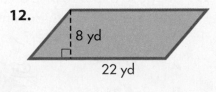

8 yd

22 yd

*For another example, see Set B on page 294.

Step 1

The shaded triangle of the parallelogram can be cut off.

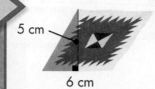

5 cm

6 cm

Step 2

The triangle can be placed along the other side to form a rectangle.

5 cm

6 cm

Step 3

Use the formula to find the area of a parallelogram.

$A = b \times h$

$A = 6 \text{ cm} \times 5 \text{ cm}$

$A = 30 \text{ cm}^2$

The area of the parallelogram is 30 square centimeters.

Problem Solving

13. Parallelogram *A* has a base of 12 feet and a height of 11 feet. Parallelogram *B* has a base of 13 feet and a height of 10 feet. Which parallelogram has the greater area? How much greater is the area?

14. Each morning, Kathie rides the train 9 kilometers to work. The train takes 10 minutes to travel $4\frac{1}{2}$ kilometers. How much time does she spend on the train each day to and from work?

15. Which of these figures has the greatest area?

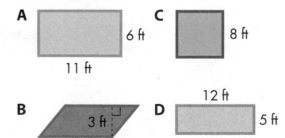

A 6 ft 11 ft

C 8 ft

B 3 ft 7 ft

D 12 ft 5 ft

16. A store display has 36 bottles of perfume on the bottom shelf, 30 bottles on the shelf above that, and 24 on the shelf above that. If this pattern continues, how many bottles will be on the next shelf above?

17. What is the area of the parallelogram lift shown below?

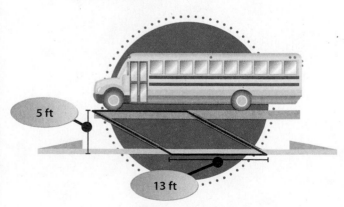

5 ft

13 ft

18. THINK SOLVE EXPLAIN
Kurt bought two items that cost a total of $100. One item cost $10 more than the other. What was the cost of each item? Explain your reasoning.

19. Algebra Paige knows that the product of a pair of factors is 54. One of the factors is an odd number. If *x* is the other factor, what are all of the possible values of *x*?

Critical THINKING

MA.5.G.5.4 Derive and apply formulas for areas of parallelograms, triangles, and trapezoids from the area of a rectangle.

Area of Triangles

How can you use a parallelogram to find the area of a triangle?

This parallelogram is divided into two congruent triangles. The area of each triangle is equal to half the area of the parallelogram.

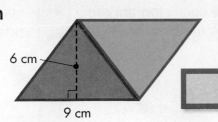

6 cm

9 cm

Guided Practice*

Do you know HOW?

In **1** and **2**, find the area of each triangle.

1.
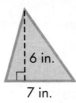
6 in.
7 in.

2.
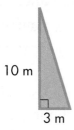
10 m
3 m

Do you UNDERSTAND?

3. **Writing to Explain** In the example above, how do you know the area of the triangle is equal to half the area of the parallelogram?

4. In the example above, find the area of the red triangle if the base measures 12 cm and the height remains the same.

Independent Practice

In **5** through **10**, find the area of each triangle.

5.

6 in.
5 in.

6.
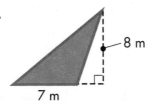
8 m
7 m

7.
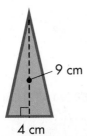
9 cm
4 cm

8.
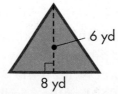
6 yd
8 yd

9.

3 ft
2 ft

10.
10 cm
4 cm

*For another example, see Set B on page 294.

Step 1

Find the area of the red triangle.

Identify the measures of the base and **height** of the triangle.

base (b) = 9 cm
height (h) = 6 cm

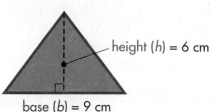

Step 2

To find the area of a triangle, multiply the base by the height and divide by 2.

Substitute the values into the formula.

$$\text{Area} = \frac{\text{base} \times \text{height}}{2}$$

$$A = \frac{b \times h}{2}$$

$$A = \frac{9 \times 6}{2}$$

$$A = 27 \text{ cm}^2$$

The area of the red triangle is 27 square centimeters.

Problem Solving

11. **Writing to Explain** Jay says that this triangle has an area of 3,000 square inches. Is Jay correct? Explain.

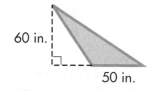

12. Terry wants to buy one pair of moccasins. She can choose from some that cost $22.50, $27.00, $20.95, and $24.75. How much will Terry save if she buys the least expensive instead of the most expensive pair?

13. **Reasoning** The difference between the prices of two bikes is $18. The sum of the prices is $258. How much does each bike cost?

14. What is the area of a triangle with a base of 7 inches and a height of 8 inches?

A 15 in²   C 56 in²

B 28 in²   D 64 in²

15. Which of the following numbers is composite?

F 2   H 7

G 5   I 9

16. Natalie is going to wallpaper her room. Each wall in her bedroom measures 10 ft × 8 ft. How much wallpaper will Natalie need to cover 3 of the bedroom walls?

17. What is the area of the dinner bell shown at the right?

18. **Algebra** A lunar module has a triangular-shaped window with a base of 60 centimeters and an area of 1,200 square centimeters. Solve the equation $\frac{60h}{2} = 1{,}200$ to find the height, in centimeters, of the window.

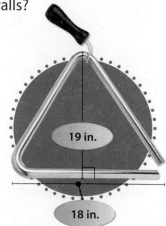

MA.5.G.5.4 Derive and apply formulas for areas of parallelograms, triangles, and trapezoids from the area of a rectangle.

Area of Trapezoids

How can you use triangles to find the area of a trapezoid?

A trapezoid is a quadrilateral that has exactly one pair of parallel sides. These parallel sides are the bases of a trapezoid. The bases of this trapezoid are 2 meters and 4 meters. The height is 3 meters. What is the area?

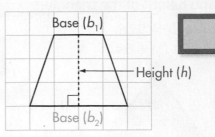

Guided Practice*

Do you know HOW?

In **1** and **2**, find the area of each trapezoid.

1.
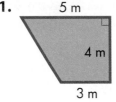
5 m
4 m
3 m

2.

2 cm
6 cm
4 cm

Do you UNDERSTAND?

3. Writing to Explain In the formula for the area of a trapezoid above, does it matter which base you use for b_1 or b_2? Explain.

4. If the height of the trapezoid above were doubled, what would be the new area?

Independent Practice

For **5** through **10**, find the area of each trapezoid.

5.
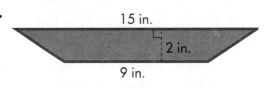
15 in.
2 in.
9 in.

6.
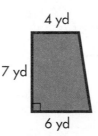
4 yd
7 yd
6 yd

7.
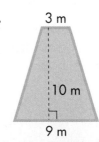
3 m
10 m
9 m

8.

10 ft
13 ft
8 ft

9.
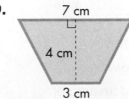
7 cm
4 cm
3 cm

10.
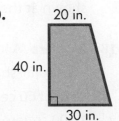
20 in.
40 in.
30 in.

*For another example, see Set C on page 294.

<table>
<tr><td>

One Way

Divide the trapezoid into 2 triangles to find the area. First, find the area of each triangle.

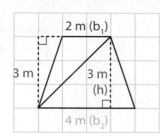

Area of First Triangle:

$$\frac{b_1 \times h}{2} = \frac{2 \times 3}{2} = \frac{6}{2} = 3 \text{ m}^2$$

Area of Second Triangle:

$$\frac{b_2 \times h}{2} = \frac{4 \times 3}{2} = \frac{12}{2} = 6 \text{ m}^2$$

Then add the areas of the triangles: $3 \text{ m}^2 + 6 \text{ m}^2 = 9 \text{ m}^2$
So the area of the trapezoid is 9 square meters.

</td><td>

Another Way

Use the formula for area of a trapezoid.

$$A = \frac{(b_1 + b_2)}{2} \times h$$

$$A = \frac{(2 + 4)}{2} \times 3$$

$$A = 3 \times 3 = 9 \text{ m}^2$$

So the area of the trapezoid is 9 m².

</td></tr>
</table>

Problem Solving

11. Tammy and Gordon cut trapezoids out of construction paper. Tammy's trapezoid has bases of 6 in. and 8 in. and a height of 2 in. Gordon's trapezoid has bases of 3 in. and 9 in. and a height of 2 in. Whose trapezoid has the greater area? How much greater is the area?

12. Which trapezoid has the least area?

A 1 m

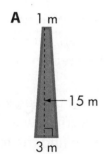

15 m

3 m

B 13 m

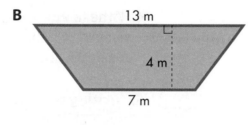

4 m

7 m

C 4 m

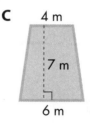

7 m

6 m

D 6 m

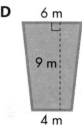

9 m

4 m

13. Robert slices a large loaf of bread to make 12 sandwiches. He makes 3 turkey and 5 cheddar cheese sandwiches. The rest are ham sandwiches. What fraction of the sandwiches Robert makes are ham? Use simplest form.

14. The Millers need to know the area of their front porch for a neighborhood survey. Their porch is the shape of a trapezoid with bases of 7 feet and 5 feet and a height of 5 feet. How many square feet is their front porch?

15. Reasoning Does the way that you divide a trapezoid into two triangles affect the area? Explain.

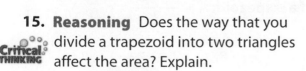

16. Keith wants to see a movie at 3:10 P.M. The bus that he takes to the movie theater runs every 40 minutes, beginning at 1:00 P.M. If it takes 25 minutes for the bus to go from Keith's stop to the movie theater, what is the departure time for the latest bus he can take?

17. A triangle and a rectangle have the same measurements for the base and the height. Do the figures have the same area? Explain why or why not.

MA.5.G.5.4 Derive and apply formulas for areas of parallelograms, triangles, and trapezoids from the area of a rectangle.

Using Area Formulas

How can you use area formulas to solve problems?

A garden has the shape and size shown at the right. Mr. White wants to find the area of the garden to know how much fertilizer he will need to buy. What is the area of the garden?

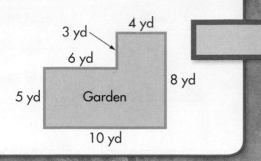

3 yd
4 yd
6 yd
8 yd
5 yd   Garden
10 yd

Guided Practice*

Do you know HOW?

Use the area formula of a rectangle to find the area of each figure.

1.

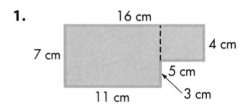

16 cm
7 cm
4 cm
5 cm
11 cm
3 cm

2.

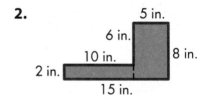

5 in.
6 in.
10 in.
8 in.
2 in.
15 in.

Do you UNDERSTAND?

3. In the example above, how did separating the garden shape into two rectangles make it possible to find the area of the garden?

4. Draw a Picture Show a different way to separate the garden, from the example above, into two rectangles.

5. Writing to Explain If the garden were separated into two trapezoids, would you still add their areas to find the total area? Explain.

Independent Practice

Use area formulas of familiar shapes to find the area of each figure.

Area of a rectangle: $A = b \times h$ **Area of a parallelogram:** $A = b \times h$

Area of a triangle: $A = \dfrac{b \times h}{2}$ **Area of a trapezoid:** $A = \dfrac{(b_1 + b_2)}{2} \times h$

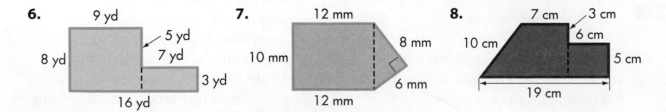

6.
9 yd
5 yd
8 yd
7 yd
3 yd
16 yd

7.
12 mm
8 mm
10 mm
6 mm
12 mm

8.
7 cm   3 cm
6 cm
10 cm
5 cm
19 cm

The garden can be separated into two rectangles. Identify the base and height of each rectangle.

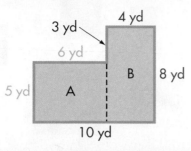

Use the formula $A = b \times h$ to find the area of each rectangle.

Area of Rectangle A	Area of Rectangle B
$A = b \times h$	$A = b \times h$
$= 6 \times 5$	$= 4 \times 8$
$= 30 \text{ yd}^2$	$= 32 \text{ yd}^2$

Add to find the total area.

$30 + 32 = 62 \text{ yd}^2$

The area of the garden is 62 yd^2.

Problem Solving

In **9** and **10**, use the diagram of a city park shown at the right.

9. It will cost $2 per square foot to plant grass in the park. What will be the total cost, in dollars, of planting the grass?

10. The cost of installing iron fencing with gates is $12 per foot. What will be the total cost of installing a fence with gates around the entire perimeter of the park?

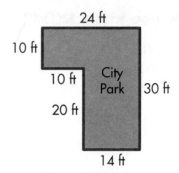

11. **Science** The largest breed of rabbit is the White Flemish Giant, which can have a mass as much as 8 kilograms. In a report, Rebecca said that the mass of this kind of rabbit could be as much as 800 grams. Was Rebecca's report correct? Explain.

12. **Writing to Explain** When can one of the two congruent sides of an isosceles triangle be used as the height of the triangle? Include a picture as part of your explanation.

Critical THINKING

13. Kevin drew a 180° angle and classified it as obtuse. Is Kevin correct? Explain why or why not.

14. The figure below can be separated into 3 rectangles and 2 triangles. What is the area of the figure?

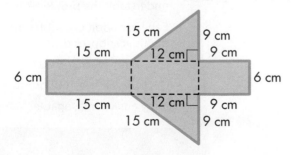

15. What is the area of this figure?

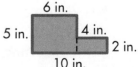

A 8 in²

B 30 in²

C 38 in²

D 50 in²

MA.5.A.6.5 Solve non-routine problems using various strategies including "solving a simpler problem" and "guess, check, and revise."

Problem Solving

Guess, Check, and Revise

Which of these square tiles can be used to completely cover the area of this floor without cutting tiles, or combining tiles of different sizes?

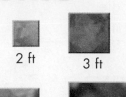

2 ft   3 ft

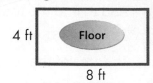

4 ft | Floor |

8 ft

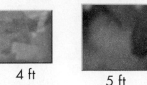

4 ft   5 ft

Guided Practice*

Do you know HOW?

1. Which of these tiles can be used to cover a 10 × 10 ft floor without cutting any tiles: 2 × 2 ft, 3 × 3 ft, 4 × 4 ft, or 5 × 5 ft tile?

2. What size rectangular tile floor can be completely covered by using only 2 × 2 ft tiles OR 3 × 3 ft tiles? Remember, you can't cut tiles or combine the two tile sizes.

Do you UNDERSTAND?

3. How do you use *Guess, Check, and Revise* to help you find the solution to a problem?

4. Write a Problem Write a real-world problem that involves common factors and can be solved using the *Guess, Check, and Revise* strategy.

Independent Practice

For **5** through **9**, use *Guess, Check, and Revise* to solve.

5. Bert is planning to tile a floor that measures 9 ft × 11 ft. What size square tile can he use to completely cover it?

6. Mrs. Gonzales wants to tile her floor with a pattern that repeats every 3 feet. Can she cover the floor without cutting off part of the pattern? Explain.

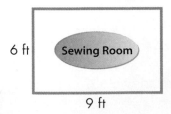

6 ft | Sewing Room |

9 ft

Stuck? Try this....

- What do I know?
- What am I asked to find?
- What diagram can I use to help understand the problem?
- Can I use addition, subtraction, multiplication, or division?
- Is all of my work correct?
- Did I answer the right question?
- Is my answer reasonable?

Use reasoning to make good guesses. Then check.

One side of the floor is 4 feet so I think the 4 x 4 ft tile is the only one that works.

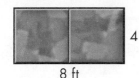

4 ft

8 ft

It works!

Next I'll try the 3 × 3 ft tile.

4 ft

8 ft

3 does not work for the 4 ft width and 8 ft length because 3 is not a factor of 4 or 8.

Revise what you know.

4 works for the 4 ft width.

4 works for the 8 ft length.

5 is not a factor of 4 or 8, so the 5 × 5 ft tile won't work.

2 is a factor of 4 and 8, so the 2 × 2 ft tile will work too.

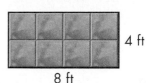

4 ft

8 ft

7. You buy a baseball and a bat and spend $31. The bat costs $19 more than the baseball. What is the price of the baseball? What is the price of the bat?

8. The difference between the prices of two bikes is $22. The sum of the prices is $328. How much does each bike cost?

For **9**, use the picture at the right.

9. Kyle's mother spent $115 on shirts and pairs of socks for him. If she bought at least 3 shirts, how many pairs of socks and how many shirts did she buy?

$3

$17

$22

For **10**, draw a picture, write an equation, and solve.

10. Each of the 13 members of a basketball team bought a team emblem. The emblems cost the team $78. How much did it cost each member of the team to buy an emblem?

Critical THINKING

11. A group of 168 students are going to a ball game. They will travel on buses that hold 36 students. How many buses could be completely filled? How many buses will be needed? How many seats are left on the bus that is not filled?

12. It costs $2 for each person to ride the bus in the city. A transfer costs $0.50. If 10 people get on the bus, and 2 of those people want a transfer, what is the total amount the bus driver collects?

13. A farmer has 9 cows, 10 pigs, and 25 sheep on his farm. Special food for all the animals costs $3 a pound. If the farmer needs to buy 100 pounds of food for each animal, what will his total cost be?

1 Which of the following is the area of a parallelogram whose base measures 20 meters and height measures 12 meters? (12-3)

    A. 64 m

    B. 120 m^2

    C. 240 m^2

    D. 480 m^2

2 Which of the following is closest to the measure of the angle shown? (12-1)

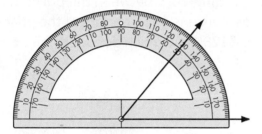

    F. 40°

    G. 50°

    H. 130°

    I. 140°

3 A counter in Karen's kitchen is shaped like a trapezoid. If the measures of the bases of the trapezoid are 7 feet and 5 feet and the measure of the height is 2 feet, what is the area of the trapezoid? (12-5)

    A. 35 ft^2

    B. 24 ft^2

    C. 12 ft^2

    D. 10 ft^2

4 The area of the rectangle is 120 square yards. Which of the following can be used to find the area of the shaded triangle? (12-4)

    F. 120

    G. 120 ÷ 2

    H. 120 − 40

    I. 120 − (2 × 40)

5 A rectangular window has a base of 36 inches and a height of 48 inches. What is the area of the window? (12-2)

    A. 1,728 in^2

    B. 1,488 in^2

    C. 864 in^2

    D. 168 in^2

6 Which is the area of the parking lot? (12-4)

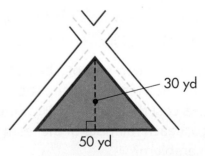

    F. 80 yd^2

    G. 750 yd^2

    H. 1,500 yd^2

    I. 1,800 yd^2

7 A patio has the shape shown, separated into a rectangle and a triangle. What is the area of the patio? (12-6)

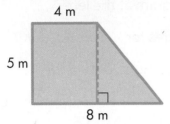

A. 20 m²

B. 24 m²

C. 26 m²

D. 30 m²

8 Casey needs to tile an area that is 56 square feet. Each blue tile has an area of 2 square feet and each white tile has an area of 3 square feet. If Casey would like to use 2 more white tiles than blue tiles, how many of each tile should Casey use to make an area of exactly 56 square feet? (12-7)

F. 12 blue tiles and 10 white tiles

G. 8 blue tiles and 10 white tiles

H. 10 blue tiles and 12 white tiles

I. 8 blue tiles and 14 white tiles

9 How should this angle be classified? (12-1)

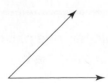

A. Right

B. Acute

C. Obtuse

D. Straight

10 The floor in Johnson's room is a square. The measure of one of the sides of the floor is 12 feet. Which expression can be used to find the area of the floor in his room? (12-2)

F. 12 × 12

G. 12 × 4

H. 12 + 12 + 12 + 12

I. 2 + 12

11 What is the area of the figure shown below? (12-6)

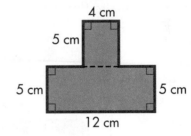

A. 20 cm²

B. 60 cm²

C. 80 cm²

D. 108 cm²

12 Chase draws a parallelogram on grid paper. The base is 14 units and the height is 11 units. How many square units is the area? (12-3)

13 THINK SOLVE EXPLAIN

Georgia wants to make a quilt that is 60 inches × 40 inches and uses a pattern of same-size squares. She has patterns for squares that measure 12 inches, 8 inches, 6 inches, or 5 inches on each side. Which pattern size should she use for the squares so the quilt has only whole squares? Explain. (12-7)

Set A, pages 278–279

The figure below shows the center of a protractor placed on the vertex at Point *K*. Use this diagram to complete the exercises.

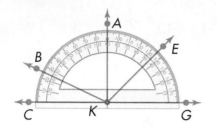

Remember to use the scale on the protractor that lines an angle side with 0°.

For **1–3**, use the diagram at the left.

1. Find the measures for ∠*GKE* and ∠*GKB*.

2. Is ∠*CKA* an acute, right, obtuse, or straight angle?

3. How would you classify ∠*AKE*?

Set B, pages 280–285

You can use a formula to find each area.

Rectangle
$A = b \times h$
$A = 8 \times 6 = 48 \text{ in}^2$

6 in.
8 in.

Parallelogram
$A = b \times h$
$A = 5 \times 3 = 15 \text{ ft}^2$

3 ft
5 ft

Triangle
$A = \dfrac{b \times h}{2}$
$A = \dfrac{11 \times 8}{2} = 44 \text{ m}^2$

8 m
11 m

Remember that area is measured in square units.

Find each area.

1.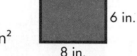
8 m

2.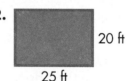
20 ft
25 ft

3.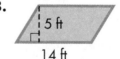
5 ft
14 ft

4.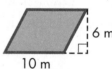
6 m
10 m

5.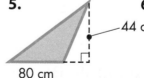
44 cm
80 cm

6.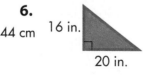
16 in.
20 in.

Set C, pages 286–287

You can use a formula to find the area of a trapezoid.

$A = \dfrac{(b_1 + b_2)}{2} \times h$

$A = \dfrac{(14 + 18)}{2} \times 9$

$A = \dfrac{32}{2} \times 9$

$A = 144 \text{ in}^2$

14 in.
9 in.
18 in.

Remember that a trapezoid has one pair of parallel sides, and these sides are the bases of the trapezoid.

Find each area.

1.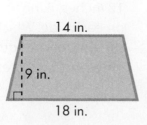
14 m
11 m
10 m

2.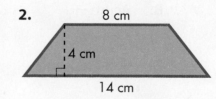
8 cm
4 cm
14 cm

Set D, pages 288–289

Find the area of the figure.

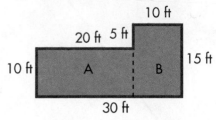

Separate the figure into two rectangles.

Use the formula $A = b \times h$ to find the area of each rectangle.

Rectangle A

$A = 20 \times 10$

$\quad = 200 \text{ ft}^2$

Rectangle B

$A = 10 \times 15$

$\quad = 150 \text{ ft}^2$

Add the areas of the rectangles to find the total area:

$200 + 150 = 350$

The area of the figure is 350 ft².

Remember that some shapes can be separated into regular shapes.

Find the area of each figure.

1.

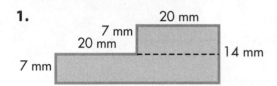

2.

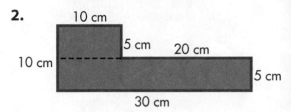

3.

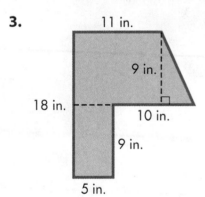

Set E, pages 290–291

When you *guess*, *check*, and *revise* to solve a problem, follow these steps:

Step 1

Make a reasonable first guess.

Step 2

Check by using information given to you.

Step 3

Use your first guess to make a reasonable second guess.

Step 4

Keep checking until you find the answer.

Remember *guess*, *check*, and *revise* can help to solve a problem.

1. Mr. Herrera wants to tile his floor with a pattern that repeats every 3 feet. Could he cover the floor without cutting off part of the pattern? Explain.

20 ft.

8 ft.   Living Room

Three-Dimensional Shapes

1

The Louvre Pyramid serves as the main entrance to the Louvre Museum in Paris, France, and is an example of a polyhedron. How can you make a net for this solid figure? You will find out in Lesson 13-3.

2

What kinds of solid figures can you find in this torii gate? You will find out in Lesson 13-1.

Review What You Know!

Vocabulary

Choose the best term from the box.

> • quadrilateral • square
> • triangle • pentagon

1. A polygon with only 3 sides is a __?__.

2. Every rectangle is a __?__.

3. A rectangle with all sides the same length is a __?__.

Area

Find the area of each figure.

4.

6 ft

10 ft

5.
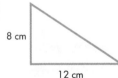
8 cm

12 cm

Operations

Multiply or divide.

6. 16×6 7. 3×42 8. $216 \div 3$

9. $364 \div 14$ 10. 475×25 11. $128 \div 4$

Geometry

Writing to Explain Write an answer for the question.

12. How are parallel lines different from perpendicular lines?

3

How could you classify the shape of this bar of solid gold? You will find out in Lesson 13-2.

Topic Essential Question

• How can three-dimensional shapes be represented and analyzed?

MA.5.G.3.1 Analyze and compare the properties of two-dimensional figures and three-dimensional solids (polyhedra), including the number of edges, faces, vertices, and types of faces.

Three-Dimensional Shapes

What is a solid figure?

A three-dimensional shape, or solid, takes up space. One solid is the cube. It has flat polygon-shaped surfaces called faces. All the faces of a cube are squares. Faces meet along segments called edges, and edges meet at points called vertices. The singular of vertices is vertex.

Hands-On
Power Solids

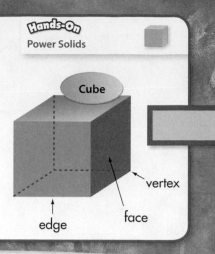

Cube

vertex

edge   face

Guided Practice*

Do you know HOW?

For **1** through **3**, use the solid shown.

1. Give the number of vertices.

2. Give the number of faces.

3. Give the number of edges.

Do you UNDERSTAND?

4. Which type of solid figure is shown at the left?

5. Which of the solid figures shown at the top have curved surfaces?

6. Writing to Explain Why is a cube a prism and not a pyramid? Explain.

Independent Practice

For **7** through **9**, tell which type of solid figure each object resembles.

7.

8.

9.

For **10** through **12**, use the solid shown at the right.

10. Give the number of vertices.

11. Give the number of faces.

12. Give the number of edges.

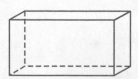

DIGITAL Animated Glossary, eTools
www.pearsonsuccessnet.com

Some solid figures have curved surfaces, while others have all flat surfaces.

Prism
A solid with two congruent parallel bases and faces that are parallelograms.

Cylinder
A solid with two circular bases that are congruent and parallel.

Cone
A solid with one circular base. The points on this circle are joined to one point outside the base.

Pyramid
A solid with one base that is a polygon and whose other faces are triangles with a common vertex.

Problem Solving

13. Which of the following decimals is equivalent to 12.45?

   A 12.0045

   B 12.0450

   C 12.4500

   D 124.5000

14. Which of the following solids has a curved surface?

   F Pyramid

   G Cube

   H Prism

   I Cone

15. Luke's tent weighs $6\frac{1}{2}$ pounds. His fishing tackle weighs $5\frac{1}{4}$ pounds. What is the total weight of both items?

16. Reasoning Can a prism have an odd number of vertices? Explain.

Critical THINKING

17. Torii gates are often found in Japan, where they originated. What kinds of solids can you find in a torii gate?

18. Which of the following is NOT a rectangular prism?

   A   **C**

   B   **D**

19. Algebra Fillmore Park had 75 spruce trees. Volunteers planted 39 more. Solve $75 + 39 = t$ to find the total number of spruce trees in the park now.

MA.5.G.3.1 Analyze and compare the properties of two-dimensional figures and three-dimensional solids (polyhedra), including the number of edges, faces, vertices, and types of faces.

Polyhedrons

How are some polyhedrons classified?

A polyhedron is a three-dimensional shape made of flat polygon-shaped surfaces. Prisms and pyramids are two general classes of polyhedrons.

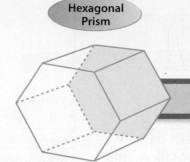

Hexagonal Prism

Another Example How do you name the parts of a three-dimensional shape?

You can use symbols to name the segments that form the edges of polyhedrons. For example, an edge that is formed by the vertices *A* and *B* can be labeled $\overline{AB}$.

You can use symbols to name the faces of a polyhedron. For example, a triangular-shaped face having vertices *A*, *B*, and *C* can be labeled $\triangle ABC$.

Name the vertices, edges, and faces of the triangular prism.

Vertices: *A*, *B*, *C*, *X*, *Y*, and *Z*

Edges: $\overline{AB}$, $\overline{AC}$, $\overline{BC}$, $\overline{XY}$, $\overline{XZ}$, $\overline{YZ}$, $\overline{AX}$, $\overline{BY}$, and $\overline{CZ}$

Faces: $\triangle ABC$ and $\triangle XYZ$; $\square ABYX$, $\square CBYZ$, and $\square AXZC$

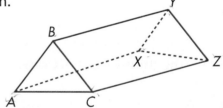

Name the vertices, edges, and faces of the pentagonal pyramid.

Vertices: *A*, *B*, *C*, *D*, *E*, and *F*

Edges: $\overline{AF}$, $\overline{BF}$, $\overline{CF}$, $\overline{DF}$, $\overline{EF}$, $\overline{AB}$, $\overline{BC}$, $\overline{CD}$, $\overline{DE}$, and $\overline{AE}$

Faces: $\bigcirc ABCDE$; $\triangle ABF$, $\triangle BCF$, $\triangle CDF$, $\triangle DEF$, and $\triangle EAF$

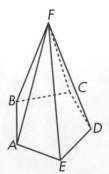

Explain It

1. How many edges of the pentagonal pyramid above meet at the vertex outside its base?

2. What is the name of a prism whose bases each have 8 sides?

Prisms

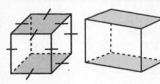

| Cube | Rectangular prism | Pentagonal prism | Triangular prism |

A prism is named by the shape of its bases. The other faces are parallelograms.

Pyramids

Triangular pyramid   Rectangular pyramid   Hexagonal pyramid

A pyramid is named by the shape of its base. Triangular faces join the edges of the base to a point outside the base, which is called a vertex.

Guided Practice*

Do you know HOW?

Classify each polyhedron. Name all faces, edges, and vertices.

1.
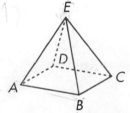

2.
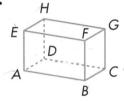

Do you UNDERSTAND?

3. Explain the difference between a vertex and an edge.

4. Explain the difference between a pyramid and a prism.

5. What would you look for if you were classifying polyhedrons?

Independent Practice

For **6** through **9**, classify each figure.

6.
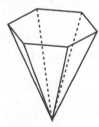

7.
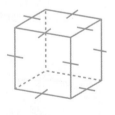

8.
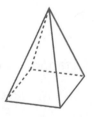

9.

For **10** through **13**, classify each polyhedron. Name all faces, edges, and vertices.

10.
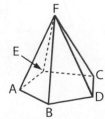

11.
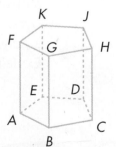

12.
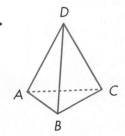

13.
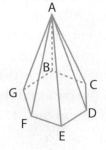

*For another example, see Set A on page 312.

Use the table at the right for **14** through **17**.

Polyhedron	Faces (F)	Vertices (V)	F + V	Edges (E)
Trianglar Pyramid				
Cube				
Pentagonal Prism				

14. The Swiss mathematician Leonhard Euler (OY-ler) and the French mathematician Rene Descartes (dā KART) both discovered a pattern in the numbers of edges, vertices, and faces of polyhedrons. Complete the table to look for a pattern.

15. Number Sense Describe any pattern you see in the table that relates the number of edges to the number of faces and vertices.

Critical THINKING

16. Algebra Write a formula to describe your pattern. Does the pattern work for a hexagonal prism?

17. Writing to Explain If a rectangular prism has 12 edges and 6 faces, how could you use a formula to find the number of vertices the figure has?

18. Classify the shape of this bar of gold. How many faces does it have? How many vertices? How many edges?

19. Why are the faces on a pyramid triangular, regardless of the shape of its base?

THINK SOLVE EXPLAIN

20. What is the name of a prism that has bases with 6 edges?

    A Hexagonal prism   **C** Octagonal prism

    B Pentagonal prism   **D** Heptagonal prism

21. An octagonal pyramid has 9 faces and 9 vertices. How many edges does an octagonal pyramid have?

    F 9   **H** 18

    G 16   **I** 20

22. Keshia made a pentagonal pyramid as a prop for the school play. All of the triangular faces are congruent and each of them needs to be painted green. What is the total area of the pyramid that Keshia will paint green?

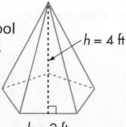

$h = 4$ ft

$b = 2$ ft

23. The shape at the right is not a prism or a pyramid. Is it a polyhedron? Explain.

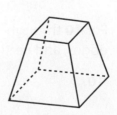

Mixed Problem Solving

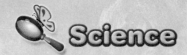

Mixtures of solids can be separated based on observable properties. For **1** through **10**, observe the solids shown below to answer each exercise.

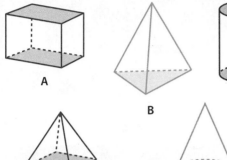

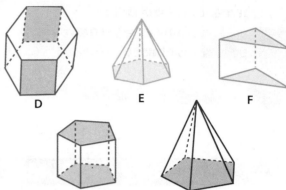

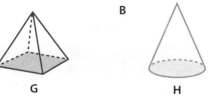

1. Which of the solids are prisms?

2. Which of the solids have 7 faces?

3. Which of the solids are polyhedrons?

4. Which of the solids have 12 edges?

5. Which of the solids have more than 1 triangular face?

6. Which of the solids are orange?

7. Which of the solids have more than 1 edge, and less than 10 edges?

8. Which of the solids have an equal, non-zero number of faces and vertices?

9. Which of the solids are purple?

10. Which of the solids have 6 vertices?

- -

11. Which of these solid shapes could be stacked up repeatedly like blocks to fill space?

   A Cone

   B Sphere

   C Rectangular prism

   D Rectangular pyramid

12. Which is NOT true about a pyramid?

   F It has an equal number of faces and vertices.

   G It has an even number of edges.

   H It has triangular shaped faces.

   I It always has a square base.

13. Strategy Focus Solve using the strategy *Act It Out and Use Reasoning*. Suppose the centers of the 5 faces of a square pyramid are connected by line segments. Which solid shape would these segments form the edges of?

Lesson
13-3

MA.5.G.3.1 Analyze and compare the properties of two-dimensional figures and three-dimensional solids (polyhedra), including the number of edges, faces, vertices, and types of faces.

Nets

How can you use a two-dimensional shape to represent a three-dimensional solid?

A net is a plane figure which, when folded, will make a solid.

How can you draw a net for this solid figure?

Guided Practice*

Do you know HOW?

Predict what solid each net will make.

1.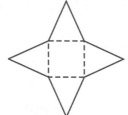

2.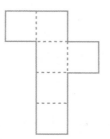

Do you UNDERSTAND?

3. **Writing to Explain** How did you make your predictions in Exercises 1 and 2?

4. A solid may have different nets. Draw a different net for the solid you identified in Exercise 2.

Independent Practice

For **5** through **7**, predict what solid each net will make.

5.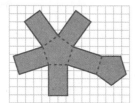

6.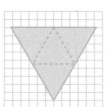

7.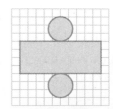

In **8** through **10**, draw a net for each solid.

8.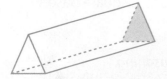

9.

10.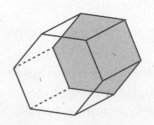

Animated Glossary
www.pearsonsuccessnet.com

DIGITAL

*For another example, see Set B on page 313.

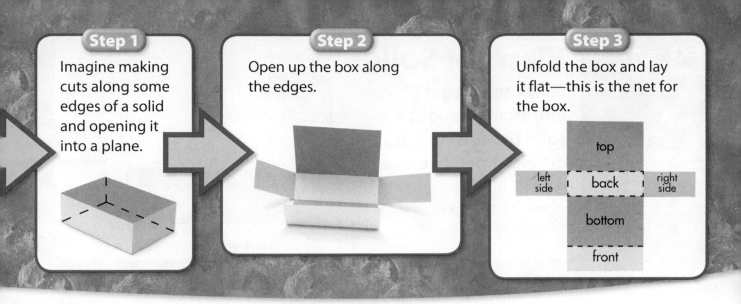

Step 1

Imagine making cuts along some edges of a solid and opening it into a plane.

Step 2

Open up the box along the edges.

Step 3

Unfold the box and lay it flat—this is the net for the box.

top

left side | back | right side

bottom

front

Problem Solving

11. A net has 4 large rectangles and 2 small rectangles. What solid figure might it make?

  A Rectangular prism

  B Square pyramid

  C Triangular prism

  D Rectangular pyramid

12. Molly spent $120 on two items. One cost $10 more than the other. Which shows the correct cost for each?

  F $70, $50

  G $50, $60

  H $60, $70

  I $55, $65

13. Strategy Focus When some rock music is played unamplified its sound has been measured at 62 decibels. Sound for amplified music can be measured at 124 decibels. Draw a picture and write an equation to find the difference between the number of decibels measured.

Critical THINKING

14. Algebra Diane is thinking of a number. She doubles it and adds 10. Her result is 50. Which equation could you use to find Diane's number?

  A $(2 \times n) - 10 = 50$

  B $2 \times 10n = 50$

  C $2 \times n = 50$

  D $(2 \times n) + 10 = 50$

15. 🎨 **Art** The Louvre Museum, located in Paris, France, displays many of the world's art treasures. The Louvre Pyramid serves as an entrance to the museum. This is an example of a rectangular pyramid. Draw a net for this polyhedron.

MA.5.G.3.1 Analyze and compare the properties of two-dimensional figures and three-dimensional solids (polyhedra), including the number of edges, faces, vertices, and types of faces.

Views of Solids

How can you get information about a solid by viewing it from different perspectives?

What do the different views of this stack of cubes look like?

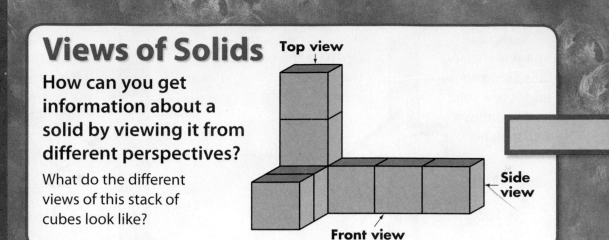

Top view

Side view

Front view

Guided Practice*

Do you know HOW?

1. Sketch the front, top, and side views of the solid figure below.

Do you UNDERSTAND?

2. How many cubes are not visible in the diagram at the left?

3. Which two views would be the same for the solid shown below?

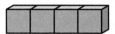

Independent Practice

In **4** through **9**, draw front, side, and top views of each stack of cubes.

4.
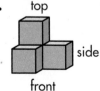
top
side
front

5.
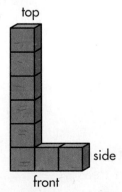
top
side
side
front

6.
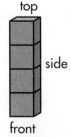
top
side
front

7.
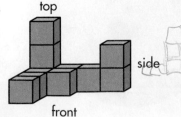
top
side
front

8.
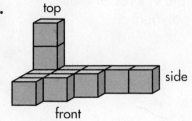
top
side
front

9.
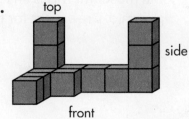
top
side
front

*For another example, see Set C on page 313.

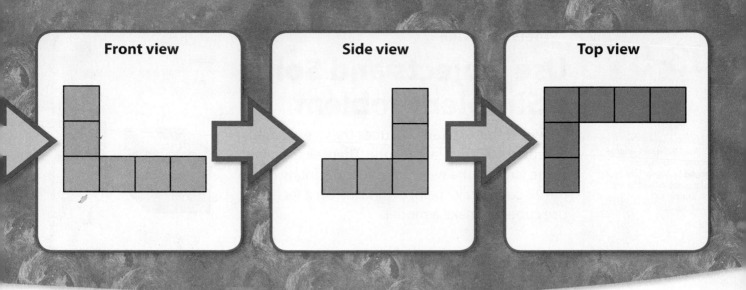

Front view	Side view	Top view

10. 🔬 **Science** The world's biggest bird is the ostrich. It can weigh 345 pounds and have a height of 9 feet. Which of the following is NOT equal to 9 feet?

A 3 yards

B $\frac{9}{5,280}$ mile

C 108 inches

D $\frac{1}{100}$ mile

11. How many cubes are not visible from the front view?

Critical THINKING

Front view	Side view	Top view

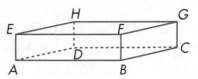

12. Draw the front, side, and top views of this stack of cubes.

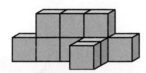

13. A bag contains 5 red marbles, 1 green marble, and 1 yellow marble. What fraction of the marbles are red?

F $\frac{1}{7}$

G $\frac{1}{5}$

H $\frac{5}{7}$

I $\frac{5}{5}$

14. How many cubes are not visible from the top view?

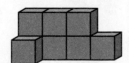

15. In the rectangular prism below, which face is parallel to $\square ABCD$?

16. If 10 cubes are stacked vertically, how many cubes are not visible from the top view?

A $\square BCGF$

B $\square ADHE$

C $\square EFGH$

D $\square DCGH$

MA.5.A.6.5 Solve non-routine problems using various strategies including "solving a simpler problem" and "guess, check, and revise." Also MA.5.G.3.1

Problem Solving

Use Objects and Solve a Simpler Problem

Hands-On
cubes

Shown at the right are 27 cubes that were glued together to form a larger cube. Then, all 6 faces of the larger cube were painted. How many of the 27 cubes have paint on 1 face? On 2 faces? Use cubes to make a model.

Guided Practice*

Do you know HOW?

1. Use cubes and the example of the simpler problem above to build a larger cube with 4 layers. Each layer will have 4 rows of 4 cubes. How many cubes will the larger cube contain?

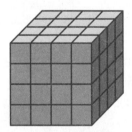

Do you UNDERSTAND?

2. Think of gluing the cubes together for the $4 \times 4 \times 4$ cube you made. Then, think of painting the outside faces. How many cubes will have paint on 1 face? On 2 faces? On 3 faces?

3. **Write a Problem** Write a real-world problem that involves using objects to help solve a simpler problem.

Independent Practice

In **4** through **9**, use objects to help you solve a simpler problem. Use the solution to help you solve the original problem.

4. Alicia uses wood timbers to build steps. The pattern is shown for 1, 2, 3, and 4 steps. How many timbers will she need to build 10 steps?

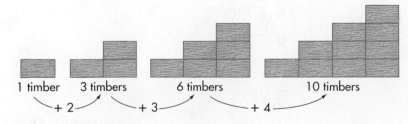

1 timber   3 timbers   6 timbers   10 timbers

+ 2   + 3   + 4

Stuck? Try this....

- What do I know?
- What am I asked to find?
- What diagram can I use to help understand the problem?
- Can I use addition, subtraction, multiplication, or division?
- Is all of my work correct?
- Did I answer the right question?
- Is my answer reasonable?

How many cubes have paint on 1 face?

The center cube on each of the 6 faces of the larger cube has paint on 1 face.

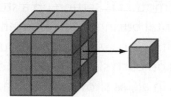

Six of these cubes have paint on 1 face.

How many cubes have paint on 2 faces?

Only 1 cube on each of the 12 edges of the larger cube has paint on 2 faces.

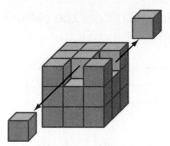

Twelve of these cubes have paint on 2 faces.

5. Four people can be seated at a table. If two tables are put together, six people can be seated. How many tables are needed to make a long table that will seat 20 people?

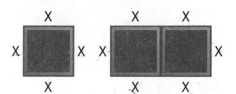

6. Jeremiah wants to make a display of CD boxes. He wants a single box on the top layer. Layers that are below the top layer must form a square, with each layer being 1 box wider than the layer above it. The display can only be 4 layers high. How many total boxes will be in the display? Use cubes.

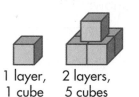

1 layer,   2 layers,
1 cube   5 cubes

7. Katherine is constructing a patio using the design shown at the right.

   a How many total blocks will she need in order to have 5 blocks in the middle row?

   b How many total blocks will she need in order to have 6 blocks in the middle row?

   c What do you notice about the number of blocks in the middle row compared to the total number of blocks?

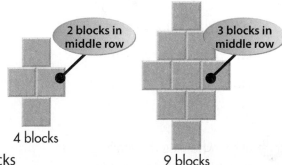

4 blocks

9 blocks

8. An artist wants to cut 1 square sheet of copper into 16 equal pieces. Before he cuts, he will draw segments on the sheet of copper showing where to make the cuts. How many horizontal and vertical segments will he need to draw?

9. There are 24 balls in a large bin. Two out of every three are basketballs. The rest are footballs. How many basketballs are in the bin?

eTools
www.pearsonsuccessnet.com

Which solid does the picture below resemble? (13-1)

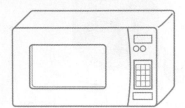

A. Cone

B. Pyramid

C. Cube

D. Prism

2 What solid can be made with the net shown? (13-3)

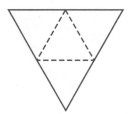

F. Triangular pyramid

G. Triangular prism

H. Rectangular pyramid

I. Cube

3 Which names the base of the polyhedron below? (13-2)

A. △PQR

B. △TUV

C. ○QRSTUV

D. ○PQRSTU

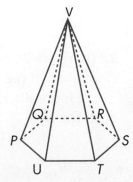

4 Todd's mother is setting up a storage unit rental business. She is arranging the units in an L-shape. If she puts 3 units on each side of the L, she has 5 units in all, as shown. How many units does she have if she puts 8 units on each side of the L? (13-5)

F. 13

G. 15

H. 16

I. 17

5 Nita stacked some crates to make a bookshelf as shown. Which of the following is the top view of the crates? (13-4)

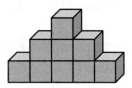

A.

B.

C.

D.

6 Henry made a tower using 9 cubes. How many cubes are NOT visible from the front view? (13-4)

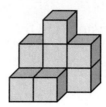

F. 0

G. 1

H. 2

I. 3

7 Which names an edge of the rectangular pyramid? (13-2)

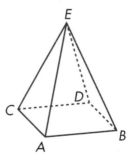

A. $\overline{CB}$

B. $\overline{CA}$

C. $\triangle DBE$

D. E

8 Gordon's net has 2 circles and 1 rectangle. What solid can be made from this net? (13-3)

F. Rectangular prism

G. Cube

H. Cone

I. Cylinder

9 Which names a face of the rectangular prism? (13-2)

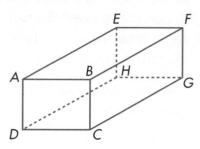

A. ▱$ABCD$

B. ▱$ADCE$

C. $\overline{DC}$

D. G

10 How many edges does a rectangular pyramid have? (13-1)

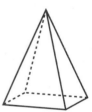

11 Angelo has the cardboard box shown below. He wants to cut along the edges to see the net of the solid. Draw a net for this solid. (13-3)

THINK
SOLVE
EXPLAIN

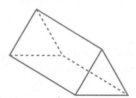

Set A, pages 298–299; 300–302

A **three-dimensional shape**, or solid, takes up space. Three-dimensional shapes that are made up of flat polygon-shaped flat surfaces, called **faces**, are **polyhedrons**. Two types of polyhedrons are prisms and pyramids.

A **prism** is a solid with two parallel bases and faces that are parallelograms.

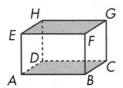

Prism

A **pyramid** is a solid with a base that is a polygon and whose other faces are triangles with a common vertex.

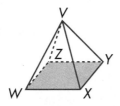

Pyramid

Faces meet along segments called **edges**, and edges meet at points called **vertices**. The singular of vertices is vertex. Prisms and pyramids can be named by the shapes of their bases.

Name the pyramid shown above. How many faces does it have? Name the faces.

The pyramid has a rectangular base, so it is a rectangular pyramid. It has 5 faces, including its base. The faces are □WXYZ, △WXV, △XYV, △YZV, and △ZWV.

Remember A prism has two congruent parallel bases, but a pyramid has only one base.

1. Which of the following is NOT a polyhedron?

   A

   B

   C
   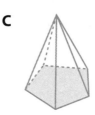

   D

For **2** through **6** use the solid shown below.

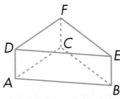

2. Name the figure.

3. Give the number of faces.

4. Give the number of edges.

5. Name the vertices.

6. Do the bases of the prism change if the prism is placed on one of its sides? Explain.

Set B, pages 304–305

A net is a plane figure which, when folded, gives a solid. The net below can be folded to make a rectangular prism.

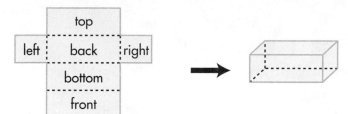

Remember that dashed lines are used to represent where a net should be folded.

Predict what solid each net will make.

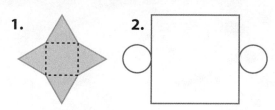

1.

2.

Draw a net for each solid.

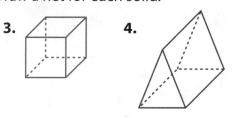

3.

4.

Set C, pages 306–307

Draw the front, top, and side views of the solid made from stacked cubes.

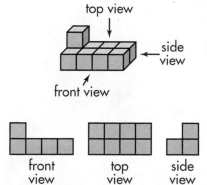

top view

side view

front view

front view

top view

side view

Remember to consider cubes that are hidden from your view.

Draw the front, top, and side views of each solid made from stacked cubes.

1.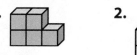

2.

Set D, pages 308–309

To solve a simpler problem, follow these steps:

Step 1

Break apart or change problem into one that is simpler to solve.

Step 2

Use objects to solve the simpler problem.

Step 3

Use the answers to the simpler problem to solve the original problem.

Remember that objects can be used to see patterns or relationships.

1. After folding a piece of paper one time, there are two sections. How many sections are there after 2 folds? After 3 folds? If you fold the paper 5 times, how many sections would you have?

Topic 14

Measurements of Three-Dimensional Shapes

1

Over 1.6 million one-inch-square glass tiles cover the walls of the Outer Bay exhibit. What is an estimate for the volume of the main viewing window of this exhibit? You will find out in Lesson 14-4.

2

How can you find the surface area of the outer walls and roof of one of these pueblo houses? You will find out in Lesson 14-2.

Review What You Know!

Vocabulary

Choose the best term from the box.

> • area
> • perimeter
> • polyhedron
> • prism

1. __?__ is the number of square units to cover the inside of a two-dimensional shape.

2. A solid with two congruent parallel bases and faces that are parallelograms is called a(n) __?__ .

3. Any solid made up of flat polygon-shaped surfaces is a(n) __?__ .

Multiplication

Find each product.

4. $10 \times 8 \times 5$ 5. $20 \times 40 \times 5$

6. $15 \times 10 \times 10$ 7. $2 \times 10 \times 8$

8. $3 \times 30 \times 9$ 9. $50 \times 33 \times 2$

Area

Find the area of each figure.

10. A rectangle with dimensions 4 feet × 7 feet.

11. A triangle with a base of 14 inches and a height of 9 inches.

12. A square with a side 3 meters long.

Writing to Explain Write an answer for the question.

13. How is finding the area of a triangle different from finding the area of a rectangle?

3

Some antique boxes, like this one, were made from special cuts of wood and included intricate carvings. How can you find the volume of this box? You will find out in Lesson 14-4.

Topic Essential Question
• What do the surface area and the volume of a three-dimensional shape mean and how can each be found?

Lesson
14-1

MA.5.G.3.2 Describe, define and determine surface area and volume of prisms by using appropriate units and selecting strategies and tools.

Models and Surface Area

How can you use a model to measure surface area?

The surface area (SA) of a polyhedron is the sum of the areas of all of its faces. You can use a net to show the faces of a polyhedron. What is the surface area of the rectangular prism on the right?

Hands-On
grid paper

Guided Practice*

Do you know HOW?

1. Find the surface area of the rectangular prism represented by the net below. Show your work.

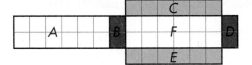

Do you UNDERSTAND?

2. How could you model the surface area of a cube with an edge that measures 4 units?

3. Draw a net that models the surface area of a cube with an edge that measures 3 units.

4. List the congruent faces of the net in Exercise 1.

Independent Practice

In **5** and **6**, find the surface area of the rectangular prism represented by each net below.

5.

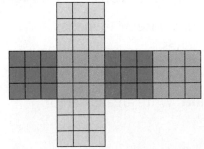

6.

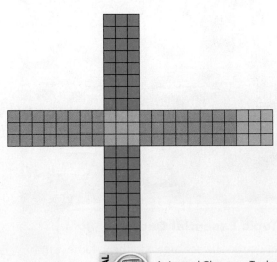

For another example, see Set A on page 334.

Animated Glossary, eTools
www.pearsonsuccessnet.com

Use a net to model the surface area. Then count the number of square units for each face.

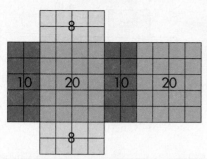

Add the areas of all the faces to find the surface area.

side	side	front	back	top	bottom

$$SA = 10 + 10 + 20 + 20 + 8 + 8$$

$$= 76 \text{ square units}$$

The surface area of the rectangular prism is 76 square units.

Problem Solving

7. A net has 4 triangular faces. What solid figure does it make?

   A Cone   **B** Cube   **C** Cylinder   **D** Pyramid

For **8** and **9**, use the nets at the right.

James

8. James and Mary make nets to use as scale models for the storage sheds they plan to build. The nets represent sheets of metal. Whose storage shed requires more metal to build? How many square units more?

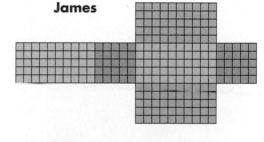

9. If each square unit on their nets represents $15 of metal, how much will it cost to buy metal for each of the storage sheds?

Mary

10. The walls, floor, and ceiling of Judith's room can be represented by the model shown below. If each square on the grid measures 1 square inch, how many square inches of paint does she need to paint the entire model?

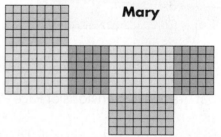

11. Writing to Explain Find the surface area of this rectangular prism by counting the squares on the faces that you can see and multiply the result by 2. Why is this number equal to the surface area? Explain.

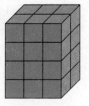

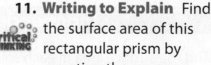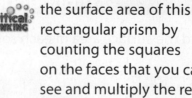

MA.5.G.3.2 Describe, define, and determine surface area and volume of prisms by using appropriate units and selecting strategies and tools.

Surface Area

How can you find the surface area of a rectangular prism?

Use what you know about nets and the formula for area of a rectangle to find the surface area of the rectangular prism shown at the right.

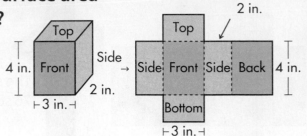

Guided Practice*

Do you know HOW?

For **1** and **2**, use the net of the rectangular prism shown below.

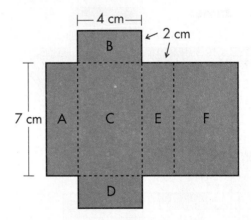

1. What are the dimensions of Face F?

2. What is the surface area of the figure?

Do you UNDERSTAND?

3. List the congruent faces of the net at the left.

4. For which type of rectangular prism could you find the surface area by finding the area of 1 face and multiplying that area by 6?

5. What is the surface area of a cube with an edge that measures 5 cm?

6. Writing to Explain A child's shoebox is 8 in. × 5 in. × 9 in. Carla said that the surface area of the box equals 314 inches. Is Carla correct? Why or why not?

Independent Practice

In **7** through **9**, find the surface area of each solid.

7.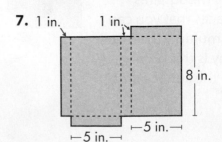

8.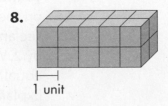

9.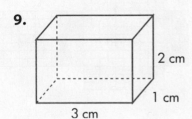

For another example, see Set B on page 334.

You can use the formula for the area of a rectangle to find the area of each face.

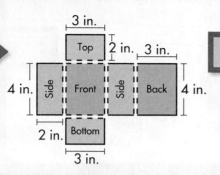

Add the areas of all the faces to find the surface area (SA).

        side   side   front   back   top   bottom

$$SA = (4 \times 2) + (4 \times 2) + (4 \times 3) + (4 \times 3) + (3 \times 2) + (3 \times 2)$$
$$= 8 + 8 + 12 + 12 + 6 + 6$$
$$= 52 \text{ square inches (in}^2)$$

The surface area of the rectangular prism is 52 in².

Problem Solving

For **10** and **11**, use the diagram at the right.

10. Draw a net to represent Mylah's cupboard. Find the surface area.

11. Writing to Explain If Mylah wants to put a wood trim around the base of the cupboard, would she need to find the perimeter or the area of the base?

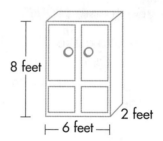

12. What type of transformation is shown below?

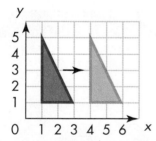

13. Morgan receives a crate that is 4 feet × 2 feet × 3 feet. Kenley receives a crate that is 3 feet × 1 foot × 5 feet. Whose crate has the greater surface area? Explain.

Critical THINKING

14. The bottom of a vase forms a right triangle with a base of 4 inches and a height of 6 inches. How many square inches of space will the vase occupy on a tabletop?

15. Kori's softball team played 18 games. Her team won 4 more games than they lost. How many games did they win?

For **16**, use the diagram at the right.

16. **Social Studies** The Pueblo tribe of New Mexico lived in houses that looked like boxes stacked on top of one another. What would the surface area of the outer walls and roof of a pueblo house be if it had the dimensions shown?

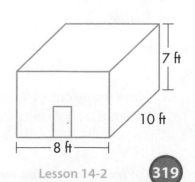

Lesson
14-3

MA.5.G.3.2 Describe, define, and determine surface area and volume of prisms by using appropriate units and selecting strategies and tools.

Models and Volume

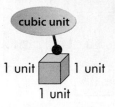
Hands-On
unit cubes

How can you measure space inside a solid figure?

Volume is the <u>number of cubic units</u> <u>needed to fill a solid figure.</u>

A cubic unit is <u>the</u> <u>volume of a cube</u> <u>1 unit on each edge.</u> What is the volume of this solid?

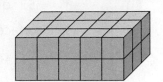

cubic unit

1 unit   1 unit
1 unit

Guided Practice*

Do you know HOW?

Use cubes to make a model of each rectangular prism. Find the volume by counting the number of cubes needed to make the model.

1.   2.

Do you UNDERSTAND?

3. Make a model of a rectangular prism with a base that is 3 cubes long by 3 cubes wide. The height of the prism is 2 cubes. Then draw a picture of your model.

4. If you add another layer to the top of the prism in Exercise 1, what would the new volume be in cubic units?

Independent Practice

In **5** through **10**, find the number of cubic units needed to make each rectangular prism. You can use unit cubes or you can count the cubes by looking at the drawing.

5.   6.   7.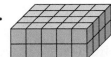

8.   9.   10.

11. How many cubes would it take to make a model of a rectangular prism that is 4 units long × 5 units wide × 3 units high?

DIGITAL   Animated Glossary, eTools
www.pearsonsuccessnet.com

Use cubic units to make a model.

bottom layer

Count the number of cubes.
There are 15 cubes in the bottom layer.

There are two layers.

second layer

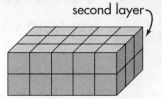

Multiply the volume of the bottom layer by 2.
The volume of the prism is 2 × 15 or 30 cubic units.

Problem Solving

For **12** through **16**, use the table at the right.

Compare the volumes of the prisms.
Write >, <, or = for each ◯.

12. Prism A ◯ Prism B

13. Prism B ◯ Prism C

14. Prism C ◯ Prism A

Prism	Model
A	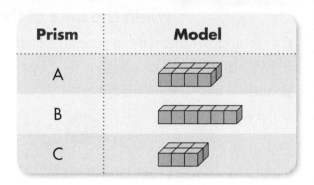
B	
C	

15. If you added another layer of unit cubes on top of Prism A, what would its volume be in cubic units?

16. If you put Prism C on top of Prism A, what would the volume of the new solid be in cubic units?

17. Number Sense A jaguar is 80 inches long. A school's jaguar mascot is 7 feet long. Is the mascot longer or shorter than a real jaguar?

18. Reasoning Ms. Kellson's storage closet is 3 feet long, 3 feet wide, and 7 feet high. Can she fit 67 boxes that each have a volume of 1 cubic foot in her closet? Explain your answer.

Critical THINKING

19. 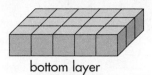 **About the Process** One carton of books had a mass of 8.4 kilograms. Ramon put a book with a mass of 1.2 kilograms into the carton and removed 2 books each with a mass of 1.1 kilograms. Which number sentence could be used to find the final mass of the carton?

A 8.4 + 1.2 + 2.2

C (8.4 + 1.2) × 2 − 1.1

B 8.4 + 1.2 − (2 × 1.1)

D 8.4 + 1.2 + 2(1.1)

MA.5.G.3.2 Describe, define, and determine surface area and volume of prisms by using appropriate units and selecting strategies and tools.

Volume

How can you use a formula to find the volume of a rectangular prism?

Remember that volume is the number of cubic units (units³) needed to fill a solid figure.

Find the volume of the rectangular prism at the right if each cubic unit represents 1 cubic foot.

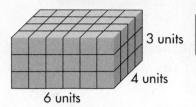

3 units

4 units

6 units

Another Example How can you find the volume of a rectangular prism when the area of the base is given?

If a rectangular prism has a base area B and a height h, use this formula:

Volume = base area × height

$V = B \times h$

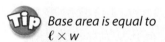 **Tip** Base area is equal to $\ell \times w$

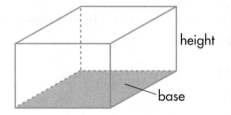

height

base

Find the volume of a rectangular prism with a base area of 56 cm² and a height of 6 cm.

$V = B \times h$

$V = 56 \times 6$

$V = 336 \text{ cm}^3$

The volume of the rectangular prism is 336 cm³.

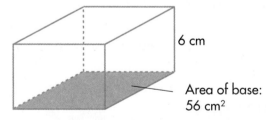

6 cm

Area of base: 56 cm²

Explain It

1. In the example above, what are possible length and width dimensions of the base of the rectangular prism shown? Explain.

2. How is counting cubes related to the formulas for finding volume?

3. How do you know which formula for volume to use?

If the measurements of a rectangular prism are given in length ℓ, width w, and height h, then use this formula to find volume V:

Volume = (length × width) × height

$$V = \ell \times w \times h$$

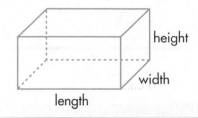

Use the formula to find the volume of the rectangular prism.

$$V = \ell \times w \times h$$
$$V = 6 \times 4 \times 3$$
$$V = 72 \text{ ft}^3$$

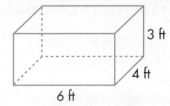

The volume of the rectangular prism is 72 ft³.

Guided Practice*

Do you know HOW?

In **1** through **3**, find the volume of each rectangular prism.

1.

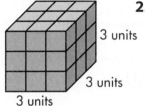

3 units
3 units
3 units

2.

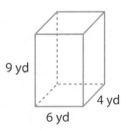

9 yd
6 yd
4 yd

3. Base area: 26 m²
    height: 4 m

Do you UNDERSTAND?

4. In the example above, could you first multiply the height by the width?

5. A cereal box measures 6 in. × 2 in. × 10 in. Draw a rectangular prism and label it. What is the volume of the figure you drew?

6. Writing to Explain How can you use different methods to find the volumes of the prisms in Exercises 1–3?

Independent Practice

In **7** through **12**, find the volume of each rectangular prism.

7.

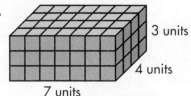

3 units
4 units
7 units

8.

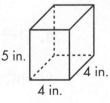

5 in.
4 in.
4 in.

9.

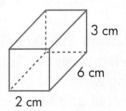

3 cm
6 cm
2 cm

10.

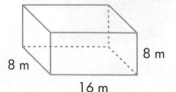

8 m
8 m
16 m

11.

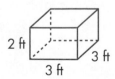

2 ft
3 ft
3 ft

12.

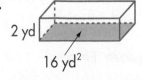

2 yd
16 yd²

Independent Practice

For **13** through **15**, find the volume of each rectangular prism.

13. Length: 8 in., width: 7 in., height: 5 in.

14. Base area: 100 ft², height: 17 ft

15. Base area: 72 yd², height: 8 yd

Problem Solving

For **16** through **18**, use the information below.

Sixty-four students are planning a field trip to an art museum. Each student will pay $9. Each van can hold 7 students and 1 driver.

16. How much money will be collected if all the students attend?

17. How many vans will be needed if all the students travel to the museum?

18. The school pays each driver $60 to drive the van. If the round trip takes 4 hours, how much does each driver make per hour?

19. A refrigerator measures 6 feet tall, 4 feet wide, and 3 feet deep. What is the volume of the refrigerator?

20. Only 3 students in each event win medals at the track meet. If 9 students are running the mile, what fraction of them will win a medal?

21. What is the perimeter of this figure?

16 cm
9 cm   11 cm
20 cm

22. Algebra Last week 22 people worked a total of 1,100 hours. Each person worked the same number of hours, h. Which equation represents this situation?

A $1,100h = 22$ **C** $h \div 1,100 = 22$

B $22 \div h = 1,100$ **D** $22h = 1,100$

23. Harry is in line at the store. He has 3 items that cost $5.95, $4.25, and $1.05. Explain how Harry can add the cost of the items mentally before he pays for them.

THINK
SOLVE
EXPLAIN

24. Estimation The Outer Bay exhibit at the Monterey Bay Aquarium has a viewing window that is 56.5 feet long, 17 feet tall, and 13 inches thick. Estimate its volume in cubic feet. HINT: 13 inches is about 1 foot.

Critical THINKING

26. Algebra Find $3c - 17$ if $c = 20$.

25. Think About the Process Which expression can be used to find the volume of this antique box?

3 in.   4 in.   6 in.

F $(6 \times 4) \times 3$ **H** 6×4

G $(6 \times 4) + 3$ **I** $2 \times (6 \times 4 \times 2)$

Mixed Problem Solving

Tangrams are ancient Chinese puzzles made up of geometric shapes. All tangrams have the same seven pieces, which fit together to form a square. The objective is to create a design using all seven pieces, called tans. The tans must all be touching, but they may not overlap.

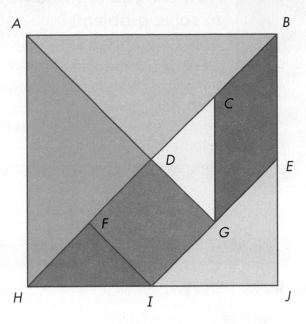

Use the above tangram for **1** through **7**.

1. What shape do the 7 pieces of the tangram make?

2. What shape is formed by points *A*, *D*, and *H*?

3. Identify three pairs of parallel line segments.

4. Identify a pair of perpendicular line segments.

5. What shape is formed by points *C*, *B*, *E*, and *G*?

6. What shape is formed by points *H*, *B*, and *J*?

7. How many triangles do you see in the tangram?

On a separate sheet of paper, use the above design to create your own tangram. Using the tans from your tangram, try to make the design at the right, using all seven tans. Make sure none of them overlap. Use the puzzle for **8** through **10**.

8. Describe the shape the tangram puzzle forms.

9. Make a Design Make your own tangram puzzle from the pieces. Name your design and describe what shape your design makes.

10. Writing to Explain Explain how you created your own shape in Exercise 9.

MA.5.G.3.2 Describe, define and determine surface area and volume of prisms by using appropriate units and selecting strategies and tools.

Combining Volumes

How can you use volume formulas to solve problems?

A storage building has the shape and size shown at the right. The warehouse supervisor wants to find the volume of the building to determine how much storage space is available. What is the volume of the building?

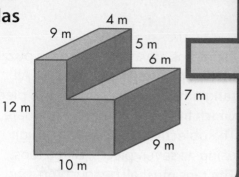

Guided Practice*

Do you know HOW?

Find the volume of each solid figure.

1.

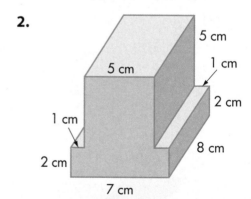

5 in.
6 in.
7 in.
8 in.
7 in.
10 in.
2 in.
7 in.
15 in.

2.

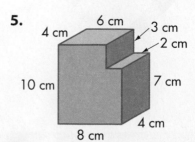

5 cm
5 cm
1 cm
2 cm
1 cm
8 cm
2 cm
7 cm

Do you UNDERSTAND?

In **3** and **4**, use the shape below. The dashed line separates it into two rectangular prisms, A and B.

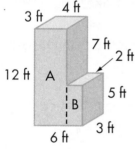

3 ft   4 ft
7 ft
2 ft
12 ft   A
5 ft
B
6 ft   3 ft

3. What are the length, width, and height of Prism A? What are the length, width, and height of Prism B?

4. **Draw a Picture** How else could you separate the shape into two rectangular prisms?

Independent Practice

In **5** through **7**, find the volume of each solid figure.

5.

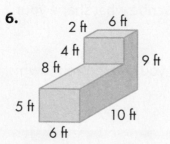

6 cm
4 cm
3 cm
2 cm
10 cm
7 cm
4 cm
8 cm

6.

2 ft   6 ft
4 ft
8 ft   9 ft
5 ft
6 ft   10 ft

7.

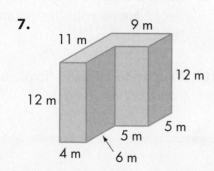

9 m
11 m
12 m
12 m
5 m
4 m   6 m   5 m

*For another example, see Set E on page 335.

The building can be separated into two rectangular prisms. Identify the measurements for the length, width, and height of each prism.

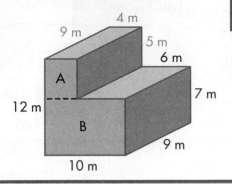

Use the formula $V = \ell \times w \times h$ to find the volume of each rectangular prism.

Volume of Prism A	Volume of Prism B
$V = \ell \times w \times h$	$V = \ell \times w \times h$
$= 4 \times 9 \times 5$	$= 10 \times 9 \times 7$
$= 180 \text{ m}^3$	$= 630 \text{ m}^3$

Add to find the total volume.

$180 + 630 = 810 \text{ m}^3$

The volume of the storage building is 810 m³.

Problem Solving

8. The rectangle shows the dimensions of Richard's patio. Find the perimeter of the patio in feet.

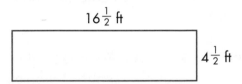

9. **Draw a Picture** Join these two rectangular prisms to make one solid figure. Find the volume.

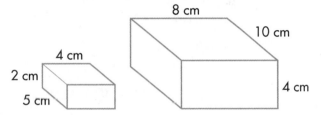

10. **Writing to Explain** In the example at the top of the page, why do you add the volumes of the rectangular prisms?

11. **Algebra** Write an expression you can use to find the surface area of the cube.

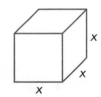

12. What is the volume of this solid figure?

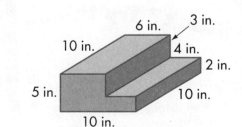

A 50 in³

B 260 in³

C 380 in³

D 500 in³

13. **Science** About 78% of the Earth's atmosphere is made up of nitrogen. Write 78% as a decimal and as a fraction in simplest form.

14. Cynthia is making a table to record the mass of objects for her science fair project. Which power of 10 can she use to convert grams to kilograms?

F 10^1

G 10^2

H 10^3

I 10^4

MA.5.G.3.2 Describe, define, and determine surface area and volume of prisms by using appropriate units and selecting strategies and tools. Also MA.5.A.6.5.

Use Objects and Reasoning

Hands-On
unit cubes

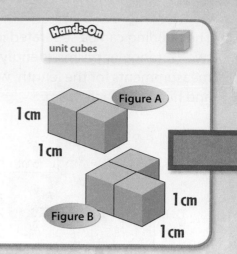

Figure A has a volume of 2 cubic centimeters (cm³). It has a surface area of 10 square centimeters (cm²).

Find the volume and surface area of Figure B.

Then use cubes to make a solid figure with a volume of 4 cm³ and a surface area of 18 cm².

Guided Practice*

Do you know HOW?

1.

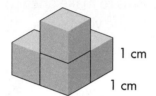

1 cm
1 cm

a What is the volume of this solid?

b What is the surface area of this solid?

Do you UNDERSTAND?

2. How can using cubes help you answer questions about volume and surface area?

3. Write a Problem Arrange 5 cubes, each measuring 1 centimeter on each edge, to form a solid figure. Draw the solid. Write questions about the volume and surface area for a partner to answer. Include the answer.

Independent Practice

Find the volume and surface area of each solid.

4.

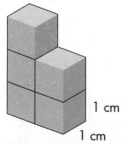

1 cm
1 cm

5.

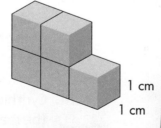

1 cm
1 cm

6.

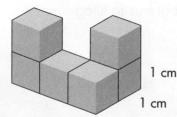

1 cm
1 cm

7.

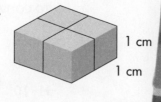

1 cm
1 cm

Stuck? Try this....

- What do I know?
- What am I asked to find?
- What diagram can I use to help understand the problem?
- Can I use addition, subtraction, multiplication, or division?
- Is all my work correct?
- Did I answer the right question?
- Is my answer reasonable?

Count the cubes to find the volume.

I see 3 cubes. None are hidden.

The volume is 3 cm³.

Count all the outside faces of the cubes in the solid figure to find the surface area.

I see 7 faces, and 7 more faces on the bottom and the back of the solid figure are hidden.

The surface area is 14 cm².

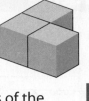

7 faces are hidden

Use centimeter cubes to make a solid figure with 4 cubes that has 18 outside faces.

Think I counted the number of cubes to find the volume and the outside faces to find the surface area.

It has a volume of 4 cm³ and a surface area of 18 cm².

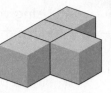

For **8** through **11**, use centimeter cubes to make a solid with the given volume and surface area. Draw your answers.

8. Matt used centimeter cubes to make a solid that had a volume of 5 cubic centimeters and a surface area of 22 square centimeters. What might his solid have looked like?

9. April and Julie each made differently shaped solids with a volume of 4 cubic centimeters and a surface area of 18 square centimeters or less. What might their 2 solids have looked like?

10. Sebastian made a solid with a volume of 6 cubic centimeters and a surface area greater than 21 square centimeters. What might his solid have looked like?

11. Alberto made a solid with a volume of 8 cubic centimeters and a surface area of 24 square centimeters. What might his solid have looked like?

Use the solid figure at the right for **12** and **13**. Draw your answers.

12. Use 7 centimeter cubes to make a different solid figure with the same surface area.

13. Use centimeter cubes to make a solid figure that has the same volume as the illustration but a smaller surface area.

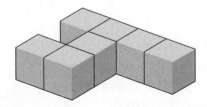

eTools
www.pearsonsuccessnet.com

DIGITAL

Lesson 14-6   329

14. You can use a formula to find the surface area of a tower of centimeter cubes.

 Critical THINKING

   a Using your cubes, make a stack *x* cubes tall. Fill in the table with the surface area of your tower.

Cubes, x	2	3	5	7	10
Surface area, y	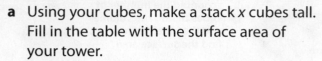				

   b Find a pattern and make a conjecture. Look at your table. What pattern do you see? Write an equation for the pattern.

   c Test your conjecture. Substitute the value 6 for *x* in the formula. What is the value of *y*? Build a tower 6 cubes tall. Count the faces to determine the surface area. Is your conjecture correct?

15. How does the sum of the volume of 4 individual cubes compare to the volume of a stack of 4 cubes?

For **16** and **17**, use centimeter cubes to help draw your pictures.

16. Draw a cube that has twice the length, width, and height of the 1 cm cube. What are the volume and surface area of the new solid?

17. Draw a cube that has triple the length, width, and height of the 1 cm cube. What are the volume and surface area of the new solid?

Volume = 1 cubic centimeter
Surface area = 6 square centimeters

18. Writing to Explain Why can two solids with the same volume have different surface areas?

Think About the Process

19. Which expression shows how to find the total surface area of 4 individual 1 cm cubes? The cubes are not touching each other.

   A 4×4

   B $4 \times 1 + 2$

   C $4 \times 4 + 2$

   D 4×6

20. How can you find the surface area of the solid figure on the right?

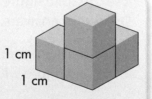

1 cm
1 cm

   F Count the number of faces.

   G Count the number of cubes.

   H Count the number of cubes and subtract 2.

   I Count the number of cubes and multiply by 6.

Classify each figure. Identify whether or not the solid is a polyhedron.

1.   2.   3.   4.

For **5** through **7**, complete the following table.

	Number of Faces	Number of Vertices	Number of Edges
5.			
6.			
7.			

For **8** through **10**, find the volume of each solid.

8.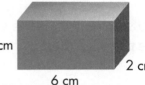
3 cm
6 cm
2 cm

9.
2 ft   2 ft
8 ft

10.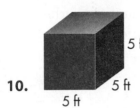
5 ft
5 ft
5 ft

Error Search Determine if each volume is correct. If the volume is incorrect, write it correctly and explain the error.

11.
length: 3 cm
width: 5 cm
height: 18 cm
volume: 270 cm^2

12.
length: 12 in.
width: 3 in.
height: 15 in.
volume: 540 in^3

13.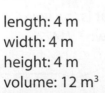
length: 6 ft
width: 1 ft
height: 1 ft
volume: 6 ft^3

14.
length: 4 m
width: 4 m
height: 4 m
volume: 12 m^3

Number Sense

Estimating and Reasoning Write whether each statement is true or false. Explain your answer.

15. A cube with a volume of 27 cm^3 can have a height of 9 cm.

16. The volume of an 8 cm cube will be less than 100 cm^3.

The rectangular prism below is made up of unit cubes. What is the volume of the prism? (14-3)

A. 18 cubic units

B. 54 cubic units

C. 72 cubic units

D. 108 cubic units

2 The solid figure below is made up of cubes and has a volume of 4 cm³. What is the surface area of the solid figure? (14-6)

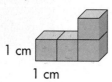

1 cm

1 cm

F. 18 cm²

G. 20 cm²

H. 22 cm²

I. 24 cm²

3 What is the volume of the step stool shown? (14-5)

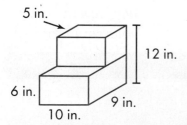

5 in.

12 in.

6 in.

9 in.

10 in.

A. 320 in³

B. 790 in³

C. 840 in³

D. 1,080 in³

4 What is the surface area of the prism formed by the net shown? (14-2)

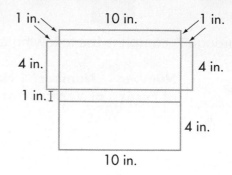

1 in.   10 in.   1 in.

4 in.   4 in.

1 in.

4 in.

10 in.

F. 100 in²

G. 108 in²

H. 118 in²

I. 120 in²

5 How many square units is the surface area of the prism formed by this net? (14-1)

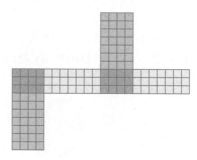

A. 61 square units

B. 84 square units

C. 110 square units

D. 122 square units

6 What is the surface area of the trunk shown? (14-2)

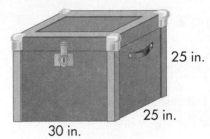

25 in.

25 in.

30 in.

F. 320 in²

G. 3,000 in²

H. 4,250 in²

I. 18,750 in²

7 What is the volume of the bale of hay? (14-4)

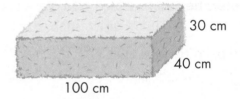

30 cm

40 cm

100 cm

A. 120,000 cm²

B. 120,000 cm³

C. 12,000 cm²

D. 12,000 cm³

8 The rectangular prism below is made from cubes that each measure 1 cubic meter. What is the volume of the prism? (14-3)

F. 9 m³

G. 12 m³

H. 21 m³

I. 36 m³

9 Which trunk has a volume of 30 cubic feet? (14-4)

A.

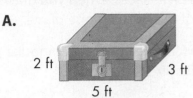

2 ft   3 ft

5 ft

B.

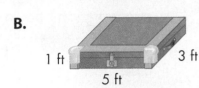

1 ft   3 ft

5 ft

C.

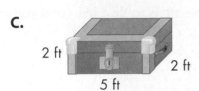

2 ft   2 ft

5 ft

D.

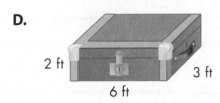

2 ft   3 ft

6 ft

10 Todd's cube has an edge that measures 5 inches. Kara's cube has an edge of 3 inches. How many more cubic inches is the volume of Todd's cube than the volume of Kara's cube? (14-4)

11 The solid figure below is made up of unit cubes. Explain how you can use objects or reasoning to find the surface area of this solid figure. What is the surface area? (14-6)

THINK
SOLVE
EXPLAIN

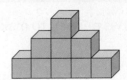

Set A, pages 316–317

The surface area (*SA*) of a polyhedron is the sum of the areas of all its faces. When you draw a net, you can see all of the faces on one plane.

Find the surface area of the rectangular prism that can be formed from this net.

Count the number of square units for each face.

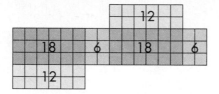

Then add the areas to find the total surface area.

SA = 18 + 18 + 12 + 12 + 6 + 6
= 72 square units

Remember to count the square units to find the area of each face.

For **1** and **2**, use the net below.

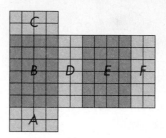

1. Find the area of each face.

2. What is the surface area of the solid formed by the net?

Set B, pages 318–319

The net below folds to make a rectangular prism. Find the surface area by adding areas of the faces.

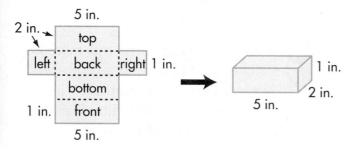

$SA = (5 \times 2) + (5 \times 2) + (2 \times 1) +$
$(2 \times 1) + (1 \times 5) + (1 \times 5) = 34 \text{ in}^2$

Remember that surface area is always measured in square units, such as m².

Find each surface area.

1.
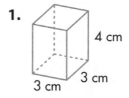

2.
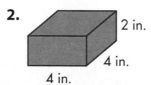

Set C, pages 320–321

Find the number of cubes needed to make this rectangular prism.

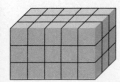

There are 3 rows of 5 cubes in the bottom layer. There are 3 layers.

So the total number of cubes is 3 × 5 × 3 or 45. The volume is 45 cubic units.

Remember that you can find the number of cubes in each layer and then multiply by the number of layers.

Find each volume.

1.    **2.**

Set D, pages 322–324

Find the volume of this rectangular prism.

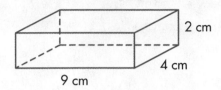

Volume = length × width × height.

$V = \ell \times w \times h = 9 \text{ cm} \times 4 \text{ cm} \times 2 \text{ cm}$
$V = 72 \text{ cm}^3$

The volume of the prism is 72 cm³.

Remember if you know the base area of a rectangular prism, use the formula $V = B \times h$, where B is the base area.

Find each volume.

1. Base area = 42 m²,
   height = 3 meters

2.
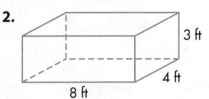

Set E, pages 326–327

Some solid figures can be separated into two rectangular prisms.

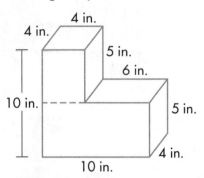

Add the volumes of both prisms to find the total volume of the solid figure.

$V = (4 \times 4 \times 5) + (10 \times 4 \times 5) = 280 \text{ in}^3$

Remember to identify the length, width, and height of each prism part so that you can calculate the volume of each part.

1. Find the volume.

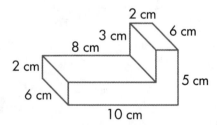

Set F, pages 328–330

You can use objects and reasoning to find patterns and solve problems. Find the volume and surface area of the solid figure.

Volume

1 cube = 1 cm³, so volume of 2 cubes = 2 cm³.

Surface Area

Faces on 1 cube: 6   Faces on 2 cubes: 12
Shared faces on 2 cubes together: 2

Surface Area: 12 cm² – 2 cm² = 10 cm²

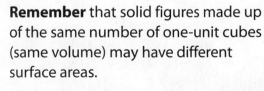
Shared surface
1 cm
1 cm   1 cm

Remember that solid figures made up of the same number of one-unit cubes (same volume) may have different surface areas.

Find the volume and surface area. The solid figures are made of 1-centimeter cubes.

1.

2.
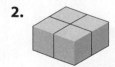

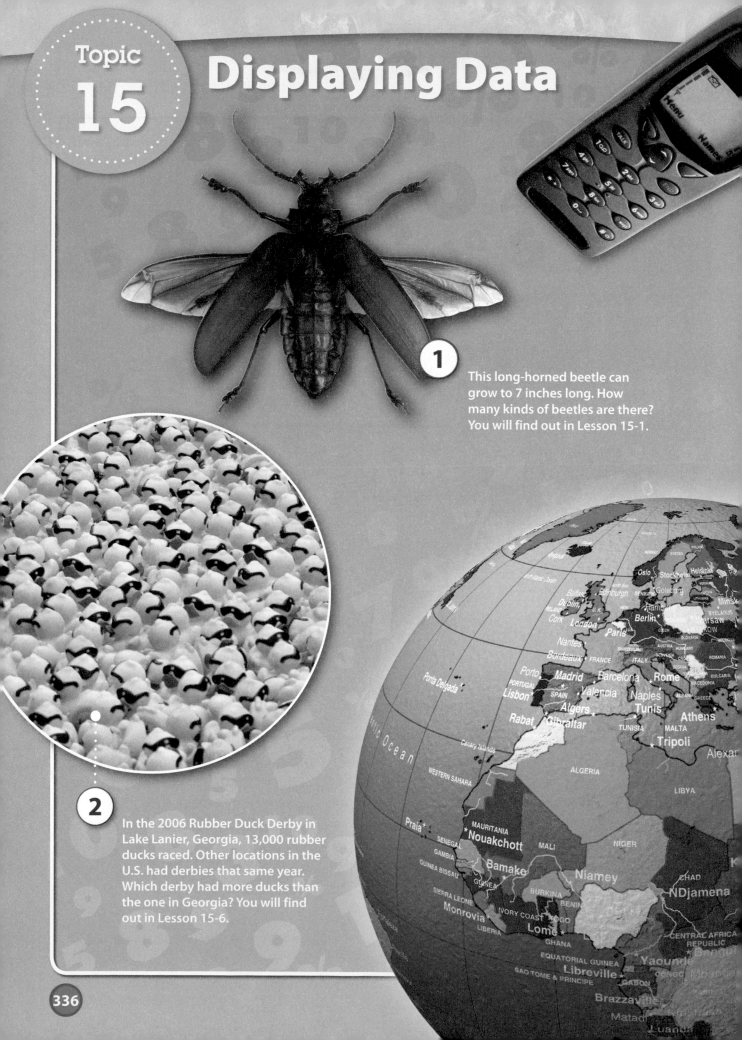

Displaying Data

1

This long-horned beetle can grow to 7 inches long. How many kinds of beetles are there? You will find out in Lesson 15-1.

2

In the 2006 Rubber Duck Derby in Lake Lanier, Georgia, 13,000 rubber ducks raced. Other locations in the U.S. had derbies that same year. Which derby had more ducks than the one in Georgia? You will find out in Lesson 15-6.

3

American households spend hundreds of dollars every year on telephone service. How many more dollars did Americans spend on phone service in 2004 than in 2001? You will find out in Lesson 15-5.

4

Cities are located on a globe by using ordered pairs of latitude and longitude. What city is located at the coordinates (30°N, 30°E)? You will find out in Lesson 15-5.

Review What You Know!

Vocabulary

Choose the best term from the box.

- axis
- point
- ordered pair
- origin

1. A(n) __?__ is either of two perpendicular lines in a graph.

2. A(n) __?__ is an exact location in space.

3. A pair of numbers used to locate a point on a graph is called a(n) __?__.

Line Plots

Use the line plot below to answer the questions.

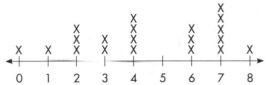

Number of Soccer Goals Scored by 20 Teams

4. How many teams scored 3 goals or less?

5. What was the greatest number of goals scored by a team?

Coordinate Grids

Write the ordered pair for each point.

6. A   7. C

8. G   9. D

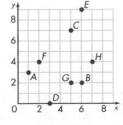

10. **Writing to Explain** Describe the steps you would take to plot a point at (6, 5).

Topic Essential Questions

- What type of graph is most appropriate for representing different types of data?

- How can graphs be analyzed to answer questions and make predictions?

15-1

MA.5.S.7.2 Differentiate between continuous and discrete data and determine ways to represent those using graphs and diagrams. Also MA.5.S.7.1

Bar Graphs

What do bar graphs show?

A bar graph uses bars to show and compare data. About how many more species of animals are in the Minnesota Zoo than the Phoenix Zoo?

The scale consists of numbers that show the units used on a graph.

The interval is the amount between tick marks on the scale.

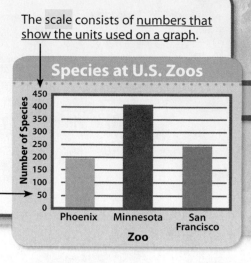

Species at U.S. Zoos

Guided Practice*

Do you know HOW?

For **1** and **2**, use the bar graph below.

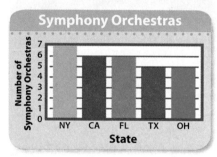

1. Which state shown on the graph has the most symphony orchestras?

2. Which state has the same number of symphony orchestras as Florida?

Do you UNDERSTAND?

3. What is the interval of the scale for the bar graph above?

4. The Miami Metro Zoo has 300 species of animals. In the example above which zoos have fewer species than the Miami Metro Zoo?

5. **Writing to Explain** Explain how the graph in the example above shows discrete data.

Independent Practice

For **6** through **8**, use the bar graph at the right.

6. About how much longer does a lion live than a giraffe?

7. Which animals have the same average lifespan?

8. The average lifespan of a gorilla is 20 years. How would you change the graph to add a bar for gorillas?

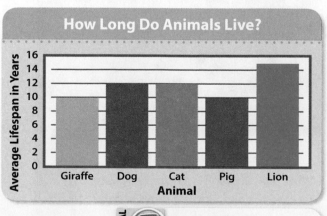

How Long Do Animals Live?

Animated Glossary, www.pearsonsuccessnet.com

Species at U.S. Zoos

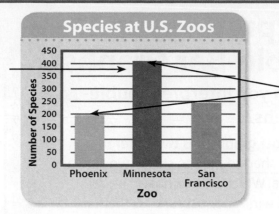

The purple bar is just above the number 400. The Minnesota Zoo has about 400 species of animals.

Skip count by 50s from the top of the green bar (Phoenix Zoo) until you are even with the top of the purple bar (Minnesota Zoo). Count: 50, 100, 150, 200.

Bar graphs are useful for comparing data. Data like the number of species are discrete data because only whole numbers are possible. The Minnesota Zoo has about 200 more species than the Phoenix Zoo.

Problem Solving

For **9** through **11**, use the graphs at the right.

9. How many more students were in the band in 2008 than in 2007?

10. Which of these is NOT true of the data in the graphs?

  A Drama club membership decreased in 2008.

  B Spelling club was the least popular for both years.

  C Spelling club membership increased in 2008.

  D There were fewer band members than drama club members in both years.

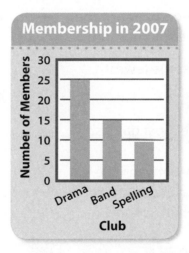

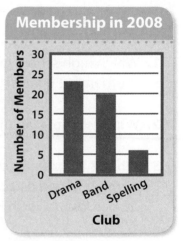

11. How could the information on these two graphs be shown more efficiently?

Critical THINKING

For **12** and **13**, use the graph at the right.

12. 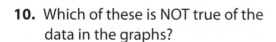 **Science** There are over 350,000 species of beetles. How does this compare to the number of species shown for moths and butterflies?

13. Which two types of insects have about the same number of species?

Number of Insect Species

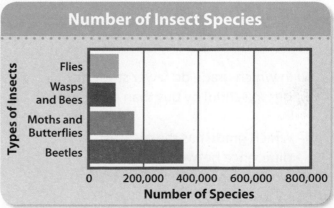

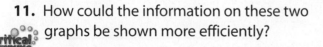
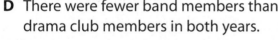

Lesson

15-2

MA.5.S.7.1 Construct and
analyze line graphs and
double bar graphs.

Interpreting Double-Bar Graphs

How can you interpret double-bar graphs?

A double-bar graph uses two different-colored or shaded bars to show two similar sets of data. Which school has an equal number of wins and losses?

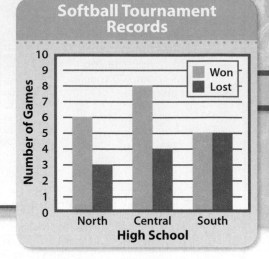

Guided Practice*

Do you know HOW?

In **1** and **2**, use the double-bar graph in the example above to answer each question.

1. Which high school lost the fewest tournament games?

2. Which school won the most games?

3. What is the difference between the number of games won and number of games lost at North High School?

Do you UNDERSTAND?

4. In the example above, what would happen if the key was not included as part of the graph?

5. Describe another set of data that could be presented as a double-bar graph and what the two colors would represent on the graph.

Independent Practice

In **6** through **9**, answer the questions about the double-bar graph at the right.

6. How many students in Grade 6 get to school by bus? In Grade 7?

7. In which grade do the most students get to school by bus?

8. In which grade do fewer students get to school by bus than other ways?

9. Which grade has the greatest difference between students who get to school by bus and by other ways?

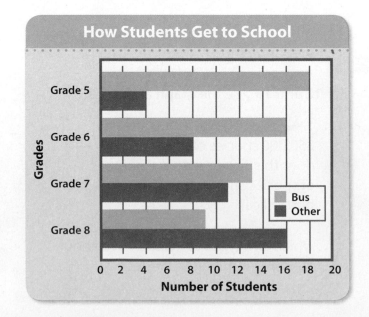

*For another example, see Set B on page 358.

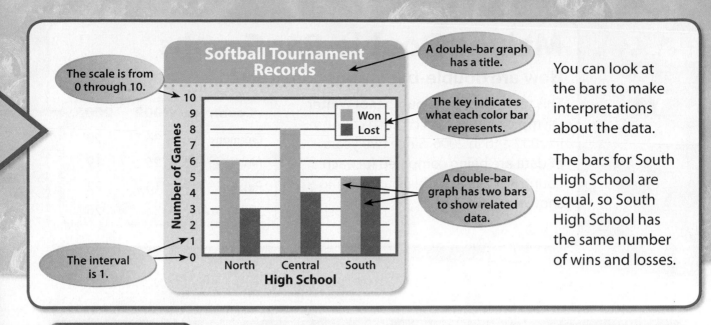

Softball Tournament Records

A double-bar graph has a title.

The scale is from 0 through 10.

The key indicates what each color bar represents.

Won
Lost

A double-bar graph has two bars to show related data.

The interval is 1.

Number of Games

North   Central   South
High School

You can look at the bars to make interpretations about the data.

The bars for South High School are equal, so South High School has the same number of wins and losses.

Problem Solving

For **10** through **12**, use the graph of 2000 and 2007 national park attendance.

10. How many million visitors are being represented by one interval on the scale?

11. Estimate the total number of people who visited the Grand Canyon in 2000 and 2007.

12. In 2007, about how many more people visited Olympic Park than Grand Teton Park?

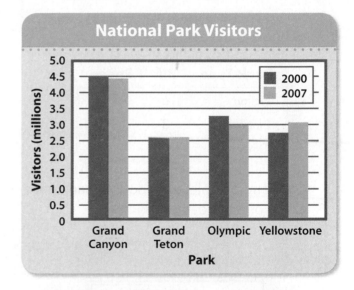

National Park Visitors

2000
2007

Visitors (millions)

Grand   Grand   Olympic   Yellowstone
Canyon   Teton
Park

13. **Think About the Process** Julio bought 3 dozen eggs. He had 13 eggs left after making egg salad for the picnic. Which expression shows how to find the number of eggs Julio used?

A $(13 - 12) \times 3$ **C** $(13 \times 12) - 3$

B $(12 - 3) - 13$ **D** $(3 \times 12) - 13$

14. **Writing to Explain** A school has 12 soccer teams with 10 students on each team. The school wants to place all of the players on only 8 soccer teams. Explain how to find the number of students that will be on each team if there are only 8 teams.

Critical THINKING

15. Point *A* represents which mixed number on the number line below?

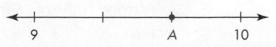

9   *A*   10

MA.5.S.7.1 Construct and
analyze line graphs and
double bar graphs.

Making Double-Bar Graphs

How are double-bar graphs constructed?

This table shows the number of Winter Olympic medals won by each country in 2002 and in 2006. Since two years of data are being compared for each country, make a double-bar graph to show the data.

Country	2002	2006
Germany	36	29
Norway	25	19
Russia	13	22
United States	34	25

Guided Practice*

Do you know HOW?

1. Bill and Renee kept track of the types of books they read.

Book Type	Bill	Renee
Fiction	6	4
Biography	3	7
Other	2	1

Copy and complete the double-bar graph of these data.

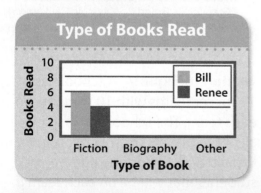

Do you UNDERSTAND?

2. Why are two bars used for each category in a double-bar graph?

3. What interval is used in the Winter Olympic Medals graph above?

4. For which of the following situations would making a double-bar graph to display the data be most appropriate?

   A To show the number of students in each class

   B To show the number of boys in each class

   C To show the number of girls in each class

   D To show the number of boys and the number of girls in each class

---

Independent Practice

5. The table shows information about school activities. Make a double-bar graph to display the data.

6. **Writing to Explain** How did you decide what interval to use for the graph you made in Exercise 5?

Number of Members		
Activity	Boys	Girls
Chess Club	6	7
Band	9	12
Basketball	8	8

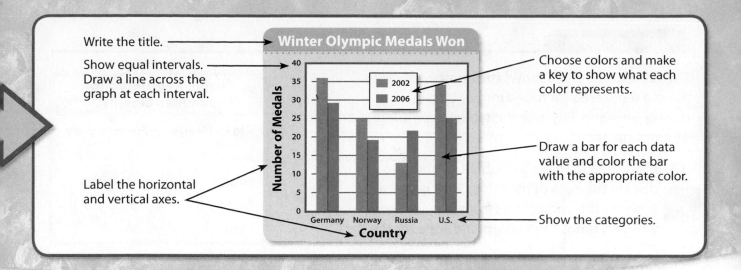

Write the title.

Show equal intervals. Draw a line across the graph at each interval.

Label the horizontal and vertical axes.

Winter Olympic Medals Won

Key: 2002, 2006

Number of Medals: 40, 35, 30, 25, 20, 15, 10, 5, 0

Germany, Norway, Russia, U.S.

Country

Choose colors and make a key to show what each color represents.

Draw a bar for each data value and color the bar with the appropriate color.

Show the categories.

Independent Practice

For **7** through **11**, use the data in the table at the right.

7. **Science** Make a double-bar graph of the data.

8. How many bars are shown for each city on your graph?

9. What interval did you use for your graph?

10. Other than using color, how could you distinguish the bars on your graph?

Critical THINKING

11. What label did you use for the vertical axis? Explain why.

Precipitation by City (inches)		
City	2000	2007
West Palm Beach, FL	42	64
Albuquerque, NM	8	10
Seattle, WA	29	39

For **12** through **15**, use the data in the table at the right.

12. The table at the right gives monthly bank balances for Kelly and Jess. Make a double-bar graph using the data in the table.

	Jan.	Feb.	Mar.	Apr.	May	June
Jess	$14	$45	$27	$34	$44	$10
Kelly	$23	$35	$41	$45	$51	$60

13. Explain how you can use your graph to determine whose bank balance increased each month.

14. Use your graph to determine who had the greater increase from one month to the next. Between which two months did this increase occur?

15. During which month were Jess's and Kelly's bank balances the closest? During which month did they have the greatest difference in their balances?

The table at the right shows the number of people registered for four summer classes during June and July. Use the table to complete **16** through **18**.

People Registered for Summer Classes		
Class Name	June	July
Jujitsu	5	8
Yoga	7	7
Painting	9	11
Orchestra	8	9

16. Kiki wants to make a double-bar graph to display the data in the table. She creates a scale for the vertical axis from 0 to 10. Explain why this is not the appropriate scale for the data.

THINK SOLVE EXPLAIN

17. Make a double-bar graph using the information in the table.

18. Which class had the greatest increase in students from June to July?

For **19** and **20**, use the frequency table.

19. Think About the Process Explain why you should NOT make a double-bar graph to display these data.

20. How many more U.S. residents visited France than Italy in 2004?

    F 49,000   **H** 1,285,000

    G 492,000   **I** 4,322,000

Top 5 Destinations of U.S. Residents, 2004	
Destination	Number of Travelers
Mexico	19,360,000
Canada	15,056,000
United Kingdom	3,692,000
France	2,407,000
Italy	1,915,000

For **21** through **23**, use the graph.

21. According to the graph at the right, which professional sport is reported to have higher minimum salaries for its players—football (NFL) or basketball (NBA)?

22. How do years of experience affect salaries in both leagues?

23. About how much more money will a basketball pro earn than a football pro if both have 1 year of experience and earn the minimum salary?

24. Rob wants to make a double-bar graph comparing the average cost of diesel fuel to the average cost of unleaded fuel in Florida, Louisiana, Oklahoma, and Virginia. How many pairs of bars will Rob's graph have?

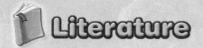
Venn diagrams are graphic organizers that may use two overlapping loops or circles. A Venn diagram can be used to compare and contrast two characters in a story, for example. The Venn diagram below shows some ways that plays and short stories may be alike and different.

Plays   Short Stories

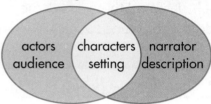

actors
audience

characters
setting

narrator
description

Venn diagrams can also be used to analyze mathematical relationships. Describe the relationship shown by the sets of numbers in the Venn diagram below.

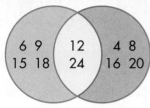

6 9   12   4 8
15 18   24   16 20

The numbers in the green loop are divisible by 3. The numbers in the orange loop are divisible by 4. The numbers in the yellow area of overlap are divisible by 3 and 4.

- -

For **1** and **2**, describe the relationship shown by each set of numbers.

1.

6 3
12 9   15
21 18   30
24   27

5
10
20
25

2.

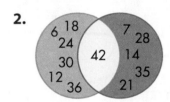

6 18
24
30   42
12 36

7
28
14
35
21

For **3** and **4**, read the exercise and make a Venn diagram to compare and contrast the main ideas of the two topics discussed.

3. **Customary and Metric Measures** Customary and metric measures are two systems used to measure volume. Both *measure volume in cubic units.* Customary units include *cubic inches (in³)* and *cubic feet (ft³).* Metric units include *cubic centimeters (cm³)* and *cubic meters (m³).*

4. **Pyramids and Prisms** Pyramids and prisms are *three-dimensional (3D) figures.* Both have *edges, vertices, bases,* and other polygon-shaped *faces.* A pyramid has *one base.* The *other faces* of a pyramid are *triangular.* A prism has *two bases.* The other faces of a prism have *parallelogram shapes.*

MA.5.S.7.2 Differentiate between continuous and discrete data and determine ways to represent those using graphs and diagrams. Also MA.5.S.7.1

Interpreting Line Graphs

How do you read and interpret line graphs?

A line graph connects points and often shows how data changes over time.

What was the population of Iowa in 1965?

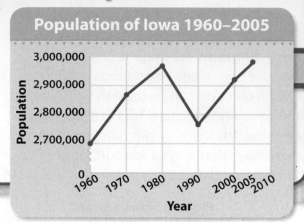

Guided Practice*

Do you know HOW?

1. Use the line graph below. About how long did it take the cyclist to travel 4 miles?

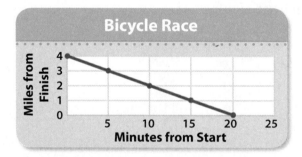

Do you UNDERSTAND?

2. **Writing to Explain** In the example above, did Iowa's population increase more between 1970 and 1980 or between 1990 and 2000? Explain.

3. How can you tell when there is an increase in the data on a graph?

4. How can you tell when there is a decrease in the data on a graph?

Independent Practice

For **5** through **8**, use the graph at the right.

5. About how many miles were traveled in the first 8 hours?

6. About how long did it take to travel 250 miles?

7. About how many miles were traveled between Hour 6 and Hour 10?

8. **Reasoning** What is the trend in the data?

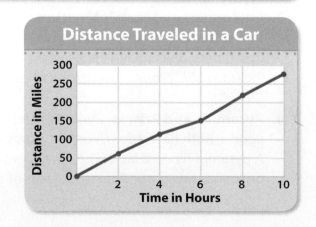

Animated Glossary
www.pearsonsuccessnet.com

For another example, see Set D on page 360.

Use the line graph to find the population of Iowa in 1965.

The grid line for 2,800,000 crosses the graph between 1960 and 1970.

The population was about 2,800,000 in 1965.

What was the general trend in the population? A pattern in the data showing an increase or decrease is the trend.

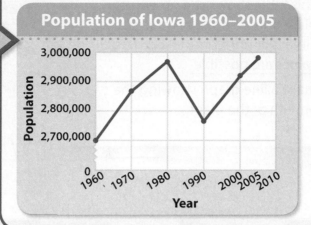

Population of Iowa 1960–2005

The line goes up from 1960 to 1980, decreases from 1980 to 1990, and then increases from 1990 to 2005.

The trend in the population was an increase.

Problem Solving

For **9** through **11**, use the graph at the right.

9. Between which times did Mary ride the fastest?

10. What do you think happened between 9:00 and 9:30?

11. How many miles did Mary ride in two hours and thirty minutes?

Mary's Charity Bike Ride

For **12** through **16**, use the graph at the right.

12. **Science** About how many species of mammals were endangered in 1996?

13. During which four-year periods did the number of endangered mammals increase the most?

14. **Estimation** About how many more species of endangered mammals were there in 2004 than in 1992?

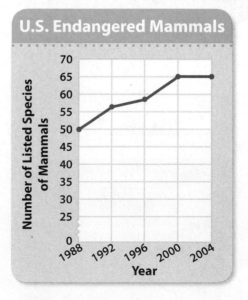

U.S. Endangered Mammals

15. Between which four years did the number of endangered mammals stay the same?

16. **Reasoning** What does this graph tell you about the number of endangered species of reptiles?

A   1988–1992   C   1996–2000

B   1992–1996   D   2000–2004

Lesson
15-5

MA.5.S.7.1 Construct and analyze line graphs and double bar graphs.

Making Line Graphs

How are line graphs constructed?

This table shows the growth of a plant at the end of several weeks. Time is continuous data since all values are possible.

Make a line graph showing the growth of the plant.

Hands-On
metric ruler
grid paper

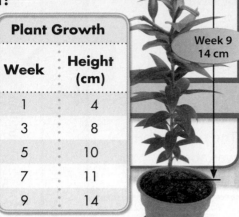

Plant Growth	
Week	**Height (cm)**
1	4
3	8
5	10
7	11
9	14

Week 9
14 cm

Guided Practice*

Do you know HOW?

1. One day last summer Sam kept track of the temperatures in Fahrenheit degrees at 8 A.M., 10 A.M., noon, and 2 P.M. Copy the line graph below. Use the data in the table to complete the line graph.

Temperatures During the Day	
Time	**Temp (°F)**
8 A.M.	63
10 A.M.	70
noon	77
2 P.M.	81

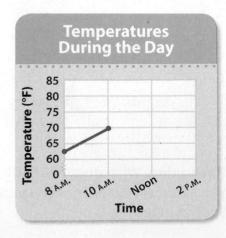

Do you UNDERSTAND?

2. **Writing to Explain** Why is a line graph a good way to display continuous data?

3. In the problem above, if the line connecting the points for two weeks in a row were horizontal, how much taller would the plant have grown between those weeks?

4. For which of the following situations would making a line graph to display the data NOT be appropriate?

   A To show the growth of a palm tree each year for five years

   B To show the number of laps Connie swims in 5-minute intervals

   C To show the number of phone calls received at an office in intervals during a day

   D To show the number of boys and girls who attended the school play on Friday

Animated Glossary, eTools
www.pearsonsuccessnet.com

*For another example, see Set E on page 360.

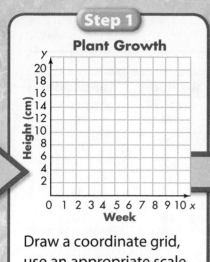

Step 1

Plant Growth

Draw a coordinate grid, use an appropriate scale, and label each axis. Title the graph.

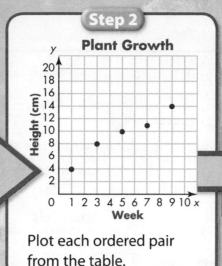

Step 2

Plant Growth

Plot each ordered pair from the table.

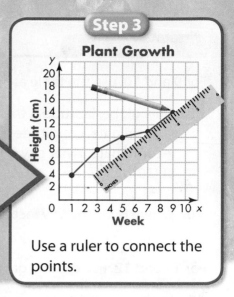

Step 3

Plant Growth

Use a ruler to connect the points.

Independent Practice

In **5** through **7**, use each set of data and the given interval to make each line graph.

5.

Reading Log

Hours	Total Pages Read
1	20
2	60
3	80
4	90
5	120

Interval: 20 pages

6.

Rainfall at Sunshine Elementary

Month	Total Rainfall (in.)
1	3
2	5
3	10
4	14
5	14

Interval: 2 inches

7. Ants live in many different environments all over the world. The table at the right gives the distance an ant crawls for a given number of seconds.

A Crawling Ant

Seconds	5	10	15	20
Total Distance (m)	1	2	4	5

Interval: 1 meter

8. **Science** Record the outside temperature at regular intervals over a 5-hour period. Organize the data and make a line graph to display the data. Then make one observation about any trend you see.

For **9** and **10**, use the table at the right.

9. On a globe, latitude is the *x*-coordinate. Longitude is the *y*-coordinate. What city is located at (30°N, 30°E)?

10. Where is Milan, Italy located?

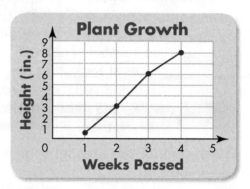

City	Latitude Approx. °N	Longitude Approx. °E
Cairo, Egypt	30	30
London, England	50	0
Bordeaux, France	45	0
Milan, Italy	45	10

For **11** and **12**, use the line graph at the right.

11. Look for a trend. How many inches do you predict the plant will have grown by the end of Week 5?

12. How many more inches did the plant grow from the end of Week 2 to the end of Week 4?

Plant Growth

13. Use the graph at the right. About how much more money was spent on telephone service in 2004 than in 2001?

14. **Think** **About the Process** If a line graph

Critical THINKING shows an upward trend in population growth for the past five years, what do you know about the population size during that time?

F The population decreased.

G The population inceased and then decreased.

H The population stayed the same.

I The population increased.

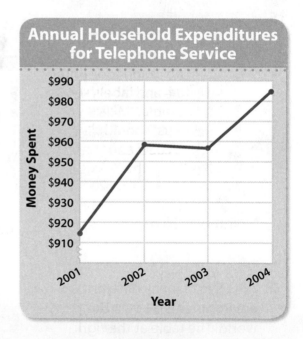

Annual Household Expenditures for Telephone Service

For **15** and **16**, use the table at the right.

15. Make a line graph of the data. Use a scale from 0 to 12 and an interval of 2 for the miles hiked. Write a sentence about the trends represented on the graph.

16. During which day did the hikers hike the greatest distance?

Four-day Hike				
By End of Day	1	2	3	4
Total Miles Hiked	2	6	8	11

Line Graphs

Use tools
Spreadsheet/Data/Grapher

Draw a line graph of the data in the table.

Step 1 ⬈ Go to the Spreadsheet/Data/Grapher eTool. Use the arrow tool to select 6 rows and 2 columns. Set the number of decimal places at zero using the .00 pull-down menu. Type in the data shown in the table to the right.

Data

Elementary (K–8) Students in the United States	
Year	**Millions of Students**
1950	19
1960	27
1970	33
1980	28
1990	30
2000	34

Step 2 ⬈ 📈 Use the arrow tool to select the data. Click on the line graph tool. Enter the title and labels shown in the table. "Millions of Students" should be the Y-Axis Label and "Year" should be the X-Axis Label. Set the interval at 5, the minimum at 0, and the maximum at 40. Click OK.

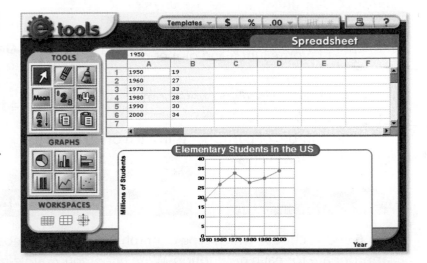

Practice

Use the line graph you created to answer the following questions.

1. Which year showed the only decrease in the number of elementary students?

2. Between which two years did the largest increase take place?

3. Based on the trend in the graph, how many elementary students would you predict in 2010?

4. How many more elementary students were enrolled in the United States in 1960 than in 1950?

MA.5.S.7.2 Differentiate between continuous and discrete data and determine ways to represent those using graphs and diagrams. Also MA.5.S.7.1

Choose an Appropriate Graph

Hands-On grid paper

How do you choose the best type of graph for displaying a set of data?

Charlie made a table of the distance he traveled over the course of a five-day road trip. What type of graph would be most appropriate to display this data? Explain your reasoning and make the graph.

Charlie's Road Trip Log

Day of Trip	Total Distance Traveled (miles)
1	353
2	735
3	760
4	1,200
5	1,468

Guided Practice*

Do you know HOW?

In **1** through **3**, choose which type of graph would be the most appropriate for each description. Write *bar graph*, *double-bar graph*, or *line graph*.

1. Results of a survey of 20 people about their favorite lunch and dinner choices

2. Your height since you were born

3. The number of participants in each of three track events

Do you UNDERSTAND?

4. **Writing to Explain** In the problem above, why isn't a bar graph the better choice for displaying the data? Explain.

5. Write a survey question that would generate data best shown on a bar graph. How can you conduct your survey so that the data would allow for a double-bar graph?

Independent Practice

For **6** and **7**, choose which type of graph would be the most appropriate for each description. Write *bar graph*, *double-bar graph*, or *line graph*.

6. The population of Orlando over the last ten years

7. Number of male and female manatees found in three different rivers

8. Before changing the design of their labels, a company surveyed 30 customers at each of two major locations to find out which design was preferred. The table shows the results of the survey. What would be the most appropriate type of graph for displaying these data? Make the appropriate graph.

Label Design Survey

Store Location	Old Design	New Design
East	12 votes	18 votes
West	16 votes	14 votes

What You Think

Line graphs show data that often change over time.

Bar graphs compare discrete data.

I know that Charlie's data were collected over the course of a five-day road trip. These data were continuous, so a line graph would be the appropriate way to display the data.

What You Show

Make a line graph of Charlie's data.

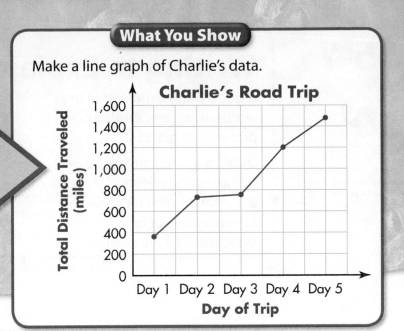

Charlie's Road Trip

Problem Solving

Sonya gathered data about the number of ducks in some of the 2006 rubber duck derbies. Use her table for **9** through **12**.

Rubber Duck Derbies, 2006				
Location	Congaree River, SC	Lake Lanier, GA	St. Louis Riverfront, MO	Meinig Memorial Park, OR
Number of Rubber Ducks	5,000	13,000	15,000	1,000

9. Are the data discrete or continuous?

10. Display the data using the most appropriate type of graph.

11. Write a Problem Write a problem that can be solved accurately by looking at your graph.

12. How many more ducks raced in the St. Louis Riverfront derby than the Lake Lanier derby?

13. Writing to Explain Ben and Eliza made graphs to show the number of soccer fields in four different counties. Who made the more appropriate graph? Explain.

Critical THINKING

Ben's Graph

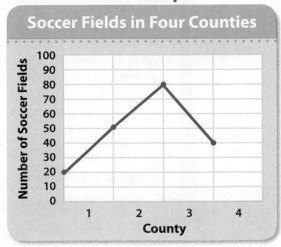

Eliza's Graph

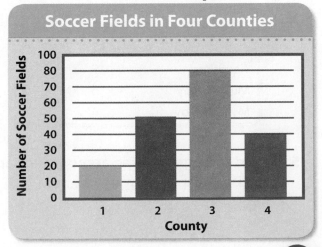

MA.5.S.7.2 Differentiate between continuous and discrete data and determine ways to represent those using graphs and diagrams.

Writing to Explain

Hands-On
grid paper

A good math explanation uses words, numbers, symbols, pictures, or graphs.

Data for a company's sales of mountain bicycles and skateboards are shown in the table. Explain how the sales of bicycles and skateboards have changed.

Year	Number of Bicycle Sales	Number of Skateboard Sales
2005	800	200
2006	900	400
2007	1,000	800
2008	1,000	999
2009	1,100	1,100

Guided Practice*

Do you know HOW?

1. In a survey, students were asked to name their favorite pet. The results are shown in the table below. Explain the results of the survey. Include an appropriate graph with your answer.

Dog	Cat	Bird	Other
12	6	4	2

Do you UNDERSTAND?

2. How can including a graph be helpful when writing to explain some data sets?

3. **Write a Problem** Write a real-world problem that can be solved by making a graph as part of the explanation.

Independent Practice

4. Mr. Lauer surveyed his students to find out what kind of field trip they preferred. Which field trip is most popular? Make a bar graph and use it to explain your answer.

Field Trip	Number of Votes
Zoo	12
Aquarium	9
Musical Play	5
Mystery Play	4

5. Would a line graph be an appropriate graph in Exercise 4? Explain why or why not.

Stuck? Try this....

- What do I know?
- What am I asked to find?
- What diagram can I use to help understand the problem?
- Can I use addition, subtraction, multiplication, or division?
- Is all of my work correct?
- Did I answer the right question?
- Is my answer reasonable?

I can make a line graph for bicycle sales.

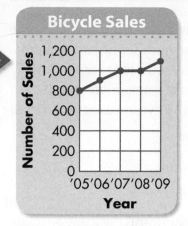

Bicycle Sales

I can make a line graph for skateboard sales.

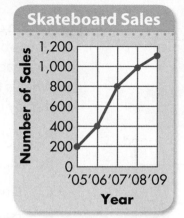

Skateboard Sales

I can write an explanation to answer the question.

The sales for skateboards have been increasing more rapidly than bicycles over the years.

The difference between the number of bicycle sales and the number of skateboard sales is becoming smaller.

6. Ella and Toby competed in a 1,200-meter race. Write two statements that can be supported by the two line graphs at the right.

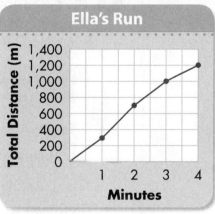

7. Writing to Explain

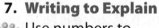

Use numbers to explain how you know that 2 is a factor of all multiples of 10.

8. The data about bicycle sales and skateboard sales at the top of the page could also be shown using a double-bar graph. Copy andcomplete the graph at the right. How is this a better way to show that the difference in sales decreased?

9. A café sells turkey, roast beef, ham, or cheese sandwiches; milk, water, or juice; and yogurt or fruit. How many different meals are possible for a person who wants a sandwich, drink, and dessert?

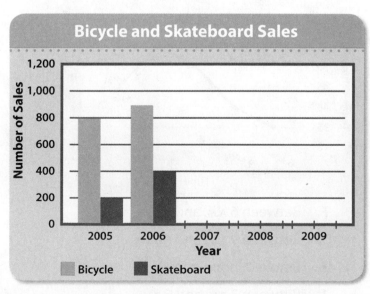

Bicycle and Skateboard Sales

1 Mrs. Chi made a bar graph of the number of books students read over summer break.

Books Read During Summer Break

A bar graph is a good way to display what kind of data? (15-1)

A. Equal data

B. Continuous data

C. Discrete data

D. Random data

2 Between which times did the temperature increase 10°F? (15-4)

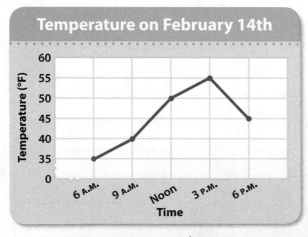

Temperature on February 14th

F. Between 6 A.M. and 9 A.M.

G. Between 9 A.M. and noon

H. Between noon and 3 P.M.

I. Between 3 P.M. and 6 P.M.

3 Peyton collected data from two different cities about the number of people who own each of four different car models. What is the most appropriate graph to display the data Peyton collected? (15-6)

A. Bar graph

B. Picture graph

C. Line graph

D. Double-bar graph

4 The data show the Fahrenheit temperature in Old Town measured every hour after 8:00 A.M.

Hours after 8:00 A.M.	1	2	3	4	5	6
Temperature (°F)	35	39	47	54	59	60

If you use the table to complete the line graph below, which of these is NOT an appropriate step? (15-5)

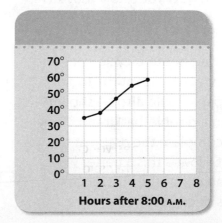

Hours after 8:00 A.M.

F. Plot a point for Hour 6 at 60° and connect it to the point for Hour 5.

G. Insert a title.

H. Connect the origin at Hour 0 and 0° to the point for Hour 1.

I. Label the vertical axis "Temperature in Fahrenheit."

5 The graphs below show the number of times an answer choice was used on two different tests.

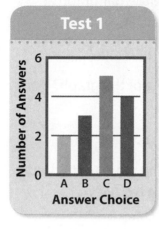

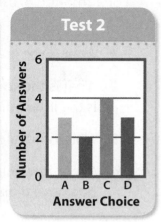

Mr. Rodriguez wants to make a double-bar graph to compare the data more efficiently. Which of the following describes one of the steps he should take to do this? (15-3)

A. Add to find the number of times A was used on both tests and graph that sum with one bar.

B. Double the scale on the vertical axis so the new graph shows 0 through 12.

C. Choose one color for each test and make a key to indicate what each color represents.

D. Select two answer choices so the new graph only shows the data for those two choices.

6 Cora wants to make a line graph to show how the weight of her cat has changed over the past five years. Why is a line graph the most appropriate to use? (15-6)

F. The weight doesn't change.

G. There are two sets of data.

H. There are more than three years of recorded data.

I. The data changes over time.

7 The graph shows the number of students who plan to compete in different events at the next track meet.

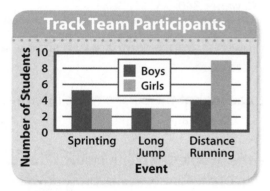

How many more boys than girls plan to participate in sprinting events? (15-2)

8 The graph below shows a company's profits between 2004 and 2010.

THINK
SOLVE
EXPLAIN

How can this graph be used to explain why 5 million dollars is a good prediction for profits in 2012? (15-7)

Set A, pages 338–339

Which animal has about 34 teeth?

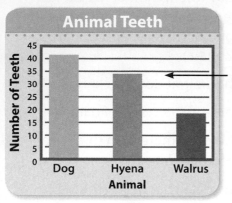

The top of the bar for hyenas is below the line for 35.

Hyenas have about 34 teeth.

Remember that a bar graph can be a good way to compare discrete data.

For **1** through **4**, use the bar graph at the left.

1. What is the graph about?

2. What is the scale of the graph? What is the interval?

3. Which animal has 18 teeth?

4. About how many more teeth does a dog have than a hyena?

Set B, pages 340–341

Double-bar graphs compare two similar sets of discrete data.

You can look at the bars to make interpretations about the data.

Use the double-bar graph below. What does the length of the longest bar represent? How much more did Brand A cost in 2007 than in 2000?

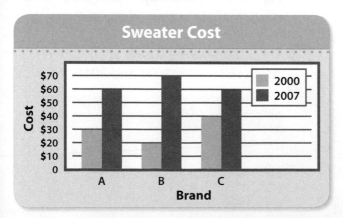

The longest bar shows that Brand B cost $70 in 2007.

In 2007, Brand A cost $30 more than it did in 2000.

Remember that a double-bar graph compares two similar sets of data, represented as bars, on one graph.

For **1** and **2**, use the double-bar graph at the left.

1. Which brand increased the most in price from 2000 to 2007?

2. What does the length of the shortest bar represent?

For **3**, use the graph below.

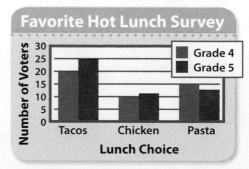

3. Which lunch choice got the most votes overall? The least votes overall?

Set C, pages 342–344

Use the data below to make a double-bar graph.

Favorite Fourth of July Activity		
Activity	Children	Adults
Watching the Parade	30	30
Watching Fireworks	50	20
Barbeque	20	50

Step 1 Write a title and label the horizontal and vertical axes.

Step 2 On the vertical axis, mark and label equal intervals beginning with zero. Draw a line across the graph at each interval.

Step 3 On the horizontal axis, write the categories at equal intervals.

Step 4 Choose colors and make a key to show what each color represents.

Step 5 Draw a bar for each data value and color each bar with the appropriate color.

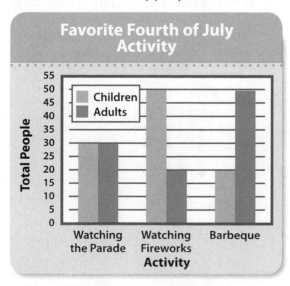

Remember that a double-bar graph uses two different-colored or shaded bars to show two similar sets of data.

Use the data table below.

Number of Minutes on Phone	Students	Adults
0–15 minutes	10	30
16–30 minutes	25	40
31–45 minutes	20	10
46–60 minutes	40	15

1. Copy and complete the double-bar graph.

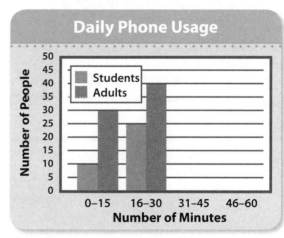

2. Make a double-bar graph using the data in the table below.

Number of Family Members	Grade 4	Grade 5
3	10	5
4	12	7
5	5	15

Set D, pages 346–347

Look at the line graph below.

How much money was made in charity donations in the year 2000?

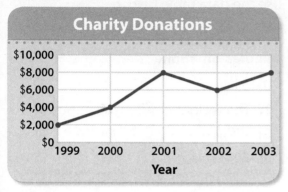

In 2000, the donations were $4,000.

When did donations decrease?

When the value along the vertical axis decreases, the graph will appear to go downhill.

Donations decreased from 2001 to 2002.

Remember that line graphs can display continuous data.

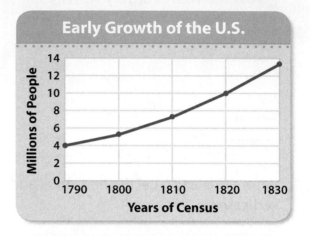

1. In what year was the population about 10 million?

2. What is the change in population from 1790 to 1820?

3. What is the overall trend?

Set E, pages 348–350

Make a line graph for the data.

Day	Books Sold
1	6
2	8
3	9
4	10
5	12

To make a line graph:

• Use grid paper to draw a coordinate grid.

• Label the axes.

• Number each axis with a consistent scale.

• Plot the ordered pairs and connect the points.

Remember that line graphs can show trends in data that change over time.

1. Make a line graph for the data.

Week	CDs Sold
1	10
2	5
3	20
4	15

2. Describe the trend.

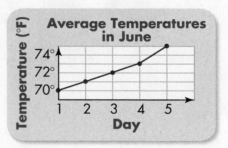

Set F, pages 352–353

Look at the table and decide which type of graph is the most appropriate for displaying the data.

Family Member	CDs Owned
Dad	18
Mom	15
Bobby	10
Alexandria	7

A bar graph is appropriate for these data because they compare **discrete data** that can be counted.

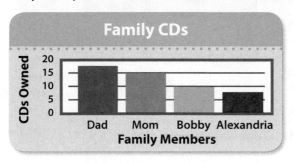

Remember that line graphs often show data that are continuous. **Continuous data** has all values possible.

1. Why isn't a line graph the best graph for the data at the left?

In **2** through **6**, choose the appropriate graph for the data described.

2. The weight of Alfonzo's puppy at the end of every 6 months

3. A survey asking students about their favorite Olympic event

4. Changes in the cost of milk over a two-week period

5. The number of people who watched five different television shows during Seasons 1 and 2

6. The number of cups of each type of juice in a fruit punch recipe

Set G, pages 354–355

Which animal is the most popular? Explain.

Favorite Animal	
Penguin	7
Elephant	6
Lion	3
Monkey	4

Make a graph to help explain your answer.

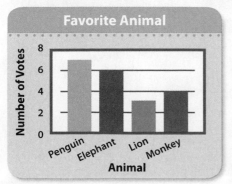

The tallest bar corresponds with the most popular animal.

The penguin is the most popular because it received the most votes.

Remember that a good math explanation uses words, numbers, symbols, pictures, or graphs.

Monthly Snowfall				
Month	Dec.	Jan.	Feb.	Mar.
Inches	6	12	18	4

1. Make a line graph of the data.

2. Which month has a snowfall 3 times as great as December? Use the graph to help explain your answer.

Topic 16

Integers

1 The Mariana Trench is the deepest ocean trench in the world. How can the depth of this trench be expressed as an integer? You will find out in Lesson 16-1.

2 Death Valley is located in the Mojave Desert and the Great Basin. This valley has the lowest elevation in the United States. What is the elevation of Death Valley? You will find out in Lesson 16-3.

3

The Great Blizzard of 1899 was the only time on record that Florida recorded subzero temperatures. How cold did it get in Tallahassee during the blizzard? You will find out in Lesson 16-4.

Review What You Know!

Vocabulary

Choose the best term from the box.

- variable
- decimal
- fraction
- percent

1. A number that shows a comparison to 100 is called a __?__.

2. A number that contains a point to separate the ones place from the tenths place is a __?__.

3. A number used to name a part of a whole is a __?__.

Number Lines

Write the fraction for each point.

4. C   **5.** A   **6.** B   **7.** D

Adding and Subtracting Decimals

Add or subtract.

8. $0.19 + 1.2$ **9.** $4.5 - 0.66$

10. $0.551 + 0.136$ **11.** $8.75 - 8.3$

Adding and Subtracting Fractions

Add or subtract. Write your answer in simplest form.

12. $\frac{1}{2} + \frac{2}{12}$ **13.** $\frac{7}{8} - \frac{1}{3}$

14. $2\frac{3}{5} + 4\frac{7}{10}$ **15.** $8\frac{7}{50} - 4\frac{8}{25}$

16. Writing to Explain To add two fractions with unlike denominators, do you need to find the LCM of the denominators? Explain.

Topic Essential Questions

- What numbers on the number line are opposites of the whole numbers?

- How can integers be compared and ordered?

MA.5.A.6.3 Describe real-world situations using positive and negative numbers.

Understanding Integers

What are integers and what situations can integers represent?

The highest point in Louisiana is Driskill Mountain at five hundred thirty-five feet above sea level. The lowest point is New Orleans at eight feet below sea level.

How can you write those highest and lowest points with integers?

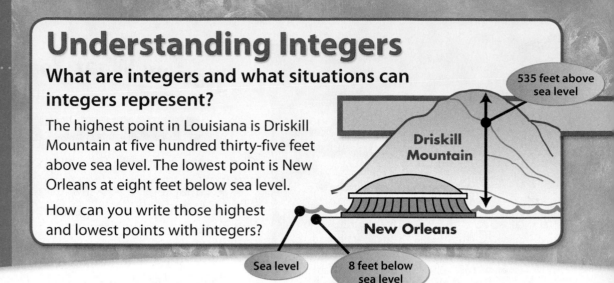

535 feet above sea level

Driskill Mountain

New Orleans

Sea level

8 feet below sea level

Guided Practice*

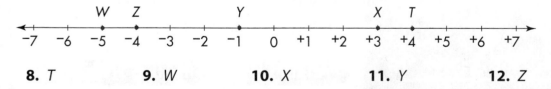

Do you know HOW?

In **1** through **4**, write an integer for each word description.

1. Ten degrees below zero

2. Seventy degrees above zero

3. Two hundred thirty feet above sea level

4. Fifty-two feet below sea level

Do you UNDERSTAND?

5. In the example above, what is the opposite elevation of Driskill Mountain, written as an integer?

6. How far away from sea level is 512 feet below sea level?

7. How would you represent sea level as an integer?

Independent Practice

In **8** through **12**, use the number line to identify the integer at each point.

```
      W   Z           Y              X   T
←———•———•———•———•———•———•———•———•———•———•———•———•———•———•———→
  -7  -6  -5  -4  -3  -2  -1   0  +1  +2  +3  +4  +5  +6  +7
```

8. *T*   9. *W*   10. *X*   11. *Y*   12. *Z*

In **13** through **20**, write an integer for each word description.

13. A withdrawal of $20

14. A deposit of one hundred dollars

15. A gain of three inches

16. A loss of six yards

17. A loss of 7 pounds

18. A temperature drop of 2 degrees

19. 6 steps forward

20. 10 seconds before blastoff

Animated Glossary
www.pearsonsuccessnet.com

For another example, see Set A on page 378.

Distance above sea level is greater than zero. It is represented by a positive integer. $^+535$

Distance below sea level is less than zero. It is represented by the negative integer. $^-8$

Integers name magnitude (distance) and direction from 0.

```
        0
  ←──┼─┼──────────────────┼──→
    ⁻8                   ⁺535
```

The magnitude of $^-8$ is 8. The direction is negative.

The magnitude of $^+535$ is 535. The direction is positive.

Integers are the whole numbers and their opposites; 0 is its own opposite.

Numbers that are opposites of each other have the same magnitude (distance from 0).

$^-5$ and $^+5$ are the same distance from 0.

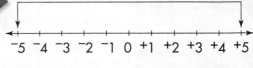

```
  ←┼──┼──┼──┼──┼──┼──┼──┼──┼──┼──┼→
   ⁻5  ⁻4  ⁻3  ⁻2  ⁻1  0  +1  +2  +3  +4  +5
```

Negative integers are less than zero.

Positive integers are greater than zero.

$^-5$ is read "negative five."

$^+5$ is read "positive five."

$^-2$ is the opposite of $^+2$.
$^+4$ is the opposite of $^-4$.

Problem Solving

21. A football team started at the 20-yard line. In the first two plays, the team lost 4 yards and gained 4 yards. Where did they end up?

22. Adam has 7.5 feet of aluminum wire and 6.29 feet of copper wire. How many more feet of aluminum wire than copper wire does Adam have?

23. A movie company announced that one of its releases lost two million, eight hundred fifty-seven thousand, nine hundred dollars. Write that number as an integer.

24. At midnight, the temperature was 2 degrees. It went down 5 degrees, then it went up 3 degrees, and then dropped 2 degrees. What was the final temperature?

25. Number Sense Julie needs to select an integer that is two less than $^-11$. What number should she choose? How did you find the number?

Critical THINKING

26. The Mariana Trench is located in the floor of the western North Pacific Ocean. It is 35,798 feet below sea level. Express this depth as an integer.

27. Think About the Process While setting up for a dinner party, Flo folds each napkin into a triangle. Each triangle has a base of 8 inches and a height of 5 inches. Which expression can you use to find the area of each triangular shape in square inches?

A 8×5

B $2 \times (8 + 5)$

C $(8 \times 5) \div 2$

D $(8 + 5) \div 2$

28. Writing to Explain Describe how to find the surface area of the rectangular prism shown below. Then find the surface area.

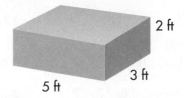

29. Write integers to represent earning $26 on Saturday and spending $15 that evening.

MA.5.A.6.4 Compare, order, and graph integers, including integers shown on a number line.

Graphing Integers on a Number Line

Hands-On
centimeter ruler

How can you graph integers on a number line?

You can represent temperatures as integers. At the right is a table of the lowest recorded temperatures in several major U.S. cities during the last 50 years. Graph these integers on a number line.

Record Lowest Temperatures

City	Temperature (°F)
Boston, MA	⁻12
Chicago, IL	⁻27
Dallas, TX	⁻1
Juneau, AK	⁻22
Los Angeles, CA	⁺24
Tallahassee, FL	⁺6

Guided Practice*

Do you know HOW?

In **1** through **6**, graph each set of integers on a number line.

1. ⁺1, ⁺4, ⁺7, ⁺10
2. ⁻8, ⁻4, 0, ⁺4

3. ⁺50, ⁻20, ⁻50, ⁺60
4. ⁺14, ⁺2, ⁻8, ⁺1

5. ⁺7, ⁻13, ⁺27, ⁻2
6. ⁻17, ⁺55, ⁺31, ⁺10

Do you UNDERSTAND?

7. In the example above, describe where you would plot ⁺17°F, the lowest recorded temperature for Phoenix, AZ.

8. **Writing to Explain** How do you choose an interval for a number line?

Independent Practice

Leveled Practice In **9** through **20**, copy both number lines below. Then graph each integer.

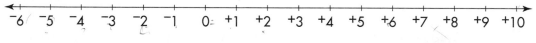

9. ⁺1   10. ⁺3   11. ⁻4   12. ⁺10   13. ⁻5   14. ⁺7

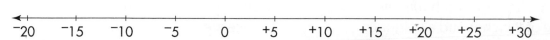

15. ⁻15   16. ⁺24   17. ⁺6   18. ⁻12   19. ⁻1   20. ⁺25

In **21** through **26**, graph each set of integers on a number line.

21. ⁻1, ⁻4, 0, ⁺6, ⁺2, ⁻7   22. ⁺5, ⁻8, ⁻9, ⁻13, ⁻4, ⁺2   23. ⁻19, ⁺20, ⁺5, ⁺15, ⁺16, ⁻10

24. ⁻2, ⁻5, ⁺1, ⁺6, ⁺4, ⁺2   25. ⁺20, ⁺59, ⁻45, ⁻10, ⁺50   26. ⁻1, ⁻18, ⁻12, ⁺3, ⁻9, ⁻17

DIGITAL
eTools
www.pearsonsuccessnet.com

*For another example, see Set B on page 378.

Step 1	Step 2	Step 3	Step 4
Choose an appropriate interval to represent the data.	Draw the number line, labeling positive integers to the right of zero and negative integers to the left of zero.	Graph a point for each integer of the data set on the number line.	Insert labels and a title if appropriate.

Since the temperatures range from ⁻27°F to ⁺24°F, you can use an interval of 5°F.

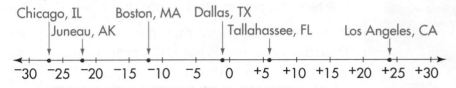

Chicago, IL   Boston, MA   Dallas, TX
  Juneau, AK   Tallahassee, FL   Los Angeles, CA

⁻30 ⁻25 ⁻20 ⁻15 ⁻10 ⁻5   0   ⁺5 ⁺10 ⁺15 ⁺20 ⁺25 ⁺30

Record Lowest Temperatures (°F)

Problem Solving

27. Number Sense Kathy claims that there are at least 5 integers that are between ⁻20 and ⁻15. Jeffrey thinks that there are fewer than 5 integers. Who is correct?

28. Aaron remembers the pass code to his computer because the code is the common factors of 40 and 60, in increasing order. What is Aaron's pass code?

For **29** and **30**, use the table at the right. The table shows the highest temperatures over the last 50 years in several U.S. cities.

29. Show the temperatures on a number line. Include the title. Since the lowest temperature is 96°F, begin the number line at ⁺95.

30. How would your number line change if you had to include ⁺134°F, the highest temperature ever recorded for the United States?

Data

Highest Temperatures Recorded in United States

City	Temperature (°F)
Baltimore, MD (A)	⁺105
Birmingham, AL (B)	⁺106
Montpelier, VT (C)	⁺96
Seattle, WA (D)	⁺100
Tampa, FL (E)	⁺99

31. Which of the following is NOT always an integer?

A The number of wheels on a car

C The number of planets in the solar system

B The home team's score in a baseball game

D The price of one gallon of milk

32. Geometry What is the volume of a rectangular prism, in cubic feet, with a base area of 12 square feet and a height of 8 feet?

33. What is the surface area of the rectangular prism at the right?

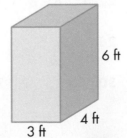

6 ft

3 ft   4 ft

Lesson
16-3

MA.5.A.6.4 Compare, order, and graph integers, including integers shown on a number line.

Comparing and Ordering Integers

How do you compare and order integers?

Alan's family spent a week at a resort in Utah. The resort newspaper listed the low temperature for each night that week.

Which night had a lower temperature, Thursday or Friday? What is the order from least to greatest of the low temperatures?

This week's temperatures (°F)		
Day	**Low**	**High**
Monday	6°	30°
Tuesday	0°	28°
Wednesday	4°	21°
Thursday	⁻7°	17°
Friday	⁻3°	19°

Data

Guided Practice*

Do you know HOW?

In **1** through **4**, compare. Use >, <, or = for ◯.

1. ⁺4 ◯ ⁺3   **2.** ⁻2 ◯ ⁺2

3. ⁻1 ◯ ⁻4   **4.** ⁻10 ◯ ⁻11

In **5** and **6**, order from *least* to *greatest*.

5. ⁺8, ⁻5, ⁻2   **6.** ⁻10, ⁺2, ⁻3

Do you UNDERSTAND?

7. Compare ⁻7 and ⁻3. Use the > sign.

8. In the example above, if the temperature on Wednesday night was ⁻9°F, which night would have been colder, Wednesday or Thursday?

9. In the example above, order the week's high temperatures from *least* to *greatest*.

Independent Practice

In **10** through **17**, compare. Use >, <, or = for ◯.

10. ⁺1 ◯ ⁺3   **11.** ⁻4 ◯ ⁺9   **12.** ⁺5 ◯ ⁻2   **13.** ⁻11 ◯ ⁻10

14. ⁻8 ◯ ⁻15   **15.** ⁺10 ◯ ⁺11   **16.** ⁻7 ◯ ⁻6   **17.** ⁻1 ◯ 0

In **18** through **33**, order from *least* to *greatest*.

18. ⁺1, ⁻7, ⁻5   **19.** 0, ⁻3, ⁺6   **20.** ⁻5, ⁺10, ⁻1   **21.** ⁻4, ⁺11, ⁻6

22. 0, ⁺8, ⁻8   **23.** ⁺3, ⁺1, ⁺5   **24.** ⁻2, ⁻8, ⁻1   **25.** ⁻23, ⁻50, ⁻42

26. ⁺15, ⁻5, ⁺6, ⁻2   **27.** ⁻20, ⁻1, ⁻9, ⁻13   **28.** 0, ⁻19, ⁺5, ⁻4   **29.** ⁻5, ⁻20, ⁻10, ⁻15

30. ⁺6, ⁻3, ⁻2, ⁺7   **31.** ⁻18, ⁻3, ⁺3, ⁻8   **32.** ⁻5, 0, ⁺1, ⁻20   **33.** ⁻6, ⁻7, ⁻8, ⁻9

*For another example, see Set C on page 379.

Compare the integers $^-7$ and $^-3$.

Locate $^-7$ and $^-3$ on a number line. Integers, just like whole numbers, fractions, and decimals, increase in value as you move from left to right.

Thursday night   Friday night

$^-8$ $^-7$ $^-6$ $^-5$ $^-4$ $^-3$ $^-2$ $^-1$ 0 $+1$ $+2$

The integer $^-7$ is farther to the left on a number line than $^-3$. So, $^-7$ is less.

$^-7 < {^-3}$

Thursday night was colder than Friday night.

Order the integers 6, 0, 4, $^-7$, and $^-3$.

Locate the numbers on a number line.

$^-7$ $^-6$ $^-5$ $^-4$ $^-3$ $^-2$ $^-1$ 0 $+1$ $+2$ $+3$ $+4$ $+5$ $+6$

From least to greatest, the week's low temperatures are $^-7$, $^-3$, 0, 4, and 6.

Tip *Positive numbers are often written without the $^+$ sign.*

Problem Solving

34. **Science** The table shows the lowest elevations, relative to sea level, for four states. Order the elevations from *greatest* to *least*.

Location	Lowest Elevation (ft)
Colorado River, AZ	$+70$
New Orleans, LA	$^-8$
Death Valley, CA	$^-282$
Lake Champlain, VT	$+95$

Data

35. **Algebra** Write an integer for x to make each statement true.

   a $x > {^-3}$

   b $x < {^+1}$

   c $^-13 < x$

36. **Reasoning** A number, x, is four units to the left of $^-5$ on the number line. What is the value of x? Is x greater than or less than $^-5$?

Critical Thinking

37. **Writing to Explain** Is the explanation below correct? If not, tell why not and write a correct response.

   $^-13$ is less than $^-12$ because it is farther to the left on the number line.

In **39** through **41**, use the map at the right.

39. Of the states shown, which had the lowest record temperature?

40. Which state had the warmest record low temperature?

41. List the record low temperatures in order from least to greatest.

38. **Number Sense** Which integer is neither positive nor negative?

Lowest/Highest Temperatures (°F)

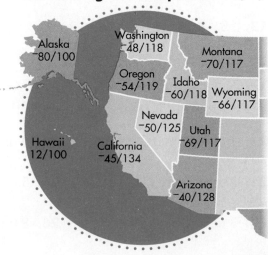

Alaska $^-80/100$

Washington $^-48/118$

Montana $^-70/117$

Oregon $^-54/119$

Idaho $^-60/118$

Wyoming $^-66/117$

Nevada $^-50/125$

Utah $^-69/117$

Hawaii 12/100

California $^-45/134$

Arizona $^-40/128$

MA.5.A.6.3 Describe real-world situations using positive and negative numbers.

Distance on a Number Line

How do you find a distance on a number line?

The temperature at midnight was ⁻2°F. By noon, the temperature rose to 4°F. What was the amount of the increase in temperature?

You can think of the two temperatures as integers on a number line.

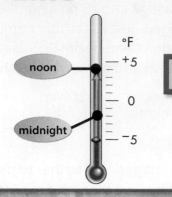

°F
+5
0
⁻5

noon

midnight

Guided Practice*

Do you know HOW?

In **1** through **3**, use the number line to find the distance between each pair of integers.

⁻6 ⁻5 ⁻4 ⁻3 ⁻2 ⁻1 0 ⁺1 ⁺2 ⁺3 ⁺4 567

1. ⁻6, ⁻2   **2.** ⁺1, ⁺4   **3.** ⁻3, ⁺3

In **4** through **6**, find the distance between each pair of integers on a number line.

4. ⁻4, ⁺3   **5.** ⁻5, ⁻1   **6.** ⁺4, ⁺7

Do you UNDERSTAND?

7. Find the distance between ⁻3 and ⁺7 without drawing a number line. What is this distance?

8. Writing to Explain How is the thermometer in the picture above similar to a number line? How is it different? Explain.

Independent Practice

In **9** through **20**, find the distance between each pair of integers on a number line.

9. ⁻6, ⁻4   **10.** ⁺1, ⁺5   **11.** ⁻2, ⁺7   **12.** ⁻7, ⁺2

13. ⁺3, ⁺4   **14.** ⁻2, 0   **15.** 0, ⁺6   **16.** ⁻5, ⁺5

17. ⁻8, ⁻5   **18.** ⁻7, ⁺5   **19.** ⁻1, ⁺1   **20.** ⁺3, ⁻1

In **21** through **29**, name two integers that match each description.

21. 1 unit from 0   **22.** 4 units from ⁺1   **23.** 6 units from ⁺4

24. 2 units from ⁻2   **25.** 5 units from ⁺10   **26.** 7 units from ⁻6

27. 3 units from ⁻9   **28.** 8 units from ⁻5   **29.** 10 units from ⁺3

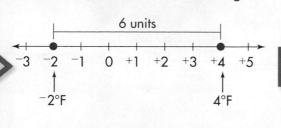

One Way

Count the units between the integers.

6 units

-3 -2 -1 0 $+1$ $+2$ $+3$ $+4$ $+5$

$-2°F$ $4°F$

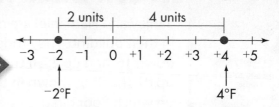

Another Way

Count the units between each integer and 0.

2 units | 4 units

-3 -2 -1 0 $+1$ $+2$ $+3$ $+4$ $+5$

$-2°F$ $4°F$

Add the distances: 2 units + 4 units = 6 units

The amount of the increase was 6°F.

Problem Solving

30. Elena, Tran, and Lee live along the same straight road. Lee lives between Elena and Tran. Tran lives 6 miles from Elena and 2 miles from Lee. What is the distance between Elena's house and Lee's house?

31. Toby planted a seed 2 inches below the surface of the soil. Weeks later, the top of the sprout was 7 inches above the surface of the soil. How many inches away from the seed did the top of the sprout grow?

For **32** through **34**, use the table shown at the right.

32. **Social Studies** The Great Blizzard of 1899 was an unusually severe cold wave that caused many cities to experience temperatures that still stand as the record lows. The table shows a few of these cities and their lowest temperatures. Graph these data on a number line. Include a title.

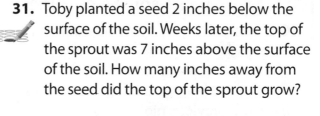

Blizzard Temperatures	
City	**Temperature (°F)**
Pittsburgh, PA	-20
Cleveland, OH	-16
Tallahassee, FL	-2
Charlotte, NC	-5
Erie, PA	-12

33. How many degrees warmer is the record low temperature for Tallahassee, FL, than the low for Erie, PA?

34. Which of these cities experienced the lowest temperature?

35. **Number Sense** Alexis says that 10 and $+10$ are the same. Is she correct? Explain.

36. What integer on a number line is the same distance from 0 as $+6$?

37. Barry buys 12 lemons, but only uses the juice from $8\frac{1}{2}$ lemons.

Which equation can be used to find how many lemons Barry has left?

A $8\frac{1}{2} + 12 = y$ **B** $12 - 8\frac{1}{2} = y$ **C** $(12 - 8) + \frac{1}{2} = y$ **D** $(12 + 8) \div 2 = y$

MA.5.A.6.5 Solve non-routine problems using various strategies including "solving a simpler problem" and "guess, check, and revise."

Problem Solving
Work Backward

Sanjay and Nathaniel are riding the elevator in their building. They rode up 10 floors, down 16, and up 25. If the elevator ended up on the floor shown in the picture, on which floor did they start?

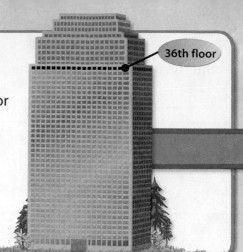

36th floor

Another Example ## When do you work backward to solve a problem?

One summer night, the temperature dropped 17°F between 8 P.M. and 6 A.M. By 10 A.M., the temperature had increased 6°F. The temperature increased another 12°F from 10 A.M. to noon, making the temperature 92°F. What was the temperature at 8 P.M. the previous night?

Read and Understand

What do I know?

The temperature changed after 8 P.M., and the temperature at noon the next day was 92°F.

What am I being asked to find?

The temperature at 8 P.M. the previous night

Plan and Solve

Think Work backward when there is an end result after a series of steps, and you are asked to find the information in the first step.

8 P.M.	6 A.M.	10 A.M.	Noon
°F →	°F →	°F →	92°F
− 17°	+ 6°	+ 12°	

Work backward from the temperature at noon.

91°F ⟵ 74°F ⟵ 80°F ⟵ 92°F
+ 17°   − 6°   − 12°

The temperature was 91°F the previous night.

Explain It

1. Why can you work backward to solve the problem?

2. What can you do to check your answer?

What do I know? They went up 10, down 16, up 25, and ended on the 36th floor.

What am I being asked to find? On which floor did they start riding the elevator?

If you know the ending position and each change made, then you can use the inverse of each change to work backward.

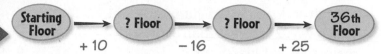

Work backward from the 36th floor.

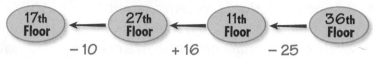

They started on the 17th floor.

Guided Practice*

Do you know HOW?

Solve. Check your answer.

1. Gustavo chose a number, added 3 to it, divided the sum by 2, and subtracted 1. The result was 4. What was Gustavo's number?

Do you UNDERSTAND?

2. In the elevator problem, what operation undoes adding 25?

3. **Write a Problem** Write a word problem that can be solved by working backward.

Independent Practice

Solve. Check your answers.

4. Jessie's mom had a bowl of apples. Liz took three to a picnic, Jessie packed one in her lunch, and Jessie's dad ate one. There were only three left. How many apples were in the bowl to start with?

5. Amy spent $9 at the movies, earned $18 for babysitting, and bought a book for $7. She had $13 left. How much money did she have at the start?

6. Arnie rode 14 miles on his bike. He started from his house and rode to Nick's house. They rode 4.6 miles to the park, 2.4 miles to the store, and 3 miles back to Arnie's house. What is the distance from Arnie's house to Nick's house?

Stuck? Try this....

- What do I know?
- What am I asked to find?
- What diagram can I use to help understand the problem?
- Can I use addition, subtraction, multiplication, or division?
- Is all my work correct?
- Did I answer the right question?
- Is my answer reasonable?

*For another example, see Set E on page 379.

7. Scott, Adrian, and Juan are jumping at the skate park. Scott jumped twice as high as Juan. Adrian jumped 4 feet, which was 2 feet less than Scott. How many feet did Juan jump?

8. Algebra Solve each equation to find the missing number.

a $7 + \blacksquare = 12$ **b** $3 - \blacksquare = 1$

c $6 \times \blacksquare = 36$ **d** $\frac{x}{2} = 4$

9. A famous unsolved problem referred to as *Goldbach's conjecture* states that every even number greater than 2 can be written as the sum of two prime numbers. For example, $4 = 2 + 2$ and $8 = 3 + 5$. Write 32 as the sum of two prime numbers.

10. Allie is saving for new computer equipment that costs $110. She started saving in week one. She saved $26 in week two, spent $14 in week three, and saved $47 in week four. She now has $91. How much did she save during week one?

11. It takes Lisa 30 minutes to ride her bicycle from her house to the ballet studio. One afternoon, she rode her bicycle to her ballet lesson, which lasted 90 minutes. She talked to friends after practice for 10 minutes before riding home. If Lisa arrived back at her house at 6:00 P.M., what time did she leave?

12. Strategy Focus Mike has a rain gauge in his backyard. He empties it every night before he goes to bed. There was rain in the gauge when Mike took his first measurement before breakfast. At 10 A.M., Mike measured an increase of 0.3 inch. At lunch, he measured an increase of 0.6 inch. Before dinner, Mike noted an increase of 0.1 inch, and before he emptied it that night there was an increase of 0.4 inch. There was a total of 2.7 inches of rain in the gauge. How much did it rain during the previous night before breakfast?

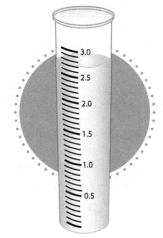

 Think About the Process

13. Jordan is thinking of a number. If you triple the number, add 9, and divide by 10, you end up with 3. What order of operations would you do to work backward to find the number?

    A Addition, multiplication, subtraction

    B Multiplication, subtraction, division

    C Division, addition, multiplication

    D Multiplication, addition, division

14. Ursula is filling treat bags each with 4 granola bars. She made 36 granola bars and plans on giving them all away. If *b* equals the number of treat bags, which equation can be used to determine how many treat bags Ursula needs?

    F $4 + b = 36$ **H** $36 - b = 4$

    G $36 \times 4 = b$ **I** $4 \times b = 36$

Mixed Problem Solving

This map of the United States shows the six different time zones.

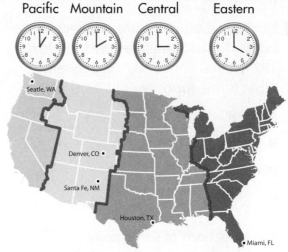

Pacific   Mountain   Central   Eastern

Alaska

Anchorage, AK

Hawaii

Honolulu, HI

1. In which time zone are you located?

3. What time does your school start in the morning? What time is it in each of the other time zones? Draw clock hands to show each time.

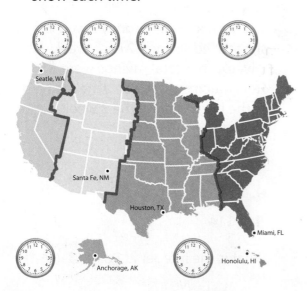

2. The President gave a speech in Denver, CO, at 7:30 P.M. It was broadcast live in each of the other time zones. The speech lasted 2 hours 15 minutes. Determine when the President's speech began and ended in each of the following cities:

  a Seattle, WA: Start _____
                           End _____

  b Santa Fe, NM: Start _____
                           End _____

  c Houston, TX: Start _____
                           End _____

  d Miami, FL: Start _____
                           End _____

  e Honolulu, HI: Start _____
                           End _____

  f Anchorage, AK: Start _____
                           End _____

4. Your favorite television program is scheduled for 7:00 P.M. Eastern Time. What time does that program start in each of the following time zones?

  a Pacific   **c** Alaska

  b Hawaii   **d** Mountain

5. Strategy Focus Solve using the strategy *Write an Equation*. Theo earns $7 an hour washing cars. How many hours will he need to work to earn $847?

Let h = the number of hours of work.

1 The lowest temperature ever recorded in the United States was in Alaska in 1971. It was about ⁻80° Fahrenheit. What is the opposite of ⁻80? (16-1)

   A. ⁻80

   B. ⁻79

   C. ⁺80

   D. ⁺81

2 The elevations of some points of interest are given in the table. These elevations are above, at, or below sea level.

Location	Elevation (feet)
Potomac River	1
New Orleans	⁻8
Delaware River	0
Lake Champlain	95

Which of the following lists the elevations from *least* to *greatest*? (16-3)

   F. ⁻8, 0, ⁺1, ⁺95

   G. 0, ⁺1, ⁻8, ⁺95

   H. ⁻8, ⁺1, 0, ⁺95

   I. ⁺95, ⁻8, ⁺1, 0

3 What is the distance between ⁻3 and ⁺4 on a number line? (16-4)

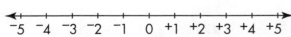

   A. 1 unit

   B. 3 units

   C. 4 units

   D. 7 units

4 Which of the following can be used to represent a deposit of $132? (16-1)

   F. ⁺132

   G. ⁺1

   H. 0

   I. ⁻132

5 Look at the number line. Which comparison is true? (16-3)

⁻15 ⁻10 ⁻5   0   ⁺5 ⁺10 ⁺15

   A. ⁻12 < ⁻6

   B. ⁻12 > ⁻6

   C. ⁻8 > ⁻4

   D. ⁺3 < ⁻3

6 Amelia had some money saved before she started saving $2 each week. After 3 weeks, her total savings were $16. How much money had Amelia saved at the beginning of the 3 weeks? (16-5)

   F. $2

   G. $8

   H. $10

   I. $14

7 What is the integer at Point *L*? (16-1)

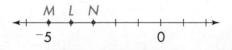

   A. ⁻6

   B. ⁻5

   C. ⁻4

   D. ⁻3

8 Which number line shows the graph of Point *M* at ⁻5? (16-2)

F.

M

⁻10 ⁻8 ⁻6 ⁻4 ⁻2 0 ⁺2 ⁺4 ⁺6 ⁺8 ⁺10

G.

M

⁻10 ⁻8 ⁻6 ⁻4 ⁻2 0 ⁺2 ⁺4 ⁺6 ⁺8 ⁺10

H.

M

⁻10 ⁻8 ⁻6 ⁻4 ⁻2 0 ⁺2 ⁺4 ⁺6 ⁺8 ⁺10

I.

M

⁻10 ⁻8 ⁻6 ⁻4 ⁻2 0 ⁺2 ⁺4 ⁺6 ⁺8 ⁺10

9 What is the distance between Point *T* and Point *S*? (16-4)

T   S

⁻8 ⁻7 ⁻6 ⁻5 ⁻4 ⁻3 ⁻2 ⁻1 0 ⁺1 ⁺2 ⁺3

A. 8 units

B. 7 units

C. 5 units

D. 1 unit

10 Which description could be used to represent the integer ⁻14? (16-1)

F. A 14-yard loss in a football game

G. A bank deposit of $14

H. A gain of 14 yards

I. A temperature 14 degrees above 0

11 Which shows the integers in order from *greatest* to *least*? (16-3)

A. ⁻15, ⁺14, ⁻16, ⁺15

B. ⁺15, ⁺14, ⁻15, ⁻16

C. ⁻15, ⁻16, ⁺14, ⁺15

D. ⁺14, ⁺15, ⁻16, ⁻15

12 Which number line shows the graph of the following numbers? (16-2)

⁻20, ⁻14, ⁻1, ⁺4, ⁺9, ⁺13

F.

⁻20⁻18⁻16⁻14⁻12⁻10 ⁻8 ⁻6 ⁻4 ⁻2

G.

⁻20 ⁻15 ⁻10 ⁻5 0 ⁺5 ⁺10 ⁺15

H.

⁻14 ⁻12 ⁻10 ⁻8 ⁻6 ⁻4 ⁻2 0

I.

⁻30 ⁻20 ⁻10 0 ⁺10 ⁺20 ⁺30

13 Which two integers are 6 units from ⁻8 on a number line? (16-4)

A. ⁺2 and ⁺14

B. ⁻2 and ⁺14

C. ⁻14 and ⁻2

D. ⁻14 and ⁺2

14 What is the distance, in units, between ⁻20 and ⁺20 on a number line? (16-4)

15 Tobias wins some tickets playing a ring toss game at a carnival. He uses 53 of the tickets to get an action figure and 15 tickets to get a yogurt. He then wins 48 more tickets bowling. Tobias now has 70 tickets. How many tickets did he win from the ring toss? Describe what you did to find the answer. (16-5)

THINK SOLVE EXPLAIN

Set A, pages 364–365

Integers are the whole numbers and their opposites; 0 is its own opposite.

Write an integer for each point.

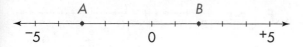

Point *A* is three units from zero and to the left of zero. Point *A* is at ⁻3.

Point *B* is two units from zero and is to the right of zero. Point *B* is at ⁺2.

Remember that the + and − signs name a direction from zero.

Write an integer for each description.

1. Two degrees below zero

2. Taking the elevator up two floors

3. A hole that is four feet deep

Write an integer for each point.

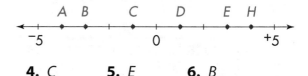

4. *C* 5. *E* 6. *B*

Set B, pages 366–367

The table shows the low temperatures during 5 days in a northern U.S. state. Graph the data as integers on a number line.

Low Temperatures for January 21–25					
Day	M	TU	W	TH	F
Temperature (°F)	⁻4	0	⁺6	⁻1	⁻7

Choose an appropriate interval.
Since the range of these integers is from ⁻7 to ⁺6, use an interval of 1 or 2.

Draw a number line.
Include 0 and enough tick marks for the integers you'll be graphing. Write the integers under the tick marks.

Plot the points.
Plot a point above the appropriate integer for each low temperature from the table.

Give your graph a title.
If necessary, put a title at the bottom of the graph.

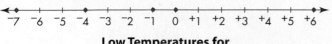

Low Temperatures for
January 21–25 (°F)

Remember that negative integers are to the left of 0 and positive integers are to the right of 0.

Graph each set of integers on a number line. Consider the interval you will use in your number line.

1. ⁻1, ⁻2, 0, ⁺2, ⁺1, ⁺5

2. ⁻19, ⁻2, ⁻11, 0, ⁺3, ⁺7, ⁺14

3. ⁻33, ⁻20, ⁻28 ⁻9, ⁻14, ⁻11, ⁺15, ⁺27

4. The table below shows low temperatures from a northern U.S. state recorded each month for 5 months. Graph the data on a number line.

Low Temperatures for December–April					
Month	Dec	Jan	Feb	Mar	Apr
Temperature (°F)	⁺23	⁻6	⁻9	⁺5	⁺16

Set C, pages 368–369

Compare ⁻4 and ⁺3. Use >, < or = .

Plot the numbers on a number line.

```
←——+——•——+——+——+——+——+——+——•——+——+——→
  ⁻5  ⁻4  ⁻3  ⁻2  ⁻1   0  +1  +2  +3  +4  +5
```

As you move to the right from any point on a number line, the numbers increase in value.

⁺3 > ⁻4   ⁺3 is to the right of ⁻4.

⁻4 < ⁺3   ⁻4 is to the left of ⁺3.

Remember that numbers increase in value as you move to the right on a number line, and decrease as you move to the left.

Compare. Use <, >, or = for each ◯.

1. ⁺3 ◯ ⁻3   **2.** ⁻9 ◯ ⁻7

3. ⁺1 ◯ ⁻16   **4.** ⁻14 ◯ ⁻10

Order from least to greatest.

5. ⁺42, ⁻29, 0, ⁻3

6. ⁻8, ⁻17, ⁺20, ⁻12

Set D, pages 370–371

Find the distance between ⁻2 and ⁺4 on a number line.

```
←——+——+——+——•——+——+——+——+——•——+——+——→
  ⁻5  ⁻4  ⁻3  ⁻2  ⁻1   0  +1  +2  +3  +4  +5
```

There are 6 units between ⁻2 and ⁺4 on the number line.

Remember that you can count units to find the distance between points on a number line.

Find the distance between each pair of integers on a number line.

1. ⁻3 and ⁺5   **2.** ⁻7 and ⁻1

3. ⁻6 and 0   **4.** ⁻4 and ⁺4

5. ⁻1 and ⁺8   **6.** ⁻2 and ⁺1

7. ⁻10 and ⁻8   **8.** ⁻3 and ⁺9

Set E, pages 372–374

To work backward, follow these steps.

Step 1 Identify the unknown initial amount.

Step 2 List each change, starting with the initial amount.

Step 3 Start at the end result. Work backward using the inverse of each change.

Remember addition and subtraction undo each other.

1. Jean spent 1 hour on math homework and 1 hour on English. Then she spent 2 hours baking. If she finished baking at 8:00 P.M., what time did she start doing her homework?

Glossary

acute angle An angle whose measure is between 0° and 90°.

acute triangle A triangle whose angles are all acute angles.

Addition Property of Equality The same number can be added to both sides of an equation and the sides remain equal.

algebraic expression A mathematical phrase involving a variable or variables, numbers, and operations.
Example: $x - 3$

angle Two rays that have the same endpoint.

area The number of square units needed to cover a surface or figure.

Associative Property of Addition Addends can be regrouped and the sum remains the same.
Example: $1 + (3 + 5) = (1 + 3) + 5$

Associative Property of Multiplication Factors can be regrouped and the product remains the same.
Example: $2 \times (4 \times 10) = (2 \times 4) \times 10$

axis (plural: axes) Either of two lines drawn perpendicular to each other in a graph.

bar graph A graph that uses bars to show and compare data.

base (exponent) The number that is multiplied by itself when raised to a power. *Example:* In 5^3, the 5 is the base.

base (of a polygon) The side of a polygon to which the height is perpendicular.

b

base (of a solid) The face of a solid that is used to name the solid.

Base

bases of a trapezoid The two parallel sides of a trapezoid.

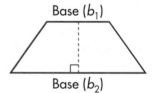
Base (b_1)
Base (b_2)

benchmark fraction Common fractions used for estimating, such as $\frac{1}{4}, \frac{1}{3}, \frac{1}{2}, \frac{2}{3}$, and $\frac{3}{4}$.

capacity The volume of a container measured in liquid units.

Celsius (°C) A unit of measure for temperature in the metric system.

centimeter (cm) A metric unit of length. 100 centimeters is equal to 1 meter.

common denominator A common multiple of the denominator of two or more fractions.

common factor A number that is a factor of two or more given numbers.

common multiple A number that is a multiple of two or more numbers.

Commutative Property of Addition The order of addends can be changed and the sum remains the same.
Example: 3 + 7 = 7 + 3

Commutative Property of Multiplication The order of factors can be changed and the product remains the same.
Example: 3 × 5 = 5 × 3

compatible numbers Numbers that are easy to compute with mentally.

composite number A whole number greater than 1 that has more than 2 factors.

cone A solid with one circular base; the points on the circle are joined to one point outside the base.

congruent figures Figures that have the same size and shape.

conjecture A generalization that you think is true.

continuous data Data, like time, that has all values possible.

coordinate grid A grid that makes it easy to locate points in a plane by using an ordered pair of numbers.

coordinates The two numbers in an ordered pair.

cube A solid with six flat surfaces called faces. All of the faces are squares.

cubed A name for a number to the third power.

cubic unit The volume of a cube that measures 1 unit on each edge.

cup (c) A customary unit of capacity. One cup is equal to 8 fluid ounces.

cylinder A solid with two circular bases that are congruent and parallel.

data Collected information.

decimal A number with one or more places to the right of a decimal point.

degree (°) A unit of measure for angles and temperature.

denominator The number below the fraction bar in a fraction.

difference The number that results from subtracting one number from another.

digits The symbols used to show numbers: 0, 1, 2, 3, 4, 5, 6, 7, 8, 9.

discrete data Data where only whole numbers are possible.

dividend The number to be divided.

divisible A number is divisible by another number if there is no remainder after dividing.

Division Property of Equality Both sides of an equation can be divided by the same nonzero number and the sides remain equal.

divisor The number used to divide another number.

double-bar graph A bar graph that uses two different-colored or shaded bars to show two similar sets of data.

edge A line segment at which two faces meet in a solid.

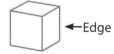

elapsed time The difference between two times.

equation A number sentence that uses an equal sign to show that two expressions have the same value. *Example:* 9 + 3 = 12

equilateral triangle A triangle whose sides all have the same length.

equivalent decimals Decimals that name the same amount. *Example:* 0.7 = 0.70

equivalent fractions Fractions that name the same part of a whole region, length, or set. *Example:* $\frac{1}{4} = \frac{2}{8}$

estimate To give an approximate value rather than an exact answer.

evaluate To find the numerical value of an expression by substituting numbers for any variables and using the order of operations.

expanded form A way to write a number that shows the place value of each digit. *Example:* 3,000 + 500 + 60 + 2

exponent A number that tells how many times the base is used as a factor. *Example:* In 5^3, the 3 is the exponent.

exponential notation A way to write a number using a base and an exponent. *Example:* 5^3

expression A mathematical phrase that can involve variables, numbers, and operations.

face A flat polygon-shaped surface of a polyhedron.

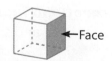

factor pair A pair of whole numbers whose product equals a given whole number.

factors Numbers that are multiplied to get a product.

factor tree A diagram that shows the prime factorization of a composite number.

Fahrenheit (°F) A unit of measure for temperature in the customary system.

fluid ounce (fl oz) A customary unit of capacity equal to 2 tablespoons.

foot (ft) A customary unit of length. One foot is equal to 12 inches.

formula A rule that uses symbols.

fraction A symbol, such as $\frac{2}{3}$, $\frac{5}{1}$, or $\frac{8}{5}$, used to describe one or more parts of a whole that is divided into equal parts. A fraction can name a part of a whole, a part of a set, a location on a number line, or a division of whole numbers.

gallon (gal) A customary unit of capacity. One gallon is equal to 4 quarts.

generalization A general statement. *Example:* A generalization about rectangles applies to all rectangles.

gram (g) A metric unit of mass. 1,000 grams is equal to 1 kilogram.

greatest common factor (GCF) The greatest number that is a factor of two or more given numbers.

height (of a polygon)
The length of a segment from one vertex of a polygon perpendicular to its base.

hexagon A polygon with 6 sides.

hundredth One part of 100 equal parts of a whole.

Identity Property of Addition The sum of any number and 0 equals that number.

Identity Property of Multiplication The product of any number and 1 equals that number.

improper fraction A fraction whose numerator is greater than or equal to its denominator.

inch (in.) A customary unit of measure; 12 inches is equal to 1 foot.

inequality A mathematical sentence that contains one of the symbols >, <, ≥, or ≤.

integers The whole numbers and their opposites; 0 is its own opposite.

intersecting lines Lines that pass through the same point.

interval The amount between tick marks on the scale of a graph.

inverse operations Operations that undo each other. *Example:* Adding 6 and subtracting 6 are inverse operations.

isosceles triangle A triangle with two sides of the same length.

kilogram (kg) A metric unit of mass. One kilogram is equal to 1,000 grams.

kilometer (km) A metric unit of length. One kilometer is equal to 1,000 meters.

least common denominator (LCD) The least common multiple of the denominators of two or more fractions.

least common multiple (LCM) The least number that is a common multiple of two or more numbers.

line A straight path of points that goes on forever in two directions.

linear equation An equation whose graph is a straight line.

line graph A graph that connects points and often shows how data changes over time.

line of symmetry The fold line in a symmetric figure.

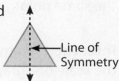
Line of Symmetry

line plot A display of responses along a number line with X's recorded above the numbers on a number line to indicate how many times a response occurred.

line segment Part of a line having two endpoints.

line symmetry A figure has line symmetry when it can be folded along one or more lines that create congruent parts, which can fit on top of each other exactly.

liter (L) A metric unit of capacity. One liter is equal to 1,000 milliliters.

mass The amount of matter that something contains.

meter (m) A metric unit of length. One meter is equal to 1,000 millimeters.

mile (mi) A customary unit of length. One mile is equal to 5,280 feet or 1,760 yards.

milligram (mg) A metric unit of mass. 1,000 milligrams is equal to 1 gram.

milliliter (mL) A metric unit of capacity. 1,000 milliliters is equal to 1 liter.

millimeter (mm) A metric unit of length. 1,000 millimeters is equal to 1 meter.

mixed number A number that has a whole-number part and a fractional part.

multiple The product of a given whole number and any other whole number.

multiple of 10 A number that has 10 as a factor.

Multiplication Property of Equality Both sides of an equation can be multiplied by the same nonzero number and the sides remain equal.

net A plane figure which, when folded, gives the original shape of a solid.

numerator The number above the fraction bar in a fraction.

obtuse angle An angle whose measure is between 90° and 180°.

135°

obtuse triangle A triangle in which one angle is an obtuse angle.

octagon A polygon with 8 sides.

order of operations The order in which operations are done in calculations. Work inside parentheses is done first. Next, terms with exponents are evaluated. Then multiplication and division are done in order from left to right, and finally addition and subtraction are done in order from left to right.

ordered pair A pair of numbers used to locate a point on a coordinate grid.

origin The point at which the x-axis and y-axis of a coordinate plane intersect. The origin is represented by the ordered pair (0, 0).

ounce (oz) A customary unit of weight. 16 ounces are equal to 1 pound.

overestimate The result of using larger numbers to estimate a sum or product. The estimate is larger than the actual answer.

parallel lines In a plane, lines that never cross and stay the same distance apart.

parallelogram A quadrilateral with both pairs of opposite sides parallel.

partial products Products found by breaking one of two factors into ones, tens, hundreds, and so on, and then multiplying each of these by the other factor.

pentagon A polygon with 5 sides.

percent A number that shows a comparison to 100. The symbol for percent is %. *Example:* 50% means 50 per 100 and can be written as a fraction, $\frac{50}{100}$, or as a decimal, 0.50.

perimeter The distance around the outside of any polygon.

period A group of 3 digits in a number. Periods are separated by a comma and start from the right of a number.

perpendicular lines Two lines that intersect to form square corners or right angles.

picture graph A graph that uses pictures or symbols to compare data that can be counted. Each picture represents a certain amount in the data.

pint (pt) A customary unit of capacity equal to 2 cups.

place value The position of a digit in a number that is used to determine the value of the digit.
Example: In 5,318, the 3 is in the hundreds place. So, the 3 has a value of 300.

plane An endless flat surface.

point An exact location in space.

polygon A closed plane figure made up of line segments.

polyhedron A three-dimensional shape made up of flat polygon-shaped surfaces.

pound (lb) A customary unit of weight. One pound equals 16 ounces.

prime factorization The process of writing a whole number as a product of all of its prime factors.

prime number A whole number greater than 1 that has exactly two factors, 1 and itself.

prism A solid with two congruent parallel bases and faces that are parallelograms.

product The number that is the result of multiplying two or more factors.

protractor An instrument used to measure and draw angles.

pyramid A solid with one base that is a polygon and whose other faces are triangles with a common vertex.

quadrilateral A polygon with 4 sides.

quart (qt) A customary unit of capacity equal to 2 pints.

quotient The number that is the result of dividing.

ray Part of a line that has one endpoint and extends forever in one direction.

rectangle A parallelogram with four right angles.

reflection The change in the position of a figure that gives the mirror image of the figure.

regular polygon A polygon that has sides of equal length and angles of equal measure.

remainder In division, the part that is left over after the division is complete.

rhombus A parallelogram with all sides the same length.

right angle An angle whose measure is 90°.

right triangle A triangle in which one angle is a right angle.

rotation The change in the position of a figure that moves it around a point.

rotational symmetry A figure has rotational symmetry when it can rotate onto itself in less than a full rotation.

rounding A process that determines which multiple of 10, 100, 1,000, etc., a number is closest to.

scale Number that shows the units on a graph.

scalene triangle A triangle in which no sides have the same length.

sides (of an angle) The two rays that form an angle.

simplest form A fraction in which the greatest common factor of the numerator and denominator is 1.

solid A figure that has three dimensions and takes up space.

solution The value of a variable that makes an equation true.

sphere A solid with all points the same distance from the center point.

square A rectangle with all sides the same length.

squared A name for a number to the second power. *Example:* six squared is written as 6^2 and means 6×6.

standard form A common way of writing a number with commas separating groups of three digits starting from the right. *Example:* 3,458

straight angle An angle measuring 180°.

Subtraction Property of Equality The same number can be subtracted from both sides of an equation and the sides remain equal.

sum The number that is the result of adding two or more addends.

surface area (SA) (polyhedron) The sum of the areas of all faces.

survey A question or questions used to gather information.

T

table of x- and y-values A table used to show how *x* and *y* relate.

tenth One out of ten equal parts of a whole.

thousandth One out of 1,000 equal parts of a whole.

three-dimensional shape A solid figure that takes up space.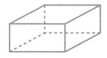

ton (T) A customary unit of weight. One ton equals 2,000 pounds.

transformation A move such as a translation, reflection, or rotation that does not change the size or shape of a figure.

translation The change in the position of a figure that moves it up, down, or sideways.

trapezoid A quadrilateral that has exactly one pair of parallel sides.

tree diagram A diagram used to find the prime factorization of a composite number.

trend A pattern in the data showing an increase or decrease.

triangle A polygon with 3 sides.

U

underestimate The result of using lesser numbers to estimate a sum or product. The estimate is smaller than the actual answer.

V

value (of a digit) The number a digit represents, which is determined by the position of the digit. See also *place value*.

variable A letter or symbol that represents a number that can vary or change.

vertex (plural: vertices) a. The common endpoint of the two rays in an angle. **b.** The point at which three or more edges meet in a solid. **c.** The point of a cone.

volume The number of cubic units needed to fill a solid figure.

W

weight A measure of how heavy something is.

whole numbers The numbers 0, 1, 2, 3, 4, and so on.

word form A way to write a number using words.

x-axis The horizontal axis in a graph or coordinate grid.

x-coordinate The first number in an ordered pair, which names the distance from the origin along the *x*-axis.

yard (yd) A customary unit of length. One yard is equal to 36 inches or 3 feet.

y-axis The vertical axis in a graph or coordinate grid.

y-coordinate The second number in an ordered pair, which names the distance from the origin along the *y*-axis.

Zero Property of Multiplication The product of any number and 0 equals 0.